Early Innings

A

Documentary

History of

Baseball,

1825–1908

Early Innings

Compiled & Edited by

Dean A. Sullivan

Introduction by

Benjamin G. Rader

University of Nebraska Press

Lincoln & London

Library of Congress Cataloging in Publication Data

Early innings : a documentary history of baseball, 1825–1908 / compiled and
edited by Dean A. Sullivan ; introduction by Benjamin G. Rader.

p.   cm.

Includes bibliographical references and index.

ISBN 0-8032-4237-9 (cl)

1. Baseball—United States—History—19th century—Sources.   2. Baseball—
United States—History—20th century—Sources.   I. Sullivan, Dean A., 1963–   .

GV863.A1E27   1995

796.357′0973′09034—dc20   94-30847

CIP

Contents

Illustrations

Preface

Many baseball fans today read newspapers, magazines, and books to gain a better understanding and appreciation of their sport. They examine how racial tensions, labor disputes, gambling scandals, rule changes, and other issues affect baseball; they enjoy preseason assessments as well as in-depth coverage of games from opening day to the postseason. Their nineteenth-century counterparts also read about these issues in the popular press.

Early Innings is a collection of articles, book excerpts, and other material published between 1825 and 1908. It includes the basic documents upon which the early history of the game rests and many others. A general introduction by Benjamin G. Rader as well as brief introductions to each chapter and document place the documents more fully within the context of baseball history. Through this guided immersion into the past, readers will gain a sense of how baseball was viewed in the nineteenth century. Those interested in particular aspects of baseball history may want to supplement this material by consulting the books mentioned in the introductions or listed among the references at the end of this book.

I have preserved the orthography, capitalization, and grammar used in the original documents; obvious errors in names and dates have been silently corrected.

I would like to thank Society for American Baseball Research (SABR) members Frederick Ivor-Campbell, Jerry Malloy, Frank Phelps, Jean Ardell, Bob Bailey, and David Q. Voigt for encouraging me to complete this project and for sending me copies of important documents. The staffs of the Library of Congress and the National Baseball Library and Archive in Cooperstown, New York (NBLA), patiently provided me with much-needed assistance. Special thanks go to NBLA chief librarian Tom Heitz, who not only reviewed the text but also sent me a document for use in *Early Innings*, and to the anonymous reviewers who did so much to improve the book.

Most of all, however, I must thank my family—my father Donald Sullivan, brothers Steve and Jay Sullivan, and sisters Lisa Rodriguez and Laurie Barden—for giving me the inspiration to complete what at times seemed a hopeless task. Tragically, my mother, Ruth Sullivan, did not survive to see the completion and publication of *Early Innings*. During the last year of her life we often discussed the book, and her contributions to its content and spirit, as well as to my spirit, are too numerous to list.

Introduction Benjamin G. Rader

Less-informed fans are likely to date the origins of modern baseball to the beginning of this century. Although they may vaguely recall hearing that Abner Doubleday invented the game much earlier, they assume that the game really took hold around 1900 with the creation of the current major league system and the playing of a World Series. Indeed, even the sportswriters who selected the charter members for the Hall of Fame at Cooperstown, New York, completely ignored nineteenth-century ball players.

As these marvelous documents collected by Dean A. Sullivan demonstrate, such a perception of baseball history is profoundly mistaken. The sport had become an integral part of American life long before the turn of the century. In the first decades of the nineteenth century, ball games were simple and informal, played mostly by boys. In the 1840s and 1850s, these games evolved into the club based, fraternal pastime of young men living in the larger northeastern cities. While remnants of the fraternal game lingered on, as early as the 1860s commercial considerations began to dictate the main contours of baseball history; the formation of the National League in 1876 signaled the full arrival of baseball as a business enterprise. Finally, in 1903, the National and American Leagues signed a pact that established the present major league structure.

Before the Civil War, the informal bat and ball games boys played on empty lots, village greens, and cow pastures reflected the casual ways of preindustrial America. The boys had no formal teams and no league. The rules of the game differed from one place to another. Then, as the United States entered the industrial era, the various bat and ball games merged into one. This game—initially called "base," "base ball," or "base-ball"—quickly became the nation's most popular team sport.

During the 1850s, young men, especially those clerks and artisans who lived in impersonal boardinghouses in the nation's largest cities, and who were experiencing profound changes in their work, turned to baseball with enthusiasm. In the game and its associated activities, they found excitement, male camaraderie, and opportunities to exhibit other skills. Led by New Yorkers, the young men organized dozens of formal "base ball" clubs. Representatives of these clubs wrote and revised the rules of play, appointed game officials, scheduled matches, and in 1858 organized the first national association.

The early players belonged to what contemporaries called a "fraternity." The use of the word "fraternity" was by no means accidental or insignificant; it implied that all ball players—regardless of their membership in distinct clubs, their ethnicity, social class, or religion—were members of a single brotherhood. They distinguished themselves by donning colorful uniforms similar to those worn by volunteer fire departments and militia units of the day. They not only played ball together but ate, drank, wagered, talked, and more. Winning clubs typically hosted gala dinners in honor of the losers. Clubs even held formal dances; sometimes the players seem to have been as busy on the dance floor as they were on the playing field. For example, in the winter of 1860–61, Brooklyn's Eckford club, whose members were shipbuilders, scheduled eight "invitation hops" and an annual ball, where club captain Frank Pidgeon exhibited his special talents in the "Parisian style" of dancing.

Today's fans would find the fraternity's game both familiar and strange. Just as today, the bases were ninety feet apart and the infield was diamond-shaped. Three strikes swung at and missed retired a batsman, but umpires only gradually began to call balls and strikes. Initially the umpire (who might be dressed in tails and a tall black top hat) sat at a table along the third base line. He rendered decisions only when controversies arose between the team captains. The fielders wore no gloves, and the catchers, hoping to catch pitches on the first bounce, stood several feet behind the "striker," or batter. From a running start, the pitcher, or "feeder," would pitch the ball underhanded with a straight arm from a distance of forty-five feet. In the early days, the pitcher was obligated to toss the ball gently so that the batter could have a pitch to his liking.

At the very height of its success, the baseball fraternity began to disintegrate. In 1862, the same year that Alexander T. Stewart opened the nation's first department store in downtown Manhattan, an ambitious Brooklynite, William H. Cammeyer, drained his pond, which served as a skating rink during the winter. He filled it with dirt, built a fence around it, nailed together some wooden benches for spectators, invited ball teams to play at his newly created Union Grounds, and charged fans a fee to watch games there. The "enclosure movement," as the drive to build fences around fields and charge an admission fee was called, introduced a new era of baseball history. To seize the opportunities presented by gate fees, teams began to play more games, to embark on long summer tours, to recruit athletes on the basis of their playing skills rather than their sociability, and even to pay outstanding players. It was, as the distinguished contemporary sportswriter Henry Chadwick declared, "really the beginning of professional base ball playing" in the United States.

The professional game helped to satisfy Americans' yearnings for a sense of belonging and identity. Given their astonishing geographic mobility, the very newness of the country, and the absence of a hereditary aristocracy, a rigid class system, or a state church, representative baseball teams helped to define the character of particular urban communities, providing their citizens with a sense of place and furnishing them with cherished collective memories.

Professional baseball thrived on urban rivalries. The success in 1869 of the nation's publicly acknowledged first all-salaried nine, Cincinnati's Red Stockings, provoked the envy of countless cities elsewhere. Across the nation, businessmen, politicans, and civic boosters, among others, joined forces to form joint-stock company baseball clubs. Like most small businesses then and since, the clubs usually lasted just a year or two, but out of their ashes, new clubs frequently arose to replace them. From the 1871 through 1875 seasons, several of these professional clubs competed for a championship pennant sponsored by a loose confederation known as the National Association of Professional Base Ball Players.

Professional baseball entered a new phase in 1876 when William A. Hulbert, president of the Chicago club, and Albert G. Spalding, player, manager, and soon-to-be sporting goods magnate, set about organizing a replacement for the National Association. Spalding and Hulbert's new National League was more tight-knit; it shared many features of today's major league baseball cartel. Determined that the league would become the premier circuit of professional clubs representing only the larger cities, the National League prohibited clubs in cities with less than 75,000 inhabitants from joining, required any club wishing to join the circuit to have the approval of the existing clubs, and provided each team with a territorial monopoly. By banning Sunday games, prohibiting the sale of liquor at ballparks, and charging a fifty cent admission fee, the league also sought to obtain the patronage of proper Victorians.

In the 1880s professional baseball shared in the nation's booming prosperity. National League attendance soared, and no fewer than seventeen other leagues of representative professional teams appeared (although several expired after only a season or so). In 1882 the American Association, dubbed the "Beer Ball League" because it permitted beer to be sold at games, challenged the National League's hegemony over big league baseball. The following year the two leagues (plus the Northwestern League) signed an agreement that ended fierce competition for players and recognized the territorial exclusivity of existing franchises. During the 1880s, the predecessor of baseball's modern World Series also began to take shape. Beginning in 1884 and ending in 1890, the National League champions met the American Association flagbearers in a postseason championship series.

In the meantime, conflicts between the franchise owners and the players escalated. First they clashed over player drinking. Young, away from home, and with large amounts of idle time on their hands, the players, in the owners' opinion, wasted their energy and talents, and damaged the image of baseball, by carousing and drinking too much. The players, on the other hand, resented restrictions on their personal behavior and opposed the player reservation system that the National League had instituted in 1879. A reserve clause in the players' contracts prevented them from offering their services to the highest bidders. Moreover, the players believed that they were not getting a fair share of baseball's additional earnings. Player grievances climaxed in the formation of a separate Players' League in 1890. With three big leagues competing for the loyalties of fans, the superior leadership offered by Albert Spalding enabled the National League to crush the upstart league after only one season. In 1891, the American Association also collapsed, leaving only the twelve-team National League as a major league circuit.

The National League drifted aimlessly through the 1890s. Faced with a terrible industrial depression in the middle years of the decade, game attendance fell. The league failed to develop an adequate substitute for the popular "World Championship series" of the 1880s. The absence of good teams in New York, Philadelphia, and Chicago, the nation's most populous cities, adversely affected the league's potential attendance. With twelve teams, too many cities fielded nines with terrible won-lost records; at the end of each season, as many as 84 games separated the last- and first-place clubs. While the league previously had cultivated an image of Victorian propriety, in the 1890s it acquired a notorious reputation for brawling, both on the field and in the stands.

As the National League wandered through the 1890s without direction, Byron Bancroft (Ban) Johnson began laying the foundations for a new league to challenge the senior loop. Johnson, a Cincinnati sportswriter, accepted the presidency of a revived minor league, the Western League, in 1894. In 1900 he renamed his loop the American League and proceeded to plant franchises in Chicago, Cleveland, Baltimore, and Washington, D.C. An all-out war for players soon erupted between the two leagues. Finally, in 1903, the leagues signed a peace pact in which they agreed to recognize each other's reserved players and established a three-man commission to oversee all of professional baseball. Although the National Agreement of 1903 did not provide for a postseason championship series, in 1905 the leagues agreed upon a mandatory postseason World Series.

Most fans cared little if at all about what had occurred behind the closed doors of the executive suites. They were far more excited about what was transpiring between the foul lines. And there the game also underwent a series of profound changes.

Long ago the pitchers had stopped tossing the ball gently underhanded to the hitters. As early as the 1860s, they increased the speed of their pitches and began to throw curveballs. A gradual relaxation of the rules permitted overhanded pitching in 1884. In 1887 the hitters lost the privilege of asking for a pitch above or below the waist. Finally, in 1893, the league adopted the modern pitching distance; in that year the rules required that the pitcher deliver the ball with his back foot anchored on a rubber slab and lengthened the pitching distance to sixty feet six inches, ten feet longer than it had been a dozen years earlier.

Offensive and defensive tactics slowly grew more sophisticated. In the 1860s, infielders inched away from their respective bases, and managers began to place their quickest man at shortstop. During the next decade, a few catchers donned masks and fielders put on gloves; at first the skintight gloves (with the ends cut off to improve throwing) were used exclusively to protect the hands from the sting of the ball. In the 1890s, with the extension of the pitching distance, teams increasingly turned to bunting and the ingenious hit-and-run play.

During the first decade of the twentieth century, baseball came of age. By then, the way baseball was played bore striking similarities to today's game. The World Series had become a widely celebrated rite, equaling the sheer excitement of Independence Day, Washington's Birthday, and even tippling on New Year's Eve. Giant new stadiums made of concrete and steel soon began to join newly built skyscrapers in the inner cities. The decade sported a galaxy of national heroes: Ty Cobb, Nap Lajoie, Honus Wagner, Walter Johnson, and Christy Mathewson among others. Only one thing was missing, it seemed, and that was an official account of the game's origins. As the last chapter of *Early Innings* reveals, the custodians of big league baseball solved that problem by inventing the myth of the game's American conception.

Early Innings

1

The Emergence of a National Game, 1825–60

Long before Abner Doubleday allegedly invented baseball at Cooperstown, New York, in 1839, American boys (and some girls) played a wide variety of bat and ball games. By the 1850s these games began to evolve into a single game that bears a striking resemblance to modern baseball. During the same decade, dozens of "base ball" clubs formed in the greater New York City area. The foundation built by these clubs, their players, and their supporters quickly grew to the point where baseball was widely considered a national game.

The Earliest Known Newspaper Report of a "BASS-BALL" Challenge (1825)

Source: Delhi (New York) *Gazette*, July 13, 1825, as reprinted in the *New York Times*, June 3, 1991

To date, this notice is the earliest printed evidence of a challenge to play a game called "BASS-BALL." Given the variety of names applied to similar bat and ball games, and the inconsistencies in spelling of the day, the newspaper might have printed the challenge as a game of "Base," "Base Ball," "Base-Ball," "Goal Ball," or perhaps "town ball." As research continues on the origins of modern baseball, references to even earlier challenges and games may yet be found. Indeed, there are several earlier mentions of the game of "base" (variously spelled) in English literature. See Henry Chadwick, "The Ancient History of Base Ball," Ball Players' Chronicle, July 18, 1867.

A CHALLENGE

The undersigned, all residents of the new town of Hamden, with the exception of Asa C. Howland, who has recently removed into Delhi, challenge an equal number of persons in any town in the County of Delaware, to meet them at any time at the house of *Edward B. Chace*, in said town, to play the game of BASS-BALL, for the sum of one dollar each per game. If no town can be found that will produce the required number, they will have no objection to play against any selection that can be made from the several towns in the county.

ELI BAGLEY,
EDWARD B. CHACE,
HARRY P. CHACE,
IRA PEAK,
WALTER C. PEAK,
H. B. GOODRICH,
R. F. THURBER,
ASA C. HOWLAND,
M. L. BOSTWICK.

Hamden, July 12, 1825.

2

Baseball in Rochester, New York (1825)

Source: Thurlow Weed, *Autobiography of Thurlow Weed*, ed. Harriet A. Weed (Boston: Houghton, Mifflin and Co., 1884), p. 203

Thurlow Weed, author of the following selection, was a powerful New York newspaperman and Whig politician. His recollection of a baseball team in his home town may be apocryphal. In the 1880s and 1890s many reminiscences of baseball teams and games from the distant past were published. By this time baseball, firmly established as the national pastime, had become a symbol of an idyllic, rural American past, an expression of nostalgic desire for the "good old days." Perhaps Weed intended to portray his boyhood in this manner.

. . . Though an industrious and busy place, its [Rochester's] citizens found leisure for rational and healthy recreation. A base-ball club, numbering nearly fifty members, met every afternoon during the ball-playing season. Though the members of the club embraced persons between eighteen and forty, it attracted the young and the old. The ball-ground, containing some eight or ten acres, known as Mumford's meadow, by the side of the river above the falls, is now a compact part of the city. Our best players were Addison Gardiner, Frederick Whittlesey, Samuel L. Selden, Thomas Kempshall, James K. Livingston, Dr. George Marvin, Dr. F. F. Backus, Dr.

A. G. Smith and others. Messrs. E. Delafield and Augustus F. Smith, who are prominent and successful in the practice of law in the city of New York, are the sons of Dr. A. G. Smith.

3

A Description of "Base, or Goal Ball" (1834)

Source: Robin Carver, *The Book of Sports* (Boston: Lily, Wait, Colman, and Holden, 1834)

The original version of this document appeared in Britain in William Clarke's The Boy's Own Book *(first U.S. edition, 1829). Five years later Robin Carver reprinted it in his own book, but he changed the name of the game from "rounders" to "base." As baseball grew in popularity, provisions for having runners retired by hitting them with a thrown ball ("soaking" or "plugging") and having all the hitters on a side bat in each inning were dropped from the rules.*

BASE, OR GOAL BALL

This game is known under a variety of names. It is sometimes called "round ball," but I believe that "base" or "goal ball" are the names generally adopted in our country. The players divide into two equal parties, and chance decides which shall have first innings. Four Stones or stakes are placed from twelve to twenty yards asunder, as a, b, c, d, in the margin; another is put at e. One of the party, who is out, places himself at e. He tosses the ball gently forward, toward a, on the right of which one of the in-party places himself, and strikes the ball, if possible, with his bat. If he miss three times, or if the ball, when struck, be caught by any of the players of the opposite side, who are scattered about the field, he is out, and another takes his place. If none of these accidents takes place, on striking the ball he drops the bat and runs toward b, or, if he can, to c, d, or even to a again. If, however, the boy who stands at e, or any of the out-players who may happen to have the ball, strike him with it in his progress from a to b, b to c, c to d, or d to a, he is out. Supposing he can only get to b, one of his partners takes the bat, and strikes the ball in turn. If the first player can only get to c, or d, the second runs to b, only, or c, as the case may be, and a third player begins; as they get home, that is, to a, they play at the ball by turns, until they all get out. Then, of course, the out-players take their places.

Ball Playing among Native Americans (1837)

Source: Anonymous, *Female Robinson Crusoe: A Tale of the American Wilderness* (New York: J. W. Bell, 1837), pp. 176–78

This description of a ball game played by Native Americans captures the enthusiasm players had for their sport. Whether the author actually witnessed such a game is unclear. Stuart Cullin, in Games of the North American Indians *(1907; Lincoln: University of Nebraska Press, 1992, 2 vols.), 2:616–47, describes several varieties of Native American ball games, including "shinny," a game that usually entailed hitting a ball with a curved stick and running between two bases.*

Some of the male adults were playing ball, which article was, as he afterwards ascertained it to be on examination, portion of a sturgeon's head, which is elastic, covered with a piece of dressed deerskin. Another ball which he noticed was constituted of narrow strips of deerskin, wound around itself, like a ball of our twine, and then covered with a sufficiently broad piece of the same material.

In playing this game, they exhibited great dexterity, eagerness, and swiftness of speed. The party engaged, occupied an extensive surface of open ground, over whose whole space, a vigorous blow with the hickory club of the striker, would send the ball, and also to an amazing height. On its coming down, it was almost invariably caught by another player at a distance, and as instantly hurled from his hand to touch, if possible, the striker of the ball, who would then drop his club, and run, with a swiftness scarcely surpassed by the winds, to a small pile of stones, which it was part of the game for him to reach. If the runner succeeded in attaining to the desired spot, before the ball touched him, he was safe. Otherwise, he had to resign his club to the fortunate thrower of the ball against him, and take his place to catch. The runner, by watching the coming ball, was almost always enabled to avoid its contact with him, by dodging or leaping, which was effected with all the nimbleness of one of the feline race. If that was effected, another person, in his own division of the playing party (there being two rival divisions), assumed the dropped club, to become a striker in his turn.

Their principal object seemed to be, to send the ball as far as possible, in order to enable the striker of it, to run around the great space of ground, which was comprised within the area formed by the piles of stones, placed at intervals along the line of the imaginary circle.

Two rival parties would thus contrive in eager contest for hours, and their captive, has actually known them to keep up the game for several days, regardless of food or drink, which, however, their fellow savage spectators, who became interested, would bring, and persuade them to partake of, in order to sustain in vigour, their drooping strength and spirits. When the darkness of night had involved the scene, and they could no longer discern the ball, they would drop asleep in the very spot where they had stood, at the time that the obscurity in the air, obliged them to suspend playing; and at the earliest gray of dawn, some arose, and immediately making the welkin ring with their shouts, thus awakened the others, and at it again they all went, with scarce a moment's cessation, until night again temporarily stopped the sport.

5

The Constitution of the Olympic Ball Club of Philadelphia (1837)

Source: *Constitution of the Olympic Ball Club of Philadelphia*, published privately in 1838

The Olympic Ball Club, founded in Philadelphia in 1831, was apparently the first town ball club to draft and publish a constitution. The following excerpts include not only the obligations of the membership but a provision for keeping records of the games played.

PREAMBLE

WHEREAS—Field Sports having from time immemorial been the favourite recreation of all classes of men, not merely for the amusement they afford, the bracing and healthy vigour they impart to the human frame, and the hilarity and good feeling they promote; but for their manly and athletic character, and the generous and friendly emulation they encourage and uphold. The undersigned, therefore, well assured that these characteristics of gymnastic sports have in no manner degenerated, and that the present age is not behind the past in a taste for their enjoyment, when exercised with decorum and moderation; hereby unite ourselves in a social compact for purposes hereafter specified; and for the proper management of the Association, agree to be governed by the following

CONSTITUTION

Article I

This Institution shall be denominated "THE OLYMPIC BALL CLUB."

. . .

Article VI

Of the Recorder.
    SECT. 1. The Recorder shall be President of the Board of Directors, and shall be the medium through whom they shall report to the Club, and to whom all applications to the Board shall be made.
    SECT. 2. It shall be his duty to record in a book, to be provided for the purpose

at the expense of the Club, an accurate account of all the games played on Club days, date of the same, names of the players, the number of points made by each, and the ground used on each occasion.

SECT. 3. He shall be the umpire between the captains on Club days, in the event of a disputed point of the game, and from his decision there shall be no appeal, except to the Club, at its next stated meeting.

SECT. 4. He shall be in attendance on the ground on Club days, provided with a minute book to note down the game, in which he shall be assisted by a member from each party who shall be designated by him, observing rotation in the selection as nearly as possible.

SECT. 5. Should he be unable to attend on any Club day, he shall cause his book for rough notes to be conveyed to the ground by a member whom he shall nominate, and who shall be Recorder for that occasion.

SECT. 6. He shall report to each stated meeting of the Club, such general information in regard to occurrences on Club days and other matters as he may deem useful or interesting.

SECT. 7. He shall have charge of the pattern uniform owned by the Club.

SECT. 8. He shall be fined as follows, viz.:

For absence of himself or substitute from roll-call on Club days, ...12½ cts.

For absence of himself or substitute on Club days, ...25 "

For neglect to have the roll and minute books, .25 "

For absence from roll call at a meeting of the Club, ... 6¼ "

For absence from a meeting, ...25 "

For neglecting to have the record book kept in proper order, or for not

    bringing it to each stated meeting, ...50 "

For neglecting or refusing to perform any other duty incumbent upon

    him, not exceeding, ...50 "

. . .

Article VIII

Of the Board of Directors.

SECT. 1. The Board of Directors shall be elected semi-annually at the stated meetings in June and December of each year.

SECT. 2. They shall organize themselves within three days after their election, and appoint a Secretary. They shall have the power to frame laws and impose fines on their members, provided they are consistent with the laws of the Club.

SECT. 3. They shall have all the Bats, Balls and other implements belonging to the Club under their particular care, and it shall be their duty to have them kept in good order, repair the same when necessary, and report their condition at each stated meeting of the Club, with such other information or remarks as they may deem useful or interesting.

SECT. 4. They shall be provided, at the expense of the Club, with a suitable box or chest wherein to deposit the articles belonging to the Club, under their care, for safe keeping.

SECT. 5. All expenses incurred by them in the repair and preservation of the property of the Club, the transportation of the same to the ground on Club days, and in the execution of such other duties as may devolve upon them, shall be repaid from the funds of the club.

SECT. 6. It shall be their duty to select a suitable spot of ground for practice, at least four days previous to each Club day, and they shall cause notices to be prepared by their Secretary and delivered to the Clerk, not less than forty-eight hours prior to the hour which they may appoint for the meeting, designating time and place.

SECT. 7. Should the weather prove unfavourable on the regular Club day, the Directors shall select a day for the purpose as soon thereafter as practicable, and notify the members thereof.

SECT. 8. They shall have all the necessary implements of the game conveyed on Club days to the ground selected by them for the occasion.

SECT. 9. They shall, upon the written application of ten members, permit them to have the use of such articles belonging to the Club, and under their care, as they may wish for playing volunteer games; exacting as a condition that they shall be safely returned to their custody; in default of which they shall report such applicants at the next stated meeting, who shall be held responsible for the value of any article lost or injured on the occasion.

SECT. 10. The Bats, Balls, or other property of the Club, shall not be used for any purpose not provided for by the Constitution, without the consent of the Board of Directors, under a penalty of one dollar for each offence.

SECT. 11. Each Director shall be fined for not keeping the implements belonging to the Club, under their charge, in proper order, in a sum not exceeding fifty cents; and for refusing or neglecting to perform any other duty imposed upon them twenty-five cents.

Article IX

Of Members.

SECT. 1. The Club shall consist of persons above the age of twenty-one years, and the number of members shall not exceed thirty.

SECT. 2. Each person, on being admitted into membership, shall pay into the hands of the Treasurer *Five Dollars*, and be subjected to a monthly contribution of 12½ cents, payable yearly in advance, at the stated meetings in March.

SECT. 3. Each member shall provide himself with a uniform, similar in all respects to the pattern uniform owned by the Club; for neglect thereof he shall be fined 25 cents per month, until this requisition is complied with.

SECT. 4. When a member changes his place of residence, he shall notify the Secretary thereof, under a penalty of 12½ cents for each month's omission.

SECT. 5. No resignation of the right of membership shall be accepted, until the member has paid the amount he is indebted to the Club, or been excused by a vote of the Club.

SECT. 6. A member shall be fined as follows:

For absence from roll-call, at a meeting or Club day, ... 6½ cts.

For absence from a meeting or Club day, ... 12½ "

For absence from a special meeting, after signing the call therefor, ... 25 "

For withdrawal from a meeting without the permission of the President,
    or from the ground on Club day, without the consent of the Captain of his
    party, ... 25 "

For disorderly conduct at a meeting or on Club day, not exceeding . . . . 50 "

For appearing on Club days out of uniform, or with it unclean, ... 12½ "

. . .

Article XIV

Of Club Days.

SECT. 1. The second Thursday in each month shall be set apart for practice, and shall be denominated Club day.

SECT. 2. At the appointed hour of meeting the roll shall be called by the Recorder, (noting thereon the absentees and those unequipped or with soiled uniform,) and after the selection of Captains, the Club shall forthwith proceed to make the requisite arrangements to play the game which may be agreed upon.

Article XV

Of the Captains.

SECT. 1. The Captains shall be chosen by the members present on Club days, and they shall alternately select their players.

SECT. 2. They shall have command of the Club when on duty, and in the event of a disputed point of the game, shall have the settlement thereof, and if they are unable to agree, the Recorder shall be umpire.

SECT. 3. Any member disobeying their orders, or acting improperly in any way, shall be reported by them to the Club, at its next stated meeting, with a statement of the offence committed; which, should the Club find correct, shall subject such member to a fine not exceeding one dollar.

A Canadian Ball Game (1838)

Source: *Sporting Life*, May 5, 1886

In this letter, Dr. Adam E. Ford recalls a ball game he witnessed on June 4, 1838, in Beechville, Ontario, "which closely resembled our present national game." Ford's letter provides additional evidence that bat and ball games were widely played in North America. See Nancy B. Bouchier and Robert Knight Barney, "A Critical Examination of a Source on Early Ontario Baseball: The Reminiscences of Adam E. Ford," Journal of Sport History 15 (Spring 1988): 75–87.

VERY LIKE BASE BALL

A Game of the Long-ago Which Closely Resembled Our Present National Game

DENVER, Col., April 26.—Editor SPORTING LIFE—The 4th of June, 1838, was a holiday in Canada, for the Rebellion of 1837 had been closed by the victory of the Government over the rebels, and the birthday of His Majesty George the Fourth was set apart for general rejoicing. The chief event at the village of Beechville, in the county of Oxford, was a base ball match between the Beechville Club and the Zorras, a club hailing from the townships of Zorra and North Oxford.

The game was played in a nice, smooth pasture field just back of Enoch Burdick's shops. I well remember a company of Scotch volunteers from Zorra halting as they passed the grounds to take a look at the game. Of the Beechville team I remember seeing Geo. Burdick, Reuben Martin, Adam Karn, Wm. Hutchinson, I. Van Alstine, and, I think, Peter Karn and some others. I remember also that there were in the Zorras "Old Ned" Dolson, Nathaniel McNames, Abel and John Williams, Harry and Daniel Karn and, I think, Wm. Ford and William Dodge. Were it not for taking up too much of your valuable space I could give you the names of many others who were there and incidents to confirm the accuracy of the day and the game. The ball was made of double and twisted woolen yarn, a little smaller than the regulation ball of to day and covered with good, honest calf skin, sewed with waxed ends by Edward McNamee, a shoemaker.

The infield was a square, the base lines of which were twenty-one yards long, on which were placed five bags. . . . The distance from the thrower to the catcher was eighteen yards; the catcher standing three yards behind the home bye. From the home bye, or "knocker's" stone, to the first bye was six yards. The club (we had bats in cricket but we never used bats in playing base ball) was generally made of the best cedar, blocked out with an ax and finished on a shaving horse with a drawing knife. A wagon spoke, or any nice straight stick would do.

We had fair and unfair balls. A fair ball was one thrown to the knocker at any height between the bend of his knee and the top of his head, near enough to him to be fairly within reach. All others were unfair. The strategic points for the thrower to aim at was to get it near his elbow or between his club and his ear. When a man struck at a ball it was a strike, and if a man struck at a ball three times and missed it he was out if the ball was caught every time either on the fly or on the first bound. If he struck at the ball and it was not so caught by the catcher that strike did not count. If a struck ball went anywhere within lines drawn straight back between home and the fourth bye, and between home and the first bye extended into the field the striker had to run. If it went outside of that he could not, and every man on the byes must stay where he was until the ball was in the thrower's hands. Instead of calling foul the call was "no hit."

There was no rule to compel a man to strike at a ball except the rule of honor, but a man would be dispised and guyed unmercifully if he would not hit at a fair ball. If the knocker hit a ball anywhere he was out if the ball was caught either before it struck the ground or on the first bound. Every struck ball that went within the lines mentioned above was a fair hit; everyone outside of them no hit, and what you now call a foul tip was called a tick. A tick and a catch will always fetch was the rule given strikers out on foul tips. The same rule applies to forced runs that we have now. The bases were the lines between the byes and a base runner was out if hit by the ball when he was off of his bye. Three men out and the side out. And both sides out constituted a complete inning. The number of innings to be played was always a matter of agreement, but it was generally from 5 to 9 innings, 7 being most frequently played and when no number was agreed upon seven was supposed to be the number. The old plan which Silas Williams and Ned Dolson (these were gray-headed men then) said was the only right way to play ball, for it was the way they used to play it when they were boys, was to play away until one side made 18 or 21, and the one getting that number first won the game. A tally, of course, was a run. The tallies were always kept by cutting notches on the edge of a stick when the base runners came in. There was no set number of men to be played on each side, but the sides must be equal. The number of men on each side was a matter of agreement when the match was made. I have frequently seen games played with 7 men on each side and I never saw more than 12. They all fielded.

The object in having the first bye so near the home was to get runners on the base lines so as to have the fun of putting them out or enjoying the mistakes of the fielders when some fleet-footed fellow would dodge the ball and come in home. When I got older I played myself, for the game never died out. I well remember when some fellows down at or near New York got up the game of base ball that had a "pitcher" and "fouls," etc., and was played with a ball hard as a stick. India rubber had come into use, and they put so much into the balls to make them lively that when the fellow tossed it to you like a girl playing "one o'd cat," you could knock it so far that the fielders would be chasing it yet, like dogs hunting sheep, after you had gone clear around and scored your tally. Neil McTaggart, Henry Cruttenden, Gordon Cook, Henry Taylor, James Piper, Almon Burch, Wm. Herrington and others told me of it when I came home from the University. We, with a "lot of good fellows more," went out and played it one day. The next day we felt as if we had been on an overland trip to the moon. I could give you pages of incidents, but space forbids. One word as to prowess in those early days. I heard Silas Williams tell Jonathan Thornton that old Ned Dolson could catch the ball right away from the front of the club if you didn't keep him back so far that he couldn't reach it. I have played from that day to this, and I don't intend to quit as long as there is another boy on the ground. Yours, DR. FORD.

7

The First Reported Baseball Games between New York City–area Clubs (1845)

Source: New York Morning News, October 22 and 25, 1845

The earliest known published citations of baseball games played in the New York area appeared in 1845. On September 11, the New York Morning News *reported that "the Iowa Indians had a game of ball play, at Hoboken, yesterday," and on October 21, the* New York Herald *noted that "the New York Base Ball Club will play a match of base ball against the Brooklyn Club, to-morrow afternoon, at 2 o'clock, at the Elysian Fields, Hoboken." The following two accounts describe this match and a return match played in Brooklyn. It is clear that "the time-honored game of Base" was already popular, since the* Morning News *remarked that "two more Base Clubs are already formed."*

Several features of these games distinguish them from modern baseball. First, the games ended when a club scored twenty-one or more "aces," or runs, after both clubs had completed the same number of innings. Second, each club fielded only eight players, as team size had not yet been standardized. Third, following each game the victorious club honored its opponents at a banquet, a common ritual in the antebellum era.

[October 22, 1845]

Base Ball Match

A friendly match of the time-honored game of Base was played yesterday at the Elysian Fields, Hoboken, between eight members of the New York Ball Club and the same number of players from Brooklyn. A cold wind from the North made the day somewhat unpleasant for the spectators, yet a large number, among whom we noticed several ladies, assembled to witness the sport. Play was called at 3 o'clock, P.M. Umpires—Messrs. Johnson, Wheaton and Chase. The toss was won by the Brooklyn players, who decided in favor of giving their antagonists the first innings, and accordingly Hunt took up the bat, and the game commenced. The match was for the first twenty-one aces—three out, all out. Hunt made a single ace, but before another was added to the score, three of the New Yorkers went out in rapid succession, and the bats were yielded to Brooklyn. Many of the Brooklyn players were eminent cricketers, but the severe tactics of the N. Y. Club proved too effective, and they soon resigned their innings to their opponents, not scoring one.

New York now took her second chance, and the score began slowly to tell. During this innings, four aces were made off a single hit, but by the arbitrary nature of the game, a single mistake sometimes proving fatally irretrievable, they were soon driven to the field again. The second innings of the Brooklyn players proved alike disastrous, and the close of the third still left them, all their tickets blank. On the fourth innings the New York Club made up their score to twenty-four aces. The Brooklyn players then took their fourth, against hopeless odds, but with undiminished spirits. They were, however, forced to yield with a score of four only, and the New Yorkers were declared winners with a spare three and a flush of twenty. The fielding of the Brooklyn players was, for the most part, beautiful, but they were evidently not so well practiced in the game as their opponents.

The following abstract shows the aggregate of the four innings:

NEW YORK BALL CLUB

	Runs	Hands out		Runs	Hands out
Davis	5		Case	2	2
Tucker	2	3	Vail	3	1
Miller	4	1	Kline	2	3
Winslow	4	2		24	12
Murphy	2				

BROOKLYN PLAYERS

	Runs	Hands out		Runs	Hands out
Hunt		2	Sharp		1
Gilmore	1	2	Whaley	1	1
Hardy	1	2	Ayres		1
Forman	1	2		4	12
Hine		1			

At the conclusion of the match, both parties sat down to a dinner prepared by McCarty in his best style; and the good feeling and hilarity that prevailed, showed that the Brooklyn players, though defeated, were not disheartened. A return match will be played on Friday next, commencing at 1 o'clock P.M., on the grounds of the Brooklyn Star Club, Myrtle avenue. Those who would witness genuine sport, should improve the opportunity.

[October 25, 1845]

BASE BALL—The return match between the New York Base Ball Club and the Brooklyn players, came off yesterday afternoon on the ground of the Brooklyn Star Club, Myrtle Avenue, Brooklyn. The Brooklyn boys, though keen players at cricket, it seems have not sufficient practice yet, to cope with their more skilful antagonists in this game, and as a consequence, have again been defeated. Give them, however, a little more drill, and their sure and agile fielding, even now, will eventually tell in their favor. Two more Base Clubs are already formed in our sister city, and the coming season may witness some extra sport. The liberal and gentlemanly bearing of the losing party is highly commendable, and on this, if on no other account, they certainly deserve ultimate success.

After the match was concluded, a bounteous supper was provided at Sharp's, during the consideration of which, the utmost harmony and good feeling prevailed.

The following is a correct record of the score.—Umpires, Messrs. Johnson, Wheaton and Van Nostrand.

NEW YORK BALL CLUB			BROOKLYN		
	Hands out	*Runs*		*Hands out*	*Runs*
Davis	2	4	Hunt	1	3
Murphy	0	6	Haines	2	2
Vail	2	4	Gilmore	3	2
Kline	1	4	Hardy	1	2
Miller	2	5	Sharp	2	2
Case	2	4	Meyers	0	3
Tucker	2	4	Whaley	2	2
Winslow	1	6	Forman	1	2*
	12	37		12	19

*Error in original; should be 3.—Ed.

8

Dr. Daniel Adams and the Knickerbockers of New York (1850s)

Source: *Sporting News*, February 29, 1896

No single baseball club was more influential in the early growth of baseball than the New York Knickerbockers, formed in 1845. Indeed, as Henry Chadwick, the game's earliest chronicler, observed in 1861, the Knickerbockers deserved "the honor of being the pioneer of the present game of Base Ball." If the following reminiscence is accurate, Dr. Daniel Adams, a cofounder and long-time member of the Knickerbocker club, was personally responsible for devising several of the important rules as well as the early manufacture of balls and bats.

DR. D. L. ADAMS

MEMOIRS OF THE FATHER OF BASE BALL

He Resides in New Haven and Retains an Interest in the Game

NEW HAVEN, Conn., February 24—SPECIAL CORRESPONDENCE:—In a pleasant home on quiet Edwards street, lives Dr. Daniel L. Adams, who undoubtedly, more than any other man in the country, is entitled to be called the Father of Base Ball. His brother-in-law, William S. Briggs of Keene, N.H., makes this claim for him, and the facts bear it out.

Dr. Adams was born in Mt. Vernon, N.H., Nov. 11, 1814. He was, therefore, 81 years old last November, but one would not think so to look at him. He is exceedingly well preserved, and his active step and unimpaired eyesight and hearing go far to prove the value of an active interest in athletics in early life. The doctor was one of the first men to belong to an organized base ball club, and quickly took the lead in all matters connected with the growth and character of the National game.

A representative of THE SPORTING NEWS learning that Dr. Adams could tell some interesting reminiscences of the old-time games, called upon him recently and found him very willing to talk about his favorite subject.

"I graduated from Yale College in 1835," said he, "and from the Harvard Medical School in [1838], after which I became a practicing physician in New York city. I was always interested in athletics while in college and afterward, and soon after going to New York I began to play base ball just for exercise, with a number of other young medical men.

"Before that there had been a club called the New York Base Ball Club, but it had no very definite organization and did not last long. Some of the younger members of that club got together and formed the Knickerbocker Base Ball Club, September 24, 1845. The players included merchants, lawyers, Union Bank clerks, insurance clerks and others who were at liberty after 3 o'clock in the afternoon. They went into it just for exercise and enjoyment, and I think they used to get a good deal more solid fun out of it than the players in the big games do nowadays.

"About a month after the organization of this club, several of us medical fellows joined, myself among that number. The following year I was made President, and served as long as I was willing to retain the office. Our playground was the 'Elysian Fields' in Hoboken, a beautiful spot at that time, overlooking the Hudson, and reached by a pleasant path along the cliff. It was a famous place in those days, but is now cut up railroad tracks. Mr. Stevens' 'castle' stands far from the site.

PRACTICED ON "ELYSIAN FIELDS"

"Twice a week we went over to the 'Elysian Fields' for practice. Once there we were free from all restraint, and throwing off our coats we played until it was too dark to see any longer. I was a left-handed batter, and sometimes used to get the ball into the river. People began to take an interest in the game presently, and sometimes we had as many as a hundred spectators watching the practice. The rules at that time were very crude. The pitching was all underhand, and the catcher usually stood back and caught the ball on the bound.

"Our players were not very enthusiastic at first, and did not always turn out well on practice days. There was then no rivalry, as no other club was formed until 1850, and during these five years base ball had a desperate struggle for existence. I frequently went to Hoboken to find only two or three members present, and we were often obliged to take our exercise in the form of 'old cat,' 'one' or 'two' as the case might be. As captain, I had to employ all my rhetoric to induce attendance, and often thought it useless to continue the effort, but my love for the game, and the happy hours spent at the 'Elysian Fields' led me to persevere. During the summer months many of our members were out of town, thus leaving a very short playing season.

"I used to play shortstop, and I believe I was the first to occupy that place, as it had formerly been left uncovered. At different times I have, however, played in every position except that of pitcher. We had a splendid catcher in the person of Charles S. Debost, who would be a credit to the position even to-day, I am sure. He was a good batter also, and a famous player in his day.

"We had a great deal of trouble in getting balls made, and for six or seven years I made all the balls myself, not only for our club but also for other clubs when they were organized. I went all over New York to find someone who would undertake this work, but no one could be induced to try it for love or money. Finally I found a Scotch saddler who was able to show me a good way to cover the balls with horsehide, such as was used for whip lashes. I used to make the stuffing out of three or four ounces of rubber cuttings, wound with yarn and then covered with the leather. Those balls were, of course, a great deal softer than the balls now in use. It was not until some time after 1858 that a shoemaker was found who was willing to make them for us. This was the beginning of base ball manufacturing. There is now, I believe, a factory in Philadelphia where 1,000 people are employed in this one industry.

HARD GETTING BATS

"It was equally difficult to get good bats made, for no one knew any more about making balls [bats] than balls. The bats had to be turned under my personal supervision, the workman stopping occasionally for me to ascertain when the right diameter and taper was secured. I was often obliged to try three or four turners to find one with suitable wood, or one willing to do the work. In fact, base ball playing for the first six or seven years of its existence was the pursuit of pleasures under difficulties.

"The first professional English cricket team that came to this country used to practice near us, and they used to come over and watch our game occasionally.

They rather turned up their noses at it, and thought it tame sport, until we invited them to try it. Then they found it was not so easy as it looked to hit the ball. Upon this discovery, they began to find fault with the ball, and so our crack pitcher took their own hard cricket ball, and gave them every opportunity, but they had no better success.

"The first club to be organized after the Knickerbockers was the Gotham Club, and its members became our special rivals. I remember one game of 12 innings which finally ended in a tie, with a score of 12 to 12. Soon other clubs began to form in rapid succession, until there were quite a number in various places. It was then possible to have matches of no mean size. There was one series of three matches between members from all the New York clubs and all the Brooklyn clubs. Our Knickerbocker catcher, Debost, played in them all, and New York won two out of the three. At one of these matches I acted as umpire. There were thousands of people present, but no admission was charged.

"The Gotham Club was organized in 1850 and the Eagle in 1852. The playing rules remained very crude up to this time, but in 1853 the three clubs united in a revision of the rules and regulations. At the close of 1856 there were 12 clubs in existence, and it was decided to hold a convention of delegates from all of these for the purpose of establishing a permanent code of rules by which all should be governed. A call was therefore issued signed by the officers of the Knickerbocker Club as the senior organization, and the result was the assembling of the first convention of base ball players in May, 1857. I was elected presiding officer. In March of the next year the second convention was held, and at this meeting the annual convention was declared a permanent organization, and with the requisite constitution and by-laws became the National Association of Base Ball Players.

HE WAS CHAIRMAN

"I was chairman of the Committee on Rules and Regulations from the start and so long as I retained membership. I presented the first draft of rules prepared after much careful study of the matter, and it was in the main adopted. The distance between bases I fixed at 30 yards—the only previous determination of distance being 'the bases shall be from home to second base 42 paces; from first to third base 42 paces equi-distant'—which was rather vague. In every meeting of the National Association while I was a member I advocated the 'fly game'—that is, not to allow first-bound catches—but I was always defeated on the vote. The change was made, however, soon after I left, as I predicted in my last speech on the subject before the convention.

"The distance from home to pitcher's base I made 45 feet. Many of the old rules, such as those defining a foul, remain substantially the same to-day, while others are changed and, of course, many new ones added. I resigned in 1862, but not before thousands were present to witness matches, and any number of outside players standing ready to take a hand on regular playing days. But we pioneers never expected the game so universal as it had now become.

"I have no idea of the number of clubs at present, nor the number of players at present, nor the number of persons employed in making base ball material, but it is an important industry. Newspapers are now obliged to report games and could not afford to neglect it.

"William F. Caldwell, still living, I [believe ?], was a newspaper man who took great interest in ball playing at that time. His paper was the New York Sunday Mercury, and it used to be all he could do to help the game in his columns. He was one of the first to report the matches and was generally a member of the base ball committees, though he did not belong to our club.

"The Knickerbocker Club had an existence of about 30 years, and my connection with it lasted about half that time. An old book of rules issued by the club in 1854, gives the officers and members at that time as follows:

"President, Fraley C. Niebuhr; Vice President, Alex. H. Drummond; Secretary, James W. Davis; Treasurer, George A. Brown. Directors, Daniel L. Adams, W. F. Ladd, Charles S. Debost; Honorary Members, James Lee, Esq., Abraham Tucker, Esq., Edward W. Talman, Esq.; Active Members, Duncan F. Curry, Charles B. Birney, Ebenezer E. Dupignac, Jr., Fraley C. Niebuhr, James Moncrief, Daniel L. Adams, William L. Tallman, Charles S. Debost, Henry S. Anthony, Alex. H. Drummond, George Ireland, Jr., Benjamin C. Lee, Benjamin K. Brotherson, George A. Brown, William F. Ladd, John Murray, Jr., Richard F. Stevens, Thos. W. Dick, Jr., John Boyle, William H. Grenelle, John Clancy (?), James W. Davis, George W. Devoe, G. Colden Tracy, William B. Eager, Jr., Otto W. Parfsen, Edgar F. Lasak, Frank W. Tyron, Edwin F. Frook, Albert H. Winslow, Louis F. Wadsworth, William F. McCutchen, Samuel E. Kissam, Gershom Lockwood, Henry C. Ellis."

SEVERAL OTHERS

"Many others were members at one time or another. Besides those named in the list I remember two brothers named O'Brien, who were brokers and afterward became very wealthy. There was also a man named Morgan, who was very successful in business. Henry T. Anthony is the photographic supply dealer who is well-known all over the country through his large New York establishment. Duncan F. Curry was an insurance man, and James Moncrief became, I think, a judge of the Superior Court.

"The best pitcher then developed was not a member of the Knickerbocker Club, but of the Excelsior Club of Brooklyn. His name was Creighton, and he won considerable note in his day.

"James W. Davis, a broker, and secretary of our club, is still living. He ought to go down to history as the first base ball fiend. Indeed, we used to call him a fiend in the old days because of his enthusiasm. He was an outfielder. We had a flag on which were the words 'Knickerbocker Base Ball Club,' and I understand that he has been given orders that when he dies he is to be wrapped in that flag. But most of the old players of the Knickerbocker Club have already 'come home.'"

OLD TIMER

9

The New York Baseball Rules (1854)

Source: Charles Peverelly, *The Book of American Pastimes* (New York, 1866), pp. 346–48

During the 1850s, when baseball exploded in popularity in the New York area, the top teams played by the Knickerbocker, or "New York," rules. In 1854 a revised version of the original Knickerbocker rules of 1846 was approved by a small committee of New York baseball officials, including Dr. Adams. This document describes the first known meeting of baseball club representatives. Three years later, a much larger convention would result in the creation of the National Association of Base Ball Players (NABBP).

At a meeting held November 18, 1853, a communication was received from the Eagle Club, asking for a committee to join them in arranging a set of rules for playing, and Dr. Adams, Curry, and Tucker were appointed.

The annual meeting, for 1854, was held at Smith's, 35 Howard street, on the 1st of April. The committee on rules presented the following as having been arranged to govern the three clubs, viz. the Knickerbockers, Gotham, and Eagle.

1. The bases shall be "Home" to second base, forty-two paces; and from first to third base, forty-two paces, equidistant; and from Home to pitcher not less than fifteen paces.

2. The game to consist of twenty-one counts, or aces, but at the conclusion an equal number of hands must be played.

3. The ball must be pitched, not thrown, for the bat.

4. A ball knocked outside the range of the first or third base is foul.

5. Three balls being struck at and missed, and the last one caught, is a hand out; if not caught is considered fair, and the striker bound to run.

6. A ball being struck or tipped and caught, either flying or on the first bound, is a hand out.

7. A player must make his first base after striking a fair ball, but should the ball be in the hands of an adversary on the first base before the runner reaches that base, it is a hand out.

8. Players must make the bases in the order of striking, and when a fair ball is struck and the striker not put out, the first base must be vacated as well as the next base or bases if similarly occupied; players may be put out, under these circumstances, in the same manner as when running to the first base.

9. A player shall be out, if at any time when off a base he shall be touched by the ball in the hands of an adversary.

10. A player who shall intentionally prevent an adversary from catching or getting the ball, is a hand out.

11. If two hands are already out, a player running home at the time a ball is struck, cannot make an ace if the striker is caught out.

12. Three hands out, all out.

13. Players must take their strike in regular rotation; and after the first inning is played the turn commences at the player who stands on the list next to the one who lost the third hand.

14. No ace or base can be made on a foul stroke.

15. A runner cannot be put out in making one base when a balk is made by the pitcher.

16. But one base allowed if the ball, when struck, bounds out of the field.

17. The ball shall weigh from five and a half to six ounces, and be from two and three-quarters to three and a half inches in diameter.

10

"The New York Base Ball Clubs" (1854)

Source: *Spirit of the Times*, December 23, 1854

The following letter, perhaps the first letter to the press on baseball, reflects the state of baseball in New York City after the 1854 season. The author of the letter, William Van Cott, an officer of the Gotham Club, refers to baseball as "the old-fashioned game" while simultaneously promoting it as a new sport. He also gives what may be the first commercial endorsement by a baseball figure.

THE NEW YORK BASE BALL CLUBS

Mr. Editor—It may be a matter of interest to some of your readers to know, what you are doubtless aware of, that there are now in this city three regularly organized Clubs, who meet semi-weekly during the playing season, about eight months in each year, for exercise in the old fashioned game of Base Ball—the Knickerbocker, Gotham, and Eagle Base Ball Clubs. The Knickerbockers and Eagles play at the Elysian-fields, Hoboken, and the Gothamites at the Red House, Harlem. These Clubs are composed of residents of this city, of various professions, each numbering about thirty members, and their affairs are conducted in such manner, in point of system and economy, as to enable all persons, who can give the necessary time for this purpose, to enjoy the advantages of this noble game.

There have been a large number of friendly, but spirited trials of skill, between the Clubs, during the last season, which have showed that the game has been thoroughly systematized, and that the players have attained a high degree of skill in the game. The season for play closed about the middle of November, and on Friday evening, December 15th, the three Clubs partook of their annual dinner at Fijux's, in Barclay-street. The Clubs were well represented, and the occasion was one of high social pleasure and enjoyment. Good feeling reigned supreme, and for several hours mirth and fun were very considerably above par.

The indications are that this noble game will, the coming season, assume a higher position than ever, and we intend to keep you fully advised, in the future, of all our doings, as we deem your journal the only medium in this country through which the public receive correct information in these matters.

Too much can scarcely be said in praise of the good things furnished on the occasion of our late dinner, either in regard to quality, or the mode of cooking and serving up. Everything, including wines and liquors, was of the A. No. 1 quality, and we cheerfully recommend the proprietor of 11 Barclay-street to all who desire the enjoyment of a similar nature and occasion.

W. H. V. C.

December 19th, 1854.

11 _____

The Growing Popularity of Baseball in New York (1855)

Source: *Spirit of the Times,* June 2, 1855

Not only was baseball growing more popular by the mid-1850s, but the game was becoming increasingly serious. Apart from playing "match" games against the nines from other clubs, the Knickerbockers, Eagles, Empires, and Gothams required that their players attend two practice sessions per week.

Base Ball.—The interest in the game of Base Ball appears to be on the increase, and it bids fair to become our most popular game. There are now four clubs in constant practice, *vis.* Gotham, Knickerbocker, Eagle, and Empire, who meet as follows:—

. . . . .

The first match game of the season will be played between the Knickerbockers and Gothams, at the Red House, Harlem, on Friday, June 1st, play to commence about 3 o'clock. A match will be played between the Eagles and Empires on Friday, June 15, at the Elysian Fields, Hoboken, play to commence at 3 o'clock. Besides the above, there will be a match game between the Knickerbockers and Eagles, and between the Gothams and Eagles, during the month of June; time and place not named.

The Knickerbockers meet on Monday and Thursday afternoons, at the Elysian Fields, Hoboken.

The Eagles on Tuesday and Friday afternoons, at same place.

The Empires on Wednesday and Saturday afternoons, at same place.

The Gothams on Tuesday and Friday afternoons, at Red House, Harlem.

The Excelsior, days not decided, at South Brooklyn.

12

A Defense of Baseball as a "Manly Exercise" (1856)

Source: *New York Times*, September 27, 1856

During the antebellum era, critics frequently charged that young American men failed to achieve the physical robustness of their English counterparts. The author of this letter denies the charge by citing the many clubs in the New York area whose players viewed "manly exercise as necessary to physical happiness."

Base Ball

To the Editor of the N. Y. Daily Times:

Noticing in your yesterday's morning issue an article commending the attachment of the English to athletic games and manly sports, and blaming severely the American youth for their devotion to "brandy cock tails" and "billiards," at the expense of sports requiring bone and muscle, I beg leave to disabuse your mind of some mistakes, at any rate.

During the whole of your editorial you make not the slightest mention of the American game—that of *Base Ball*, which here deservedly takes the place of Cricket, its English rival, though the latter has its partisans too, especially in our country towns.

The game of Base Ball is one, when well played, that requires strong bones, tough muscle and sound mind; and no athletic game is better calculated to strengthen the frame and develop a full, broad chest, testing a man's powers of endurance most severely. And if a representative from your office would take the trouble to visit the Ball grounds in Hoboken, Jersey City, Brooklyn, Harlem, or Morrisania, on almost any day in the week—he would there see youths, who, after working at the desk the greater part of the day in hard mental labor are here developing their physical force, and building up for themselves a constitution anything but "feeble and enervated." I will guarantee, that nowhere will you behold more manly forms, deep chests, and broad shoulders, with arms that a "*short boy*" might envy.

Some of these clubs have members in the prime of life, who rightly value manly exercise as necessary to physical happiness. I have no doubt that some twenty-five Clubs (limited to forty members each) could be reckoned up within a mile or two of New-York, that stronghold of "enervated" young men. I can give sixteen from memory, viz.:

Knickerbocker, of Hoboken.	Putnam, of Brooklyn, E. D.
Eagle, of Hoboken.	Continental, of Brooklyn, E. D.
Empire, of Hoboken.	Harmony, of Brooklyn, E. D.
Gotham, of Harlem.	Excelsior, of Brooklyn, E.D.
Harlem, of Harlem.	Atlantic, of Bedford.
Baltic, of Harlem.	Excelsior, of Brooklyn, proper.
Union, of Morrisania.	Astoria, of Astoria.
Pioneer, of Jersey City.	Excelsior, of Jersey City.

These Clubs, in a generous spirit of rivalry, frequently challenge each other to a contest of skill, and after seeing these matches reported in your paper, I was the more surprised at the want of credit given.

New-York has its Ball Clubs and Cricket Clubs, its Boat Clubs and its Yacht Clubs—and though they are not so largely entered into as they should be—still I for one protest against your dictum that "New-York youth knows not these enjoyments," referring to manly sports.

Trusting that I have not encroached too much upon your valuable space, I remain,

Yours truly, BASEBALL.

THURSDAY, Sept. 25, 1856.

13

Formation of the National Association of Base Ball Players (NABBP) in New York (1857)

Source: *Spirit of the Times*, January 31, 1857

In order to promote the standardization of playing rules, to regulate interclub competition, and to encourage the growth of baseball, the New York clubs formed a national association in 1857. By 1861, clubs located in New Haven, Philadelphia, Baltimore, Washington, D.C., and Detroit as well as those from the New York area would send delegates to the annual NABBP convention. A description of the association's first meeting in 1857 follows.

OUR NATIONAL SPORTS

A convention of the Base Ball Clubs of this city and the vicinity was held on Thursday evening, 22nd inst., at Smith's Hotel, Broome street, for the purpose of discussing and deciding upon a code of laws which shall hereafter be recognized as authoritative in the game. Base ball has been known in the Northern States as far back as the memory of the oldest inhabitant reacheth, and must be regarded as a national pastime, the same as cricket is by the English. It is a manly and healthful exercise, and if generally known would become popular, being full of excitement and rendering the body lithe and hardy. It is played in most of the New England schools, and those who have once engaged in it never lose their interest in the game. We should hail it as a favorable omen for the next generation if that bright specimen of humanity, yclept Young New York, would join the base ball or cricket clubs and quit his bar rooms, and other night amusements, and seek the open air. The following account is copied from the "Herald" of the 23rd:—

The Knickerbocker is the oldest base ball club now existing in this city, and seems to be the most influential. The present convention was called by that club, and is composed of three delegates appointed by the various associations. Fourteen separate and independent organizations were represented last evening by the following gentlemen, and it was stated that others would have been present but for distance, or the impossibility of getting home the same night.

Knickerbocker—Messrs. D. L. Adams, Wm. H. Grinnell, L. F. Wadsworth.
Gotham—Messrs. Wm. H. Van Cott, R. H. Cudlip, Geo. H. Franklin.
Eagle—Messrs. W. W. Armfield, A. J. Bixby, John W. Mott.
Empire—Messrs. R. H. Thorn, Walter Scott, Thomas Leary.
Putnam—Messrs. Theo. F. Jackson, Jas. W. Smith, Edw. A. Walton.
Baltic—Messrs. Phillip Weeks, Robt. Cornell, Dr. Chas. W. Cooper.
Excelsior—Messrs. Jas. W. Andrews, Jas. Rogers, P. R. Chadwick.
Atlantic—Messrs. C. Sniffen, W. Babcock, T. Tassie.
Harmony—Messrs. R. Justin, Jr., G. M. Phelps, Frank D. Carr.
Harlem—Messrs. E. H. Brown, John L. Riker, C. M. Van Voorhis.
Eckford—Messrs. Chas. M. Welling, Francis Pidgeon, James M. Gray.
Bedford—Messrs. John Constant, Chas. Osborn, Thos. Bagot.
Nassau—Messrs. Wm. P. Howell, J. R. Rosenquest, Eph. Miller.
Continental—Messrs. John Silsby, Nath. B. Law, Jas. B. Brown.

The Convention met together shortly after the hour appointed, and being satisfied with each other's personal appearance, (justly so, for most of them were splendid looking fellows,) the delegates proceeded to elect a President and officers, when the following were appointed:—

President—Dr. D. L. Adams, of the Knickerbocker.
Vice President—Reuben H. Cudlip, Gotham; John W. Mott, Eagle.
Secretary—Jas. W. Andrews, Excelsior.
Assistant Secretary—Walter Scott, Empire.
Treasurer—E. H. Brown, Harlem.

After some remarks from the President, a brisk discussion ensued on the motion that a committee of five be appointed to prepare a code of laws which shall be authoritative on the game. An amendment was offered, that twenty should form such committee; and, again, that the Convention should go into Committee of the Whole upon the laws. The various propositions were sweated down to two, and, being put to the vote, it was finally determined that the delegates from each club should appoint one member to sit on said committee. The gentlemen so appointed are as follows:—

Committee to Draft a Code of Laws on the Game of Base Ball, to be Submitted to the Convention—Messrs. L. F. Wadsworth, W. H. Van Cott, W. W. Armfield, Thos. Leavy, Thos. F. Jackson, Dr. Chas. W. Cooper, P. R. Chadwick, T. Tassie, F. D. Carr, E. H. Brown, Francis Pidgeon, John Constant, Wm. P. Howell and Nathaniel B. Law. This committee will meet next Wednesday.

Mr. Armfield moved that an assessment of $2 be made from each club, in order to defray incidental expenses, and referred to the proposed Central Park as a most suitable spot for playing matches. Provision had been made there by the Commissioners for the English national pastime of cricket, but none for base ball,* and he trusted that this convention would put itself in communication with the authorities on this subject.

Mr. R. G. Cornell submitted three specimen balls of various sizes, 6⅓ oz., 6½ oz., and 6¾ oz.; the convention will eventually be called upon to decide which is orthodox of the trio.

Mr. Francis Pidgeon proposed that a committee of five be appointed by the Chair to confer with the Central Park Commissioners in relation to a grant of public lands for base ball purposes. This being carried, the Chair named the following:—

Committee to treat with the Commissioners for a plot of ground in the Central Park—Francis Pidgeon, E. H. Brown, George F. Franklin, John W. Mott, L. F. Wadsworth.

A motion was then made and carried that each club forthwith pay the Treasurer $2, when that officer remarked, "I shall be under the necessity of notifying that I don't take Spanish quarters." The Secretary read over the names of the clubs, the money was forthcoming, and the Convention adjourned at 9½ o'clock until the third Wednesday in February.

Base ball is about becoming a great national institution. The gentlemen assembled last evening at Smith's Hotel were engaged in a work not of that trifling importance which a casual observer might suppose. *Mens sana in corpore sano* is a maxim worthy of notice in this age, when young men are forsaking the fields and out door exercise for the fumes of cellars and the dissipation of the gaming table. Let us have base ball clubs organized by the spring all over the country, rivalling in their beneficent effects the games of Roman and Grecian republics. Schoolmasters and clergymen, lend a helping hand.

*Mr. Armfield and the Convention seems to us to labor under a mistake; the Commissioners recommend that a space be set apart for a "Cricket Ground, for the encouragement of, and indulgence in, *athletic and manly sports.*" This, we should suppose, would include Base Ball, Quoits, &c., &c.—Editor "Spirit."

A Defense of Cricket as a "National Game" (1857)

Source: *New York Clipper*, May 16, 1857

This editorial indicates that baseball had not yet vanquished all contenders for the honor of being America's national game. The author believed that, as citizens of a truly democratic nation, Americans should not object to "making cricket an American pastime" solely because the game was developed in England. Another Clipper *editorial espoused lacrosse as a national pastime as well.*

CRICKET

THIS game is rapidly making its way into popular favor as one of our national games, and attaching to itself an importance of which the recent convention held here is the forerunner. Hitherto, one great obstacle to the progress of the game in this country has been the assertion made by certain ignorant and prejudiced parties, that Cricket is only played by Englishmen. Even were this the case, why it should deter Americans from enjoying and participating in the sport, we cannot imagine. But it is not so. Americans are, and have been for some time past, taking a most active interest in the game—many of them are really good players, whilst others give promise of future excellence; and, with care and practice, all are likely to make a telling mark on the general score-book. We recognise no such distinctions as Englishmen, Irishmen, &c., &c., in this country, more especially in sporting circles. We are all Americans, enjoying the same privileges, and looking up to the constitution of our country as our beacon light. Setting aside the subject of our nationality, however, we cannot conceive what objection there can be in our adoption of whatever is for the good of the community, let it come from whence it may; and that Cricket has that tendency we have evidence sufficient in the general good and gentlemanly behavior evinced by those who engage in it towards one another, as well as towards all with whom they are brought in contact, to say nothing of their general healthy appearance. Again, its laws, and the mode of carrying them out, are so in accordance with our own institutions, and so democratic in their influences, that our only wonder is that it has not been more generally fostered by native born citizens. The youth of America are much in need of an agreeable and proper kind of exercise; sunshine, and the aroma arising from the green turf and beautiful foliage, and a fine bracing air, are quite necessary to their health, vigor, and general happiness. Then what objection there can be to our making Cricket an American pastime, we are at a loss to discover.

Rules of the Massachusetts Game (1858)

Source: *The Base Ball Player's Pocket Companion* (Boston: Mayhew and Baker, 1859), pp. 20–22

In New England the "Massachusetts game," a form of town ball, had not yet been superseded by baseball. On May 13, 1858, the Massachusetts Association of Base Ball Players drafted the following rules for their sport. The association soon collapsed, however, after its players and supporters embraced the "New York game" in the early 1860s. Compare these rules with the "New York rules" found in Document 9.

1. The Ball must weigh not less than two, nor more than two and three-quarters ounces, avoirdupois. It must measure not less than six and a half, nor more than eight and a half inches in circumference, and must be covered with leather.

2. The Bat must be round, and must not exceed two and a half inches in diameter in the thickest part. It must be made of wood, and may be of any length to suit the Striker.

3. Four Bases or Bounds shall constitute a round; the distance from each base shall be sixty feet.

4. The bases shall be wooden stakes, projecting four feet from the ground.

5. The Striker shall stand inside of a space of four feet in diameter, at equal distance between the first and fourth Bases.

6. The Thrower shall stand thirty-five feet from and on a parallel line with the Striker.

7. The Catcher shall not enter within the space occupied by the Striker, and must remain upon his feet in all cases while catching the Ball.

8. The Ball must be thrown—not pitched or tossed—to the Bat, on the side preferred by the Striker, and within reach of his Bat.

9. The Ball must be caught flying in all cases.

10. Players must take their knocks in the order in which they are numbered; and after the first innings is played, the turn will commence with the player succeeding the one who lost on the previous innings.

11. The Ball being struck at three times and missed, and caught each time by a player on the opposite side, the Striker shall be considered out. Or, if the Ball be ticked or knocked, and caught on the opposite side, the Striker shall be considered out. But, if the Ball is not caught after being struck at three times, it shall be considered a knock, and the Striker obliged to run.

12. Should the Striker stand at the Bat without striking at good balls thrown repeatedly at him, for the apparent purpose of delaying the game, or of giving advantage to players, the Referees, after warning him, shall give one strike, and if he persists in such action, two and three strikes; when three strikes are called, he shall be subject to the same rules as if he struck at three fair balls.

13. A player, having possession of the first Base, when the Ball is struck by the succeeding player, must vacate the Base, even at the risk of being put out; and when two players get on one Base, either by accident or otherwise, the player who arrived last is entitled to the Base.

14. If a player, while running the Bases, be hit with the Ball thrown by one of the opposite side, before he has touched the home Bound, while off a Base, he shall be considered out.

15. A player, after running the four Bases, on making the home Bound, shall be entitled to one tally.

16. In playing all match games, when one is out, the side shall be considered out.

17. In playing all match games, one hundred tallies shall constitute the game, the making of which by either Club, that Club shall be judged the winner.

18. Not less than ten or more than fourteen players from each Club, shall constitute a match in all games.

19. A person engaged on either side, shall not withdraw during the progress of the match, unless he be disabled, or by the consent of the opposite party.

20. The Referees shall be chosen as follows: One from each Club, who shall agree upon a third man from some Club belonging to this Association, if possible. Their decision shall be final, and binding upon both parties.

21. The Tallymen shall be chosen in the same manner as the Referees.

16

The First Brooklyn–New York All-Star Match (1858)

Source: *Spirit of the Times*, July 24, 1858

No previous baseball match attracted as much attention as a three-game series between all-star squads from Brooklyn and New York in 1858. The first game, described below, was won by the New York club on July 20. Brooklyn evened the series on August 17 with a 29–8 victory, but New York rebounded on September 10 to take the final game 29–18. The box scores of all three games can be found in Seymour Church, Base Ball: The History, Statistics, and Romance of the American National Game from Its Inception to the Present Time (San Francisco, 1902), pp. 25–26. It is evident from the box score below that detailed statistics—including pitch counts—were already a feature of baseball coverage.

Two recent baseball histories, by Charles Alexander and Benjamin Rader, begin with this game, reflecting the importance of this event. Not only does the playing of an all-star game show that baseball's popularity grew tremendously during this era; it also demonstrates a general acceptance that baseball teams represented their communities on the field.

THE GREAT BASE BALL MATCH

Tuesday last, the day fixed upon for the great match at Base Ball between the Brooklyn and New York players, was as fine as the most ardent lover of the game could desire, either for play or for the drive out to witness the match. An immense concourse of people were upon the course before the time announced for commencing the game, and the cry was "still they come!" up to five o'clock. Every imaginable kind of vehicle had been enlisted in the service, milk-carts and wagons, beer wagons, express wagons, stages, and the most stylish private and public carriages. The Excelsior Club figured in a large stage drawn by fourteen handsomely caparisoned horses; the Eagle Club, of Jersey City, boasted an eight-horse team, with a band of music; the Pastime eight horses; the Empire two stages, each drawn by six horses; the Putnams and St. Nicholas each with six; and the Nassau, Union, Monument, Oriental, and Columbian, each with four-in-hands, while several other Clubs were represented in a more unpretending, but not less enthusiastic manner. The ladies (God bless them!) turned out in large numbers, and many of them seemed to enter into the spirit of the game in a manner worthy of the most ardent devotee, betting kids and other trifles on the result, and applauding heartily a good catch, a good run, and often a noble *attempt*. The stands were well filled, while the entire homestretch was filled with a triple row of carriages, besides hundreds which were upon the field and outside the course. The Flushing cars and stages brought out a large number of persons, most of whom occupied the field, forming an arena which the players occupied, the front ranks seating themselves on the grass, so that those in the rear could have an uninterrupted view, while the stages and other vehicles completed the outside circle, which presented not only an animated but a very beautiful spectacle to those upon the stands. When we state that Sheriff Boyd superintended the Police arrangements, our readers will understand that perfect order was maintained, and that pickpockets were scarce.

The Brooklyn nine went first to the bat, and the play on both sides was of the very highest order. Indeed it would be unjust to particularise. Holder was the only one who made a clear home strike, and a beauty it was, clear out of the middle field, which brought him to the home base amidst the most unbounded applause. Other players received their share of applause, particularly Van Cott, for stealing runs—judiciously—and Wright and P. O'Brien for catches on the fly in the long fields.

After the match was concluded, the players and some invited guests were invited to the Committee room, and refreshments were furnished. Judge Van Cott, of the Gotham Club, proposed as a toast—"Health, success, and prosperity to the members of the Brooklyn Base Ball Clubs," which was received with all the honors, and three times three and a tiger. Dr. Jones, President of the Excelsior Club, appropriately responded in like terms, and with much good taste, hoping that on the return match victory might favor Brooklyn. Three times three and a tiger. Judge Van Cott toasted "the health and success of the members of the Niagara Base

Ball Club of Buffalo," which was enthusiastically received, and responded to by Mr. Williams, of that Club. Everything passed off in the most good-humored manner, and the Base Ball match between the Brooklyn and New York nines will be long remembered with pleasure by all lovers of this noble and invigorating game.

The following is the score in full:

BROOKLYN	Hands Lost.	Runs.	NEW YORK	Hands Lost.	Runs.
Leggett, catcher	3	1	Pinckney, 2d base	3	3
Holder, 2d base	4	2	Benson, right field	3	3
Pigeon, short	2	1	Bixby, 3d base	4	1
Greene, middle field	2	4	De Bost, catcher	3	2
P. O'Brien, left field	3	2	Gelston, short	3	1
J. Price, 1st base	3	3	Wadsworth, 1st base	4	3
M. O'Brien, pitcher	3	3	Hoyt, left field	2	4
Masten, 3d base	4	1	T. G. Van Cott, pitcher	1	5
Burr, right field	3	1	Wright, middle field	4	0
Total	27	18	Total	27	22

Innings—	1st	2d	3d	4th	5th	6th	7th	8th	9th	Total Runs
New York	0	1	2	4	7	2	1	5	0	22
Brooklyn	3	2	2	0	4	2	1	4	0	18

New York—Number of balls pitched by Van Cott	198
" —Most in one innings	55
" —Least "	12
" —Average to an innings	22
Brooklyn—Number of balls pitched by M. O'Brien	264
" —Most in one innings	69
" —Least "	20
" —Average to an innings	29
New York—Number of balls passing De Bost	6
Brooklyn— " " " Leggett	12
New York—Number of balls caught on the fly	6
Brooklyn— " " "	6
New York— " " " the first bound	11
Brooklyn— " " " " "	7
New York— " " " bases	5
Brooklyn— " " " "	5

Umpire—Mr. E. H. Brown, of the Metropolitan.
Scorers—Brooklyn, Mr. J. B. Bach.
" —New York, Mr. W. H. Van Cott.

17

A Song Celebrating "Uncle Samuel's Sport" (1858)

Source: Henry Chadwick, *The Game of Base Ball* (1868; reprint, Columbia, S.C.: Camden House, 1983), pp. 178–80

During the antebellum era, drink and song often accompanied the elaborate postgame dinners hosted by the home club. At a supper given for the Excelsiors by the Knicker-bockers on August 20, 1858, the players sang the following song to the tune of "Uncle Sam's Farm." A verse may be missing or the last two verses misnumbered.

"BALL DAYS" IN THE YEAR A.D. 1858

I

Come, base ball players all and listen to the song
About our manly Yankee game, and pardon what is wrong;
If the verses do not suit you, I hope the chorus will,
So join with us, one and all, and sing it with a will.

CHORUS

Then shout, shout for joy, and let the welkin ring,
In praises of our noble game, for health 'tis sure to bring;
Come, my brave Yankee boys, there's room enough for all,
So join in Uncle Samuel's sport—the pastime of base ball.

II

First a welcome to our guests, the brave Excelsior boys,
They play a strong and lively game, and make a lively noise;
They buck at every club, without breaking any bones,
Assisted by their president, the witty Doctor Jones.

III

They well deserve their motto, and may they ever keep
Their men from slumbering, till their score "foots up a heap;"
And their name will resound through village and through town,
Especially by older clubs, who've been by them done brown.

IV

They have Leggett for a catcher, and who is always there,
A gentleman in every sense, whose play is always square;
Then Russell, Reynolds, Dayton, and also Johnny Holder,
And the infantile "phenomenon," who'll play when he gets older.

V

But if I should go on singing of each and every one,
'Twould require another day, till the setting of the sun;
But they need no voice of mine to glorify their name,
Their motto's "Ever Onward," and may it never wane.

VI

The Nestors and the parents of this our noble game,
May repose on laurels gathered and on records of their fame;
But all honor and all glory to their ever fostering hand,
That is multiplying ball clubs in towns throughout the land.

VII

Then treat the fathers kindly, and please respect their age,
Their last appearance is not announced, as yet, on any stage;
Some vigor yet remains, as you very well must know—
It shines out like a star in our agile Charles De Bost.

VIII

Now we'll sing to the Gothams—they hold a foremost rank;
They have taken many prizes, and they seldom draw a blank;
Their players are hard to beat, with Van Cott in the race,
And Wadsworth is bound to die on the very first base.

IX

There's a club that's called the Eagle, and it soars very high;
It clipped the parent's wing, and caught them on the fly;
Little Gelston plays behind, and Bixby pitches well,
And Hercules he bats the ball—oh! dreadfully to tell.

X

And here we have the Putnams—they bear a gallant name;
They are jovial, good fellows, as every one will claim—
For Dakin is a trump, as the Brooklyn boys well know,
And with Masten for a catcher, they have a right to crow.

XI

See the conquering hero comes from the broad *Atlantic's* ocean,
And the Nestors' hearts do swell with grateful, glad emotion;
They've so many star players, you can hardly name the lions,
But I think you'll all agree they are the O'Briens.

XII

But we'll cross to the westward, where Empire takes its way,
At our home, the Elysian Fields, this club enjoys its play;
They've Benson, Hoyt, and Miller, Leavy, Thorne, and Fay,
And are noted for their even play on every practice day.

XIII

There's the aspiring Eckford boys, justly considered some;
When they send a challenge, that club looks very *Grum*;
Their *Pidgeon's* ne'er caught napping, and they never are cast down,
With such splendid fielders as Manolt and Ed. Brown.

XIV

There's a club at Morrisania, that's a very strong bulwark;
It forms a solid "Union" 'twist Brooklyn and New York—
They've Gifford for their pitcher, and Booth plays well behind,
And Pinckney, on the second base, is hard to beat you'll find.

XVI

The young clubs, one and all, with a welcome we will greet,
On the field or festive hall, whenever we may meet;
And their praises we will sing at some future time;
But now we'll pledge their health in a glass of rosy wine.

XVII

Your pardon now I crave—this yarn is spun too long—
The Knickerbocker's "fiend," you know, he always goes it strong;
On America's game of base ball he will shout his loud acclaim,
And his "tiger" shall be telegraphed to Britain's broad domain.

THE END

18 _____

The First Intercollegiate Ball Game (1859)

Source: *Pittsfield (Mass.) Sun*, July 7, 1859

Although this match between Amherst and Williams has been described as the first intercollegiate baseball game, the contest was actually played by "Massachusetts game" rules. The first intercollegiate ball game pairing nine-man teams and playing by New York rules occurred several months later, on November 3, when Xavier met Fordham.

THE BALL AND CHESS GAMES BETWEEN THE STUDENTS OF AMHERST AND WILLIAMS COLLEGES.—The match games of Ball and Chess between Amherst and Williams Colleges, which had been talked about for some time, came off in this town last week—the Ball game on Friday and the Chess game on Saturday. The weather on Friday being delightful, a large number of ladies and gentlemen were gathered on the grounds, east of the Maplewood Institute, to witness the exciting affair. From Amherst there were present but few students except the players and chess champions, the authorities of the College not having granted a holiday to the students generally, but from Williams, where the Faculty *were more liberal,* nearly all the students were in attendance, and some of them were accompanied by ladies from Williamstown. The field where the friendly contest took place, reminded us of what was seen "a long time since" in Berkshire, when "General Training" was in vogue. The game commenced at about 11 A.M., and was not concluded until past 3 P.M.

The players were as follows:—On the part of Williams—H. S. Anderson, Captain; Players, H. F. C. Nichols, R. E. Beecher, John E. Bush, J. H. Knox, S. W. Pratt, 2d., A. J. Quick, B. F. Hastings, J. L. Mitchell, C E. Simmons, G. P. Blagden, H. B. Fitch, G. A. Parker; Umpire, C. R. Taft.

On the part of Amherst—J. F. Claflin, Captain; Players, E. W. Pierce, S. J. Storrs, F. E. Tower, M. B. Cushman, J. A. Evans, E. M. Fenn, H. D. Hyde (thrower—one of the best we have ever seen), J. A. Leach, II, H. C. Roome, H. Gridley, J. L. Pratt, F. Thompson; Umpire, L. R. Smith; Recorder of Score, A. Maddock.

William R. Plunkett, Esq., President of the Pittsfield Club, was chosen arbiter or referee, and it is somewhat remarkable, that his services were required to decide every point, the Umpires not being able to agree upon any question proposed for their decision.

It is due to the students of Williams to say, that previous to the reception of the challenge from Amherst, there was no organized Ball club at that institution, while at Amherst there has long been a famous Club.

Amherst had the first innings, and 25 rounds were played and recorded. The results of each player and each club appear in the following table; the Amherst players winning a victory with a score twice that of their rivals:—

AMHERST CLUB			WILLIAMS CLUB		
Players	Tallies	Outs	Players	Tallies	Outs
Claflin	7		Parker		4
Pierce	5	2	Fitch		5
Storrs	7	1	Blagden	1	5
Tower	7	1	Simmons	4	1
Cushman	4	3	Brown	3	3
Evans	5	4	Hastings	4	1
Fenn	5		Quick	3	1
Hyde	4	3	Pratt...........	2	2

AMHERST CLUB			WILLIAMS CLUB		
Players	Tallies	Outs	Players	Tallies	Outs
Leach	7		Knox	4	
Roome	5	4	Bush	4	1
Gridley	3	4	Beecher	3	2
Pratt	7	2	Nichols	2	
Thompson	6		Anderson	3	1
Total	73*		Total	33	

*The figures (as best I can read them) add up to 72.—Ed.

At the close of the contest the Pittsfield Base Ball Club gave a dinner to the two College Clubs at the U.S. Hotel, Mr. Henton having provided an excellent Dinner for the occasion. Toasts and speeches followed the repast, and all who participated had "a glorious time," as we are assured.

The match game of Chess was played on Saturday, and occupied from 9 A.M. to 3 P.M., resulting in the triumph of Amherst. At the 49th move Williams resigned, and Amherst was pronounced the winner. A large number of amateurs were present in an adjoining room.

The names of the Amherst players were—Messrs. J. F. Claflin, A. Maddock and A. G. Biscoe; Umpire, F. A. Williams. Williams—Messrs. E. E. K. Royce, E. S. Bowsterr, Henry Anstice; Umpire, E. B. Parsons. Referee, Geo. B. Hunt of Canaan, Ct.

19 _____

The First Reported African American Baseball Games (1859 and 1862)

Sources: *New York Anglo-African*, December 10, 1859, and *Brooklyn Eagle*, October 17, 1862

The earliest known account of a ball game involving African Americans appeared in the New York Anglo-African on July 30, 1859. In this Fourth of July contest, "the venerable Joshua R. Giddings made the highest score, never missing the ball when it came near him." Giddings was a sixty-four-year-old white Republican Congressman known for his passionate opposition to slavery. The following articles indicate that at least one all-black club, the Unknown of Weeksville, New York, existed at this time.

Not only did the Unknown play in the two games reported below, but, according to baseball historian Harry Simmons, they also defeated the Union Club of Williamsburg, New York, 11–0 on September 28, 1860. (The Negro Baseball Leagues: A Photographic History, ed. Phil Dixon and Patrick J. Hannigan, Mattituck, N.Y.: Amereon, 1992, pp. 31–32). The existence of at least four all-black teams during this period indicates that baseball was firmly established in the African American community. It also suggests that such clubs may have existed prior to 1859, especially since the December 10 article implies that the Unknown and the Henson club had played at least once previously.

BASE BALL

MR. EDITOR:—A match was played between the Henson Base Ball Club of Jamaica, and the Unknown, of Weeksville, at Jamaica, L.I., on Tuesday, Nov. 15th, which resulted in another victory for the Henson. The following is the score:

HENSON	O	R	UNKNOWN	O	R
Johnson, c.	2	10	Poole, p.	4	4
Henson, p.	4	6	H. Smith, c.	1	8
Vanwyck, s. b.	3	4	Ricks, f. b.	4	5
Hanke, f. b.	4	5	Anderson, s. b.	2	6
G. Anthony, t. b.	0	9	J. Thompson, t. b.	4	3
Ferris, s. s.	3	4	J. Smith, s. s.	2	4
Wilmore, c. f.	2	8	A. Thomson, r. f.	2	6
J. Anthony, r. f.	4	4	Wright, c. f.	5	3
Hewlett, l. f.	2	4	Johnson, l. f.	2	3

RUNS MADE IN EACH INNING

Innings	1	2	3	4	5	6	7	8	9	
Henson	6	1	6	17	3	9	3	9		—54
Unknown	7	5	4	4	7	0	2	3	11	—43*

SCORERS—Henson Club, Wm. Austin; Unknown, Wm. Johnson.
UMPIRE—Charles English.

Base Ball

A NEW SENSATION IN BASE BALL CIRCLES—
SAMBO AS A BALL PLAYER, AND DINAH AS AN EMULATOR
UNKNOWN OF WEEKSVILLE VS. MONITOR OF BROOKLYN

The return match between the Atlantic and Harlem Clubs did not take place as appointed yesterday afternoon, but was postponed on account of the unfit condition of the grounds for playing. Among the large crowd that visited the ground was our reporter, who, on learning that the match would not be played, went on a perambulating tour through the precincts of Bedford, waiting for something to "turn up." He had not proceeded far when he discovered a crowd assembled on the grounds in the vicinity of the Yukaton Skating Pond, and on repairing to the locality, found a match in progress between the Unknown and Monitor Clubs— both of African descent. Quite a large assemblage encircled the contestants, who were every one as black as the ace of spades. Among the assemblage we noticed a number of old and well known players, who seemed to enjoy the game more heartily than if they had been the players themselves. The dusky contestants enjoyed the game hugely, and to use a common phrase, they "did the thing genteely." Dinah, all eyes, was there to applaud, and the game passed off most satisfactorily. All appeared to have a very jolly time, and the little piccaninnies laughed with the rest. It would have done Beecher, Greeley, or any other of the luminaries of the radical wing of the Republican party good to have been present. The playing was quite spirited, and the fates decreed a victory for the Unknown. The occasion was the first of a series. We append the score:

UNKNOWN	HL	R	MONITOR	HL	R
Pole, 3d b.	5	2	Dudley, 1st b.	3	2
V. Thompson, l. f.	2	7	W. Cook, r. f.	2	2
Wright, 2d b.	5	3	Williams, s. s.	2	1
J. Thompson, p.	5	1	Marshall, 3d b.	4	1
Smith, c. f.	0	9	G. Abrams, p.	3	2
Johnson, c.	7	2	Brown, c.	3	3
A. Thompson, 1st b.	5	4	Cook, l. f.	4	1
Durant, r. f.	4	5	Orater, 2d b.	3	2
Harvey, s. s.	3	4	J. Abrams, c. f.	3	1
		41*			15

RUNS MADE IN EACH INNING

	1	2	3	4	5	6	7	8	9	
Unknown	3	4	3	7	14	1	7	2	0	—41
Monitor	3	3	0	0	2	1	1	5	0	—15

Umpire—C. Ophate, of the Hamilton of Newark.

Scorers—Baker, Unknown; Jones, Monitor.

This is the first match to our knowledge that has been played in this city between players of African descent.

*In this era box scores frequently did not balance. In the 1859 game, the Unknown's run column adds up to 42, not 43; in 1862, their run column adds up to 37, not 41. It is impossible to determine at this date which figures are correct, but in such cases historians usually accept the stated totals as accurate.—Ed.

20 _____

The Functions of Each Defensive Player (1860)

Source: *Beadle's Dime Base Ball Player* (New York: Beadle and Co., 1860), pp. 21–26

In the mid-nineteenth century, Beadle's was one of the nation's leading publishers of the inexpensive, mass-produced novels known as "dime" novels. In 1860 the company hired Henry Chadwick, arguably the leading authority on baseball, to produce an annual guide to satisfy the rapidly growing market of "cranks," or fans. Since the guide—containing some of Chadwick's newspaper articles, rules and statistics, and a summary of the benefits of the sport—allegedly sold fifty thousand copies, imitators soon followed. "The Positions on the Field" was reprinted frequently (usually without attribution) throughout the century, including in Seymour Church's book Base Ball: The History, Statistics, and Romance of the American National Game from Its Inception to the Present Time (San Francisco, 1902).

THE POSITIONS ON THE FIELD

THE CATCHER

This player is expected to catch or stop all balls pitched or thrown to the home base. He must be fully prepared to catch all foul balls, especially tips, and be able to throw the ball swiftly and accurately to the bases, and also keep a bright lookout over the whole field. When a player has made his first base, the Catcher should take a position nearer the striker, in order to take the ball from the pitcher before it bounds; and the moment the ball is delivered by the pitcher, and the player runs from the first to the second base, the Catcher should take the ball before bounding and send it to the second base as swiftly as possible, in time to cut off the player before he can touch the base; in the latter case it would be as well, in the majority of cases, to send the ball a little to the right of the base. The same advise holds good in reference to a player running from the second base to the third. As the position occupied by the Catcher affords him the best view of the field, the person filling it is generally chosen captain, although the pitcher is sometimes selected for that honor. We would suggest, however, that some other player than the pitcher be selected as captain, from the fact that the physical labor attached to that position tends to increase the player's excitement, especially if the contest is a close one, and it is requisite that the captain be as cool and collected as possible. We would suggest to the Catcher the avoidance of the boyish practice of passing the ball to and from the pitcher when a player is on the first base; let the discredit of this style of game fall on the batsman, if anyone, as then the umpire can act in the matter; we have referred to this matter elsewhere, as it is a feature of the game that is a tiresome one. The Catcher, whenever he sees several fielders running to catch a ball, should designate the one he deems most sure of taking it, by name, in which case the others should refrain from the attempt to catch the ball on the fly, and strive only to take it on the bound in case of its being otherwise missed.

THE PITCHER

This player's position is behind a line four yards in length, drawn at right angles to a line from home to second base, and having its center upon that line at a point distant forty five feet from the former base. He should be a good player at all points, but it is especially requisite that he should be an excellent fielder, and a swift and accurate thrower. He must pitch the ball, not jerk or throw it; and he must deliver the ball as near as possible over the home base, *and for the striker*, and sufficiently high to prevent its bounding before it passes the base. When in the act of delivering the ball, the Pitcher must avoid having either foot in advance of the line of his position, or otherwise a baulk will be declared; this penalty is also inflicted when he moves his arm with the apparent purpose of delivering the ball, and fails to do so. He should be exceedingly cautious and on the alert in watching the bases when the players are attempting to run, and in such cases should endeavor his utmost to throw a swift and true ball to the basemen. When a player attempts to run in to the home base when he is pitching, he should follow the ball to the home base as soon as it leaves his hand, and be ready at the base to take it from the catcher. The Pitcher will frequently have to occupy the bases on occasions when the proper guardian has left it to field the ball. And in cases where a foul ball has been struck, and the player running a base endeavors to return to the one he has left, he should be ready to retrieve the ball at the point nearest the base in question, in order to comply with Section 16 of the rules, wherein, in such cases, it is required that the ball be settled in the hands of the Pitcher before it is in play. The Pitcher, who can combine a high degree of speed with an even delivery, and at the same time can, at pleasure, impart a bias or twist to the ball, is the most effective player in that position. We would remind him that in cases where a player has reached his first base after striking, it is the Pitcher's duty to pitch the ball to the bat, and not to the catcher; and should the batsman refuse to strike at good balls repeatedly pitched to him, it will be the umpire's duty to call one strike, etc., according to Section 37 of the rules.

SHORT STOP

This position on the field is a very important one, for on the activity and judgment of the Short Stop depends the greater part of the in-fielding. His duties are to stop all balls that come within his reach, and pass them to whatever base the striker may be running to—generally, however, the first base. In each case his arm must be sure, and the ball sent in swiftly, and rather low than high. He must back up the pitcher, and when occasion requires, cover the third base when the catcher throws to it; also back up the second and third bases when the ball is thrown in from the field. He should be a fearless fielder, and one ready and able to stop a swift ground-ball; and if he can throw swiftly and accurately, it would be as well to be a little deliberate in sending the ball to the first base, as it is better to be sure and just in time, than to risk a wild throw by being in too great a hurry. His position is generally in the center of the triangle formed by the second and third bases and the pitcher's position, but he should change it according to his knowledge of the striker's style of batting. He must also be on the alert to take foul balls on the bound that are missed on the fly by either the third baseman or pitcher, or indeed any other player he can get near enough to to be effective in this respect. In doing this, however, he should be careful not to interfere with the fielder who is about catching the ball; so as to prevent him doing so, the catcher will call to that fielder who he thinks will best take a ball on the fly. An effective Short Stop and a good first base player, especially if they are familiar with each other's play, will materially contribute to the successful result of a well-contested game.

The First Baseman should play a little below his base and inside the line of the foul-ball post, as he will then get within reach of balls that would otherwise pass him. The moment the ball is struck, and he finds that it does not come near him, he should promptly return to his base, and stand in readiness, with one foot on the base, to receive the ball from any player that may have fielded it. The striker can be put out at this base without being touched by the ball, provided the fielder, with the ball in hand, touches the base with any part of his person before the striker reaches it. The player will find it good practice to stand with one foot on the base, and see how far he can reach and take the ball from the fielder; this practice will prepare him for balls that are thrown short of the base. In the same manner he should learn to jump up and take high balls. This position requires the player filling it to be the very best of catchers, as he will be required to hold very swiftly-thrown balls. The moment he has held the ball, he should promptly return it to the pitcher, or to either of the other bases a player is running to, as in some instances two and sometimes three players are put out by promptitude in this respect. For instance, we will suppose a player to be on each of the first, second, and third bases, and the striker hits the ball to short field, the latter sends it to First Base (he should, however, send it to the catcher, that being the proper play), in time to cut off the striker running to it; the First Baseman seeing the player on the third base running home, immediately sends the ball to the catcher, who, in turn, sends it to the third base; and if this be done rapidly in each case, all three players will be put out, as it is only requisite, under such circumstances, for the ball to be held—not the player to be touched with it—for each player to be put out. Should, however, there only be players on the second and third bases when the striker is put out at the first, and the ball is sent to the catcher as above, and by him to the third baseman, it will be requisite that each player be touched with the ball, as in the first case they are *forced* from their bases, but in the latter they are not. We give this as an illustration of a very pretty point of the game. For the rule in reference to it, see Sections 15 and 16.

This position is considered by many to be the key of the field, and therefore requires an excellent player to occupy it. He should be an accurate and swift thrower, a sure catcher, and a thorough fielder. He should play a little back of his base, and to the right or left of it, according to the habitual play of the striker, but generally to the left, as most balls pass in that direction. He should back up the pitcher well, allowing no balls to pass both that player and himself too. When the striker reaches the first base, the Second Baseman should immediately return to his base and stand prepared to receive the ball from the catcher, and put out his opponent by touching him with the ball, which it is requisite to do on this base as well as on the third and home bases, except in the cases of balls caught on the fly, or foul balls, in both of which instances a player can be put out in returning to the base he has left, in the same manner as when running to the first base,—see rule 16. When the catcher fails to throw the ball with accuracy to the Second Baseman, the latter should by all means manage to stop the ball, if he can not catch it, in time to put out his opponent. He should also promptly return the ball to the pitcher.

THIRD BASE

The Third Base is not quite as important a position as the others, but it nevertheless requires its occupant to be a good player, as some very pretty play is frequently shown on this base. Its importance, however, depends in a great measure upon the ability displayed by the catcher, who, if he is not particularly active, will generally sacrifice this base by giving his principal attention to the second. A player who catches with his left hand will generally make a good Third Baseman. The same advice in regard to the proper method of practice for the first base, is equally applicable to the second and third, but it is not quite as necessary to the two latter as to the former. Should a player be caught between the bases, in running from one to the other, it is the surest plan to run in and put the player out at once, instead of passing the ball backward and forward, as a wild throw, or a ball missed, will almost invariably give the player the base. All three of the basemen should avoid, by all fair means, obstructing the striker from reaching the base, as the penalty for any willful obstruction is the giving of the base to the striker. We scarcely need to remind each of the basemen that whenever they ask for judgment from the umpire, on any point of play, that they should forbear from commenting on the same, be it good or bad, but receive it in entire silence. Such is the course a gentleman will always pursue.

LEFT FIELD

This position requires the fielder who occupies it to be a good runner, a fine thrower, and an excellent and sure catcher; as probably three out of every six balls hit are sent toward the left field.

CENTER FIELD

The same qualities are requisite also in this position, as necessary in the left field, but not to the extent required by the latter fielder. The Center Fielder should always be in readiness to back up the second base, and should only go to long field in cases where a hard-hitter is at the bat.

RIGHT FIELD

This is the position that the poorest player of the nine—if there be any such—should occupy; not that the position does not require as good a player to occupy it as the others, but that it is only occasionally, in comparison to other portions of the field, that balls are sent in this direction.

2

Baseball Becomes a Commercial Spectacle, 1861–71

As the following documents reveal, baseball quickly became a commercial spectacle. As early as 1858, fans had to pay a gate fee in order to watch a match between the all-star squads of Brooklyn and New York. In 1862 William Cammeyer of Brooklyn enclosed a field and began to charge admission to games on a regular basis. The 1861 "benefit match" described in the first document in this chapter provides evidence that players could receive financial rewards for their play. Gamblers also began to profit from the sport. In 1865 the NABBP expelled three players for "dumping" games. By then, many differences between amateur and professional play had begun to develop. Acknowledged professionalization dates from the formation in 1869 of an all-salaried team—the famed Red Stockings of Cincinnati.

A Benefit Match for Two Famous Players (1861)

Source: *Brooklyn Eagle*, November 1, 1861

Although the baseball fraternity publicly frowned on paying players directly for their play, benefit matches provided a convenient, if less-than-convincing, subterfuge. The following account describes a benefit game scheduled for two of the game's stars—Dickey Pearce and Jim Creighton. Pearce, who began his career with the Atlantics in 1856, is credited with redefining the shortstop position by ranging farther afield to catch pop flies and stop ground balls than his predecessors. He also pioneered and popularized the bunt.

Creighton became baseball's first great pitcher by introducing a wrist snap, which enabled him to throw faster and with more spin.

THE BENEFIT MATCH—In yesterday's EAGLE a paragraph stated that a match was talked of, for the benefit of Messrs. Richard Pierce [sic], of the Atlantic, and James Creighton, of the Excelsior Club. We have not as yet learned the full particulars regarding the arrangements. The gentlemen for whom the benefit is gotten up, are well known to the Base Ball Fraternity,—the names of Pierce and Creighton, being names of players not to be forgotten, the latter noted for his superior pitching. The large circle of friends of Mr. Pierce, conceived the idea and arranged the match for *his* benefit, but he generously desired Mr. Creighton to be included, and thus the two are to share in the proceeds, and to judge from the large circle of their acquaintances the proceeds will amount to something handsome. We are requested [to] state that tickets for this match can be purchased at the store of Dick & Haynes, corner of Fulton avenue and St. Felix street, Brooklyn. Price 10 cents. Match to come off November 7th, on the St. George Cricket grounds, Hoboken.

22

Prospects for the Baseball Season in Brooklyn (1862)

Source: *Brooklyn Eagle*, April 7, 1862

In the 1860s, as today, the press prepared special articles reviewing the prospects for the upcoming baseball season. The article below, written by Henry Chadwick, contains an analysis of Brooklyn-area teams in 1862 and closes with a reference to William H. Cammeyer's new enclosed ballpark. Three days later, the Eagle *reported that Cammeyer would charge an admission fee for the games played in his park. His decision represented an important turning point in the commercialization of baseball.*

The Incoming Base Ball Season

ARRANGEMENTS FOR 1862

With the approach of summer the base ball grounds in the suburban districts of our city are beginning to put on nature's universal robe—refreshing green, and once more the ball which was set aside for the winter months is again in requisition, and the healthy and exhilarating game again monopolize the attention of the youth of our city and the ball-playing community generally. Even at this early period of the season there is an unusual interest manifested by the fraternity, and if we take this as a criterion, we may anticipate a long and brilliant season. Already extensive preparations have been made, such as levelling and rolling the ground, erecting and repairing club houses, and other arrangements, as will enable the various clubs to mutually participate in the manly sport.

The champion club (the Atlantic) contemplate changing their grounds, those they now occupy being so encroached upon for building purposes as to be unfit for use, and will occupy the ground formerly used by the Long Island Cricket Club and Pastime Base Ball Club, or the Putnam grounds; but to the latter there was an objection, the out-of-the-way situation of the grounds; but this is not now a serious drawback, as the DeKalb avenue cars pass within two blocks of them. The Atlantics have an engagement on hand to play a match which is looked forward to with great interest—the home and home match with the Mutuals—the most powerful club in New York, and as each club has won a game, this one cannot fail to prove very interesting, as both muster fine players and will make strenuous efforts to win. The Champions intend treating several of the other clubs to a display of their skill by a pacific game with them. The return contest for the silver ball between New York and Brooklyn is also anticipated with much interest, and already is attracting some attention. The Excelsiors, who remained inactive last season, anticipate taking a prominent part in the campaign of 1862, and with the officers who are at the head of the club, no doubt they will. The rumor which obtained credence in the base ball community, that Mr. James Creighton, the pitcher *par excellence* of the United States, long a member of the Excelsior Club, had joined the Atlantics, is untrue, as we learn from reliable authority. The Putnams, who remained in *statu quo* last season, will make an appearance this year, and will present quite a strong front—this and the Brooklyn club we understand having amalgamated. They will play on their grounds, on Lafayette avenue, corner of Broadway—the best ground in Brooklyn—which is also occupied by the Constellations, who played as juniors last season, but were admitted at the last Convention; and if they play as seniors as well as they did when juniors, we bespeak for them many laurels. The same remark will also apply to the Resolutes, last year champions of the juniors, but at the Convention were made seniors.

Both of these clubs will "tackle" the Enterprise club for certain, and no doubt through the season, the other crack clubs. The Enterprise boys, although unsuccessful last season, are not a whit less enterprising, and will make their appearance as usual on the ball grounds. They have an old score to settle with the Gotham of Hoboken, and we believe the Eurekas of Newark, besides several others with Brooklyn clubs. They will probably occupy the Pastime grounds. The Eckfords will muster strong and intend playing the Eagles of New York, the Enterprise of this city, and several others. They have already commenced practicing and have had a scrub game with the Favorites, which club intends taking an active part in the enjoyment of this exhilarating sport. The ball grounds on Fifth avenue will not be much used, except by the junior clubs, as they have been so encroached upon for building purposes, and the Greenwood cars running through them, that they are rendered too small. The Exercise, fast rising to be one of the first clubs of the city, will this season occupy the Carrol Park grounds, and share the new, large and commodious club-house recently erected, with the Star club. The last mentioned club are true to their name—bright in good playing, and the Carrol Park grounds will be the centre of attraction this summer, and while one club is star-ing it, the other will be playing it only for exercise. They had the honor of inaugurating the season, and the manner in which they did it was worthy of them and the ball-players of Brooklyn. The Charter Oaks of South Brooklyn will, in a short time make their *debut*, and the Waverly club, prominent as a junior, has disbanded, and its members have circulated themselves among the Star and other clubs: The Olympic and one or two other South Brooklyn organizations which occupy the grounds near Carrol Park, will make their appearance in a short time. The junior organizations remain rather quiet and we hear very little of them, and will probably be late in making their *entre*. We must remind them that the "National Association of Junior Ball Players" meet in the latter part of April, and they must not neglect to send their delegates. The Association is in a flourishing condition, and the aid of the Brooklyn clubs must not be wanting to keep it so. The retirement of the Constellation and Resolute from the Juniors has left quite a vacuum, and the Niagara are next on the list, and they no doubt will take a hand in the proceedings this season. The Powhatan will probably make their appearance to play with the Stars, with whom they have an old score to settle up. The Hamiltons are deprived of their ground, and as yet have not selected one, and therefore will be rather late in making their *debut*. On the 9th instant they have a meeting for the election of officers for the ensuing year.

The great disadvantage attached to the Ball Clubs—which every year is increasing—is that of procuring grounds. The vacant lots and unfenced fields in the suburban districts and the vicinity of the city are every year becoming in more demand, and the Ball Clubs have to make way for the giant of Time—improvement—and as he makes rapid strikes, are deprived of their grounds. But still, notwithstanding this onward movement—an every day evidence of Brooklyn's rivaling its neighbor over the water—there are enough ball grounds remaining to accommodate the clubs, as three can easily occupy the same ground, and each practice two days in the week. And with the growth of our city, the more necessary does out-door exercise become, and the advantages of ball playing grows daily apparent.

The first of May is the regular day for opening the season, but in this, as in former years, it was opened earlier and matches played a month or so before that date. Several interesting matches between New York and Brooklyn clubs will be made for this season, and there is some talk of getting up a series of "Muffin Matches," on the plan of those played upon the Putnam grounds, a few years ago, which afforded so much merriment for the spectators and pleasure for the participators. We shall have a series of the "Donkey Matches" this season. Among the members of the Cricket Clubs there are many Base Ball players who are as well acquainted with the liveliness of Base Ball as they are with the intricacies of Cricket, and we may look forward to several matches between "Cricketers and Ball

Players," like that one played at Hoboken last season, between eleven Ball players and twenty-two Cricketers, and in which the Ball players came off victorious.

The Cricket season also promises very fair, but as this is not an *American* game, but purely an English game, it never will be in much vogue with the Americans, especially the New Yorkers, who are all for fast and not slow things. The five Brooklyn Cricket Clubs are of good standing. They are as follows: The Satellite, Willow, East Williamsburgh—a new association, recently organized in the Eastern District, composed mostly of "Old Countrymen"—and the American and Long Island Club. The two latter, it is rumored, contemplate amalgamating, thereby forming a very powerful club, and possessing some very fine players. Besides these there are the East New York and Queens County Clubs. But of the Cricket Clubs we shall have more to say hereafter through the columns of the EAGLE.

A NEW CLUB AND NEW BALL GROUNDS.—The grounds used last winter by the "Union Skating Association" have been enlarged and converted into commodious ball grounds, which will be ready for use by the 1st of May. The grounds are located on the corner of Rutledge street and Leo avenue, convenient to the Greenpoint, Flushing avenue car routes. The grounds under the charge of the gentlemen who have the matter in hand, will be put and kept in the finest order, and like the Skating Association, will be an honor to that section of the city where it is located. A new club has been organized to play upon this ground, by the patriotic name of "Union Club," and will make their *debut* in the base ball world on the 4th of May next. We wish them much success, and hope they may exist in unity and win many matches.

23 ───

The Premature Death of Baseball's First Superstar (1862)

Source: *Brooklyn Eagle*, October 20, 1862

According to baseball folklore, which the following article supports, star pitcher Jim Creighton died from an injury suffered in an October 14 baseball game while running out a home run. However, some historians cite an October 25 New York Clipper article as proof that Creighton actually suffered his fatal injury in a cricket match played on October 7. Whatever the cause, Creighton's premature death contributed to the growth of a potent legend concerning his athletic abilities.

A brief Eagle *editorial, which comments ironically on the benefits of baseball, follows the article.*

OBSEQUIES OF A CELEBRATED BALL PLAYER—

The remains of the late James P. Creighton, familiar in Base Ball and Cricket circles as one of the best players in the Union, were yesterday conveyed to their last resting place, followed by a large number of friends and relatives. There are few who have not heard of Mr. Creighton. As the Pitcher, *par excellence*, the Base Ball people loose [sic] a valuable member by his untimely decease. As a general player, he had few equals; as a cricketer, he displayed unusual abilities. Although very young, Mr. Creighton had obtained an enviable position as a member of the Excelsior Base Ball and St. George Cricket Clubs. He first became a member of the Young America Junior Club, and soon after, of the Niagara. We next find him in the Star Club—then in its prime—and while here he displayed such promising qualities as a pitcher, that the attention of the older ball players was attracted, and he subsequently joined the Excelsior Club, with which organization he continued until his death. To him belongs the reputation the Excelsiors have acquired, for it was he who obtained it.

Mr. Creighton was endowed with many of those qualities which attracted friends. He was warm to his attachments, gifted with a large measure of humor, an enthusiastic and practical musician, and a most agreeable conversationalist. Poor Creighton has gone leaving behind him a memory that will ever be held fresh and green by his many sorrowing friends.

The circumstances of his death are very touching. In the late match with the Union (Tuesday inst.) the deceased sustained an internal injury occasioned by a strain while batting. After suffering for a few days he expired on Saturday afternoon last, at the residence of his father, 307 Henry st. The remains were encased in a handsome rosewood coffin, with silver mountings, and upon a silver plate was inscribed the name, age, etc., of the deceased—James P. Creighton, 21 years, 7 months, 2 days. The funeral services were conducted at the house, by the Rev. Dr. North, and at four P.M. the funeral cortege moved off for Greenwood Cemetary, where the remains were deposited a lot adjoining the Fireman's Monument. Messrs. Leggett, Polhemus, Lent and Flanley officiated as pall bearers.

Even a good thing may be carried too far. Base-ball, that was at first commendable as furnishing an agreeable out-door exercise for our young men, has been run into the ground. One of the most proficient players of Brooklyn, and one of the most estimable young men of the city, last week ruptured himself while engaged in playing a match game, died in a day or two afterwards, and was buried yesterday. In the melancholy death of James Creighton there is a warning to others. Exercise is a good thing; but like other good things, one may take too much of it.

24

Three Players Expelled for "Selling" a Game (1865)

Source: *New York Clipper*, November 11, 1865

When baseball's popularity soared following the Civil War, wagering on the outcome of games became commonplace. Charges that players had been bribed by gamblers soon followed. One of the most notorious cases of game dumping, or "hippodroming," is described below.

"HIPPODROME" TACTICS IN BASE BALL

HOW TO "HEAVE" A GAME

THE FIRST AND LAST INSTANCE OF SELLING A GAME OF BALL

On Thursday, Sept. 28th, the Eckford Club, of Brooklyn, played their return match with the Mutuals, of Hoboken, the result being the success of the Eckfords. In our report of the match we took occasion to doubt the truth of certain charges made against Wm. Wansley—the catcher of the Mutual Club—of "selling" or "heaving" the game, as it is technically termed. In analyzing the play in our report, we showed that Duffy, the 3d base player, and Devyr, the short stop, as well as McMahon—who took Wansley's place after the 5th innings had been played—were nearly equally to blame with Wansley for errors in fielding, in the shape of wild throws and passed balls. Singularly enough, the correctness of our analysis has been borne out nearly to the very letter, as will be seen from the annexed documents, the result of an investigation which has been made by the Mutual Club in regard to the truth of the alleged charges against Wansley. In our report we stated that "McMahon went behind in Wansley's place in the 6th innings," and the errors he was charged with, in wild throws and passed balls, were committed after the game had been, to all intents and purposes, lost; and the throws which were charged to him were to 3d base to Duffy. But without further comment we proceed to give a full and reliable account of the proceedings of the Mutual Club on the matter of investigating the charges of selling the game made against Wansley. The preliminary step in the matter was the serving of a copy of the charges preferred on Wansley, the document in question being as follows:—

COPY OF THE CHARGES MADE

At a meeting of the Mutual Base Ball Club, held at the rooms at Hoboken immediately after the match between the said club and the Eckford Club, certain charges were then and there made against one William Wansley, catcher of the said Mutual Club, of inattention to said game, and that such inattention was upon the part of the said William Wansley, wilful and designedly, with a view of causing the said Eckford Club to defeat the said Mutual Club in the said match; and it was further charged, and believed, that the said William Wansley was paid, and did receive from certain parties at the present time unknown to the said Mutual Club, a certain consideration for his acts in being a party to aid and assist in the defeat of the said Mutual Club; and at such meeting, hereinbefore mentioned, a committee of seven members of the said Mutual Club was by such meeting duly appointed to investigate and ascertain if such charges against the said William Wansley were true, and could be substantially proven; therefore, the said William Wansley is hereby notified, and made acquainted of such charges being preferred against him; and if proven, he the said William Wansley will be by action of the said Mutual Club expelled therefrom, and he is therefore for the purpose of responding and answering to the said aforementioned charges, to appear before the said committee and vindicate himself from such imputation and charges, and that if the said William Wansley does not appear before the said committee on the evening of Friday, the 20th inst., at 8 P.M., at the Study, 397 Hudson street, the said committee will take such action as such charges will warrant them, and that the said William Wansley will be accordingly expelled.

SIMON BURNS, Chairman,
WM. C. GOVER, Secretary,
HENRY ROGERS,
ANDREW HOLLEY,   Committee.
JOHN BRADY,
WILLIAM KANE,
R. H. THORNE,
JOHN WILDEY, President of the Club.
WILLIAM H. DONGAN, Secretary of the Club.

The above document having been duly placed in the hands of the accused, a committee of investigation was appointed, and through the unremitting exertions of the President of the club, Coroner Wildey, and the chairman of the committee, Mr. Burns, together with the able assistance afforded by others of the committee, the whole plot was laid bare, and the charge against Wansley not only fully established, but Duffy and Devyr's criminal complicity in the matter was also proved.

The following is the report of the committee of investigation:

REPORT OF THE COMMITTEE

We, the undersigned committee, appointed to investigate the charges preferred against Wm. Wansley and others, in reference to the match between the Mutual and Eckford Clubs, on Sept. 28th, 1865, after strict and diligent inquiry into this matter, find that Wm. Wansley, catcher, and E. Duffy, 3d base, and Thos. Devyr, s. s., received from a person known by the name of Kane McLoughlin, the sum of one hundred dollars, as a bribe for the purpose of allowing the said McLoughlin to win money on the game, and this committee do hereby recommend that the said W. Wansley, E. Duffy and Thomas Devyr be expelled.

SIMON BURNS, Chairman,
WM. GOVER,
WILLIAM KANE,
R. H. THORNE,   Committee.
JOHN N. BRADY,
ANDREW HOLLEY,
JOHN WILDEY,
HENRY ROGERS,

We now come to the most interesting document of the series, viz., the written confessions of young Devyr. It will be seen by this, that one of the party at least has not yet become so accustomed to transactions of the kind as to be indifferent to the opinions of those by whom he was once thought well of. His letter is a redeeming point of his conduct in the affair, and on this account the jury of the ball playing community will no doubt recommend him to mercy. The letter is as follows:

DEVYR'S CONFESSION

WILLIAMSBURGH, Oct. 25.

TO CAPT. WILDEY AND THE MUTUAL B. B. C.—

Gentlemen—As words can make no apology for the injury done your Club or the disgrace brought on myself by my connection with this affair, the briefer I am with this statement the better; but in order that I may put myself in the true light (which, God knows, is bad enough) I have concluded to write you a full and true account of all I know about it. Between eleven and twelve o'clock on the morning of the match, I was going toward the ferry, ready to go over to the ground, when I met Wansley, Duffy and another man in a wagon. Bill pulled up and asked me where I was going. I told him I was getting down toward the ferry, and that I was going over to the ground in about an hour. He says, "Do you want to make three hundred dollars?" I says "I would like to do anything for that." He says "You can make it easy." I asked how? He says, "We are going to 'heave' this game, and will give you three hundred dollars if you like to stand in with us; you need not do any of the work, I'll do all that myself and get all the blame. Let them blame, I can stand it all. We can lose this game without doing the club any harm, and win the home and home game. Now, you ain't got a cent, neither has Duffy. You can make this money without any one being a bit the wiser of it. You needn't do anything toward (heaving) it, I will do that myself." I said, "Bill, if you don't want me to help you why do you let me into it?" He says, "I want to give you a chance to make some money, and make O'Donnell sure that it can be done." Well, to make a long story short, not having a cent, I agreed. We went over to O'Donnell's house, received a hundred dollars, of which I got thirty, which was all I did receive since or before it. This is the whole substance of it.

I do not write this to vindicate myself more than the rest, nor to make you believe I am any less guilty than any of the others; on the contrary, as I entered into this affair and received my share of the gains, it is but fair that I should stand my share of the censure and punishment which the publicity of this thing will bring upon us. I simply write it to let you see how my connection with this unhappy affair was brought about. For what! for thirty dollars, which I could do nothing with but lose playing faro; and now, I have 30 hundred worth of disgrace, all to myself, never to lose, and without one envious eye to wish one cent's worth. One word about Duffy, and I will close. I saw him last night. He says that Bill came to him the day before the match and asked him if he would go in with him in 'heaving' the game; he says he refused unless I was into it. Bill says "all right, leave him to me, I can talk to him;" which he did, and with the result already too well known. I have now fulfilled a duty which devolved on me to place before you the facts of the case. I am sorry I had anything to do with it; but my sorrow, like this statement, comes too late to help me any. I close this by wishing the club a more prosperous and luckier season next year than they have this, and hope they will get no more such ungrateful players as Wansley, Duffy, and

Your humble servant,   THOS. H. DEVYR.

The perusal of this letter must lead every reader to regret that a young man of good promise, like Devyr, should have been led into such a discreditable transaction. It shows the evils of not keeping young men steadily employed in honest labor.

The following affidavits tell their own story, and are the last chapters in this disgraceful portion of the annals of our National Game. William Wansley, Edward Duffy and Thomas Devyr will be henceforth debarred from all participation in any match game of ball played by any club belonging to the National Association; and no club of which they are members will be permitted to join the National Association. A rule to this effect will be introduced at the next Convention, and will of course be unanimously adopted. The affidavits of Messrs. Wildey and Burns are appended.

AFFIDAVITS

CITY AND COUNTY OF NEW YORK, SS:

John Wildey, being duly sworn, says that he was one of the committee appointed by the Mutual B. B. Club to investigate certain charges preferred against William Wansley, Edward Duffy and Thos. H. Devyr, and from information obtained went with witnesses and saw Thomas H. Devyr, William Wansley, and Kane McLoughlin, who acknowledged to him that the late game between the Mutual and Eckford B. B. Clubs, played at Hoboken, was sold, and that Wm. Wansley, Edward Duffy and Thos. H. Devyr received at the house of S. D. O'Donnell the sum of $100 from Kane McLoughlin, which they divided before going to Hoboken to play the match.

JOHN WILDEY, President M. B. B. C.

Sworn to before me this first day of November, 1865,

GEO. H. MCKAY, Notary Public.

CITY AND COUNTY OF NEW YORK, SS:

Simon Burns, being duly sworn, says he was one of the committee appointed by the Mutual B. B. Club to investigate charges preferred against W. Wansley and others, and he was with John Wildey when the confessions were made referred to in Wildey's affidavit.

SIMON BURNS.

Sworn to before me, this first day of November, 1865,

GEO. H. MCKAY, Notary Public.

The following is the notice of expulsion from the club:

At a special meeting of the Mutual Base Ball Club, held at the house of Mr. H. A. Jennings, 397 Hudson street, the committee on Wm. Wansley and others, reported that after a thorough investigation of the charges preferred, they would recommend that Wm. Wansley, Thomas Devyr, and Edward Duffy, be expelled from this club; and on motion of Mr. Wildey, the report was received and the above named parties were expelled, unanimously, for selling the match game played with the Eckford Club on Thursday, Sept. 28, 1865.   JOHN WILDEY, President.

WM. H. DONGAN, Secretary.

25

The Tenth Annual Convention of the NABBP (1866)

Source: Charles Peverelly, *The Book of American Pastimes* (New York, 1866), pp. 501–8.

The following excerpt from the first post–Civil War meeting of the NABBP demonstrates the remarkable growth of baseball, in terms of both the sheer number of clubs represented at the convention and the geographic expansion of clubs. Moreover, the reader should recognize that the figures presented here radically undercount the total number of clubs: the great majority of clubs did not have written constitutions or belong to the association.

TENTH ANNUAL BASE BALL CONVENTION

Never before, in the history of the National Association, was there such a numerous and influential body of the fraternity gathered in convention, as marked the tenth annual meeting of the National Association of Base Ball Players, held at

Clinton Hall, New York, December 12, 1866. The great majority were up to the highest standard of assemblages of the kind, and reflected credit upon the base ball fraternity of the country.

A noteworthy feature of this great meeting was, that representatives from State Associations were present; Messrs. Griggs and Chambers, of the North-Western Base Ball Association, and Judge Rose, President of the Pennsylvania Association, being guests of the National Association on the occasion, and occupants of honorary seats on the platform with the President thereof.

Clubs from Oregon, on the extreme West, to Maine, on the East; and from Missouri, Tennessee, and Virginia, on the South, to Vermont, on the North, sent delegates to this Convention, and the flattering reception given them as their names were announced, and especially the applause which greeted the responses from the Southern clubs, afforded ample proof of the truly conservative feeling which prevailed in the Convention. But if anything more was needed it was presented in the form of the compliment paid the Southern delegation, in the selection of a candidate for the presidency of the association from among their number.

As early as 2 P.M., delegates began to throng the hall of the building known as Clinton Hall, and promptly at the hour of 3 P.M., the President was in the chair and the meeting called to order. The calling of the roll, receiving credentials, and payment of dues of clubs belonging to the Association having been got through with, the report of the nominating committee was received, and the names of the new clubs applying for admission being favorably reported upon, they were all duly elected members of the Association, and as the roll of the new clubs were called, their delegates stepped up to the Secretary's desk, presented credentials, paid their dues, and received tickets to entitle them to seats in the Convention. Nearly three hours were occupied in this business, and on motion, a temporary adjournment was held until 7½ P.M. . . .

TOTAL CLUBS REPRESENTED

New York State, 73; Pennsylvania, 48; New Jersey, 26; Connecticut, 20; District of Columbia, 10; Maryland, 5; Ohio, 4; Massachusetts, 2; Iowa, 2; Tennessee, 2; Missouri, 2; Kansas, 2; and Delaware, Virginia, West Virginia, Kentucky, Oregon and Maine, one each; making a grand total of 202 clubs, representing 17 States and the District of Columbia.

In addition to the above list of clubs there were present at the Convention, Messrs. Griggs and Chambers of the North-Western Association, and Judge Rose of the Pennsylvania Association, as representatives of over two hundred additional clubs. . . .

26

The Incorporation of the Louisville Base Ball and Skating Park Company (1866)

Source: *Acts of the General Assembly of the Commonwealth of Kentucky* (1866), chapter 206, pp. 168–70

One of the many new NABBP members was the recently incorporated Louisville club. Incorporation, a common practice among clubs during this era, allowed investors to pool their resources and sell stock in order to raise money for the purchase of land and the construction of facilities like ballparks and clubhouses. By embracing standard business practices, incorporated baseball clubs of the 1860s foreshadowed the strategy that would be used to form the National League in 1876.

AN ACT to incorporate the Louisville Base Ball and Skating Park Company.
Be it enacted by the General Assembly of the Commonwealth of Kentucky:

§1. That R. A. Browinski, Geo. B. Blanchard, Barry Coleman, Geo. P. Nash, Archie M. Quarrier, J. Lewis Shallcross, and Thos. C. Timberlake, and their successors, be, and they are thereby, created a body corporate and politic, by the name of the "Louisville Base Ball and Skating Park Company," for the term of twenty-five years, with all the powers and authority incident to corporations for the purposes hereinafter mentioned.

§2. The corporation is hereby authorized and empowered to buy, lease, construct, maintain, and operate a Base Ball and Skating Park and appendages in the city of Louisville or county of Jefferson.

§3. The capital stock of the Louisville Base Ball and Skating Park Company shall be ten thousand dollars; it shall be divided into shares of ten dollars each, and be issued and transferred in such manner and upon such conditions as the board of said corporation may direct.

§4. The affairs of said corporation shall be managed by seven directors, one of whom shall be president, all of whom shall be stockholders in said corporation; the first board of directors shall consist of R. A. Browinski, Geo. B. Blanchard, Barry Coleman, Geo. P. Nash, Archie M. Quarrier, J. Lewis Shallcross, and Thos. C. Timberlake, who shall continue in office until their successors shall be elected by a majority in interest of the stockholders of said corporation; and the board of directors chosen by the stockholders shall continue in office for one year or until their successors are elected and qualified; if any of the above named directors shall decline or refuse to act, a majority of the others shall fill the vacancy by appointing or choosing someone else. They may adopt such by-laws, rules and regulations, for the government of said corporation, and the management of its affairs and business, as they may deem proper, not inconsistent with the laws of this State. The said corporators may open books of subscriptions and receive subscriptions to the capital stock of the

Louisville Base Ball and Skating Park Company herein incorporated, and such books of subscription may be opened and subscriptions received at such times and places and upon such notices thereof as any four of said corporation may deem right and proper.

§5. That at every subscription of the stock to the capital stock of said Louisville Base Ball and Skating Park Company, there shall be paid at the time of subscribing, to said corporation or such agent as may be duly appointed, ten per cent. of the amount so subscribed; and so soon as the ten per cent. of the capital stock is subscribed and paid in, the said corporators, or any four of them, shall give notice of the time and place at which an election shall be held for a new board of directors, who shall hold and continue in office as provided herein. The board of directors of said corporation may fill all vacancies in their body which may happen by death, resignation, or otherwise, and may make such calls of payment of stock as they deem proper.

§6. The said corporation are authorized and empowered to acquire and hold and convey real estate to an amount not to exceed twenty thousand dollars. The said corporation may borrow money to an amount not to exceed the capital stock of the company, and may pledge and mortgage the property and all appurtenances and real estate belonging to said corporation.

§7. This act to be in force and take effect from its passage: *Provided,* That nothing in this act shall authorize the establishment of drinking saloons or other establishments calculated to promote dissipation, nor shall this act be so construed as to authorize banking or lottery privileges.

Approved January 26, 1866.

27

"Base Ball Fever" (1867)

Source: Performing Arts Reading Room, Library of Congress

Baseball quickly became an integral part of American culture. Baseball articles and stories could be found in the print media, baseball images in lithographs. Baseball became a theme for vaudeville skits and songs, too. Long before vaudevillian Jack Norworth composed the music and Albert von Tilzer wrote the lyrics for "Take Me Out to the Ball Game" in 1908, a song that would become baseball's unofficial anthem, "Base Ball Fever" sought to capture the emotional power of the game.

All 'round about we've queer complaints,
Which needs some Doctors patching;
But something there is on the brain,
Which seems to be more catching,
'Tis raging too, both far and near,

Or else I'm a deceiver,
I'll tell you what it is now, plain,
It is the Base Ball fever.

CHORUS:
O my, O my, O my, O my, We want a safe releiver
O my, O my, O my, O my, We want a safe releiver

28

A Fourth of July Game in Kansas (1867)

Source: *Lawrence Daily Kansas State Journal, July 3 and 5, 1867*

In those communities where baseball was not yet firmly established, clubs often arranged games by issuing challenges to other clubs in local newspapers. Published challenges helped to promote and legitimize baseball in areas where the sport was still new. Once there were enough local clubs to sustain a schedule of practices, practice games, and match (official) games, such challenges were no longer necessary.

On July 3 the Journal *published the Kaw Valley Base Ball Club's challenge, and the University Base Ball Club's acceptance, to play a game the following day. The game account appeared on July 5.*

A PRACTICE GAME.—The Kaw Valley Ball Club will meet for practice on the grounds south of the park, opposite South Lawrence House, to-day at 5 o'clock p.m.

S. S. HORTON, Sec'ry.

BASE BALL.—By the following correspondence it will be seen that our base ball players are to furnish sport for themselves and the lovers of the "noble science" on July 4th.

To the Secretary of the University Base Ball Club:

At a regular meeting of the Kaw Valley Base Ball Club, held July 2d, 1867, it was voted that a challenge be given to the University Club to play a match game at such time and place as they may choose.

S. S. HORTON, Sec'ry.

———

To the Secretary of the Kaw Valley Base Ball Club:

The challenge of the Kaw Valley Base Ball Club is hereby accepted. Game to be played July 4th, 1867, on the State Fair Grounds. Game to be called at 1 o'clock p.m.

J. H. LANE, Capt. 1st Nine U. C.

THE GAME OF BASE BALL

An interesting game of base ball was played on the fair grounds in the afternoon between the Kaw Valley and the University Clubs of this city. Quite a number of persons were present to witness this most interesting of field games. The Kaw Valley Club distinguished itself in some three very fine plays, putting out three of the Universities at one time and two at two other times. The University Club, though beaten, won respect from their opponent and applause from the spectators. It is due them to state that a number of their best players are absent from the city. We have no doubt that another game will be played, and they certainly will have no hesitancy in meeting any Club in the state. We notice the Frontier Club of Leavenworth, issued a card stating that they are ready to play. If they are anxious to play a game with either of our Clubs we doubt not they can be accommodated by sending a challenge. We are requested to state that such a note may be addressed to S. S. Horton, Secretary of the Kaw Valleys, or to Wm. L. Bullens of the University Club. The Frontiers will be kindly treated, and need feel no worse over a defeat than do the Leavenworth horsemen. The umpire of the game, Mr. W. S. White, by the manner and promptness of his decisions gave universal satisfaction. He is a thorough gentleman, a good player and an ardent lover of the game. The score is as follows:

KAW VALLEY VS. UNIVERSITY, JULY 4, 1867

Kaw Valley,	O	R	University,	O	R
Haskell, c	2	4	Barber, c	2	3
Whitman, 2d b & p	2	3	Chambers, r f	3	2
Wilder, 1st b	3	3	Hadley, c f	4	1
Horton, p & 2d b	4	1	Bullene, 2d b	4	2
Guest, 3d b	4	1	Drew, s s	2	2
Taylor, s s	3	4	Lane, p & l f	2	3
Riggs, c f	2	4	J. Rankin, 3d b	2	0
Farrel, r f	3	3	Snow, 1st b	4	0
W. Rankin, l f	4	3	Eager, l f & p	4	2

RUNS MADE EACH INNING

Inn'gs—	1st	2d	3d	4th	5th	6th	7th	8th	9th
K. V.	8	2	3	1	6	2	0	0	4—26
U.	0	1	7	3	0	2	0	0	2—15

Fly Catches—Kaw Valley: Haskell 4, Guest 2, Taylor 2, Whitman 1—9. University: Barber 5, Snow 3, Hadley 2, Bullene 1, Lane 1, Drew 1, Eager 1—14.

Foul Bound Catches—Kaw Valley: Haskell 3, Wilder 1—4. University: Barber 1.

Number of times left on Bases—Kaw Valley: Haskell 1, Whitman 2, Wilder 1, Horton 2, Guest 2, Farrell 1, Riggs 1—10. University: Hadley 1, Drew 1, J. Rankin 3, Snow 2, Barber 1, Chambers 1—9.

Passed Balls—Kaw Valley, 6. University, 4.

Called Balls—Kaw Valley, 3. University, 1.

Balks—Kaw Valley, 0. University, 2.

Struck Out—Kaw Valley: W. S. Rankin, 2. University: J. C. Rankin, 1.

Time of game, two hours and twenty minutes.

Umpire, W. S. White.

Scorers—Kaw Valley: L. J. Worden. University: R. Burgess.

29

"The Ancient History of Base Ball" (1867)

Source: *Ball Players' Chronicle*, July 18, 1867

As a part of his campaign to firmly establish baseball as America's national pastime, Henry Chadwick made frequent reference to baseball's "ancient history." In this document, Chadwick produced perhaps the most detailed account of baseball's origins to appear in the nineteenth century. Chadwick's interpretation of baseball's past would be officially discarded forty years later, when organized baseball accepted the validity of the Doubleday/Cooperstown creation myth.

THE ANCIENT HISTORY OF BASE BALL

In the old days of the gallant Edward the Third, in the first half of the fourteenth century, there came into fashion, among the youths and children of England, a game called "barres," or *bars*, which consisted in running from one bar or barrier to another. It grew to be so popular that it at last became a nuisance, so that the barons of England, as they went to the Parliament House, were annoyed by the bands of children engaged in playing it. They were at last obliged to pass an act of Parliament which declared, in the quaint Norman French of the period, that *nul enfaunt ne autres ne jue a barres* in the avenues which led to Westminster Palace. The name of this game was subsequently corrupted to "base," and two hundred years after Edward's day, Spenser, in his "Faery Queen," alluded to it as follows:

> "So ran they all as they had been at *bace*,
> They being chased that did others chace."

And Shakespeare, in his "Cymbeline," shows that he was familiar with its character, for he makes one of his characters say:

> "He with two stripling lads more like to run
> The country *base*, than to omit such slaughter."

Even now men frequently indulge in this pastime, and so late as 1770 there was a celebrated game of "bars" or "base" played in London, in the field behind Montague House, which has since been transformed into the British Museum. It was played between a select party of persons from Derbyshire and another from Cheshire, and was witnessed by all London. Derbyshire won, and a great quantity of money changed hands on the occasion. In the process of time, from a peculiarity in the method of playing it, and to distinguish it from other games which had sprung out of it, it was called "prisoner's base," and as such still affords amusement to the children of England and America.

The skill in this game consisted simply in running with agility and swiftness, in such a way as not to be caught by the opposing party, from one "bar" or "base" to another. After a while somebody thought of uniting with it the game of ball, and thus formed the game of "rounders," "round ball," or "base ball." "Rounders" took its name from the fact that the players were obliged to run *round* a sort of circle of bases. The method of playing it is thus described in an English work:

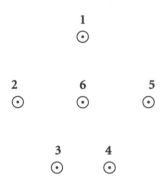

"The game is played by first fixing five spots, called 'bases,' at equal distances of fifteen or twenty yards, forming a pentagon, and marked by a stone or hole. In the centre of this is another place (6), called the 'seat,' where the 'feeder' stands to give or toss the ball to the one who has the bat, and who stands at (1) in the diagram, called 'home,' or 'house.' Two sides are chosen as in football, one of which goes in while the other is out, this being decided by tossing up the ball and scrambling for it, or by heads and tails, or any other fair mode. There should not be less than ten or twelve players in all, and twenty-four or thirty are not too many. The in-side begin by standing at the 'home,' one of them taking the bat, while the feeder, who is one of the out party, standing at his 'seat,' tosses (not throws) a ball at his knees, or thereabouts, after calling play. The rest of the out party are distributed over the field, round the outside of the pentagon. When the ball is thus given, the batsman's object is to hit it far and low over the field; and he is put out at once—first, if he fails to strike it; secondly, if he tips it and it falls behind him; thirdly, if it is caught before it falls to the ground, or after a single trap or rebound; or fourthly, if he is struck on the body after leaving the base, and while not standing at another base. The in-player may refuse to strike for three balls consecutively; but if he attempts and fails, or if he does not strike at the fourth ball, he is out. The score is made by the in party as follows: Each player, after striking the ball, runs from his base to another, or to a second, third, fourth, or even all around, according to the distance he has hit the ball, and scores one for each base he touches; and if while running between the bases he is hit by the ball, he is put out. If the ball falls among nettles or other cover of the same kind, 'lost ball' may be cried by the out party, and four only can be scored. After one of the in party has hit the ball and dropped the bat, another takes his place, and, on receiving the ball as before, he strikes it or fails as the case may be. If the latter, he is put out; but the previous striker, or strikers, if they are standing at their bases, are not affected by his failure. If the latter, he drops his bat like his predecessor, and runs round the pentagon also like him, being preceded by the previous strikers, and all being liable to be put out by a blow from the ball. The feeder is allowed to feign a toss of the ball, in the hope of touching some one of the players, who are very apt to leave their bases before the hit, in the hope of scoring an extra one by the manœuvre. When only one of the sides is left in, the others being all put out, he may call for 'three fair hits for the rounder,' which are intended to give him and his side another innings if he can effect the following feat: The outs, with the feeder, stand as usual, the rest of the striker's side besides himself taking no part. The feeder then tosses the ball as usual, which the striker may refuse as often as he pleases: but if he strikes at it, he must endeavor to run completely round the pentagon once out of three times, he being allowed three attempts to do it in. If he is struck on the body, or caught, if he falls in getting around, he and his party are finally out, and the other side go in again for another innings, but have not afterwards another such chance of redeeming their play. The out field are disposed on the same principle as at cricket, part for slight trips, and the remainder for long balls, and catch, stop or return them just as in that game."

This game of rounders first began to be played in England in the seventeenth century, and was the favorite ball game in the provinces until it was generally superseded by cricket at the close of the last century. It is still, however, occasionally practiced in remote localities. It was brought to our country by the early emigrants, and was called here "base ball" or "round ball." Sometimes the name of "town ball" was given to it, because matches were often played by parties representing different towns. But, so far as we know, the old English title of "rounders" was never used in America. The reason of this is that so many of our old New England settlers came from the eastern counties of England, where the term "rounders" appears never to have been used. In Moor's "Suffolk Words" he mentions among the ball games "base ball," while in the dialect glossaries of the northern and western counties no such word is to be found. English "base ball," or "rounders," was a mild and simple amusement compared with the American sport which has grown out of it. Even the hardy girls and women of England sometimes played it. Blaine, an English writer, says, "There are few of us, *of either sex,* but have engaged in *base ball* since our majority." Think of American ladies playing base ball! Yet the English "rounders" contained all the elements of our National game. All that it needed was systematizing and an authoritative code of rules. This it did not obtain until after 1840—and not completely until 1845. Previous to that date base ball was played with great differences in various parts of the country. Sometimes as many as six or seven bases were used; and very frequently lengthy disputes arose among the players as to the right method of conducting the game. It is a little noticeable that in laying down rules for base ball there is not one technical term that has been borrowed from cricket—a game long since reduced to a science. Of course the two sports, being both games of ball, necessarily have many terms in common, but there is not a base ball phrase which can be recognized as originating among cricketers. On the other hand, it is quite probable that cricket owed many of its peculiar words, such as "field," "fieldsman," "run," and "bat," to the older "rounders." In relation to the word "base," we may say that, in addition to the origin which we have given—namely, that it comes from a corruption of "bars" in the game styled "prison bars," or "prisoners' bars"—there is another somewhat plausible derivation. It has been suggested that as the object of each side in the game of "bars" was to keep the other party at *bay*, the places where they were so kept, that is the "bases," were styled "bays," of which "base" is a corruption. But this whole subject needs elucidation, and a careful study of the rural sports of the mother country would undoubtedly throw much light upon the history of base ball.

30

The Forest City Club Upsets the Nationals of Washington, D.C. (1867)

Source: *Ball Players' Chronicle*, August 1, 1867

In 1867 no team, or so it seemed, could stop the Nationals, a baseball nine comprised mainly of government clerks employed in the nation's capital. On a western road tour that summer, the Nationals crushed all rivals: Columbus fell to the Nationals by the lopsided score of 90–10, Cincinnati by 53–10, Indianapolis by 88–12, Louisville by 106–21, St. Louis by 53–26, and Chicago by 49–4. But then disaster befell the proud nine. As reported in the understated prose of Henry Chadwick, the Forest City club from the tiny farming community of Rockford, Illinois, upset the mighty Nationals. In the pitching box for the Rockford nine that day was seventeen-year-old Albert Goodwill Spalding, who was to become the most important figure in nineteenth-century baseball history. For Spalding's own account of this game, see Albert G. Spalding, America's National Game *(1911; reprint, Lincoln: University of Nebraska Press, 1992), pp. 109–12.*

The game between the Nationals and Forest City began at 1:40 P.M., a band of music playing an introduction to the game, besides discoursing appropriate airs, between the innings. The Forest City men led off at the bat, Addy opening play by giving Wright a chance for a catch, but George stopped in running, and missed the catch. King then tried Norton with a fly-tip, but Frank was in no condition to play and another life was given. Stearns then made his second by a good hit, but in running to third was caught napping by Wright and Fox; Williams first throwing to Wright and George to Fox. Spaulding [sic.] and Barker then retired in succession; the former at first by Norton and Fletcher and the latter at second by Norton and Wright, Barker overrunning his base. We noticed that the umpire—who gave excellent decisions as a general thing, erred in giving men out on the base when the ball was held simultaneously with the player's putting his foot on the base. Now the rule in each case requires, that if the ball be not held *before* the player reaches the bases, the latter is not out. The innings closed with the two runs scored by King and Stearns's good hits. Parker led off on the other side getting his base on three balls. Williams, after being missed on a foul-bound by Stearns, secured his first by a good grounder. Wright, after securing his first, was put out at second from over-running his base. Fox then hit one for his second, but Studley allowed Spaulding and Stearns to put him out at first; Fletcher, also, narrowly escaping being a victim of Stearns. Smith was third out from a well taken fly ball by Addy, the totals of the first innings being 3 to 2 in favor of the Nationals.

In the second innings, Wheeler led off by giving a chance to Fletcher for a foul bound, but the dead ground deceived him, and Wheeler afterwards gave Fletcher another chance to field him out, but somehow or other the Nationals could not hold the balls. Buckman was next, and Williams took his ball on the fly; and as Lightheart struck out directly afterwards, a blank would have been the result with sharp fielding. Afterwards, Addy gave Norton a chance for a foul bound, which was not taken; King followed with a chance to Smith to put him out at first, and Stearns also gave Norton a chance for a tip bound. But all were missed; and these errors, with others afterwards, and four or five good hits led to a score of eight runs for the Rockford nine; and as the Nationals only scored five for their share, through the good play of Spaulding and Addy, and well-taken catches by Light-heart and Stearns, the innings closed with the lead in the hands of the Forest City nine by the totals of 10 to 8, and the Nationals began to get serious as their opponents did to get livelier. From this time forth the Nationals failed to secure the lead; in fact, only once did they make any successful effort.

In the third innings, Barnes led off by taking his base on three balls. Addy followed by giving Smith a chance for a catch, and King offered one to Parker, but none were accepted, a kind of fatality marking the play of the majority of this game. It was the first chance they had had of playing an up-hill game, and their attempt to do so proved a failure. After five runs had been scored in this innings, Wright, Fletcher, and Norton managed to put the side out, and with the totals at 15 to 8 against them, the Nationals went in to make it even. Berthrong led off with a poor hit, but he managed to reach his base; in running to second, however, he overran it, and was put out, and Norton doing the same thing, two men were placed *hors de combat* without a run scored. Parker scratched his first afterwards, but Williams popped one up for the short stop to catch, and the third innings closed with the tally at 15 to 8 in favor of Rockfords.

Hitherto the Rockfords had looked only to getting a good score, and keeping down that of their opponents, and with no hope of a victory; now, however, they began to think victory within reach, and by earnest effort they succeeded in running up their score to 24 in the next three innings, and in keeping that of the Nationals down to 18. To show the character of the batting of the Nationals in this game, we have merely to state that in the last six innings the pitcher and short stop succeeded in putting out eight players by easy fielding to first base, every man in the six innings being put out at the in-field, the only sharp fielding necessary being that of King in taking two foul bounds, Stearns in running Studley out, and once by Barnes in putting out Norton at first. In these innings, on the National side, Berthrong's fine fielding in taking foul balls in the catcher's position, (he replacing Norton), of which he captured six in style, a good fly catch by Fox, and some good fielding by Williams, were the only efforts noteworthy, with the exception of a neat catch by Norton off Fletcher's hand.

In the sixth innings, the Forest City again opened play by giving a chance for an out; and this time it was accepted, Berthrong being behind to take the ball. Barnes then gave Smith a chance for the catch, but the ball was not held; and afterwards, when a player was on the second base, Smith had a chance to put a man out at first base, but he held the ball too long. Here would have been three out and no run but for errors of play; but for the second time the Rockford boys ran up a score of eight, when a blank score was what they earned by their batting, some very good play at the bat being shown after the lives had been given them.

As a heavy shower was impending, the Nationals, of course, desired to hurry up matters, as the probability was that no other chance than this innings would be had to get even; so they went in for a rally, George Wright opening a play with a clean home run, all the others following with good batting until Norton's turn came, and he and Parker were put out, Williams also narrowly escaping, but a wild throw sent him to third, and there he was when the umpire suspended play for fifteen minutes on account of the rain. This was rather an anxious quarter of an hour for the Nationals, as, had the rain kept on, the game would have been called, and they would have lost it by a score of 15 to 11, the tally of the even fifth innings played. The shower stopped in about ten minutes, and as it was not heavy enough to soak the ground the umpire prepared to call play. A new obstacle now sprung up, the Forest City Club refusing to play any more on account of the wet condition of the ground. By this action they showed a lack of courtesy to the visiting club in striking contrast to that of every club the Nationals had met on their tour. The umpire now very properly announced that he would give the Forest City fifteen minutes to decide whether they would take the field, and if they failed to appear and the Nationals were on the ground, he would decide the game in favor of the Nationals, as he was in duty bound to do. Before the expiration of the fifteen minutes the wise second thoughts of the Rockford Club had superseded the un-generous policy of their first decision, and they went on to the field and the game was resumed.

Two miss catches gave Wright a couple of lives on the resumption of the game, the ball being slippery from the wet ground, and afterwards by a fine hit he reached his third and sent Williams home; but then, to the surprise of all, Fox struck out and ended the inning, leaving the Foresters in the van by a score of 24 to 18. Things now began to look bad for the Nationals. They played without life or spirit, and evidently as if there was no hope of winning.

In the seventh inning, Fox woke up a bit, and caught a foul fly in style, and, as the batsman gave easy chances for outs, a blank score was the result, and the Nationals again went to the bat to make things square. Studley opened play with a fine grounder, and Fletcher followed with a fine hit to centre field, which gave him his second and Studley his third; but unluckily the fair ball for the bat which Fletcher hit was delivered with one of the pitcher's feet off the ground, and "balk" being called, the hit came dead, and both Studley and Fletcher had to return, Fletcher taking his strike again, and this time, too, he hit a good one, and as Smith followed suit three runs were scored. The next two strikers were then prettily caught out by King, Williams finally closing the inning for the three runs made, leaving the game still in favor of the Rockford players by the totals of 24 to 21. Things now looked favorable for the Nationals pulling up their score, but Fox and Smith's loose fielding allowed the Rockfords to score another run in the eighth inning, Wright and Fox's poor batting and the good fielding of Spaulding, Addy, and Stearns in running Studley out, after he had made his base by a fine grounder, led to a blank score, and the innings closed with the totals of 25 to 21 against the Nationals.

The Forest City nine now went into their last inning, and for the seventh time in the game opened play by giving a chance to the field—a fine fly-catch by Berthrong, who played well throughout the game, putting King out. Stearns ought to have been second out, but a wild throw of Fox gave him his third, and before the side was put out four runs had been added to the score, leaving the Nationals nine to get to win. This number they went in to get, but again rain necessitated a postponement for fifteen minutes, at the end of which time the sun again shown out, and the Nationals went in to win, but they were easily disposed of for two runs, and the game closed with the score of 29 to 23—and the Nationals retired from the field defeated.

The following is a full summary of the game:

BATTING SCORE

NATIONAL	O	R	FOREST CITY	O	R
Parker, l. f.	3	1	Addy, 2d b.	2	4
Williams, p.	4	3	King, c.	2	4
Wright, 2d b.	2	3	Stearns, 1st b.	3	4
Fox, 3d b.	3	3	Spaulding, p.	3	4
Studley, r. f.	2	4	Barker, c. f.	2	4
Fletcher, 1st b.	2	2	Wheeler, l. f.	3	4
Smith, c. f.	3	3	Buckman, 3d b.	5	1
Berthrong, c.	3	3	Lightheart, r. f.	6	1
Norton, s. s.	5	1	Barnes, s. s.	1	3

INNINGS	1st	2d	3d	4th	5th	6th	7th	8th	9th	
Forest City	2	8	5	0	1	8	0	1	4	—29
National	3	5	0	3	0	7	3	0	2	—23

Bases on hits—Addy 2, King 2, Stearns 2, Spaulding 3, Barker 4, Wheeler 2, Buckman 2, Lightheart 0, Barnes 0—total by Forest City, 17. Parker 0, Williams 1, Wright 5, Fox 3, Studley 4, Fletcher 2, Smith 2, Berthrong 2, Norton 2—total by Nationals, 21.

FIELDING SCORE

Fly catches—Addy 2, Barnes 1, Lightheart 1—total by Forest City, 4. Wright 4, Berthrong 3, Norton 3, Fox 1, Williams 1—total by Nationals, 12.

Foul bound catches—King 2, Stearns 1, Berthrong 3.

Catches on strikes—Norton 2, King 2.

Base play—Put out—By Stearns 11, Addy 5, Spaulding 1—total by Forest City, 17. Assisted by Barnes 5, Spaulding 5, King 3, Addy 2, Stearns 1. Put out—By Fletcher 7, Fox 1, Wright 1—total by National, 9. Assisted by Williams 4, Wright 2, Norton 2, Smith 1.

Run out—Buckman, by Fox and Berthrong.

Double plays—By Spaulding, Addy and Stearns.

Out on fouls—Forest City 9, National 3.

Time of game—2:30.

Umpire—Mr. Diedrick, of the Bloomington Club. Scorers—Messrs. Burns and Munson.

31

Henry Chadwick's "Model Base Ball Player" (1867)

Source: *Ball Players' Chronicle*, October 31, 1867

No one played a more important role in promoting baseball as a morally uplifting enterprise than Henry Chadwick. In this article he describes the moral and physical attributes of his "model" player, although he admits that such players were "not often seen."

THE MODEL BASE BALL PLAYER

This is an individual not often seen on a ball ground, but he nevertheless exists, and as a description of his characteristics will prove advantageous, we give a pen photogram of him, in the hope that his example will be followed on all occasions, for if it were, an end would at once be put to many actions which now give rise to unpleasantness on our ball grounds.

HIS MORAL ATTRIBUTES

The principal rule of action of our model base ball player is to comport himself like a gentleman on all occasions, but especially on match days, and in doing so, he abstains from *profanity* and its twin and evil brother obscenity, leaving these vices to be alone cultivated by graduates of our penitentiaries.

He never takes an ungenerous advantage of his opponents, but acts towards them as he would wish them to act towards himself. Regarding the game as a healthful exercise, and a manly and exciting recreation, he plays it solely for the pleasure it affords him, and if victory crowns his efforts in a contest, well and good, but should defeat ensue he is equally ready to applaud the success obtained by his opponents; and by such action he robs defeat of half its sting, and greatly adds to the pleasure the game has afforded both himself and his adversaries.

He never permits himself to be pecuniarily involved in a match, for knowing the injurious tendency of such a course of action to the best interests of the game, he values its welfare too much to make money an object in view in playing ball.

HIS PLAYING QUALIFICATIONS

The physical qualifications of our model player are as follows:

To be able to throw a ball with accuracy of aim a dozen or a hundred yards.

To be fearless in facing and stopping a swiftly batted or thrown ball.

To be able to catch a ball either on the "fly" or bound, either within an inch or two of the ground, or eight or ten feet from it, with either the right or left hand, or both.

To be able to hit a swiftly pitched ball or a bothering slow one, with equal skill, and also to command his bat so as to hit the ball either within six inches of the ground or as high as his shoulder, and either towards the right, centre or left fields, as occasion may require.

To be able to occupy any position on the field creditably, but to *excel in one position* only. To be familiar, practically and theoretically, with every rule of the game and "point" of play.

To conclude our description of a model base ball player, we have to say, that his conduct is as much marked by courtesy of demeanor and liberality of action as it is by excellence in a practical exemplification of the beauties of the game; and his highest aim is to characterize every contest in which he may be engaged, with conduct that will mark it as much as a trial as to which party excels in the moral attributes of the game, as it is one that decides any questions of physical superiority.

32

The Exclusion of African Americans from the NABBP (1867)

Source: *Ball Players' Chronicle*, December 19, 1867

It is presumed that whites and blacks sometimes played against and with one another during the 1860s. Yet when the Pythians of Philadelphia, an African American club, applied for membership in the NABBP in 1867, the nominating committee unanimously voted to bar any club "composed of one or more colored persons."

After the roll call the reading of the minutes of the last Convention came up in order; but as they included all the reports of the committees, the reading was, on motion, dispensed with. The reports of officers being next in order, the Recording Secretary reported verbally that he had attended to a voluminous correspondence on subjects appertaining to his office, and had written 379 letters in reply during the year. The subject of the order by the President changing Rule 10, last season, then came up. The President made an explanation of the case, stating that he had been convinced, by representations made to him by the chairman of the Committee on Rules, that the rule as printed was erroneous, and he had therefore ordered its correction. A long and rather personal discussion was about to ensue, when the Convention, taking the same view of it that the President did, by a majority vote, decided to close the discussion. This done with, the report of the Nominating Committee, through the acting chairman, Mr. James W. Davis, was presented, the feature of it being the recommendation to exclude colored clubs from representation in the Association, the object being to keep out of the Convention the discussion of any subject having a political bearing, as this undoubtedly had. The following is the

REPORT OF THE NOMINATING COMMITTEE

To the National Association of Base Ball Players:

The Nominating Committee beg leave respectfully to report:

First—That eight State Associations, representing 237 clubs, have applied for admission, and your committee recommend they be elected members, waiving such irregularities as are named in schedule No. 1 attached to this report.

Second—That they have elected eight clubs probationary members, according to Art. III, sec. 5 of the Constitution, and report favorably upon their election by the Convention, waiving such irregularities as are noted in schedule No. 2.

Third—That they report favorably upon the admission of twenty-eight clubs whose applications are correct as named in schedule No. 3.

Fourth—That they recommend the admission of eight clubs whose applications are more or less irregular, particulars of which can be found in schedule No. 4.

Fifth—That they find two memoranda received from the Recording Secretary (no doubt intended as applications from the Excelsior of Philadelphia and Crescent of ——), which are too informal to be noticed by your committee.

Sixth—Your committee would beg to add, that it has been quite impossible for them to ascertain the condition, character, and standing of all the clubs, in different parts of the country, as required by the Constitution, and can only assume that the applications made are based upon good faith. It is not presumed by your committee that any club who have applied are composed of persons of color, or any portion of them; and the recommendations of your committee in this report are based upon this view, and they unanimously report against the admission of any club which may be composed of one or more colored persons.

WM. H. BELL, M.D.

JAS. WHYTE DAVIS.

WM. E. SINN.

Philadelphia, Dec. 11, 1867.

33

Some of Baseball's "Technical Terms" (1868)

Source: Henry Chadwick, *The Game of Baseball* (1868; reprint, Columbia, S.C.: Camden House, 1983), pp. 38–46

The Game of Baseball, composed largely of excerpts from previous Beadle's *guides, was the first book exclusively about baseball. One of the most interesting sections is the glossary of baseball terms and phrases, which shows that the game had already developed a very distinctive vocabulary.*

TECHNICAL TERMS USED IN BASE BALL

AMATEUR PLAYERS.—Amateurs are divided into two classes of players in base ball, the first class of amateurs being players who play in matches for exercise and amusement only, and who are "amateurs" merely in contradistinction to "professionals." The second class of amateur players are those unskilled in playing the game, but who know more of it than the "Muffins" do. This class of players rank between muffins and second nine players. . . .

BALK.—A balk is committed when the pitcher fails to deliver a ball after making any of the preliminary movements to deliver it. Or, if he steps outside the lines of his position, before the ball leaves his hand, when in the act of pitching. Or, if he jerks or throws the ball to the batsman. . . .

BLINDER.—A "blind" is the provincial term in the Middle States for a blank score in the game.

BOUNDER.—This is the technical term for a bounding ball from the bat which strikes the ground within the lines of the in-field.

BOWLED BALLS.—A ball cannot be bowled in base ball. If a ball be bowled—that is, rolled along the ground, or tossed in so as to touch the ground before leaving the base—the umpire is empowered to call balls on the pitcher every time a ball is so bowled.

CALLED BALLS.—A called ball is the penalty inflicted on the pitcher for unfair delivery. Three called balls give a base.

CLEAN HOME RUNS.—A home run is made, in a literal sense, when the batsman—after hitting a fair ball—runs around the bases without stopping and touches the home base before being put out. But a "*clean* home run" is only made when the batsman hits a ball far enough out of the reach of the out-fielders as to enable him to run round to home base before the ball can be returned in quick enough to put him out. None other should be scored on the record as home runs. . . .

DAISY CUTTERS.—This is the term applied to a low pitched ball, hit sharply along the surface of the ground, through the grass, without rebounding to any extent. It is a hit ball very difficult to field, and, consequently, shows good batting. . . .

FACING FOR A HIT.—This is done when the batsman takes his stand, facing the position in the field he desires to send the ball. Thus, if he intends hitting a ball to third base, he faces the short-stop; if to the center field, he faces the pitcher, and if to the right field he faces the first base man. . . .

FUNGOES.—This is simply a method of affording the fielders exercise in catching the ball. The batsman tosses the ball up and tries to send it to the outer field, and the player catching it on the fly takes the bat. Of course it is of no benefit as practice at the bat, as the ball does not come to the bat as it does when delivered by a pitcher, but falls perpendicularly to the bat, hitting it as it falls. . . .

HEAD-WORK.—This is a term specially applied to the pitcher who is noted for his tact and judgment in bothering his batting opponents by his pitching. A pitcher who simply trusts to pace, in his delivery, for effect will never succeed with skillful batsmen opposed to him. A pitcher, however, who uses head-work in pitching tries to discover his adversary's weak points, and to tempt him to hit at balls, either out of his reach or pitched purposely for him to hit to a particular part of the field. Pitchers, in general, have greatly improved in this respect within the past few years. . . .

HANDS LOST.—This is the old way of recording the outs in a match. Whenever a player is put out, a "hand is lost," and an "out" is recorded in the score books. . . .

LINES OF POSITION.—There are three lines of position on the base ball field, viz., the line of the home base, six feet of length, and parallel to the line from third to first base; and the two lines of the pitcher's position, the same length and similarly parallel, the first of these two lines being forty-five from the home base, and the second forty-nine. . . .

MUFFINS.—This is the title of a class of ball players who are both practically and theoretically unacquainted with the game. Some "muffins," however, know something about how the game should be played, but cannot practically exemplify their theory. "Muffins" rank the lowest in the grade of the nines of a club, the list including first and second nine players, amateurs, and, lastly, "muffins." . . .

ONE, TWO, THREE.—This term has a double meaning. It refers to a practice game when less than six fielders on a side are present, and also to the order of going out, when the first three batsman in an inning retire in succession, in which case they are said to be put out in "one, two, three" order. The game of "One, two, three" is played as follows: The field side take their positions and a player takes the bat. When the batsman is put out—unless the ball is caught on the fly, in which case the fielder catching it changes places with the batsman—he takes his position at right field, the catcher takes the bat, the pitcher goes in to catch, and the first baseman takes the pitcher's position, and each of the other fielders advance one step towards the in-field positions. There should be at least four players on the batting side. . . .

PITCHER'S POINTS. —These are the two iron quoits placed on the two lines of the pitcher's position on a line from home to second base. . . .

PACE.—This is a term applied to the speed of a pitcher's delivery. Pitchers are divided into three classes, viz., swift pitchers, medium-paced, and slow. Creighton was the model pitcher as regards speed, and Martin is the best medium-paced pitcher. Slow pitching is merely tossing the ball to the bat in order that it may be hit high for a catch, and is only effective against very poor batsmen, except, perhaps, when a change from swift to slow pitching is made, when it sometimes proves serviceable.

PROFESSIONALS.—This is the term applied to all ball players who play base ball for money, or as a means of livelihood. The rules prohibit players from receiving compensation for their services in a match, but there is scarcely a club of note that has not infringed the rule, or that does not nullify it now in some form or other. If professionals would all act an honest part in their position much of the objection against them would be removed. But, as long as they are found to be, in a majority of cases, the mere tools of "rings," or the servants of gamblers who too frequently influence leading contests, the prejudice against professionals will naturally exist. There is no just reason except this, against a man's earning his living by base ball service. . . .

SKUNKED.—This is a slang term for a blank score. In New York a blank score is called a "skunk," in the West it is called "whitewashing," and in the East a "blinder." The Western phrase is the best of the three, but a "blank score" is the correct term. . . .

TALLY.—This term applies to the total score of the single innings played, or of the even innings, or of the totals at the close of the match.

A New Rule on Professional Players (1869)

Source: *DeWitt's Base Ball Guide* (New York: R. M. DeWitt, 1869), pp. 23–24

Following the 1868 season, the NABBP voted to recognize two classes of players: professionals and amateurs. Henry Chadwick, editor of DeWitt's, *explained that the amendment was necessary because the growing wave of professionalism could not be stopped or denied. Indeed, the following year the professionals acted to eliminate the two classes, effectively banishing the amateurs. See Document 36.*

RULE V: THE GAME

SECTION 7. All players who play base-ball for money, or who shall at any time receive compensation for their services as players, shall be considered *professional* players; and all others shall be regarded as *amateur* players.

The above is the most important amendment made to the rules, it being no less than the striking out of the whole of the section prohibiting professional players from taking part in match games, and substituing a rule officially recognizing professionals as a class of players distinct from amateurs. The necessity for some such change as this was apparent to all, and hence the Committee of Rules thought they would, at any rate, try the experiment for one year of recognizing professionals, to see how it would work. Since 1860 the professional system has been practically in vogue, though ostensibly all were amateur players, that is, all were unpaid for their services. But it is well known that nearly all the leading clubs—certainly all the prominent aspirants for the championship—employed professional players, and the fact that the rules prohibiting the custom were mere dead letters and that also it was almost impossible to frame a law on the subject that could not be evaded, had much to do in bringing about the change introduced this season. It will be seen that clubs can now openly advertise for professional players, and the latter as openly solicit employment as such. All clubs who have a majority of their nine composed of professionals are professional clubs. Amateur clubs, however, can employ a professional in their nine to take charge of their grounds or to teach them, but he cannot be played in a match without the consent of the opposing nine, unless they, too, have a professional in their nine. As soon as the experience of this season has shown the working of this new rule, no doubt a code of rules will be prepared for the government of the intercourse between the two classes of the fraternity.

Cincinnati's Red Stockings Edge
the Mutuals of New York (1869)

Source: *New York Clipper*, June 26, 1869

As many baseball fans know, the Red Stockings of Cincinnati became the first publicly acknowledged all-professional team in 1869. During that year they toured the nation and finished the season undefeated. Perhaps the best, most competitive game the Reds played was their 4–2 triumph over the Mutuals on June 15. In an era when teams rarely failed to score in double digits, such low-scoring games were hailed as milestone events.

CINCINNATI VS. MUTUAL

A WONDERFUL GAME AND A REMARKABLE SCORE

The "Red Stockings" arrived in the metropolis on the evening of the 14th from New Haven. They were to have played the Yale nine on the afternoon of that day, but rain prevented the game from taking place. The morning of the 15th was decidedly unpropitious. Rain fell during the forenoon, and it looked as though the "Red Stockings" would have to forego their meeting with the Mutuals. Toward noon, however, the clouds broke away, and the afternoon gave promise of better weather. Still, the sky bore a threatening aspect up till 3 o'clock, when it cleared off beautifully. Undoubtedly, if it had been a clear day, 5,000 or 6,000 spectators would have been present at the Union Grounds. As it was, only about 1,500 people witnessed the game, and these few persons were well repaid for the chances they took of a wetting, for a better played or more exciting game was, probably, never witnessed before. From the large and one-sided scores which the "Red Stockings" had made in nearly all their games, a heavy batting contest was looked for. Wonderful to relate, only six runs were made on both sides, and in a quickly played game of nine innings the champion Mutuals were defeated by the score of 4 to 2!

The visitors made their appearance on the ball field shortly before 3 o'clock. As they were already attired in their neat and picturesque uniform, but little time was lost in getting to work. Mr. C. D. Walker, of the Active, was selected as umpire, and at 3 o'clock the first ball was pitched. The "Red Stockings" having won the choice of innings, sent their opponents to the bat. C. Hunt led off with a mild sort of grounder right into Waterman's hands, and Charley took a back seat; Hatfield gave Sweasy a chance, and also failed at first; E. Mills did better, as the ball he sent to Waterman was thrown wildly, and Mills was safe; R. Hunt, being hard to suit, the umpire gave him his base on called balls. Even with two hands out, everything looked very favorable for a good start off for the champions. Swandel, however, did not do justice to his reputation as a safe batter, as he poked the ball into Brainard's hands, and was put out at first, with Mills and Hunt on the bases. . . . . . .

G. Wright, as he straddled the home plate and raised his bat, was looked upon as equal to knocking smithereens out of the ball, but George sent a flyer to the infield, which Hatfield attended to; Gould carried his ball out to the left centre field, and was thought sure of at least two bases; C. Hunt thought differently, however, as after a tremendous effort he got under the ball and made a difficult catch. Waterman favored his old friend, Hatfield, with a grounder, and as Johnny was slow in handling it, Fred was safe at first base; Allison sent a "daisy cutter" spinning through Eggler's legs, and sent Waterman home—just in the nick of time, as Harry Wright popped up the ball over Wolters' head, and it was nicely caught. Score 0 to 1.

The second innings saw C. Mills at the bat, but as he hit an easy one to George Wright, of course he was saved the trouble of running to first base; Eggler's ball flew off the bat into Allison's hands; Wolters also went out to Allison, but his ball bounded—another blank for the Mutuals. . . . . . Leonard sent a foul ball just off first base, and E. Mills caught it. Brainard fouled out to the other Mills. Sweasy hit easily to the right field, and made his first base, but was left there, as McVey's ball flew into the air over second base, and Hatfield nipped it—the first "whitewash" for the "Red Stockings."

On their third turn at the bat the Mutuals had a determined look, and evidently meant business. McMahon was the first striker, and he had not yet tried Brainard's "chain lightning," the spectators imagined the "old man" would find some way of getting the better of it. Billy's dodge, when he thinks it ain't safe to trust the players, is to hit the ball down near the home plate and take the chances of the umpire seeing whether it is fair or foul. After one or two attempts, he hit a fair-foul ball, which, under ordinary circumstances, would have earned him a base; but Waterman, who knows Billy of old, had been watching his manœuvres, and was playing pretty close to his base; so he easily picked up the veteran's grounder and threw it to Gould; C. Hunt, thinking he could drive his ball near to George Wright and yet be safe, tried the experiment, but found out his mistake, and sat down again; Hatfield also tried the same dodge, but George was as wide awake as ever, and the innings closed for the third application of whitewash. . . . . . The "Red Stockings," considerably encouraged by this fine display, were enabled to add another run to the single already obtained, and the third innings closed with the totals of 2 to 0. George Wright was the lucky run-getter, making his second base on a long hit to left field, and coming home on Gould's stroke to centre field; Waterman made his base on a muff of Eggler's, but was left in company with Gould, as the next two strikers flew out, Allison to Eggler, and H. Wright to Swandel.

Up to this time the game had been close and exciting, and with the exception of the errors of Hatfield and Eggler, handsomely fielded. These errors were important, however, as the two runs to the credit of the "Red Stockings" had been made through them. With the exception of Waterman's overthrow, which did no damage, the "red-legged" chaps had not committed an error. This handsome exhibition gave promise of a game of more than usual merit. And the promise was redeemed, for neither side scored in the next four innings. On the eighth the spell was broken, and as *the first run* for the Mutuals was scored cheer after cheer went up from the throats of the crowd. McMahon was the first to the bat, and trying the same dodge he attempted in the third innings, hit a fair ball, which bounded out foul, and secured two bases; C. Hunt was not so fortunate, as Leonard caught the ball Charley sent to left field, Hatfield was caught by George Wright for the third time, and again failed of reaching first base; E. Mills made a strong hit to right field, sending McMahon home; R. Hunt meant well, but George Wright was too sharp for him, and picking up the grounder Dick sent him, he threw it to second base, and Mills was sacrificed.

This was a death blow to the hopes of the Mutuals and their friends, and they seemed to lose confidence in themselves. It seemed utterly impossible to break the charm with which the "Red Stockings" appeared to be hedged. Still, notwithstanding these discouraging circumstances, the Mutuals kept up a show of courage, and went into the field determined, if possible, to prevent their opponents from adding any more runs to the two already obtained. And they were successful in this innings, for with the exception of Allison, none of the "Red Stockings" made a base. Gould, first striker, favored Eggler, and retired; Waterman hit a foul into C. Mills' hands, and H. Wright sent a long ball to right centre field, and was on his way to second base, when Dick Hunt, after a long run, caught it, while the whole field cheered their approbation.

The ninth and last innings was now entered upon, and an almost painful stillness rested upon the spectators. The Mutuals had now to do or die. One run would tie the game, while two or three would make it comparatively safe for the Mutuals. Dick Hunt commenced operations with a hit over second baseman's head; Swandel followed this up with a rattling grounder through the infield, which brought the crowd to its feet, and the excitement became intense as C. Mills sent Hunt home by carrying his ball safely to the right field. The situation was now interesting, and the friends of the Mutuals began to think the latter had broken the spell which had surrounded them so long. With one run in, two men on bases, and a good man at the bat, everything looked exceedingly lovely. Eggler, however, was not equal to the emergency, and hitting a short fly to Waterman, that usually sharp fielder, seeing a chance for a double play, caught the ball and then dropped it. Of course, Hunt and Swandel, not dreaming of any trick being played on them, hugged their bases. Fred, quickly picked the ball up, and throwing it to Wright at third, George passed it to Sweasy at second, and the unfortunates on the bases were doubled up in the shortest and most approved fashion. All this happened in less time than it takes to relate it, and was performed so quickly as to take the spectators completely by surprise. When they realized the situation, cheer after cheer rent the air at the sharpness of the Western chaps, and even the partisans of the Mutuals could not help but admire the trick. This sudden and unexpected turn in affairs had a demoralizing effect on the Mutuals, and although Wolters afterward was given his base on called balls, McMahon finished the innings by hitting a foul which Allison caught, after a long run. The score was a tie, however, and if the Mutuals could field as sharply in the last innings as they had in the five preceding ones, another innings would be necessary and then the chances would be equal. . . . . . Leonard, after getting to his base on a muff of Eggler's, was caught napping by Wolters and handsomely run out by Eggler and E. Mills; Brainard sent a sharp grounder to Swandel, which that usually careful player threw wildly to first base, and Brainard went to third and then home on a passed ball. This was the winning run, and as Brainard acrossed the home plate the wildest excitement prevailed. Sweasy now took the bat, and by a long hit to left field, made three bases, and shortly afterwards scored on a wild pitch by Wolters; McVey, hitting to Hatfield, went out at first, and G. Wright closed the innings by flying out to Dick Hunt.

Without exception, the game never had its equal and probably never will have. From first to last, the exhibition of fielding was the best ever seen in this vicinity, and we doubt its like was ever witnessed anywhere. The "Red Stockings" exceeded all expectations formed of their fielding powers, and did not make an error during the game that gave the Mutuals a run. The pitching of Brainard was remarkably even and very effective, while the catching of Allison was without fault. In fact, every man acquitted himself with credit. McVey made the only catch that calls for special mention. Of the Mutuals, Eggler, at short field, who, it is well known, is a capital out fielder and is out of place in his present position, made the most damaging errors. Swandel missed one fly catch, but it did not make any difference in the score. Hatfield made one muff, and C. Mills passed several balls which did his side no good. The most handsome plays were made by the Hunt Brothers, Dick in particular distinguishing himself. The pitching of Wolters was fully as effective as that of Brainard.

The following full score will give the reader an idea of all that occurred, which is described in the foregoing account:—

MUTUAL	H L	R	1ST B	T B	CINCINNATI	H L	R	1ST B	T B
C. Hunt, l f	4	0	0	0	G. Wright, s s	4	1	1	2
Hatfield, 2d b	4	0	0	0	Gould, 1st b	4	0	0	0
E. Mills, 1st b	2	0	3	3	Waterman, 3d b	2	1	0	0
R. Hunt, c f	2	1	1	1	Allison, c	2	0	2	2
Swandel, 3d b	2	0	1	1	H. Wright, c f	4	0	0	0
C. Mills, c	4	0	1	1	Leonard, l f	3	0	0	0
Eggler, s s	3	0	1	1	Brainard, p	3	1	0	0
Wolters, p	3	0	0	0	Sweasy, 2d b	2	1	2	4
McMahon, r f	3	1	1	2	McVey, r f	3	0	1	2
Totals	27	2	8	9	Totals	27	4	6	10

INNINGS	1st	2d	3d	4th	5th	6th	7th	8th	9th
Mutual	0	0	0	0	0	0	0	1	1—2
Cincinnati	1	0	1	0	0	0	0	0	2—4

Fly catches—C. Hunt, 1; Hatfield, 4; R. Hunt, 5; Swandel, 2; E. Mills, 1; C. Mills, 1; Eggler, 1; Wolters, 1. Total, 16. G. Wright, 1; Leonard, 2; Sweasy, 1; McVey, 1; Allison, 2. Total, 7. Foul bound catches—C. Hunt, 1; C. Mills, 3. Total, 4. Allison, 2. Out on fouls—Mutual, 4; Cincinnati, 7. Base play—Put out by

E. Mills, 6; G. Wright, 2; Gould, 12; Sweasy, 4. Total, 18. Assisted by—Hatfield, 2; Eggler, 2; Wolters, 2; G. Wright, 7; Waterman, 5; Brainard, 1; Sweasy, 2. Left on bases—E. Mills, 2; R. Hunt, 1; Swandel, 2; Eggler, 1; Wolters, 1. Total, 7. Waterman, 1; Allison, 2; Leonard, 1; Sweasy, 1; McVey, 1. Total, 6. Passed balls—C. Mills, 5. Wild pitches—Wolters, 2. Bases on "called" balls—R. Hunt, 1; Wolters, 1. Time of game—Two hours. Umpire—Mr. C. D. Walker, of the Active Club.

36

Professionals Seize Control of the NABBP (1869)

Source: *New York Clipper*, December 18, 1869

In 1869, the professionals seized control of the NABBP, promptly eliminating the distinction between amateur and professional players that the association had adopted the previous year (see Document 34). The following article from the Clipper *(probably written by Henry Chadwick) condemns the professionals' takeover of the association.*

THE BASE BALL CONVENTION

In another column we give a detailed report of the proceedings of the Annual Convention of the National Association of Base Ball Players, from which it will be seen that though the meeting was one which was less representative of the fraternity at large than any we have seen for some years past, it was one which was marked by legislation which in one sense was more important as affecting the general welfare of the game than any previous transactions since the Association became one composed of delegates from State organizations. But, unfortunately, it was important not so much from what was done to advance the interests of the game, as from what must necessarily have the reverse effect. In the first place the controling power in the Convention expunged the rule which divided the players into two classes, according as their services in the field were voluntary or paid for; by this, not only are all clubs placed on the same level as regards playing strength, but all that has been previously done to place professional ball playing upon a reputable footing has been nullified.

The experience of the past two seasons has conclusively shown how badly many of our professional clubs have been managed, and now, to cap the climax, what must they do but carry out the same blundering management in the Convention. Not content with lowering the national game to the level of the hippodroming of the turf, they aim to get control of the National Association, and especially of its Committee of Rules, the chairman of which they know to be the bitter opponent of all "ring" tactics and management, and in favor of amateur club rules in the Association, the object in view of course being to use both in the special interests of the professionals, if not of the worst phase of professional ball playing. The result of all this, it is thought, must necessarily be either the withdrawal of amateur clubs from the association or the dismissal of professional clubs. This is the issue, it seems, which the controling interest in the recent Convention has forced upon the fraternity.

At a fair estimate there are not far from a thousand regularly organized base ball clubs located in our country, from Maine to California, and from the St. Lawrence to the Gulf of Mexico. Of these not fifty can be ranked in any way as professional clubs; indeed, a contemporary limits the list to sixteen. And yet it is the ambition of this very small minority to rule the whole thousand; at least such is the conclusion forced upon us by the actions of the professional representatives in the late Convention. It is true that the apathy shown by the amateur portion of the fraternity of late years, the result, by the way, of their too great confidence in their power to rule, has afforded the other class a favorable opportunity to take the reins in their own hands; but this fact does not relieve the professional leaders from the charges of blundering management in thus arraying themselves in direct opposition to the wishes of the majority. If we mistake not there will be such a rally of the amateur clubs in the Fall of 1870, to rescue the National Association from the hands of the Philistines, that the short-sighted managers of the opposition will be made to regret the day they ever attempted to use the National Association to serve their special interests and to further their personal ends, at the expense of the great majority of the ball playing fraternity.

37 ───

The Significance of the Defeat of the Red Stockings by Brooklyn (1870)

Source: *Brooklyn Daily Eagle*, June 15, 1870

This editorial celebrates the positive effect of the Atlantics' stunning 8–7, eleventh-inning victory over the previously undefeated Red Stockings had upon Brooklyn's "local pride." The true significance of the game, claims the writer, was that it was "a Brooklyn victory won by Brooklyn boys." Although the writer hails the triumph of an indigenous, home-grown club over a squad of mercenaries hired from all over the country, many of the Atlantics themselves were professionals.

THE ATLANTIC'S VICTORY

The sporting season, or rather the season of sport, rose to its climax yesterday. The Club which never was beaten before, was vanquished by the Club that hereafter will have no excuse for being beaten, by any organization, saving, perhaps, their gallant and extraordinary adversaries of Tuesday afternoon. The story is told elsewhere: how Brooklyn led the world against the Red Stockings, and how the sun of championship was finally compelled to rise on the normal verge of the horizon, and no longer astonish mankind and perpetually outrage propriety by shooting from the chambers of the Western sky and making his bed in the Atlantic.

There are incidents about the grand victory of our local batters which make it historical. The result was opposed to the expectation of every one. The greatest achievement hoped for was a not ignominious defeat. The triumph marks the first break in the line of battle hitherto waged by the ball organization of any one city against the organization which chooses to call itself Cincinnati's, but which, in membership, as in repute, belongs to the four quarters of the country. Moreover, it was won by the fairest, staunchest, skillfullest, pluckiest playing on record. "Science and nerve" did the business. Eleven innings, a total score of fifteen, and that standing just eight to seven, tell a story to professional minds which sends the blood tingling in joy to their toes. It was the greatest game ever played between the greatest clubs that ever played, and as usual, when Brooklyn is pitted against the universe, the universe is number two.

The deep chord which the victory vibrated in the city's heart, more than anything we know of, demonstrated the depth and keenness of the sentiment of local pride, of pride in Brooklyn, which is so distinguishing a characteristic of this people. The staidest stockholder, and the doughtiest directors broke bottle over the battle of the gods. The Rink was, as to all its very full audience, marked by little conversation other than such as related to the game. The Park Theatre, Hooley's, and the Olympian braves were suffused with a like excitement. Even casual Christians in occasional prayer-meetings acknowledged the unction of victory, and exhorted the ungodly to make a home run for glory at once.

It is a Brooklyn victory won by Brooklyn boys, and Brooklyn salutes them. But let no taunt taint the triumph. The Red Stockings' honor is hardly less. They must meet with many reverses yet before their record ceases to be superior to all contemporaries. They have grafted honor and sense, and science and courtesy on to the "national game." Praise be to them for it, and better luck to them next time everywhere but in Brooklyn. And as for our own Atlantics, those veterans invincible every time they want to be, the victory of yesterday has eternized them in the affection of this people, and they are forgiven all the pangs they have ever imparted. For then once they represented all that was subtle in the science, all that was brave in the spirit and all that was bounding in the blood of Brooklyn, and after holding the enemy at bay for a terrible period, they emulated Tommy Dodd:

> They're bound to win
> When they go in—

And let them do so some more.

38

The New York State Base Ball Association Bans African Americans (1870)

Source: *New York Clipper*, November 19, 1870

Just as the NABBP *did in 1867, the New York State Base Ball Association voted to ban bl..ck clubs after several applied for membership. At the same convention, the association reinstated William Wansley, who had been expelled along with two Mutual team-mates—Thomas Devyr and Edward Duffy—for throwing a game in 1865. Devyr and Duffy were reinstated in 1867 and 1868, respectively. See Documents 24 and 32.*

NEW YORK STATE CONVENTION

The fourth annual convention of the New York State Association was held at the Delavan House, Albany, on Thursday, Nov. 10th, 1870, and, in striking contrast to the conventions of New Jersey, Pennsylvania and Connecticut, it proved to be the least successful meeting of the association yet held. Only *nine clubs* were represented by delegates when the roll was called, and but one of these clubs was located in the extensive portion of the state west of Albany, in which some of the best amateur clubs of the state exist. But for the interest taken in the association by the secretary, Mr. M. J. Kelly, not an officer of the organization would have been present, and the attendance of delegates from New York and Brooklyn alone enabled the convention to organize a meeting. Seven clubs were represented from New York city and two only from Brooklyn. No one appeared from the veteran Knickerbockers, of New York; the Unions, of Morrisania, or from the Excelsiors, Atlantics or Eckfords, of Brooklyn, clubs which have hitherto never failed to be represented. The only professional clubs represented were the Mutuals and Hay-makers. . . .

When the new clubs were proposed for election, Mr. Barnum, of the Gotham club, in order to save time, moved to suspend the rules as to elect by one ballot. Mr. W. R. Macdiarmid of the Star club of Brooklyn, then moved to amend the motion, by providing that in case any of the clubs to be elected should be composed of colored men, their claim to membership should be void. This was unanimously adopted; and thus, for the first time in the history of the National Association, was a political question introduced as a bone of contention in the council of the fraternity. The mischievous influence of this resolution will undoubtedly be felt in the forthcoming convention, and to the Star club of Brooklyn and its partisan delegate will the National Association be indebted for introducing such an element of discord into the proceedings of the National Convention. After the introduction of this fire brand, an election for officers was proceeded with. . . .

It will be seen from this selection that Capt. John Wildey, of the Mutual Club, is chairman of the New York delegation to the next convention, and that Mr. Aubrey

Wilson, an able young lawyer, also of the Mutual Club, is "Judge Advocate," the officer whose duty it is to prosecute all clubs who break the laws of the National Association.

Of course, the programme of the New York Convention would not have been complete without the introduction of something or other which would afford a field for the employment of the tactics resorted to for controlling delegations and conventions. In 1868 it was the Devyr case; in 1869 it was the Duffy case. this year Wansley is to be reinstated as "an honored and esteemed member of the fraternity."

On motion of Mr. Wildey the delegates were "instructed" to procure the remission of the penalty inflicted upon Mr. William Wansley, formerly of the Mutual Club, who has been debarred from joining the fraternity since 1865, for being guilty of the venal offence of "selling a game." Craver, of the Haymakers, was charged with doing the same thing in another way this year by the Chicago Club, and he was expelled from that club for dishonorable conduct, and yet the professional clubs have found such a charge no bar to their association with him. Under these circumstances there is no just reason why Wansley should not only be whitewashed, as Devyr and Duffy have been, but also it would be equally as advisable to expunge from the association constitution the now dead-letter rule relative to the penalty for admitting men of this class to club membership. . . .

In view of the action taken by the New York State Convention, we would suggest that the colored clubs of New York and Philadelphia at once take measures to organize a National Association of their own. In regard to the New York Convention we should like to learn how it was they managed to get a quorum together in the face of the following law of the State Constitution. We clip the rule from the published Constitution. It is from Article 8, and is as follows:—

A QUORUM

SEC. 3. Twenty delegates shall constitute a quorum for the transaction of business; but a smaller number present at any adjourned or regularly called meeting may adjourn to any specified day.

According to the statement sent us by the Secretary, but nine delegates were present when the roll was called, and the list of officers elected embraces 19. It is noteworthy, also, that the number of state delegates, elected on the basis of a list of over 80 odd regularly organized clubs, [were] regular members of the Association. As but 15 were represented at this convention, it would be interesting to know whether the balance are still members, and also how many of the clubs now on the books of the Association are defunct. In the published list of members in the State Association book are the names of at least a dozen that have no existence.

39

The Debate Continues over Professionalism (1870)

Source: James H. Haynie, *1871—Baseball Rules and Regulations* (Chicago: J. W. O. Kelley, 1871), pp. 12–13

Conflicts within the baseball fraternity over the issue of professionalism continued. However, advocates of pristine amateurism soon found themselves in retreat. In this exchange from the 1870 NABBP convention, a motion to declare professionalism "reprehensible" was debated and then defeated.

Representative Cantwell offered the following:

Resolved: That this Association regard the custom of publicly hiring men to play the game of Base Ball, as reprehensible and injurious to the best interests of the game.

For the purposes of properly considering this resolution, the Convention resolved itself into a Committee of the Whole, with Mr. Putnam, of Connecticut, as chairman.

Mr. Cantwell explained his resolution. He said it was the express wish of numerous clubs in his section of the country to have such an order passed. He believed the professional system injurious to the interests of base ball. Mr. Hubbell wanted to know how the resolution would remedy the disease. Other delegates said that the failing interest in base-ball matters was due to the hiring of professionals. Another said it encouraged gambling. Mr. Wildey wanted to know how the Convention would go to work to stop betting, and asked whether any delegates present believed that it really encouraged gambling? One delegate assailed the two Wright brothers; whereupon both of them were ably defended by Mr. Ford. Then Mr. Oberback, of Missouri, created a decided sensation, by exclaiming that if his two boys, both of whom played ball as an exercise, should turn out to be professionals, he would disown them. Mr. Dowling was in favor of professionals. Mr. Hayhurst said it was the old sore breaking out; he thought a good ball-player was worthy of his hire. Mr. Haynie and Mr. Rogers were opposed to the frowning down of professional clubs. The latter said it was the killing of the goose that laid the golden egg. The discussion, although quite animated, was at all times marked with good feeling and courtesy.

Resolution defeated, 10–17.

3

The Formation of the First
Professional Leagues, 1871–82

The uneasy division between amateur and professional clubs finally resulted in a complete rupture. In 1871 the professionals formed the National Association of Professional Base Ball Players (NA). Although the Athletics of Philadelphia won the first pennant, Boston's Red Stockings swept the next four championships. The weaknesses of the NA inspired William Hulbert, a stockholder in the Chicago NA club, to propose the formation of a new league with a strong, centralized government. The National League (NL), formed in 1876, charged fifty cents for admission (twice the standard fee) and proscribed the sale of alcohol at games and the playing of games on Sunday. After the 1881 season, a group of clubs frustrated with these restrictions formed the American Association (AA), which for the next decade would challenge the NL's monopoly over major league baseball.

40

The Formation of the National Association
of Professional Base Ball Players (NA) (1871)

Source: *New York Clipper*, March 25, 1871

In the following article, Henry Chadwick describes both the formation of the NA and the "origin of this convention." However, the delegates Chadwick believed to be "intelligent and influential" built the NA with a fatal flaw: any team could join the NA by paying a ten-dollar entry fee. As a result, the NA included not only the strongest teams from the largest cities but also a number of lesser clubs from smaller cities. The inability of the weaker clubs to attract investors and spectators contributed to the collapse of the NA following the 1875 season.

THE PROFESSIONALS IN COUNCIL

A NATIONAL ASSOCIATION ORGANIZED

AN INTELLIGENT AND INFLUENTIAL REPRESENTATION, AND A HARMONIOUS CONVENTION

The origin of this convention should be placed on record, viz., Mr. N. E. Young, the efficient Secretary of the Olympic club, of Washington who made the good suggestion in the CLIPPER last February that there should be a meeting of the Secretaries of the Professional Clubs to arrange the date of the respective tours they would take, which was approved of by all the clubs concerned, and the day selected by Mr. Young—March 17—was agreed upon. As an amendment, the able secretary of the Chicago club, Mr. J. M. Thacher, suggested that the meeting in question should take action upon the question of selecting umpires and of adopting championship rules, etc. This, too, was approved of. Seeing that in order to enforce any rules of the kind it would be necessary that they should emanate from some regularly constituted body rather than from a mere meeting of secretaries, we suggested to the professional clubs that whoever they sent to the meeting in question they should be duly empowered to act the same as delegates to a regular convention. This suggestion was endorsed and acted upon by eight of the ten clubs represented—the Mutual and Chicago clubs being the exception—and in their cases it was not that they did not endorse the idea that they failed to empower their secretaries to act fully, but that there was not time for the clubs to take the necessary action. For this reason, when the convention was held, those delegates who had not full powers were allowed to vote, subject to the endorsement of their action by their clubs. The

DELEGATES TO THE CONVENTION

assembled on the night of March 17th, which was a stormy, rainy night, at Collier's Rooms, corner of Broadway and Thirteenth street, engaged by the Mutual Club for the purpose. The representatives were as follows:

Athletic, of Philadelphia	James N. Kerns (President)
Boston, of Boston	Harry Wright (Secretary)
Chicago, of Chicago	J. M. Thacher (Secretary)
Eckford, of Brooklyn	W. H. Ray (President)
Forest City, of Cleveland	J. S. Evans (Manager)
Forest City, of Rockford	[H. H.] Waldo (Secretary)
Mutual of New York	A. V. Davidson (Secretary)
National, of Washington	O. R. Hough (Member)

Olympic, of Washington . . . . N. E. Young (Secretary)
Union, of Troy . . . . J. W. Schofield (Secretary)

At 7:30 P.M. Mr. Schofield called the meeting to order, and on motion Mr. Kerns, the President of the Athletic Club, was elected Chairman, and Mr. Young, of the Olympic Club, Secretary. The Chairman then briefly referred to the object of the meeting and to the advisability of organizing a permanent association—a course, he said, which had been forced upon them, as it were, by the action of the Convention of the amateur clubs held the previous evening. The credentials of delegates were then received, and on motion a committee of three were appointed to report on organization, consisting of Messrs. Schofield, Davidson and Wright. They retired, and shortly afterwards reported in favor of organizing a "National Association of Professional Base Ball Players," and recommended the adoption of the constitution and by-laws of the National Association as adopted at the November convention of 1870, as far as the same did not conflict with the interests of the professional clubs. The report was unanimously adopted, and the "National Association of Professional Base Ball Players" thereby sprang into existence. . . .

The next question was in reference to the championship. The first thing done was the reading of a series of resolutions adopted by the Athletic Club, of Philadelphia, governing their own actions with regard to the championship, in which they proclaim that henceforth they will play no "practice," "social" or exhibition games, but nothing but regular contests, and that their estimate of what constitutes a legitimate claim for championship honors will be based on the averages of games won and lost. The President, after reading the Athletic pronunciamento, properly stated that it would not interfere with any championship rules passed by the convention, but was simply intended to govern the Athletic Club only. Here are the resolutions above alluded to:—

WHEREAS, In the opinion of this club the championship of the United States for each respective year belongs to that club only which at the end of such respective years can show the greatest number of games with the smallest percentage of losses, played with the great professional clubs during said year: therefore,

Resolved, That from and after this date the Athletic Base Ball Club will not recognize any local, sectional, or national (so called) championship, other than as decided in the foregoing preamble, and will not permit their players to contend for any other.

Resolved, That this club will not recognize any "social," "practice" or "exhibition" games between professional clubs, nor will they permit their players to contend for any such games.

Resolved, That this club does not recognize any so called rule or obligation which prohibits any club from playing more than one series of games in any one season, with the same opponent, but on the contrary, they will play as many series or as many single games in any one season as the two contending clubs may deem proper.

Resolved, That in giving or accepting all challenges after this date, the directors of this club be instructed to forward to the opposing club a copy of the foregoing preamble and resolutions; and also to see that said resolutions are carried out by the players.

Mr. Young then offered the following

CODE OF CHAMPIONSHIP RULES,

which were unanimously adopted:—

Whereas, The title of Champion of the United States is a nominal one only, without any authority for or rule to govern it, and not being recognized by the National Association, therefore be it

Resolved, That this convention hereby authorize a championship title to be contended for by the various professional clubs in the country, and decided as hereinafter set forth, and to be governed by the following rules:—

1. All clubs desiring to contest for the championship must make application in writing to the chairman of the championship committee, hereinafter mentioned, on or before May 1st, 1871, and no club to be admitted after that date, except in case of failure of application to reach him. Each application to be accompanied by a remittance of $10. The chairman to keep a record of the clubs so applying, and to announce the names of the clubs contesting for the title by publication.

2. The series for the championship to be best three in five games, each club to play best three in five games with every other contesting club, at such time and place as they may agree upon, the first games played to be the championship series, unless otherwise specified in writing, and all games to be played before Nov. 1st, 1871.

3. The club winning the greatest number of games, in the championship series, with clubs entering for the championship during the season, shall be declared champions of the United States, and so certified to by a committee of three, who shall be appointed by the chairman of this convention, and who shall be known as the "championship committee," and to the chairman of which committee each club shall send its record on or before Nov. 1st, 1871. In case of a tie between two or more clubs, the committee shall examine the records of the clubs so tieing, and the one having the best average in championship contests, to be declared champions of the United States.

4. A championship streamer shall be purchased by the said committee, with the funds accompanying the application of clubs, who present the same on or before Nov. 15th, 1871, to the club entitled to receive it.

5. The club winning the championship at the end of the season, shall be entitled to fly the streamer until the close of the following season, and then to be given to the club that the championship committee shall declare to be entitled to receive it.

A motion was made by one of the western delegates to the effect that all professional clubs should charge half a dollar admission fee to all contests between professional clubs, and that the visiting club's share of the gate money receipts should be one third. This proposition, however, was voted down, it being desirable that the clubs should be allowed to charge according to circumstances, as in ordinary contests 25 cents admission is ample in Eastern cities, while in the west the regular charge is half a dollar. There may be occasions too, when the demand for admission may require the fee to be raised to one dollar.

The next question was that referring to the selection of umpires for championship contests. Mr. Kerns opened the discussion by referring to the absolute necessity of sustaining the integrity of umpires, and of repudiating all "scalawags" as were likely to be amenable to bribery by corrupt arrangements. The following resolution, which was among several offered to the convention, was then adopted.

HOW UMPIRES ARE TO BE SELECTED

Resolved, That the question of selecting an umpire between contesting clubs be arranged by the visiting club presenting the names of five persons to the local club to select one of their number, and that sufficient time be given before the day of play to make such arrangements. The persons named for selection shall be known as acknowledged and competent men for the position and they shall be drawn from three or more clubs. In case the umpire selected should fail, from some unknown cause, to appear on the day appointed for the game, then the umpire shall be selected by the two captains of the contesting clubs. The two latter clauses were added to the original resolution in the form of amendments. The question bearing upon revolving was then discussed, and after several resolutions had been offered, the two following were adopted, the first punishing delinquent players, and the other protecting the honest professionals.

Resolved, That any base ball player, who is under an existing and valid contract to play ball with any club belonging to this association, shall not be eligible to play with any other club in a match game until such contract is honorably cancelled.

Resolved, That in all cases where the services of a professional player are claimed by more than one club, each club so interested may elect the president of another club, and these two the president of a third, which three shall have the power to send for persons and papers and to decide the question in dispute, and their action shall be binding on the two clubs concerned.

Resolved, That in case the club, of which a player is the member, should not live up to their written engagement with him, then the player—if the club has been adjudged guilty, after a fair trial before the Championship Committee, shall be absolved from any obedience to his written contract and the same shall be declared cancelled. . . .

During the discussion on selecting the place for the next annual meeting, the subject of the proposed Convention of the late National Association was introduced. The President explained that in view of the fact of the establishment of the Amateur Association and their own, he regarded the late National Association as having become a defunct institution. Others of the delegates, too, endorsed the action of the Haymakers' delegate on the refusal of his club to attend any future meetings of that Association, as he regarded it having been superceded by the association just organized.

President Kerns is to be congratulated upon the intelligent and impartial manner in which he discharged the onerous duties of the position. His appointments, too, were creditable to his judgment, as will be seen by the following list of the committees:—

Judiciary—Messrs. Thacher, Mason, Waldo, Ray, Davidson, Wright, Schofield, Young and Haugh.
Rules—Messrs. Evans, Ray, Thacher, Waldo and Schofield.
Nominations—Messrs. Thacher, Davidson and Evans.
Printing—Messrs. Young, Schofield and Wright.
Championship—Messrs. Wright, Davidson and Young.

This gives the chairmanship of three committees to the west, and two to the east.

41

American Baseball Players' Tour of England (1874)

Source: *The Field* (London), July 11, 1874

In July and August, 1874, the Bostons and the Athletics of Philadelphia took a sabbatical from the NA to promote baseball in Great Britain. In this selection, The Field, a British "country gentleman's" sporting weekly, enthusiastically welcomed the Americans and even spelled out some advantages of baseball over cricket. In spite of this support, the tour lost money and failed to convince England of the superiority of America's national pastime.

BASE-BALL

THE COMING BASE-BALL PLAYERS

BEFORE the end of the present month we shall have seen in absolute earnest on English shores the game of which we have heard so much as the national exercise of America. For some time past there have been rumours of a visit during the summer of 1874 of a party of American players intent on affording to Englishmen a view of their own national game as it is when represented by the most skilful performers at this special amusement, and now the arrival is merely a matter of a fortnight's anticipation. The object of the Americans seems natural enough, but it is only American enterprise that could have overcome the numerous obstacles that impede the chances of such a gigantic excursion. Base-ball, says Young America, is a sport infinitely less tedious than cricket, and more exciting from the shorter duration of the games, and the consequent concentration of the interest. "Base-ball," says Young England—with a shrug of evident disparagement—"Baseball is merely a complicated form of rounders, and anyone can play at rounders." Cricket is merely a scientific adaptation, on an enlarged scale, of "cat and dog," but everyone cannot play at cricket; and the same style of argument applies equally to the depreciation of base-ball by those who know nothing of it, and who have never seen it under the most favourable circumstances. It is with a view to convince Englishmen, if possible, of the merits of base-ball that the American champions have decided on the hazardous experiment of crossing the Atlantic. Bad cricket is not a lively sport for on-lookers, but base-ball, as it is sure to be represented by incoming visitors, will at least have an excellent chance of securing popularity here under the auspices of eighteen of the recognised champions of the game. English-men will, no doubt, soon dismiss any ideas to its disadvantage when they have once seen it in full play. It is a fast game, necessitating on the part of all engaged no small amount of courage, watchfulness, and unselfishness—a combination that must commend itself to cricketers, at least, if not to every class and condition of sportsmen. It is an amusement that allow of no delays, that admits of no unequal division of labour, but keeps the interest unflagging until the finish. It has more fluctuations even than cricket, and is full of the glorious uncertainty proverbially said to be the chief recommendation of our English exercise. A match at base-ball is never won until it is lost, as the last innings may, and often does, turn a probable defeat into a certain victory, and upsets every ordinary calculation respecting the result. Base-ball with the Americans is the sport of sports, as superior to all others as cricket is to us English in the way of summer pastimes. Its influence is un-bounded and its supremacy pre-eminent over the American continent. Its popu-larity is so great that the professional exponents of the art can command salaries at which those of our professional cricketers sink into positive insignificance; and a skilful pitcher like Cummings of Chicago or Spalding of the Bostons may count on remuneration equal to that of an agile *danseuse* or an operatic star. The reason of its popularity in America is no doubt that it is essentially suited to the American disposition—fretful of restraint and less tenacious of purpose than the English stock from which they sprung; but I see no reason why with us from its many good points it should not occupy a place among our popular games, to assist in relieving the dull season that twice a year occurs when cricket and football are both in disuse. The Americans, who are coming over to England, will be twenty-two in number, eighteen of them representing the champion base-ball nines of America; the Bostons, who have the right to fly the pennant as champions; and the Athletics of Philadelphia. Besides these eighteen there will be four reserves, and the twenty-two will also play cricket against picked elevens at the different grounds at which they will appear during their brief stay in England. With commendable enterprise, in order to leave no stone unturned, the Bostons engaged one of the Nottingham Shaws to act as their coach in America preparatory to their visit; and that they are no mean performers at our own sport can be gathered from the fact that they defeated easily the Boston Cricket Club, Geo. Wright and Harry Wright, sons of the old Sam Wright, of Notts, making respectively 44 and 57 runs. The interest taken in the excursion on the American side is immense, and already several journalists have made their way to England as representatives of the chief American papers, with a view to chronicle the principal incidents in this trip. Indeed, by the end of May all the tickets for the steamer by which the players sail were taken up, and already upwards of sixty outsiders have signified their intention of accompanying the party. It is settled that the new American line from Philadelphia will carry the players, and Thursday next is the day fixed for their departure from America. They will arrive at Liverpool on the 26th of July, or at the latest on the 27th; and, as they must leave on the 27th of August on their homeward journey, they will have at the outside only one month in England. . . .

Their headquarters at Liverpool will be at the Washington Hotel; in London at the Midland Hotel, St. Pancras. Any communications on their account can be addressed to the Manager American Baseball Players, Bowles's American Reading Rooms, Strand, London, W.C. The photographs of the twenty players can be seen in the window at the *Field* office.

42

Spring Training and the Force Case (1875)

Source: *Chicago Tribune*, March 14, 1875

This document describes the Chicago White Stockings' spring training plans for 1875 as well as the controversy surrounding Davy Force. After signing a contract to play for the White Stockings in 1875, Force signed another contract with the Athletics of Philadelphia. A specially appointed NA committee initially decided in favor of Chicago, but the newly elected NA president (who was also the Athletics' president) apparently used his influence to get the decision overturned. This reversal so infuriated William Hulbert, a Chicago stockholder, that he decided to form an entirely new league. See William J. Ryczek, Blackguards and Red Stockings: A History of Baseball's National Association, 1871–1875 (Jefferson, N.C.: McFarland, 1992), pp. 183–91.

SPORTING NEWS

The White Stockings Gathering for the Fray
What Will be Done with Force—The Spring Programme

BASE BALL

THE WHITE STOCKINGS

The Chicago nine are making their way here in reply to the order from the management requiring them to be on hand by the 15th, inst. Higham, Peters, Zettlein, and Devlin have already arrived, and the others will be here tomorrow. The above-named players are looking well, and report themselves in fine condition, requiring but little practice to bring their muscles into activity. They are anxious to go to work, a very harmonious feeling seems to inspire all of them, and they are hopeful of passing through the season very successfully.

A gymnasium has been provided for their preliminary training exercise on Twenty-third street, in which they will pass most of their time, swinging clubs, throwing ball, etc., until about May 1.

About that date they will go to St. Louis, where, on the 6th and 8th, they will play their first games with the new St. Louis Club. If the weather during the month of April is inclement, and there is no chance for outdoor exercise, the Club will be taken to Louisville to spend a couple of weeks or more in practice games with some of the amateurs of that city.

The grounds at the corner of State and Twenty-third streets will be rolled and put into proper condition as soon as the weather will permit.

Few changes will be made. These will mostly be confined to the grand stand, which will be arranged for the better accommodation of spectators. The large posts which have heretofore intercepted the view from some parts of the stand will be removed, and other improvements made. Wood is to be provided with an office on the ground. A small building is to be erected for that purpose. Here he will make his headquarters, receive base-ball news, and transact the business of the Club.

The first championship games here will be the return games with the St. Louis nine, which will take place between the 8th and 12th of May.

The newly-elected Judiciary Committee, composed of three members of the Athletics, have decided that Force belongs to that club. Manager Wood has sent word to Force ordering him to put in an appearance here on the 15th inst. But it is not expected that he will obey the summons. It is only for the principle involved in the case that any dispute is urged. If a player has a right to enter into a contract with one club while already under engagement to another, it is justly thought that it will increase the unreliability of players, and make it impossible for any management to anticipate an approaching ball season in the engagement of its players. Mr. Force's services are not so valuable but that they can easily be dispensed with. He is vastly overrated. He is a base-ball hack who has seen his best days, as was amply demonstrated last season. He is intemperate, a constant kicker, a grumbler, and a constant source of trouble to any club that employs him. Let him go by all means. The management say that if he comes here they shall not play him in any of the championship games, but pay him his salary and lay him on the shelf. The course pursued in Philadelphia has caused a good deal of dissatisfaction among other clubs. The Mutuals, the Bostons, and the Hartfords have announced that they will not play with the Athletics in any games wherein Force may take a part. The loss of this played-out man does not in the least weaken the Chicago nine. Little Peters, a man of temperate habits, reliable, and faithful, will be played as short-stop, a position in which last season he made a very brilliant record. Keerls will play second base, and it is said he is likely to take care of it as well as any player in the country.

43

Problems with the NA According to William Hulbert (1875)

Source: *Chicago Tribune*, October 24, 1875

After losing the Davy Force case, William Hulbert went to work. First, in a stunning move, he signed Illinois native Albert Spalding and three other stars from the Red Stockings for the 1876 season. During the 1875 season, he detailed the flaws of the NA and made plans to establish a stronger league. These plans were published—without Hulbert's name—by friend and Tribune editor Lewis Meacham, who later played a role in the formation of the International Association (see Document 46).

SPORTING—THE PROFESSIONAL BASEBALL ASSOCIATION—

WHAT IT MUST DO TO BE SAVED—THE COMING TROUBLE FOR THE GAME AND ITS REMEDY

BASEBALL: A VITAL QUESTION FOR 1876

A glance over the ball field for the season now nearly closed presents a problem for 1876 of more than ordinary importance to the game as an exhibition. At the beginning of this season 13 clubs entered for the championship; 3 have disbanded, and 3 more—the Atlantic, New Haven, and St. Louis Reds—are out of the championship race by reason of not having played any return games. Of the last-named three, the Atlantics are a sample of too many professional clubs; they had never any organization, any association, any backing, or any elements of permanency or responsibility of any kind; they were simply a gang of amateurs and rejected professionals, who played such clubs as they could get to come to them, and shared the proceeds. They were not even a mob, for a mob must have a head. During the season so far they have played 38 different men in their nine, and it has been too evident that whenever a game was to come off someone went out into the highways and byways and picked up almost the first nine he met. No one supposes that they ever intended to play any western games; they simply entered the ring to force clubs to play as many games as possible with them, they taking two-thirds the receipts as on home ground. No large audiences have attended their games, because nobody felt any interest in the gang, and first-class visiting clubs under heavy expense have lost money every time they played with them, while the two-thirds which went to the gang was reason enough to induce them to get on as many games as they could.

A great part of this description would apply to the St. Louis Reds, whose manager is said to have announced in March that he did not intend to go east at all. The club in question was formed by a man who thought he could make something of a ball field on some ground controlled by him. In forming the club the manager calculated on nothing more than a few games on his own ground and then a country tour.

The case of the New Haven club was somewhat different, and their fault appears to have been more that they went into the ball business without counting the cost than that they meant to deal unfairly with anybody. The town is too small to support a club, and yet the intense rivalry between it and Hartford led to the establishment of one which could not be sustained.

Now this same trick is to be attempted in 1876. Already announcements are made for the following clubs for 1876, 18 in all:

Chicago	Hartford	Atlantic
St. Louis	Boston	St. Louis, Reds
Cincinnati	Athletic	Buffalo
Louisville	Philadelphia	Cleveland
Mutual	Americus	Burlington
New York	New Haven	Washington

Some of these enterprises may be still-born, but others will spring up to take their places, and the centennial year will be opened with not less than a dozen and a half professional clubs. This may be fun for the little fellows, but it will be death to the first nine clubs named, who are really the only ones in the list who have much showing of permanency.

It may be asked why the advent of more clubs and a more general interest in the game will hurt it. The answer is statistical: the ball season in Chicago lasts about 6 months, or, in round numbers, 180 days. Deduct from this Sundays, rainy days, time used in traveling and in needed rest, and it will be seen that not more than 90 (or at the outside 100) games can be played. The total expense account of the Chicago club for next year will approximate $28,000, and others in the ring will reach somewhat near the same figures. Thus it may be seen that every championship game played by the Chicago club in 1876 will cost the management not far from $300. Nine clubs have been referred to above as on a solid basis; 10 games all around, as this year, would give 80 games for each club and 40 for each city which sustains a club, and this would give the nines some leeway, to be used in playing amateurs or exhibition games. On this plan every club of the nine first named could live respectably, pay good salaries, and perhaps a modest dividend, and put the exhibition on a sound basis.

On the other hand, if the whole gang be let in, half of the games will not pay expenses. The best clubs in the country have played championship games for receipts of $10, $20, $30, when their opponents were the second class of clubs. Games of this class have been played this year with the St. Louis Reds, the Keokuks, the Washingtons, the Atlantics, and the New Havens. It doesn't require much figuring to see that this is a losing business where the game actually costs the first-class club from 10 to 20 times what it takes in.

It may be noted that the Chicago club played four games in Philadelphia on its present trip, and that their hotel bill in the city during their stay were more by $60 than their receipts from all the five games. This has a bearing on another point discussed further on.

The question which agitates the club management is, What can we do about it? They see the trouble ahead and are trying to work out their financial salvation. They know well enough that if 18 clubs come into the ring next year, the poorest half of the list will utterly swamp the whole and destroy the prospects of the whole game. At the same time, the managers say they can hardly see how to keep the duffers out. It has been the custom to vote everybody in who applied, and unless some concerted action be at once taken the same thing will be done at the professional association this winter.

The remedy is not difficult, and it lies in the hands of a few men. When the professional association meets it should at once adopt the following principles to govern the championship contests for next year:

First: No club should be allowed to enter for the championship unless it be backed by a responsible association, financially capable of finishing a season when begun.

This, if adopted, would cut off the Atlantic club and other cooperative frauds.

Second: No club should be admitted from a city of less size than 100,000 inhabitants, excepting only Hartford.

This would cut off the New Havens and other clubs in places so small that, under the most favorable circumstances, a first-class club could never expect to get its expenses paid for going to them.

Third: No two clubs should be admitted from the same city.

The evil effects of having more than one club in a city have been shown in Philadelphia this year. First, the Centennials went under, and then the Philadelphias and Athletics divided the interest, so that both of them have ended the season at a loss, poorer than poverty, and owing their players. One club can live in

Philadelphia, but two must starve—not only themselves, but visiting clubs. This is shown in the statement of White Stocking receipts given above. And it is well known that the Athletic club owes $6,000 as its showing for the year, while the Philadelphias are not much better off—or would not be but for some peculiar practices.

Fourth: The faith of the management of a club should be shown by the deposit of $1,000, or perhaps $1,500, in the hands of the association before the season begins. This sum not to be played for, but returned to each club which carries out its agreements and plays its return games. If it refuses to play all the games that it agrees to, let the sum be forfeited.

The adoption of these restrictions would limit the contestants next year to Chicago, Cincinnati, St. Louis, and Louisville in the West; Athletic, New York, and Mutual in the Middle States, and Hartford and Boston in the East; and with such an association the game would be prosperous, and the people who attended championship games would have a guaranty that they were to see the best clubs and the best games possible.

It may be doubted whether the professional association will be willing to vote the restrictions proposed, and, if they do not, it will be the plain duty of the nine clubs named to withdraw from the association as it now stands, and form an organization of their own—a close corporation, too. Every club which has a backing should discuss this matter before the meeting of professional association, and so instruct their representative that he will feel at liberty to take such action as will be for the best interests of the game.

44

Hulbert's Proposal to Form a New League (1875)

Source: *Spalding's Official Base Ball Guide, 1886* (reprint, St. Louis: Horton, 1987), pp. 8–9

William Hulbert and his St. Louis associate, Charles A. Fowle, sent the following letter proposing the formation of "a new association" to four NA clubs: the Bostons, the Hartfords, the Athletics, and the Mutuals of New York. The clubs assembled in New York two weeks later and created the National League (NL). Apparently Hulbert released a copy of this letter to the press, for it was reprinted by the New York Clipper *on February 12, 1876.*

CHICAGO, Jan. 23, 1876.

The undersigned have been appointed by the Chicago, Cincinnati, Louisville and St. Louis Clubs a committee to confer with you on matters of interest to the game at large, with special reference to the reformation of existing abuses, and the formation of a new association, and we are clothed will full authority in writing from the above named clubs to bind them to any arrangement we may make with you. We therefore invite your club to send a representative, clothed with like authority, to meet us at the Grand Central Hotel, in the city of New York, on Wednesday the 2d day of February next, at 12 M. After careful consideration of the needs of the professional clubs, the organizations we represent are of the firm belief that existing circumstances demand prompt and vigorous action by those who are the natural sponsors of the game. It is the earnest recommendation of our constituents that all past troubles and differences be ignored and forgotten, and that the conference we propose shall be a calm, friendly and deliberate discussion, looking solely to the general good of the clubs who are calculated to give character and permanency to the game. We are confident that the propositions we have to submit will meet with your approval and support, and we shall be pleased to meet you at the time and place above mentioned.

Yours respectfully,

W. A. HULBERT.

CHAS. A. FOWLE.

45

"A Startling Coup d'Etat": The National League (NL) Is Formed (1876)

Source: *New York Clipper*, February 12, 1876

Not everyone supported the establishment of the NL, particularly supporters of those NA teams that had been excluded from membership. In the following article, Henry Chadwick admitted that the professional game was badly in need of reform, but he was furious that the founders of the NL had executed their plans in secrecy and had failed to consult him earlier. Chadwick soon forgot his anger, however, and became a strong supporter of the NL.

"NATIONAL LEAGUE OF PROFESSIONAL CLUBS"

A Startling Coup d'Etat

For the past year or two we have been calling the attention of professional club-managers to the importance of doing something to put a stop to the growing abuses connected with their class of the baseball fraternity, the most prominent of which is the evil of fraudulent play in the form of "hippodroming," or the "selling" or "throwing" of games for betting purposes, practiced by knavish members of the club-teams, and countenanced by still worse club officials. While all have acknowledged the existence of the evil in question, and lamented the fact, none have hitherto taken any direct steps towards reform—at least, not prior to the close of the season of 1875. Last December, however, a meeting of club managers of Western organizations was held in Louisville, the object of which was to take the initiatory steps in a movement calculated to remove the existing odium from the professionals, and a reform was looked forward to by the best friends of the national game which could not but greatly add to the success, pecuniary and otherwise, of the professional clubs about to enter upon the promising campaign of the centennial year. In this business of reform it was evident that those who undertook it would have serious work to do; but it was expected that the issue would be met boldly and openly. The evil in question had begun to sap at the very foundations of the national game. It was necessary that the removal of the cancer from the system should be thorough and complete, and it was requisite, therefore, that the operation should be placed in experienced hands. Judging from what took place in the metropolis this past week, it would seem that this important work was not entrusted to men of experience; for, in our opinion, a sad blunder has been committed by the delegates to this club primary-meeting—it cannot be called a convention—which, on Wednesday night, Feb. 2, terminated in the organization of the "National League of Professional Clubs."

What was the work of reform the clubs in question had to do? It was to put a stop to fraudulent play among professional players, and to punish the clubs and their officials who countenanced it; and with this primary object there was the secondary one of revising the National Association laws so that knavish players could not be engaged after having become "marked" or suspected men. Then, too, by way of supplement, there remained the business of confining the contests of the championship arena to those stock-company organizations who are capable of carrying out the season's programme of tours and club engagements to a satisfactory issue. The business of revising the playing rules of the game was a matter outside of the "reform movement," and therefore was something of secondary importance. Now, what was there to prevent this work from being entered upon boldly, manfully, consistently and openly, at the general convention of the National Association? The object in view was one naturally commanding professional baseball-playing. The opposition to be expected to such a commendable movement was unimportant, and entirely inadequate to any successful resistance to the carrying-out of the needed reformation. Why, therefore, this secret meeting, with closed doors and a star-chamber method of attaining the ostensible objects in view? The honest clubs of the professional class are in a large majority, and possess the power to carry out the needed reformation. There is nothing in the laws of the National Association of professional players to prevent them from controlling the convention in the cause of honest play. If the circumstances of the relative positions of the two classes of the professionals—the honest men and the knaves—were such as to render it questionable whether the opposition of the latter could be successfully withstood, or had the existing laws of the National Association been such as to have given the opposition a power of controlling the convention and preventing the reformers from carrying their point, there would then have been some excuse for the secrecy observed, and for the anti-American method of doing their business of reform; but nothing of the kind existed. Why, therefore, was the singular course adopted of holding a meeting prior to the regular convention, and of organizing a new association outside of the regular gathering of delegates, except that there was some secret object in view which it was not considered desirable to have made public?

Again, we ask, what was the work to be done? What was it in detail? Let us answer this question plainly. It is notorious among professional players and club officials that a great deal of what is called "crooked play" was indulged in during the season of 1875, especially in Philadelphia and Brooklyn—not exclusively in those cities, however. In view of this understood fact, what was there for those advocating reform to do? Neither more nor less than to put it out of the power of the clubs in which this "crooked" business had been engaged in and negatively sanctioned, as it were, by the re-engagement of "suspected" or "marked" men, to re-enter the arena in 1876. Has this been done by the newly-organized "National League?" Certainly not. Again, a part of the work of reform was to prevent the re-engagement of suspected players, and the adoption of rules rendering such players ineligible. Has this object been accomplished by the League? We think not.

The fact is, there was but one fair, manly way of entering upon this business of reform, and that was to have publicly issued a circular, addressed to all professional clubs, expressing in plain language the existence of the abuses to be remedied, pointing out the necessity for reform, and inviting the co-operation of all clubs favoring the movement. If, at a convention held under regular auspices, it was found, that under the rules of the National Association, and at its convention, the reform desired could not be attained, it would then be time to have done what was done at the Grand Central Hotel. We are in hearty accord with the objects put forth in the Western Club Committee's circular. Indeed, it is but carrying out the programme time and again suggested in the columns of THE CLIPPER—that is, the necessity for a reformation. But we do decidedly object to the secret and sudden *coup d'etat* of the Western club-managers, and the glaring inconsistency of their action in throwing out one club, open to the charge of crooked work last season, while retaining another club equally amenable to censure for the doubtful character of the play of its team. Inconsistent action, too, is apparent in the throwing-out of the Philadelphia Club for its "irregularities"—that is the mild term, we believe—while another club in the League is countenanced in the engagement of players guilty of the very "irregularities" for which the former is punished. Instead of boldly confronting the club thus charged, the League "whip the devil round the stump," and exclude the offenders under a rule prohibiting two League clubs from being established in the same city. Then, too, they leave out the New Haven Club—an organization which, in the high character of its officials, the strength of its team, and its reputation for carrying out its obligations, stands as high as the clubs in the League—under the rule of limiting League clubs to cities having not less than 75,000 inhabitants, while they allow the Hartford Club in their League, though that city has not so many inhabitants by 13,000 as New Haven.

By a glance at the code of rules—not the playing code—governing the inter-course of the League clubs, one with the other, which are to be attempted to be enforced this season, a series of laws will be found to have been enacted which, before half the season is over, will necessarily be dead-letters. As we said before, the action of the meeting of Feb. 2, which resulted in the organization of the National League, will be found to be of as little advantage to true reform or to the pecuniary interests of the League clubs as could well have been taken. It is to be hoped that we will be found to have been mistaken in our conclusions in this respect, but we are afraid it is an "ower (?) true tale."

What effect this secret movement will have on the coming convention of the National Association we cannot say at present. It may render the convention unnecessary, but then, again, it may not. There are plenty of the semi-professional class of clubs which would be glad of a chance of getting into the Association in question; and if one club of the organization now on the roll of the National Association concludes to hold the convention, that alone will give it a support which may cause the semi-professionals to rally to the call. In conclusion, we have to say that we regard the action of the clubs in question as hasty, inconsiderate and inconsistent with their alleged efforts at reform; and though we hope to see the movement in favor of reform successful, we are afraid that the right method to insure success has not been adopted by the League.

The Hartford Times, in commenting on the action of the Leaguers, says that "the players engaged by the Philadelphia and New Haven Clubs will be thrown out by the operation of the League laws." In other words, these twenty odd players, of whom the greater number are as honest as any in the League, are to be branded as "crooked" players unworthy of employment. Such gross injustice presents a strik-ing illustration of the absurdity of some of the laws adopted by the League. We have to say that the players of the clubs in question are to be held to service, and the clubs to their responsibilities until the National Association laws which govern them cease to be operative. The players named are as follows: Seward, Nichols, Cassidy, Sommerville, Spence, S. Wright, Pabor, Waitt, Heifert, Knowdel, Meyerle, Crawley, Craver, Schaffer, Weaver, Malone, Zettlein, Treacy, Nelson, and McMul-lin. The action of the Philadelphia Club under this hasty and crude legislation at the hands of the League organization will be looked for with curiosity.

46

Formation of the International Association (1877)

Source: *Toronto Daily Globe*, February 28, 1877

The formation of the NL by no means established the league's ascendancy over all of professional baseball. Indeed, dozens of professional teams continued to operate inde-pendently of the league; some of them were as strong as, if not stronger than, some NL clubs. In 1877 delegates representing seventeen such clubs formed the International

Association in Pittsburgh. Unlike the NL *(but like the* NA*), the association welcomed any club willing to pay a modest entry fee.*

BASE BALL

FORMATION OF THE INTERNATIONAL ASSOCIATION

A convention of the representatives of seventeen clubs was recently held at Pittsburg for the purpose of forming the International Association. Ten men represented the seventeen clubs, the more prominent being the Chelsea, Live Oak, Tecumseh, Buckeye, Allegheny. The Syracuse Stars, and other clubs of that class, were not represented. The following is a list of the delegates present:—Fairbanks club, Chicago, represented by Lewis Meacham; Resolute, Elizabeth, N.J., A. B. Rankin; Brown Stockings, Erie, Pa., James Burns; Chelsea, of Brooklyn, A. B. Rankin; Live Oaks, Lynn, Mass., W. A. Cummings, pitcher of last year's Hartfords; Alaska, New York city, A. B. Rankin; Tecumseh, London, Ontario, H. Gorman; Maple Leaf, Guelph, Ontario, H. Gorman; Manchester, Manchester, N.H., H. J. Clark; Buckeye, Columbus, O., F. A. Williams; San Francisco, San Francisco, S. C. Waite; Rochester, N.Y., S. C. Waite; Mountain City, Altoona, Pa., S. M. Crane; St. Louis Reds, St. Louis, Thomas McNeary; Active, Reading, Pa., H. D. McKnight; Allegheny, Pittsburgh, H. D. McKnight. In addition to these clubs some eight or ten others were represented by proxies. A general interchange of views relative to the management of the organization was indulged in by the candidates immediately after the assemblage had been called to order by the selection of Mr. Meacham, of Chicago, as temporary President. Among other things which it is intended to incorporate in the laws of the new Association were stringent rules which, if properly enforced, will do much toward the prevention of what is known in baseball parlance as "revolving"—that is, a person leaving one club and joining another without a proper release. It is also likely that the Association will adopt the dead ball. The name occasioned no little discussion, but finally it was decided that the new organization be called the International Baseball Association. Having thoroughly discussed and exchanged views, a Committee consisting of those having at their finger-ends all the ins and outs of the national game was selected. Having subsequently met it succeeded in dispensing of all business incident to permanent organization, and adjourned to meet on the 3rd day of February next, at the Palmer House, Chicago. The proceedings commenced with the reading of the report of the Committee on Constitution. The instrument which was finally adopted is in substance pretty much the same as that adopted and in force with league clubs. There are some changes relative to scoring, the selection of umpire, and the delivery of the pitcher, but unimportant, though the members of the newly-fledged association, on the whole, consider their rules an improvement over those of the other organization. The league alliance agreement was also adopted, with the exception of article 8. Four brands of balls were offered, and Mann's dead sphere was selected. The entrance fee of the clubs was set at $10, while those desirous of competing for the championship will be obliged to put up the additional sum of $15, making $25 in all.

It was agreed that a visiting club should receive half of the gross receipts whenever such receipts exceed the sum of $55. In case this amount is not reached by gate money the deficit must be made up by the resident club. This provision is made for visiting nines, whereby they can leave non-appreciative communities by other roads than turnpikes, and be saved the affliction of being mistaken for members of that ever-moving army without destination.

After disposing of this very important point, the Association was in readiness for the election of officers. The gentlemen selected were W. A. Cummings, Lynn, Mass., of last year's Hartfords, President; H. Gorman, London, Canada, Vice-President; J. A. Williams, Columbus, O., Treasurer and Secretary.

The Judiciary Committee is composed as follows—H. D. McKnight, Pittsburg; L. E. Waite, St. Louis; N. P. Pond, Rochester, N.Y.; A. B. Rankin, Brooklyn, and George Siceman, Guelph, Ont.

Considerable discussion followed on the price of admission to the games of the Association, many of the delegates holding out for 25 cents to all games, no matter on what day or under what circumstances. It was finally decided that 25 cents be the rate of admission to the games of the clubs of the Association between themselves. With league nines it left it optional with managers of clubs contending.

47 ──

Louisville Players Expelled
for "Cussed Crookedness" (1877)

Source: *Louisville Courier-Journal*, November 3, 1877

The NL ostensibly was formed to rid baseball of gambling and "hippodroming." When four Louisville Grays were found to have thrown the majority of games in the last two weeks of the season, causing the club to lose a pennant it had nearly clinched, shock waves reverberated throughout baseball. The immediate, permanent expulsion of the four by Louisville, backed firmly by NL president William Hulbert, helped to restore the faith of baseball "cranks" in their game. The NL also expelled the Grays from the league prior to the 1878 season.

The author of this exposé, John Haldeman, was the son of team president and Courier-Journal *editor Walter N. Haldeman. The elder Haldeman had earlier purchased one share of stock in the Grays for his son, had appointed him as the club's official scorer, and had allowed him to play center field in a game in 1876. The younger Haldeman, hardly an impartial reporter, used investigative techniques we would condemn today. A possible victim of this approach was Bill Craver, who was banned solely on the basis of circumstantial evidence.*

The players' telegrams, which comprised the bulk of the evidence against the four, are reprinted in Harry C. Palmer et al., Athletic Sports in America, England and Australia *(Philadelphia: Hubbard Bros., 1889), pp. 69–77, along with an analysis by the Grays' vice-president, Charles E. Chase.*

CUSSED CROOKEDNESS

A Complete Expose of How Four Ball Men Picked Up Stray Pennies
Hall and Devlin Bounce Themselves Out of the
League on Their Own Testimony
Nichols and Craver Also Take their Gruel for Tasting of Forbidden Fruits

A SAD, SAD STORY

When the news of the expulsion of four of the Louisville players first was made public it struck St. Louis amidships, for among the four unfortunates were found the names of Hall and Devlin, who were to be two of the mightiest war bugs in the mighty Brown Stocking nine for next season. The press of St. Louis laid all manner of mean things to the credit of the Louisville Directors, the extracts presented below being fair samples. The dose came so very sudden, and was so very unpalatable to the "big bridgettes," that they didn't even think of swallowing it. We trust the evidence published this morning will be amply sufficient to cram the dose down their throats whether they like it or not.

The Times discourses as follows:

> The action of the Louisville Club in expelling Hall, Devlin, Craver and Nichols from their club was not entirely unexpected here in St. Louis. The directors of the Louisville are not looked upon by the managers of the St. Louis Club as belonging to a very respectable class of citizens, and they could do nothing that would cause much surprise anywhere. The club has been behind with the salaries of their players all the year, and Devlin and Hall have each from $300 to $600 due them, with very little prospect of ever getting any of it. They are both charged with disobeying the orders of the club manager, though in what particular is not stated. Mr. Fowle, secretary of the St. Louis club, thinks that their action in expelling Hall and Devlin was a piece of spite work against St. Louis for having engaged them for next year, and also against the players themselves for grumbling about the club's tardiness in paying them their salaries. Devlin is known to have said some very harsh things about the managers of the Louisville club, and the managers now hope to get even with him by preventing his engagement with any first-class club next year. Neither Devlin nor Hall can play in any League game until the charges against them have been investigated and passed upon by the League Directors, who meet next month at Cleveland, and not even after that, unless the motion of the Louisville club in expelling them be set aside by the League Directors.

The Globe-Democrat goes at it in a more moderate manner and is fain to indulge in a small spark of hope, to-wit: That Hall and Devlin have only "disobeyed orders and generally misconducted themselves, all of which can be easily excused." A bucket of water will have to be thrown on this spark. But to what the G.-D says:

The announcement that Hall, Devlin, Nichols and Craver had been expelled from the Louisville club for crooked conduct was the all-absorbing topic in baseball circles yesterday, and the general impression prevailed that it would result in killing the national game "deader than a mackerel." The news, of course, created greater excitement in St. Louis than elsewhere, as two of the expelled players were relied on to help bring the championship here next season; and, if the charges against them can be sustained, it is almost a foregone conclusion that the St. Louis club will "throw up the sponge," and never again place a nine in the field. Concerning Devlin and Hall, one word should be added. The Louisville dispatch states that these men and Craver and Nichols were expelled for "selling games, disobedience of orders and general misconduct." It does not specify which of the men were expelled for "selling games." This is, of course, the gravest charge, and if Hall and Devlin are not included in it, the "disobedience of orders and general misconduct" can be easily excused, as it is a notorious fact that the Louisville players have been treated in the most shabby manner, especially as regards money matters, which may have a good deal to do with the expulsions. The League, however, was organized to protect players as well as clubs, and at the Cleveland Convention no injustice will be permitted. Contracts, unlike pie crusts, were not made to be broken, and the money owed to the Louisville players should be paid them in full if the "disobedience of orders" and "general misconduct" are based on flimsy grounds.

What Cincinnati thinks, as told by the Commercial:

The Louisville developments are still the talk in base ball circles in this city. There is general surprise and incredulity expressed in regard to Hall and Nichols. Nobody has ever thought Devlin and Craver any too good to sell a game, or do anything else for money. No player, once expelled from a League club, can ever again play without the unanimous consent of the directors of all the League clubs.

Having given some idea of how the announcements of the four expulsions were taken in some cities outside of our own, it is now the COURIER-JOURNAL's pleasant duty to go deeper into details and to explain to its readers how everything was brought about. In the first place, this paper modestly asks for its share of the credit in bringing the four unprincipled black-legs to justice. After the last Eastern tour of the Louisville club, it was satisfied that foul playing had been indulged in. A series of daily paragraphs in its columns charging crooked work; insinuating very strongly that more was known of the doings of the players than had ever been made public, and threatening damage disclosures at no distant date, all lent their aid in frightening the guilty ones and extorting confessions when the proper time came. In reality the COURIER-JOURNAL had no proof positive against any of the men, but it pretended it had, which served the purpose equally as well. A representative of the paper was in Indianapolis on the occasion of the exhibition game at that place between the Louisvilles and Bostons and while there Hall, either unwittingly through ignorance or in the hope of preparing a soft fall for himself on disclosures which he thought bound to come, let out something which acted as a first rate starter to the investigation.

As we stated yesterday, the unjust aspersions made by the St. Louis papers on the Louisville Base Ball Club because of the expulsion of two of their players who had been engaged by the St. Louis Club compels us to publish a synopsis of the testimony on which the Louisville Directors acted in expelling their dishonest players. We presume no one who reads it can for a moment doubt the entire justice and necessity of the action. The confessions alone of the principal culprits were ample, but the Directors had in addition ample corroborative testimony. The evidence as to the dissipation, late hours, card-playing and disreputable conduct of some of the players was abundantly sufficient, in the view of the Directors, for their action.

Very soon after the Directors began their investigations Hall made an admission of crookedness to one of them. Frequent meetings were held, and Hall's and Devlin's confessions were made before the Directors on Friday and Saturday evenings, October 26 and 27. Their admissions were voluminous, but it is necessary to give only the gist of them, as taken from the club's records. The first portions were given Friday evening, and the second when they were recalled on Saturday evening, and are as follows:

TESTIMONY OF GEORGE HALL

About three or four weeks after Al. Nichols joined the Louisville club, he made me a proposition to assist in throwing League games, and I said to him, "I'll have nothing to do with any League games." This proposition was made before the club went on its last Eastern trip. He never made the proposition about League games but once. In Pittsburgh he made me a proposition to throw the Allegheny game, and I agreed to it. He promised to divide with me what he received from his friend in New York, who was betting on the games. Nichols and I were to throw the game by playing poorly. While in Chicago, on the club's last Western trip, I received a telegram from Nichols, stating that he was $80 in the hole, and asking how he could get out. I told Chapman that this dispatch was from my brother-in-law who lived in Baltimore. I did not reply to the dispatch.

Devlin first made me a proposition in Columbus, Ohio, to throw the game in Cincinnati. He made the proposition either in the hotel or upon the street.

We went to the telegraph office in Columbus and sent a dispatch to a man in New York by the name of McCloud, saying that we would lose the Cincinnati game. McCloud is a pool seller. The telegraph was signed "D. & H." We received no answer to this telegram. I did not know McCloud. Devlin knew him. Mc-Cloud sent Devlin $50 in a letter, and Devlin gave me $25. One of us sent a dispatch to McCloud from Louisville, saying: "We have not heard from you." He then sent the $50 to Devlin; that was the 1 to 0 Cincinnati game. We (Devlin and Hall) telegraphed to McCloud from Louisville that the club would lose the Indianapolis game. I have never received any money for assisting in throwing this game. I think it was the 7 to 3 game. Devlin said that he did not want to sign the order to have his telegraphs inspected; said it would ruin him.

TESTIMONY OF JAMES A. DEVLIN

Was introduced to a man named McCloud in New York, who said that when I wanted to make a little money to let him know. Was to use the word "sash" in telegraphing, and he would know what was meant. Hall first made the overture to me to throw games while in Columbus, Ohio. He wrote a letter to me and left it on the table in our room. In the letter he said, "Let us make some money." Can't remember what else was in it. Called Hall one side and asked him if he meant it, and he said "Yes." I proposed to telegraph to McCloud, and we did so. We made a contract to lose the Cincinnati game. McCloud sent me $100 in a letter, and I gave Hall $25 of it. Told him that *McCloud only sent $50.* Helped to throw the game in Indianapolis. Hall was with me in it. Received $100 from McCloud for it. *Did not give any of this to Hall.* Gave it to my wife. Never had anything to do with Nichols. Hall told me that Nichols had approached him, but he never told me that he had thrown any games but those in Cincinnati and Indianapolis. Don't know F. A. Williams. Suspected Craver in one of the Hartford games, and spoke of it to Chapman. Told Hall to-day that we had better make a clean breast of it.

GEORGE HALL RECALLED

Since last night I have thought of another game Nichols and I threw. It was with the Lowell Club, of Lowell, Massachusetts. He and I agreed to throw it. He did all the telegraphing. Never got a cent from Nichols for the games he and I threw. My brother-in-law has often said "I was a fool for not making money." He has said this for several years past. His talking this way caused a coldness between us. When I was in Brooklyn the last time he asked me if we could not make some money on the games, and I told him I would let him know when we could. He bet on the Allegheny game and lost. Telegraphed him from here about the Indianapolis game. Had a talk with him in June, I think in Brooklyn, about selling games. Have sent two or three telegrams to him—not over three.

His name is Frank Powell, and he lives at 865 Fulton street, Brooklyn. Nichols asked me on the last trip if I could not get somebody to work Brooklyn for us. I can't tell where it was that Nichols first approached me about throwing League games. When I told him that I would have nothing to do with League games, I meant that I would go in with him on outside games. I made the proposition about the Cincinnati game to Devlin. Last night I said he made it to me. I made the proposition in Columbus. Nichols spoke to me in Cincinnati about selling the Cincinnati game, and I said I would see about it. Nichols said: "George, try and get Jim in." He suggested that I should write a letter to Devlin. Devlin was not in the room when I wrote it. In the note to Devlin, I think I said: "Jim, how can we make a stake?" I left the note on the marble-top table in our room at the Burnet House, Cincinnati. When I next saw Devlin he was in the room putting on his ball clothes, and it was there that he said: "George, do you mean it?" And I said: "Yes, Jim." After Devlin accepted the proposition, I told Nichols that Jim was in it. Nichols was not in with us on the Cincinnati game. Think I wrote the letter to Devlin in Columbus, but won't be certain. Think I destroyed the note at the time. Did not take it out of his pocket two or three days afterward and destroy it. Am certain of this. Never got a cent for the Indianapolis game. Devlin said that he had never heard from McCloud about the money for it. Never received but $25 from Devlin.

JAMES DEVLIN RECALLED

Hall's letter to me was written in the Neal House, Columbus. After receiving the letter I next saw him in our room when we were dressing for the game. Did not say last night that I called him on one side and asked him if he meant it. We telegraphed after the Columbus game to McCloud, saying that the Cincinnati game would be lost. Did not know that Nichols was in with Hall. Hall told me that Nichols was "in" on the Allegheny game. George took the letter he wrote me out of my pocket and tore it up. This was one or two days after he wrote it. Don't know whether it was in Columbus or Cincinnati. George told me that he took it out of my pocket and tore it up. Richard Tobin, who keeps the paper stand in Earles' Hotel, New York, introduced me to McCloud on our last trip East. Knew of McCloud, but never received any work from him before this. Tobin took me to McCloud's house, and it was there that I made the agreement with him. His address is 141 Broome street, New York. He resides there with his family. It was on Sunday afternoon that I called on him. Never received but $300 from him. This was for one Cincinnati and two Indianapolis games. Was in one Indianapolis game by myself. Hall did not know it. Was in only one game at Cincinnati. Received all money from McCloud by mail. Hall sent telegraph to him about first Indianapolis game. The telegraph was sent from here. I told him to use the word "sash." I telegraphed him about the second Indianapolis game. Nichols never spoke to me about games. Received money by telegraph from John J. Martin to amount of $100 for games won here. Got $25 for each game.

This was when we were winning so many games on our own grounds. Signed my telegraphs to Martin "J. A. D." Never signed any telegraphs except "J. A. D." or "D. & H."

TESTIMONY OF GEORGE SHAFFER

Nichols told me that he was buying pools on the games. He told me so in Indianapolis, Cincinnati and New York. Said he was betting on games through a party in New York. Nichols told me that "if *he* had a chance he would not be a sucker," meaning that if he had a chance to throw a game for money he would do it. In New York a man came up to me and asked if I knew where Craver was. Said that a friend of Craver, by the name of Snider, had got all the money out of the pool-box, and that he (the man) would blow Craver's brains out if he could catch him. Have heard of McCloud, but don't know him. Nichols said he thought some of the players were not working it on the square. I understood him to mean Craver.

TESTIMONY OF JOSEPH J. GERHARDT

I know McCloud. He is a pool-seller. Was introduced to him by Mr. Cammeyer. On the Union Grounds, Brooklyn. Fred. Treacy brought me a telegram addressed to Devlin, and I told him that I would give it to him after the game was over. But Bobby Matthews said to give to him at once, as it might be important, so I gave it to him, and afterwards Devlin said it was from a man in Philadelphia to whom he owed money. Zettlein, Treacy, Mathews and Eddy King were together.

Before his departure for Brooklyn, Nichols was before the Directors and admitted that he had been betting on games, and had sent one dispatch giving information to a friend, but denied having sold games. When asked for an order on the telegraph company for permission to examine all dispatches he had sent or received, after some hesitation he gave it. Before this examination was begun he was dismissed on the proof by Hall that he had sold the games at Lowell and Allegheny, and his own admission that he had bet on games.

The Directors, having determined to probe the matter thoroughly, requested the players to give them authority to examine all telegraphic messages they received or forwarded. All gave the order (Devlin having declined to sign—until he had first seen Hall) except Craver, who absolutely refused. Craver's play in several games had been so suspicious as to amount almost to a conviction, and his management of the men (he being assistant captain) in several instances unmistakably indicated his intention to lose games. The evidence on this point was sufficient to satisfy the Directors of crookedness. Gerhardt, Shaffer and Latham also testified that he was the direct cause of most of the errors they made, he having purposely "rattled" them. He was so strongly suspected by the manager that he was laid off in an important game. He confessed to playing cards at late and unseasonable hours on nights before important games were to be played, in direct violation of the peremptory orders of the Directors and the manager. He also disobeyed their orders in regard to drinking thus disqualifying himself from playing, and by other misconduct compelled his expulsion.

The Directors are still pursuing their investigations, and it is possible further developments may be made. The Directors are thoroughly satisfied that Latham, Shaffer, Crowley, Gerhardt and Lafferty have clean records, and that their playing was earnest, fair and honest. At one time suspicion was slightly attached to Gerhardt, but the most thorough examination acquitted him entirely, and satisfied the Directors that his suspicious errors were caused by Craver adroitly "rattling" him. Nothing was produced to show criminality on the part of Hague, although costly errors at important moments and deficient batting provoked comments. Neither was there anything to show Snyder's criminality, although his persistent efforts to screen Devlin and some of his costly errors, especially in the last Chicago game, where (after playing six games without an error) he made six errors, piling one on the other, until the Chicagos had secured a victory, caused suspicion and unfavorable remarks.

The convicted players earnestly denied ever having sold any League games, and no evidence has yet been produced to show this; but there is not a man in Louisville who is not thoroughly satisfied that the last games with the Bostons and Hartfords were purposely lost. The Directors believed that men who would sell games with Alliance clubs for one hundred dollars would not hesitate to sell League games for a consideration.

At a meeting of the Louisville directors, held Tuesday night, October 30, after the statements of Hall and Devlin, as given on October 26 and 27, had been read, the following resolutions were adopted:

Resolved: That for selling games, conspiring to sell games, and tampering with players, A. H. Nichols, by a unanimous vote, the ayes and noes being called, be and hereby is expelled from the Louisville club.

Resolved: That W. H. Craver, because of disobedience of positive orders, of general misconduct and of suspicious play, in violation of his contract and the rules of the League, be and hereby is expelled from the Louisville club.

Resolved: That, for selling games, conspiring to sell games and tampering with players, George Hall be and hereby is expelled from the Louisville club.

Resolved: That for selling games, conspiring to sell games and tampering with players, James A. Devlin be, and hereby is, expelled from the Louisville club.

Resolved: That any sums to the credit of players expelled for cause be, and the same are hereby, declared forfeited.

These are the resolutions, then, that put the final quietus to any future League ball-playing on the part of Messrs. Alfred H. "Slippery-elm" Nichols, "Butcher" Craver, Jas. H. "Terror" Devlin, and "Gentleman George" Hall, unless, indeed, the League Directors think the evidence on which the "Lambs" were bounced be not conclusive enough, and that seems hardly probable in the face of what has been brought out into the bright sunlight. There they stand. A noble quartet of "Lambs," combining in themselves the first four expulsions that have ever been made from active professional service, for dabbling into certain things, which, for various reasons, are not looked upon as being directly connected with the proper workings of the "national sport." The press of the country has been talking "crooked base-ball" for years, and "crooked base-ball" has been going on for years, but it simply bordered on an impossibility to obtain sufficient proof against any of the suspected parties, so nicely did the gamblers and their very dear and efficient servants, the "Lambs," play their interesting little schemes. The "funny-work," therefore, ran on its way quite merrily; players indulged in their rascality right under the very noses of fair-minded people, who were intuitively conscious of a mass of corruption somewhere around but who couldn't, to save their gizzard, bring the body compos-ing the corruption to light, so skillfully was it concealed. The Louisville Directors would have found it a hopeless task to have fastened guilt on a single player on their nine had they been dealing with human beings gifted with even an ordinary degree of shrewdness. Their coat-tails might have been crammed with all the suspicion the world produces, and they would have been compelled to have remained content with the suspicion, without the accompanying proofs, had they been dealing with other than the most ignorant of rascals. Had Devlin and Hall locked their jaws, had they refused to answer a single question put to them, or had they worked the thing on a lying ticket all the way through, they could have had a jolly time skipping around on the St. Louis grounds next season. Craver could have carried out his little contract with the new Hartford club; and Nichols—bless his dear, lovely hide—could have looked around and discovered a more extended field for his peculiar operations than his short three months' stay on the Louisville nine opened unto him. True, the dear boy accomplished quite enough in the little time allowed him, but a standing engagement for the season is better calculated to draw him out and show what fine engineering capacities the young man is really gifted with. Hall and Devlin, however, like two true-blooded numskulls, became possessed of the idea that some of their "secret service" manipulations had been brought to light, and on their first appearance before the directors immediately began squealing worse than two stuck pigs. The cat escaped from its meal-bag confinement, and with the felines coming the occupations of four prominent Othellos of the green diamond took wings and gently soared away to leeward.

Nichols, it seems, became frightened before any of the others. He sniffed danger and wanted to "git." Just before the club started on its last Western trip, he told the club officials that he saw he was of no particular service to the nine, and rather than see any of the gentlemen go down to their pockets for his pay, he would take his release and the money then due him and "vamoose." This method of procedure looked exceedingly clever in him at the time, but a look at it now will reveal "the gray horse of another color," together with the fact that the young man was not altogether oblivious of a future. In his hurried departure, however, he left something behind him—his fate. By this time it has doubtless caught up with him again. May the two, he and it, be the means of manufacturing much fun in the future for each other—beyond the pale of the League, however. The "quartet" from this time out are marked men. They are deeply branded, and the marks put upon them will only disappear when their hides do. The boys must secure new skins before they can have a new deal.

This statement would not be so complete did we not add that the Directors have implicit faith in the integrity of their manager, Mr. J. C. Chapman. He has performed his arduous duties to their entire satisfaction, and leaves Louisville with a faultless record and the respect and confidence of every one connected with the club.

48

Baseball's First Unassisted Triple Play? (1878)

Source: *Providence Evening Press*, May 9, 1878

Providence center fielder Paul Hines has been credited with executing the first unassisted triple play in major league history. The article below mentions that Hines threw to second baseman Charlie Sweasy at the end of the play, but we do not know if the throw was necessary under 1878 rules to retire the final runner.

AFTER THAT PENNANT

Providence, 3; Bostons, 2

HINES SAVES US BY A TRIPLE PLAY
GREAT GAME AND LARGE CROWD

"They tell us, sir, that we are weak and unable to cope with so formidable an enemy," but yesterday's game of base ball has proved all such newspaper prophets false. The champion Bostons played the Providence team on the new Messer street grounds and suffered their second consecutive defeat, it being the third game between the two clubs. Over forty-five hundred people were present. The game was very exciting from the beginning to the very close and much applause was lavished on the two teams, the winning club of course coming in for the lion's share. The Providence team was the same that played in Boston, Saturday—Nichols pitching to Allison. The game began at 3:30, with the home club at the bat, Carey losing the toss. . . .

The eighth inning was a notable one. Higham, who had done little at the bat thus far, sent a pretty daisy-cutter past Wright and sped to second on a passed ball. Sutton took a fly off York's bat well, and Dick took third on Murnan's put out. Hines drove a fly to Leonard, who made a bad muff and Dick scored. Carey was put out by Morrill, assisted by Sutton. The score now stood Providence 3, Bostons 0. O'Rourke got his base on called balls. Manning sent a little grounder between first and second, which Sweasy hastily picked up and threw wild over Murnan's head, O'Rourke scoring on this unfortunate error and Manning taking third. Sutton got first on a muffed ball by Murnan. Burdock then struck what everybody considered was a clean base hit, about two rods back of short stop's position, the men on the bases having confidence enough to come home. Here a phenomenal and surprising play was made; Hines made a difficult and brilliant running catch of the ball, putting out the striker; the momentum acquired carried him near to third base, which he stepped on, thus forcing out Manning; Sweasy then signaled for the ball, which Hines threw to him, putting out Sutton. This triple play, saving two and perhaps more runs, created tempestuous enthusiasm, the crowd rising en masse, cheering and waving hats.

The ninth inning opened with the score 3 to 1 in our favor. That inning gave us nothing but a base hit by Allison. Burdock got his base on a fly that Carey muffed. Morrill was run out by Murnan, Burdock taking third, having previously stolen second. Bond batted a safe one and the visitor's last run came in. Bond got second on Allison's only passed ball. Wright then attempted to tie the score making a heavy fly hit to right field. Higham was in the right spot, held the ball and the victory was won.

The playing of the Providence team was even and pretty, the errors on muffed flies being excusable on account of the bright sun in the players' eyes. The pitching was good, though Nichols is rather slow in his delivery. Allison caught splendidly, his back-stopping being exceptionally fine; his batting was also a surprise to all. Hines cannot be accorded too much praise for saving the day for Providence by his extraordinary play. Snyder's errors helped to defeat his side materially. Burdock and Morrill were extra fine in their positions. As a whole the victory was a creditable one.

The innings were promptly received at the Press office on Weybosset street, and large crowds rejoiced at the successful progress of the game as bulletined at the close of each inning. At the grounds enthusiasm is no name for the joyful feeling.

49

Model Player Contract of the Chicago Club (1879)

Source: House Judiciary Committee, *Study of Monopoly Power: Organized Baseball* (Washington, D.C.: U.S. Government Printing Office, 1952), p. 1508

With the formation of the NL, a new disciplinary code was imposed upon the players. The contract below required that the player "absolutely refrain . . . from any excess of dissipation which may, in any degree, tend to impair his physical condition." Furthermore, the club reserved the right to terminate any player for insubordination, injury, illness, or loss of skills.

CONTRACT, 1879, CHICAGO NATIONAL LEAGUE CLUB (MODEL FOR FIRST UNIFORM PLAYER'S CONTRACT)

Articles of agreement between the Chicago Ball Club, of the City of Chicago, in the State of Illinois, a corporation duly organized under the laws of the State of Illinois, party of the first part, and _____, of the city of _____, in the State of _____, party of the second part.

Witnesseth, that the said _____, party of the second part, for the consideration hereinafter mentioned, covenants and agrees to play base ball, practice, attend gates, or perform such other duties as pertain to the exhibition of the game of base ball, in the City of Chicago and elsewhere, as may be required of him, for the party of the first part, and for no other organization whatever, in such positions as may be assigned him, from time to time, by the Manager of said Club or the Captain of its "Nine," for the period of _____, commencing on the _____ day of _____, A.D. 187__, and ending on the _____ day of _____, A.D. 187__.

The party of the second part further covenants and agrees to subject himself to the discipline required by the Management of the "Nine" of said Club; to play base ball with the utmost of his skill and ability; to cheerfully obey all the rules and regulations of the Club; and to absolutely refrain, during the term of this contract, from any excess or dissipation which may, in any degree, tend to impair his physical condition. It is understood and agreed that the said party of the second part shall, when thereto required by said party of the first part, subject himself to medical examination and medical treatment, and that the party of the first part shall withhold from the party of the second part a proportion of his monthly pay equal to the time he shall be, in the opinion of said party of the first part, disqualified for service in the "Nine" of said Club by reason of illness, injury, insubordination, or loss of skill in play from any cause, the said party of the first part being hereby constituted the judge of the disqualifications stated, and having the right to suspend the party of the second part therefore so long as the said party of the first part may deem necessary. It is also understood and agreed that the said Club has the right to terminate this contract, at its option, at any time, for the violation of any of the above covenants, conditions or agreements, or for any other good and sufficient reason, and that in the event of its termination by the Management of the Club, before the expiration of the time above limited, the monthly pay of said party of the second part shall thereupon cease, and no further payments shall thereafter be due or payable to said party of the second part upon this contract.

And, in consideration of the above-mentioned covenants by said party of the second part, the said Club agrees to pay the sum of _____ Dollars,

_____

_____

_____

It is also agreed by the parties hereto that this contract shall not be valid or binding until the receipt by the Secretary of the National League of Professional Ball Clubs of a notification signed by the parties hereto, of the making of this contract; and it is further agreed that should the Club party hereto lose its membership in the National League of Professional Base Ball Clubs at any time before the expiration of the period covered by this contract, then, immediately upon such loss of membership, the mutual contract obligations of the parties hereto shall at once cease and terminate.

In witness whereof the said Chicago Ball Club, through and by its _____ _____ and the said _____ in his own person, have hereunto subscribed their names and affixed their seals this _____ day of _____ A.D. 187___.

_____ [SEAL]

Manager.

_____ [SEAL]

Signed, sealed, and delivered in the presence of

_____

_____

50

The NL Adopts a Player Reservation System (1879)

Source: *Buffalo Commercial Advertiser*, September 30 and October 3, 1879

In 1879 the NL adopted a player reservation system designed to reduce salary costs. Initially each team could reserve a maximum of five players; these players were bound, in effect, to the team that initially signed them to a contract, for the duration of their playing careers in the league. Apparently the owners did not immediately recognize that the reservation system would also permit them to "buy" and "sell" players, or, more technically, to buy and sell the rights to sign specific players to contracts. Until the 1970s, when the reservation system finally collapsed, the "reserve clause" provided owners with a powerful means of controlling their work force.

BUFFALO, Sept. 29, 1879.

At a meeting of the National League of professional base ball clubs, held this day at Buffalo, after a careful review of the results, financial and otherwise, of the season of 1879, the following conclusions were arrived at, and recommendations adopted for future guidance:

The League believes that its efforts to present the only national game of this country strictly as an exhibition of skill, free from any of the evil influences which frequently surround such contests when governed and controlled by unprincipled managers, have been fully appreciated by the general public; that the stringent rules and regulations which have been adopted by this Association and rigidly enforced, have been conducive to the best interests of all concerned, elevating the moral tone of the game and educating the players to recognize the truth of the old adage, "Honesty is the best policy."

The financial results of the past season prove that salaries must come down. We believe that players in insisting upon exorbitant prices are injuring their own interests by forcing out of existence clubs which cannot be run and pay large salaries except at a large personal loss.

The season financially has been a little better than that of 1878, but the expenses of many of the clubs have far exceeded their receipts, attributable wholly to the high salaries. In view of these facts, measures have been taken by this League to remedy the evil to some extent for 1880.

It has also been decided that a uniform contract with players shall be used by each club, and that no money should be paid players until it has been earned, in other words, that no advance shall be given.

The contracts will hereafter extend from April 1st to October 31st, seven months, which will give players nearly half a year for the pursuit of other employment. It is hoped that the restrictions regarding advance money will work beneficially to the persons who risk their capital in the support of the sport.

Several clubs having signified their desire to enter the League in 1880, we deem it proper to respectfully direct the attention of such clubs to these regulations and agreements with which all clubs will be expected to comply.

W. A. HULBERT, President.

[October 3, 1879]

. . . At the recent League meeting financial matters were discussed for hours before anything like a feasible plan for making the clubs self-supporting was adopted. The principal cause of heavy losses to Associations is attributed to high salaries, the result of competition. To prevent competition it was suggested that a uniform salary list be arranged, but it did not take long to demonstrate the impracticality of this scheme. Finally, it was proposed that each delegate be allowed to name five desirable players from his own club as a nucleus for a team in 1880, and that these chosen men should not be allowed to sign with any other club without permission. This would prevent unhealthy competition and at the same time give each club a majority of its players for next season. The other four or five necessary players could easily be engaged. This plan met the approval of the delegates. After considerable telegraphing each club represented selected five players from its old team, except the Cleveland Association; there were only three men wanted for 1880 and the Directors were allowed to pick two outside men who had expressed a desire to locate in Cleveland next year. The names selected are known only to the directors of the clubs. Suppose the Buffalos selected Clapp, Galvin, Walker, Force and Richardson, none of these players could sign a contract with any other club in the League, and they must accept the terms offered or find engagements in outside clubs. Should any one of them join an outside club and that club should burst during the season the player could only return to the League by joining the Buffalos. Players need not imagine that the privilege will be abused. They will be rated according to their value and reasonable salaries will be paid. The aim of the League is to reduce expenses so that clubs can live. This object is to be further attained by charging each player fifty cents per day while travelling and by making him pay for his own uniform. The high price of admission has had in a measure an injurious effect upon the financial results, and patrons of the game may rest assured that next season there will be a material reduction in the entrance fee. All clubs hereafter joining the League will be obliged to conform to these new rules. Of course the agreement about picked players does not make the signing of contracts by them compulsory, but at the same time it is for their interest to stay in the League and there is not the slightest doubt that every sensible player who has the opportunity will remain where he receives fair recompense for his services and square treatment. We happen to know that more than a majority of this year's Buffalos would like to remain next season but just how many will have the chance is the question. The directors are in no hurry to sign players but it is safe to say the nine for 1880 will be stronger, particularly in batting, than it was this year.

51

The First Night Baseball Game (1880)

Source: *Boston Post*, September 3, 1880

Only three years after Thomas Edison invented the incandescent light bulb, the first attempt to play a baseball game under these lights was made. According to Michael Gershman, Diamonds: The Evolution of the Ballpark *(Boston: Houghton Mifflin, 1993), pp. 54–55, at least eight other night games were played in the nineteenth century. Experiments with artificial lighting occurred sporadically, but night baseball was not played on a regular basis until the early 1930s, when the Kansas City Monarchs, a prominent Negro League club, introduced a portable lighting system.*

THE ELECTRIC LIGHT

Plan for Lighting Cities from Towers of Electric Lamps— Exhibition of the System at Nantucket Beach

The problem of lighting cities and towns by electricity has been seriously considered ever since the invention of the electric light, and different parties have come forward with different solutions from the time of Edison's play single lamps down to the latest invention, the system of massed lamps. This latter invention by a Mr. Spaulding is in the hands of the Northern Electric Light Company of this city, and an exhibition of its practical workings was given at the Sea Foam House, Nantucket Beach, Thursday evening. A small party of gentlemen, consisting of representatives of the press and other individuals, were present, and preparatory to the exhibition sat down to an excellent supper at the Sea Foam House. Arrangements had been perfected during the day for the grand trial. For this purpose three wooden towers, some one hundred feet, or more had been erected, five hundred feet apart, and at each of their summits were placed a collection of twelve electric lamps having a combined strength of thirty thousand candle-power. In a small shed had been placed two engines with three electric generators, one for each tower. When the lamps were lighted after dark the effect was fine. A clear, pure bright light was produced, very strong and yet very pleasant to the sight. The light did not appear as brilliant as that from the lamps displayed nightly on Washington street, in this city, but this was explained as resulting from the light at the beach having an area of miles to shine over without interruption, while in the city it is practically confined between the walls of the streets and thereby intensified. Still where the light was reflected from the buildings it was bright enough to see to read by. On the broad lawn in the rear of the house there was sufficient light to enable a game of base ball to be played, though with scarcely the precision as by daylight. Picked nines from the stores of Jordan Marsh & Co. and R. H. White & Co. played nine innings, the score being 16 to 16, when the game was called so that the players could take the last boat. A few of the party present took a ride on the railroad as far as Point Allerton during the evening. All along the way the fields were lighted brighter than in a clear moonlight, and at Point Allerton the time by the watches could be distinguished without aid or other light than the electric a mile away. The exhibition was quite satisfactory, as showing that a bright and powerful light can be secured by the electric lamps, but it left a great deal to be demonstrated as to its efficiency in lighting cities. The proposition of the inventor is by an arrangement of towers carrying lights of at least 500,000 candle power to illuminate a city as light as by day, so that the use of gas or other lights on the streets or in houses will be done away with. By his system of massing and elevating the lamps he expects to suffuse the atmosphere with this light so that it will permeate all the streets and buildings as does the light of day. It is calculated that the expense of thus practically turning night into day will not exceed the gross sum now paid by cities for public lighting and by individuals and corporations for the lighting of their houses and other buildings. The inventor is quite confident of the success of his system and other exhibitions on a more extended scale, with a lighting power of 2,800,000 candles, instead of about 100,000, will soon be made. It is intimated that within six months a practical test of the system will be made in some city.

52

Prejudice against an African American Player in Louisville (1881)

Source: *Louisville Courier-Journal,* August 22, 1881

White teams often refused to play or to associate with black clubs. Throughout the 1880s, however, a number of talented black players earned positions on prominent white teams. Perhaps the best known of these players is Moses Fleetwood Walker, who in 1884 became the first black "major league" player, with the AA *Toledo club. This article examines the abuse Walker faced in Louisville, which was typical of the sort of treatment black players experienced in the nineteenth century. When Walker returned to Louisville in his* AA *debut, the abuse rattled him so badly that he committed five errors.*

A DISABLED CLUB

**The Clevelands, Short their Best Player, Defeated by the Eclipse
An Uncalled for Exhibition of Prejudice on the Field Towards a Quadroon**

CONSIDERABLE FEELING DISPLAYED

There were between 2,000 and 3,000 persons present to see the game at Eclipse Park yesterday between the ball-players of the White Sewing-machine Company of Cleveland and the home nine. What promised to be a very exciting game, turned out to be a very ordinary one. The Clevelands have won a fine reputation this season, and the score of six to three in favor of the Eclipse was not earned against the visitors on merit. The score might have told a very different story but for an incident which occured during the second inning, in which a great deal of feeling was exhibited, and which caused considerable comment of an unfavorable nature upon the conduct of the Eclipse Club. The Cleveland Club brought with them as catcher for their nine a young quadroon named Walker. The first trouble they experienced from Kentucky prejudice was at the St. Cloud Hotel yesterday morning at breakfast, when Walker was refused accommodations. When the club appeared on the field for practice before the game the managers and some of the players of the Eclipse Club objected to Walker playing on account of his color. In vain the Clevelands protested that he was their regular catcher, and that his withdrawal

Would Weaken the Nine.

The prejudice of the Eclipse was either too strong, or they feared Walker, who has earned the reputation of being the best amateur catcher in the Union. He has played against the League clubs, and in many games with other white clubs, without protest. The Louisville managers decided that he could not play, and the

Clevelands were compelled to substitute West. During the first inning West was "burned out" by the terrific pitching of Jones, and when the Eclipse went to the bat in the second inning, after one or two efforts, West said he could not face the balls with his hands so badly bruised, and refused to fill the position. The very large crowd of people present, who saw that the Clevelands were a strong nine laboring under disadvantage, at once set up a cry in good nature for "the nigger." Vice President Carroll, of the Eclipse, walked down to the field and called on Walker to come and play. The quadroon was disinclined to do so, after the general ill treatment he had received, but as the game seemed to be in danger of coming to an end, he consented, and started to the catcher's stand. As he passed before the grand stand

He Was Greeted with Cheers,

and from the crowd rose cries of "Walker, Walker!" He still hesitated, but finally threw off his coat and vest and stepped out to catch a ball or two and feel the bases. He made several brilliant throws and fine catches while the game waited. Then Johnnie Reccius and Fritz Pfeffer, of the Eclipse nine, walked off the field, and went to the club house, while others objected to the playing of the quadroon. The crowd was so pleased with his practice, however, that it cheered him again and again and insisted that he play. The objection of the Eclipse players, however, was too much and Walker was compelled to retire. When it was seen that he was not to play, the crowd heartily and very properly hissed the Eclipse club, and jeered their misplays for several innings, while the visitors, for whom White consented to catch, obviously under disadvantage, were cheered to the echo. Jones, the pitcher, was not supported adequately, and if Walker had caught it is probable the Eclipse would have been defeated. It was a very small piece of business, particularly when Walker was brought out as a substitute for a disabled man and invited to play by the Vice President of the Eclipse, who acted very properly in the matter. The Clevelands acted foolishly in playing. They should have declined to play unless Walker was admitted and entered suit for gate money and damages. They could have made their point because it was understood that Walker was catcher, and no rules provide for the rejection of players on account of "race, color or previous condition of servitude." The crowd was anxious to see Walker play, and there was no social question concerned. Walker shook the dust of Louisville from his feet last night and went home. The succeeding games will be totally uninteresting, since without him the Clevelands are not able to play the Eclipse a good game.

53

Formation of the American Association (AA) (1881)

Source: *Cincinnati Enquirer*, November 3, 1881

Soon after its creation, the AA was dubbed the "Beer Ball League" for permitting the sale of alcohol at games. AA owners—often brewery owners—further antagonized their staid NL counterparts by playing Sunday games and charging only twenty-five cents (half the NL base rate) for admission. The NL owners feared that these policies would demean professional baseball by unleashing a flood of undesirable, unruly blue-collar spectators, but relatively few blue-collar workers attended Cincinnati Reds games, even on Sundays. See Dean A. Sullivan, "Faces in the Crowd: A Statistical Portrait of Baseball Spectators in Cincinnati, 1886–1888," Journal of Sport History 17 (Winter 1990): 354–65. Nevertheless, the AA never shook its reputation as a lesser league, a reflection of the lack of leadership that would lead to its collapse following the 1891 season.

This account of the founding of the AA was written by O. P. Caylor, perhaps the most distinctive baseball writer of the day. He later served as manager for the AA Reds in 1885–86 and the Metropolitans in 1887.

BORN,

**And Its Name Is the American Association
Of Base-Ball Clubs— A Constitution Adopted,
Which Is Favorable in Its Policy to the Old League
And the Player—Six Clubs Enter, and the Chances Are That Eight Will Come In**

An Independent League has been formed. To-day it is a certainty, and its enemies can laugh as scornfully as they wish and ridicule it as much as they desire, still it has started out most bravely and most determinedly. The old League had not its backing when it began life, and to-day its members are not as wealthy as those who compose the new Association. The organizers of the latter have worked most zealously to perfect it, and success never crowned their efforts until yesterday. With the wreck of the International staring them in the face, the energetic founders of this last organization commenced their labors during the past months, and, although almost certain failure beset them at nearly every corner, they continued their exertions until they triumphed. [The International League collapsed following the 1880 season—Ed.] Their struggles have been crowned with brilliant success, and stand forth to this country requesting patronage in the shape of the American Association of Base-ball Clubs. The latter has chosen as its motto, "Liberty to all." It believes fully that the League has done much to foster and improve the national pastime, even advancing it to a point far beyond what it had ever reached. It fully recognizes the experience its elder rival has had with crooked professionals and black sheep, and proposes to support it in those particulars. It is doubly peaceful. It is liberal. It extends its hand to the old League and asks its co-operation in the advancement of this truly national sport.

Tuesday's issue gave the opening proceedings of the Committee on Constitution and By-Laws and the nature of its transactions. In it was noted the names of those who had arrived and those that were expected. The regular meeting was called to order yesterday morning at the Gibson House by Mr. H. D. McKnight, of Pittsburg. He detailed the facts concerning the meeting at his city [on October 10—Ed.], and stated briefly the objects of the assemblage. He referred to the revival that had taken place in base-ball matters in several cities, and said that these places, exhibiting a desire to form themselves into a protective base-ball body had gathered in this city for that purpose. His remarks were entirely explanatory.

On motion, Mr. McKnight was made Temporary Chairman and Mr. J. A. Williams Temporary Secretary. The delegates that were present in the meeting were:

J. Thorner, G. L. Herancourt and Victor Long, Cincinnati.
Wm. Barnie, Brooklyn.
Christopher Von Der Ahe, E. T. Goodfellow, David Reed, St. Louis.
H. D. McKnight, Pittsburg.
J. H. Pank and J. W. Reccius, Louisville.

In addition to these, Messrs. W. S. Appleton and James Mutrie, of the Metropolitans, of New York, and the Newark Club, of Newark, N.J.; Lewis Mahn, of Harry Wright's team of Boston, Mass., and the contesting Clubs being represented by Charles Fulmer and H. B. Phillips, were on hand. . . .

It was decided to call the organization the American Association of Base-Ball Clubs. Its objects were defined as being to promote and protect the interests of the Clubs and the players, and to establish and regulate the base-ball championship of America. The rules adopted regarding membership are the same as the old League. It was decided to elect the officers and Directors by ballot instead of by card. The duties and responsibilities of the same were made identical with those of the older body.

It was agreed, and a most sensible action it was, too, that when a Club disbands before the end of the season that a new one shall be taken in. This shall play out the schedule of its predecessors, and its games and those of the first Club shall be counted as one. This prevents any injustice to the Clubs contesting for the pennant. All particulars referring to the government of the League Alliance, which was a sort of mongrel organization, in becoming a member of which outside Clubs were enabled to play with League nines, were done away with. [The League Alliance was a loose association of independent clubs formed in 1877—Ed.]

It was decided to assess each Club $50 to pay the various expenses of the Association.

Then came the most important enactment of the day. It will prove quite a novelty in base-ball management, and, although it has weak points, it is in general quite an original idea. After some talk the proposition, which is known as the "guarantee plan," was adopted as follows:

"Each Club shall have exclusive control of its own grounds; shall be entitled to all receipts from admission or otherwise of schedule games played on the grounds; shall be permitted to play outside Clubs, or exhibition games with Association Clubs on any days not reserved for schedule games, provided that said home Club shall pay to the visiting Club in cash the sum of $60 on the day of such schedule game before leaving the grounds upon which said game is played, and in case the home Club fail to pay said sum as herein provided, it may be reported to the Board of Directors by the visiting Club, and, upon proof of such non-payment, said Club shall be expelled. These provisions shall not apply to schedule games played upon the fourth day of July, Decoration Day, or State holidays. Upon the afore-mentioned days the receipts of admission for schedule games shall be equally divided between the two contesting Clubs, and the home Club shall not be required to pay the sum herein before provided."

The Association showed its teeth plainly on the matter of releasing players. They did not deny the right of Clubs to release them, either with or without cause, but held that when the management desire to let a man go they must give him half a month's salary. Again, they altered the League's restriction, that released players can play with another team only twenty days after their release by permitting them to join another nine and participate in the games at once. This is clearly a departure in favor of the players, although it does remove the right of the Directory to remove them at their will. When a player is released through indiscretions or violations, or at his request, no portion of his salary is paid. . . .

Late yesterday afternoon the meeting adjourned without discussing the matter of a championship contest, the number of games to be played between the Clubs, &c., until this morning. The business then left unfinished will be concluded to-day. A Schedule Committee and Committee on Playing Rules will be appointed and officers will be elected.

Messrs. Appleton and Mutrie, representing the Metropolitans, did not enter the meeting, as they did not wish to bind themselves until they saw what would be the policy of the new organization. They thought the idea an excellent one, and supported it cordially. They say that they have $27,600 in the treasury, and that if they go in the Association they will also start a team in Newark, New Jersey. They are opposed to all belligerency in the League, and say that the country is large enough for both, and that they should live together quietly and peacefully.

54

Providence Defeats Detroit in Eighteen-Inning Contest, 1–0 (1882)

Source: *Providence Journal*, August 18, 1882

In an era in which both low-scoring and extra-inning games were celebrated, the following game achieved near-legendary status. Notice the coverage of future Hall of Famers John Ward, Charles (Old Hoss) Radbourn, and George Wright.

The abbreviations in the elaborate box score require some explanation: "1B" denotes all hits, not just singles; "L" stands for left on base. Unfortunately the meaning of "RB" is unknown.

A DOUBLE GAME

PROVIDENCE SCORES A VICTORY OF VICTORIES
DEFEAT OF DETROIT IN AN EIGHTEEN INNING CONTEST
CHICAGO, CLEVELAND AND BUFFALO WINNERS OF THE DAY

PROVIDENCE, 1; DETROIT, 0

"Two games in one" is what the eighth Providence–Detroit game, played at Messer Park, yesterday afternoon, might appropriately be termed in that it required eighteen innings to determine the victory by the attainment of a single tally—a contest unsurpassed in the history of the League in length, and in the wonderfully brilliant fielding which was performed by the diamond knights, as also clever and steady pitching, during nearly three hours of continuous exercise. Ward and Weidman occupied the points, and a glance at the batting columns is a suggestive commentary upon the strategy and coolness which characterized their manipulation of the sphere, yet there were batted freely into the diamond, and there received magnificent support as well as behind the bat. One singular feature of the game lies in the fact that the same number of men reached first base and were left on both sides, and Detroit sent but one man less to bat, which shows how uniform was the play of the teams. In the first half of the game, Detroit sent eight men to first base on four singles and errors of Start, Denny and Wright, three of whom were left on the third bag owing to the effective pitching of Ward at critical moments. In the fourth inning for Detroit, a run seemed imminent, when Hanlon gained first and second on wild throwing by Denny and Nava, and started for the plate on Powell's clean hit to centre-field. Hines gathered it up and made a beautiful throw to Nava, who fell upon Hanlon as he slid for the plate, retiring him very handsomely. In the seventh inning, Farrell completed a grand double play with

Start on Knight and Weidman, the former being declared out for running out of the base line, the play saving a run, as Bennett had reached third on a two-baser and poor throw by Wright to Denny. In the thirteenth inning, Farrell and Start completed another brilliant play on Jack's superb pick-up, and in the fourteenth inning, the double-play by Denny–Farrell and Start created intense excitement, so brilliantly was it executed. In the fifteenth inning for Providence, Wright drove a sharp grounder through the left-field gate-way into the street, and essayed to make a home run. Wood dashed after the ball, and fielded to Bennett in time to catch Wright at the plate to Trott. The ball went outside the grounds, and the umpire should have sent the runner back to third on a "blocked" ball, as the gate-way was filled with people, and he was unable to discover whether Wood was assisted by an outsider or not. In the last three innings not a man saw first on either side till the eighteenth, when Trott batted a single but was caught on Farrell's line catch of Knight's hit and throw to Start—a clever double-play. Radbourn was the first batsman for Providence in the eighteenth inning, and catching the sphere fairly on his bat he drove it high over the left field fence for a home run, and rounding the bases, earned the winning tally mid tremendous excitement. As said before, the burden of the fielding fell to the diamond knights, and the play of Farrell, Denny, Start and Whitney, notably that of Jack and Jeremiah, surpassed anything ever witnessed in this city in point of brilliancy and faultless skill in handling hard-hit grounders and splendid throwing. Start's record was remarkably fine, as also that of Powell and Trott. Nava supported Ward very acceptably and in fact the play of both sides was exceedingly sharp and effective, making the game one long to be remembered by those so fortunate as to be present. The JOURNAL bulletin was anxiously watched by hundreds of citizens assembled on Turk's Head, and the glorious announcement was received with deafening applause. The teams take a rest to-day, and close the series on Saturday. The score:

PROVIDENCE

		Batting		Base Running			Fielding		
	AB	1B	TB	R	RB	L	PO	A	E
Hines, c. f.	7	1	1	0	1	1	1	1	0
Farrell, 2b.	7	1	1	0	1	1	6	9	0
Start, 1b..	7	0	0	0	0	0	26	0	1
Ward, p.	7	1	1	0	1	1	0	5	0
York, l. f..	7	1	1	0	1	1	3	0	0
Radbourn, r. f.	7	1	4	1	1	0	1	0	0
Wright, s. s.	6	1	3	0	2	1	2	5	1
Denny, 3b.	6	1	1	0	2	1	5	11	1
Nava, c.	6	0	0	0	2	2	9	1	2
Totals	60	7	12	1	11	8	53*	32	5

	Batting			Base Running			Fielding		
	AB	1B	TB	R	RB	L	PO	A	E
Wood, l. f.	7	1	1	0	1	1	3	1	0
Hanlon, c. f........	7	1	1	0	2	1	5	0	0
Powell, 1b.	7	1	1	0	1	1	21	0	1
Bennett, 3b.	7	1	2	0	1	1	3	3	2
Trott, c............	7	2	2	0	1	1	13	1	2
Knight, r. f........	6	0	0	0	2	1	1	1	0
Weidman, p........	6	1	2	0	1	1	2	9	0
Whitney, s. s.	6	2	2	0	2	1	1	10	3
Foster, 2b..........	6	0	0	0	0	0	2	4	1
Totals	59	9	11	0	11	8	51	29	9

*Knight out for running out of base line.

Innings—

1	2	3	4	5	6	7	8	9	10	11	12	13	14	15	16	17	18

Providence—

| 0 | 0 | 0 | 0 | 0 | 0 | 0 | 0 | 0 | 0 | 0 | 0 | 0 | 0 | 0 | 0 | 0 | 1—1 |

Umpire—Bradley. Runs earned—Providence, 1. Home run—Radbourn. Three-base hit—Wright. Two-base hits—Bennett, Weidman. Struck out—Providence, 6; Detroit, 4. Base on called balls—Knight. First base on errors—Providence, 3; Detroit, 2. Double plays—Farrell–Start (2), Denny–Farrell–Start. Passed ball—Trott. Time—2h. 40m.

55

The First World Series? (1882)

Source: *Chicago Tribune*, October 7, 1882

The existence of two competing major leagues presented a problem: which pennant-winning team would be considered America's champion? Neither the AA nor the NL, now engaged in a bitter competition for players and supporters, would allow its clubs to play teams in the other league. Nevertheless, in an effort to determine a champion, Chicago and Cincinnati (champions of the NL and the AA, respectively) split a pair of shutouts before the leagues put an end to the contests. The brevity of the following account suggests that the championship contest was considered little more than another exhibition game.

BASE-BALL GAMES

Chicago Beaten 4 to 0 by Cincinnati—Other Games

Special Dispatch to The Chicago Tribune

CINCINNATI, O., Oct. 6—The two championship clubs of the country, the Chicagos and Cincinnatis, met today. It was an event which lovers of base-ball had looked forward to, and there were 2,700 people present. It was feared and generally supposed that the Chicagos would win the game, but instead of so doing they submitted to a whitewash. They could do nothing with White's pitching. Goldsmith was batted hard at times, and in the sixth inning the home club made four runs. In that inning Flint hit for a base, but was thrown out in trying to reach second. The Cincinnatis went to the bat, and Carpenter hit a liner to centre. Stearns followed with a safe hit to right, which sent Carpenter to third. Fulmer hit safe to centre, which let Carpenter in amid deafening cheers. McPhee then made a slashing hit between right and centre, which drove in Stearns and Fulmer, and landed the batsman himself at third. He went home on a wild pitch, giving the Cincinnatis four runs, which were the first and last they made. In the ninth inning the Chicagos tried hard to score, but a brilliant double play put out their last two men, and ended the game. Another game will be played by the same clubs tomorrow.

Innings	1	2	3	4	5	6	7	8	9
Chicago	0	0	0	0	0	0	0	0	0—0
Cincinnati	0	0	0	0	0	4	0	0	0—4

Base hits—Chicago, 11; Cincinnati, 13.
Earned runs—Cincinnati, 3.
Two-base hit—Williamson.
Three-base hits—Williamson, McPhee.
Left on bases—Chicago, 3; Cincinnati, 4.
Struck out—Sommer (2), Carpenter, Powers, Corcoran (2), Flint.
Double-play—Carpenter—Macullar—Powers.
Passed balls—Flint, 1.
Wild pitches—White, 1; Goldsmith, 1.
Umpire—C. M. Smith.
PHILADELPHIA, Oct. 6—Boston 7, Philadelphia 1.
ST. LOUIS, Oct. 6—Louisville 4, St. Louis 3.

4

Baseball Prospers, 1883–88

During the 1880s both the economy and professional baseball flourished. The signing of the Tripartite Agreement (later called the National Agreement) in 1883 not only brought an end to the hostilities between the NL and the AA but also created an atmosphere in which minor league baseball could thrive. Another indication of the strength of the major leagues was an annual postseason championship series, which remained popular throughout the decade. Yet the key element of the Tripartite Agreement—the reserve clause— generated such resentment that a third major league, the Union Association (UA), was formed after the 1883 season to attract disgruntled players. Poorly planned and undercapitalized—like most professional leagues of this era— the UA collapsed after its only season, in 1884.

Although salaries rose rapidly during the 1880s, players were not satisfied. Major league players felt that the reserve clause denied them the freedom to play with the team of their choice; by 1890 they made their displeasure known. Meanwhile, African American professional players, whose options were severely limited in the first half of the decade, found their freedom increasingly curtailed as the decade progressed. Finally, they were eliminated from the white game entirely as baseball established an unofficial color line, which would remain intact until 1946. African Americans formed a number of professional leagues and barnstorming clubs, but financial problems made them very unstable and the organizations were short-lived.

56

The Tripartite Agreement (1883)

Source: Francis Richter, *Richter's History and Records of Base Ball* (Philadelphia: Dando, 1914), pp. 209–10

The most important feature of the Tripartite Agreement was the broad institution of the reserve clause. The NL, AA, and the Northwestern League (a minor league) agreed to respect each other's player contracts. By prohibiting teams from raiding the rosters of clubs in leagues that had signed the agreement, baseball gained the stability it needed to prosper. In additon, teams were proscribed from signing players expelled or blacklisted by another team or league, thereby binding players even more closely to their clubs. With the reserve clause extended to allow nearly every player to be reserved, a player had little choice but to accept his club's best offer, since nearly every league capable of paying a comparable or superior salary had signed the agreement.

AGREEMENT AMONG NATIONAL LEAGUE OF PROFESSIONAL BASE BALL CLUBS, AMERICAN ASSOCIATION OF BALL CLUBS, NORTHWESTERN LEAGUE OF PROFESSIONAL BASE BALL CLUBS, 1883

The National League of Professional Base Ball Clubs, the American Association of Base Ball Clubs, and the Northwestern League of Base Ball Clubs, in consideration of the mutual advantages to be derived therefrom, agree each with the other, as follows:—

FIRST.—The players named in the lists hereto attached shall be deemed to be players in good standing, in their respective clubs as named in said lists, until November first, unless sooner expelled or released, as hereinafter provided, and no club member of either of the parties hereto shall contract with, or employ, either of said players for any period prior to the said November first, 1883, unless said player be duly released, and notice thereof given, as hereinafter provided.

SECOND.—Any player not named on the lists hereto attached, or who was not prior to January first, 1883, expelled, or suspended for the season of 1883, by either of the parties to this agreement, who shall be employed for the season of 1883, or any part thereof, by any club member of either of the parties hereto, shall be deemed and held to be a player in good standing, of such club, for any term of service terminating by November first, 1883, that may be stipulated in his contract of employment, provided that written notice of such contract, in accordance with the rules of the Association to which the contracting club belongs, shall be filed with the Secretary of such Association, and communicated by him in writing to the Secretaries of the other two Associations, by whom such notice shall in turn be served upon the clubs composing such other two Associations, and, on receipt of such notice, every club member of all the parties hereto, excepting the contracting club, shall be debarred from employing or playing the said player at any time prior to the expiration of the said term of service, excepting as hereinafter provided.

THIRD.—When a player is expelled, or suspended, in accordance with its rules by either of the parties hereto, notice of such expulsion, or suspension, shall be served upon the Secretaries of the other two Associations by the Secretary of the Association from whose club such players shall have been expelled or suspended, and the Secretaries of such other two Associations shall, forthwith, serve notice of such expulsion or suspension, upon the club members of such other two Associations, and, from the receipt of such notice, all club members of all the parties hereto, shall be debarred from employing, or playing with, or against, such expelled, or suspended, player until the period of suspension shall have terminated, or the expulsion be revoked by the association from which such player was expelled, and due notice of such revocation served upon the Secretaries of the other two Associations, and by them upon their respective clubs.

FOURTH.—No contract shall be made for the services of any player, by any club member of either of the parties hereto, for a longer period than seven months, beginning April first and terminating October thirty-first, in each year, and no such contract for services to be rendered after the expiration of the present year shall be made prior to the tenth day of October, of each year, nor shall any negotiation be entered into by, or between, any club, or agent thereof, with any player for services to be rendered in an ensuing year, prior to the said tenth day of October.

FIFTH.—On the twentieth day of September, of each year, each club member of the parties hereto shall transmit to the Secretary of its Association a list of names of any players, not exceeding eleven in number, on that date under contract with such club, which such club desires to reserve for the ensuing year, accompanied by a statement, over the signature of the secretary of such club, that such club is willing to pay not less than one thousand dollars as the compensation of each player, so reserved, in the contract to be made with him for the ensuing season, provided such club be a member of the National League, or American Association, and, if a member of the Northwestern League, or of an Alliance club of any party hereto, seven hundred and fifty dollars, and the secretary of each Association shall, on the twenty-fifth day of September, transmit to the secretaries of the other two Associations, parties hereto, a full list of players thus reserved. The secretary of each Association shall thereupon, on the fifth day of October, transmit to each club member of such Association a full list of all players so reserved by all clubs then composing the three Associations, and no club member of either of the parties hereto shall have the right to contract, negotiate with, or employ, any player so reserved by any other club member of either of the parties hereto, unless the club member reserving the player shall have notified the secretary of the Association to which such club member belongs of the release of such player from such reservation, and, in case of such release, the secretary of such Association shall notify the secretaries of the two Associations, parties hereto, and the secretaries of the three

Associations shall notify all the club members parties hereto of such release, and, on receipt of such notice, any club member of the parties hereto will have the right to employ the player so released from reservation, provided that twenty days shall have elapsed between the release from such reservation before such player shall be eligible to contract with another club.

SIXTH.—Any contract between a club member of any of the parties hereto and a player, made in accordance with the provisions of this agreement, shall be deemed valid and binding, and all other clubs shall be debarred from employing such player during the period of such contract, provided that such contract shall be considered to take effect upon receipt of written notice thereof by the club members of the parties hereto, and the transmission of such notice by the respective secretaries of the parties hereto is hereby made mandatory upon said secretaries, and such notice must follow immediately upon receipt of the contracting club's notice to the secretary of the Association to which such contracting club belongs.

SEVENTH.—Any disputes or complaints arising out of the performance of the stipulations of this agreement, and any alleged violations of this agreement; also, any question of interpretation of any stipulation of this agreement, shall be referred to an Arbitration Committee, to consist of three representatives of each party hereto, to be appointed prior to the thirty-first day of March, 1883, by the parties hereto; notice of such appointment to be served upon the secretaries of each Association, and the decision of such Arbitration Committee upon such matters, or any of them, shall be final and binding upon the parties hereto.

In witness whereof the said parties have, by the President of each of the parties hereto, thereunto duly authorized, signed this agreement on the dates set opposite their respective signatures.

The National League of Professional Base Ball Clubs, March 5th, 1883,
by A. G. MILLS, *President.*

The American Association of Base Ball Clubs, March 12th, 1883,
by H. D. MCKNIGHT, President.

The Northwestern League of Professional Base Ball Clubs, February 17th, 1883,
by ELIAS MATTER, President.

57

Formation of the Union Association (1883)

Source: *Sporting Life,* September 17, 1883

The article below describes the formation of a third major league, the Union Association (UA). Unlike the signatories of the Tripartite Agreement (renamed the National Agreement by the end of 1883), the UA hoped to attract players by eliminating the reserve clause. Francis Richter, the editor of Sporting Life *and the author of this document, observed that there were too few baseball fans to support another major league. His skepticism proved well founded, as the UA barely managed to survive its only season.*

NEW ASSOCIATIONS

The New Association Formed at Pittsburg—The Eastern League

Last Wednesday afternoon and evening a meeting of base ball men was held at the Monongahela House, Pittsburg, to form a new base ball association, separate and distinct from the National League and American Association. The following well known persons were present and enrolled the names of the clubs they represented in the new league: A. H. Henderson, Chicago; Thomas J. Pratt, Philadelphia; B. F. Matthews, Baltimore; M. B. Scanlon and W. W. White, Washington, D.C.; W. G. Seddon, Richmond, Va.; T. P. Sullivan, St. Louis; Jas. Jackson, N. Y., and A. G. Pratt and W. H. Camp, Pittsburg. Communications were read from Hartford, Conn.; Brooklyn, Milwaukee and Indianapolis, asking the Association to consider the applications of the writers for membership. The requests were complied with and the writers were admitted into the new League Association. After some discussion the constitution of the American Association was adopted with a few amendments relative to organization and other minor matters. It was also resolved to style the new body the "Union Association of Base Ball Clubs." One of the changes in the rules adopted was that visiting clubs shall receive $75 guarantee instead of $65, as paid by the American clubs. The following permanent officers were then elected: President, H. B. Bennett, Washington, D.C.; Vice President, Thomas J. Pratt, Philadelphia; Secretary and Treasurer, William Warren White. Directors, A. H. Henderson, Chicago; M. B. Scanlon, Washington, D.C.; Thomas J. Pratt, Philadelphia, and Al. G. Pratt, Pittsburg. Outside of the routine work disposed of the most important was the unanimous adoption of the following resolution:

> *Resolved,* That while we recognize the validity of all contracts made by the League and American Association, we cannot recognize any agreement whereby any number of ball-players may be reserved for any club for any time beyond the terms of their contracts with such clubs.

Notice was given that any clubs desiring to join the Association must make application to the secretary, Wm. Warren White, Treasury Department, Washington, D.C. After the transaction of a quantity of business pertaining to the organization, the Association adjourned to meet in annual session at the Bingham House, Philadelphia, in December.

WHAT SECRETARY WHITE THINKS

After the meeting your correspondent engaged Mr. White in conversation and elicited the following: "We have certainly started under more favorable auspices than did the American Association, and there is no reason why we should not succeed. We recognize the fact that in order to meet with success we must give the people good exhibitions of ball playing, and this we intend to do. Every city that has applied for membership has faithfully promised to put strictly first-class clubs in the field, and all of them have plenty of money to back up the undertaking. The intention is to have stronger nines in all of the cities in the new association than they ever had, and we are confident of success. The national game has attained such popularity with the masses that we can all survive, and under proper management there is no reason why the new association should not take a leading position in the base ball world."

The above is the account of the meeting sent us by our Pittsburg correspondent. The movement may now be considered fairly started, but we cannot agree with Mr. White that its prospects are brighter than were those of the American Association two years ago. Then there was but one organization in the field and a number of large cities were unprovided for. The new body might as well realize from the start that it will have a hard, unequal fight, and prepare itself accordingly. The American Association found the field ripe for it, and but little cultivation was required. With the new organization things will be different because it has in its ranks too many cities where strong clubs are already located, and it is just possible that the base ball business may be overdone. A new club in Chicago will have hard work to divide support with the popular League club. In Baltimore base ball is well patronized, but it is an open question whether two professional clubs can live there. In New York and Philadelphia there are already four professional clubs, and to put in one more in each is giving it to the public in rather heavy doses. In St. Louis the field is inviting, as but one club exists there now, and the management of that is extremely unpopular. In Washington there will be no opposition, and there the outlook is bright. In Richmond there is already a club, the Virginia, which has the best ground and good financial backing, which declares its purpose of going into the new Eastern League. In Pittsburg there is possibly room for another club, as the Association club now located there is somewhat in public disfavor, and besides the population is large. Brooklyn, Hartford and Indianapolis are good ball towns, and there is no opposition.

In the above list of clubs the East preponderates, and, besides, the number is too large, as ten clubs are about all that can be properly handled. However, all these things can be adjusted at the December meeting. The very most important point to be looked after is the financial standing of each member. None of these clubs need expect to make a fortune the first season, and some must even be prepared for losses, and we think that no club should be permitted to remain in the body unless it can show a backing of at least $10,000. This is a vital point. The new association merits the sympathies of all ball players by its opposition to the odious and unjust reserve rule, but sympathy is not bread and butter, and no very large number of players will be drawn from the ranks of the older organizations until the Union Association has demonstrated its ability to pay its way. If it be well heeled financially and weather one season its success is assured.

58

"A Base-Ball Burlesque": A Women's Game (1883)

Source: New York *Times*, September 23, 1883

A careful reader of Jane Austen's novel Northanger Abbey *(completed in 1803) will find that the heroine "prefer[red] cricket, base ball, riding on horseback, and running about the country at the age of fourteen, to books." A small number of American girls also played bat and ball games. In fact, following the Civil War, baseball teams were formed at some women's colleges in the Northeast. See Debra A. Shattuck, "Bats, Balls, and Books: Baseball and Higher Education for Women at Three Eastern Women's Colleges, 1866–1900," Journal of Sport History 19, no. 2 (Summer 1992): 91–109. The press rarely treated women's games seriously, however, partly because many of these games were exhibitions designed to exploit the public's fascination with the bizarre. One such game is described below.*

A BASE-BALL BURLESQUE

BLONDES AND BRUNETTES TOYING WITH THE BAT

A GAME IN WHICH THE GIRL PLAYERS GOT HOPELESSLY MIXED AND FURNISHED UNLIMITED FUN TO THE SPECTATORS

A crowd of about 1,500 people assembled on the Manhattan Athletic Club's grounds, at Eighty-sixth-street and Eighth-avenue, yesterday afternoon, and laughed themselves hungry and thirsty watching a game of base-ball between two teams composed of girls. There were eight girls on a side, but there was more genuine circus in those 16 girls than is popularly supposed to reside in a Mormon colony. At 3:30 the two nines—or rather eights—entered the game. One side was composed of brunettes, whose costumes were of an irritating red; the other was of blondes who wore sympathetic blue. The blondes won the toss and went to the bat with a air of determination. The brunettes took their positions in the field as follows: Miss Evans, catcher; Miss P. Darlington, pitcher; Miss Stanton, first base; Miss Fenton, second base; Miss Temple, third base; Miss Elliot, short stop; Miss Clayton, right field; Miss I. Darlington, centre field. The positions of the blondes were as follows: Miss Moore, catcher; Miss Williams, pitcher; Miss Myers, first base; Miss Bassman, second base; Miss Muir, short stop; Miss Healy, third base; Miss May, left field; Miss Brown, centre field. Both sides went to the bat in the order named. The costumes were bathing dresses of the ancient and honorable order. The loose body had a long, flowing skirt, which reached below the knee. Stockings of the regulation style, base-ball shoes, and white hats completed the outfit. The dresses were neatly, but not gaudily, trimmed with white braid. The hair was either coiled tightly at the back of the head or worn in long plaits, tied up in ribbon of a color that pleased the wearer's fancy. Miss Williams, the blue pitcher, rejoiced in a natty blue and white cap, which gave her a business-like appearance.

These young ladies, as the management of the affair announced, were selected with tender solicitude from 900 applicants, variety actresses and ballet girls being positively barred. Only three of the lot had ever been on the stage, and they were in the strictly legitimate business. One of them, Miss Daisy Muir, short stop for the blondes, once played Eva in "Uncle Tom's Cabin," and also once won a prize offered by a Philadelphia paper for the best reply to an offer of marriage. Most of the others were graduates of Sunday-schools and normal colleges, who had seen the vanity of Greek and Latin and yearned to emulate the examples of the great and good students of Yale, Harvard, and Princeton by traveling wholly on their muscle. They were of assorted sizes and shapes. Some were short and stout, some were tall and thin; others were short and thin, and still others tall and stout. They played base-ball in a very sad and sorrowful sort of way as if the vagaries of the ball had been too great for their struggling intellects. They had started out in life with a noble ambition to "hang on" to anything that came from the bat, no matter how hot, and they had seen their dreams diminish as their bruises increased. Base-ball was not what it was painted, and they were evidently sighing for the end of the season. Four of the girls had become expert—for girls. These were Misses Evans, P. Darlington, Moore, and Williams, comprising the batteries. The others, however, had original ideas. They realized the fact that when they got hold of the ball they ought to throw it and they threw. They didn't stop to wonder where the ball was going, for they were sure that it would not go too far. Each one just raised her hand to the level of her ear and then sent it forward with a push from the elbow. The ball didn't seem to mind it much. At the bat most of them preferred to strike at the ball after it passed them. Then it generally passed the catcher. First base was not made oftener than 15 times on three strikes. It was made just about as often on called balls. The girls displayed an alarming fondness for making home runs on three strikes, too. It was original and excited rapturous applause. One thing was certain, they all know the rules of the game. The blonde umpire—a young man— with a black hat which had a gaudy red band, did not rejoice in equal knowledge, and he appeared somewhat disconcerted when a stentorian voice in the crowd demanded that a dress be put on him.

When the blues went to the bat Miss P. Darlington, pitcher for the reds, who stood about 20 feet in front of the striker, proceeded to tie up her back hair a little tighter. Then she put another hair pin in her hat, seized the ball recklessly, drew back her right arm, and let fly viciously. Miss Moore responded gracefully by whacking a lively grounder to first base. The first basewoman made a wild grab, but did not touch the ball, whereupon the runner got around to third, while the other side pegged the ball all over the field. Finally Miss Williams went to the bat and hit a daisy cutter to short stop, who promptly threw it as far as she could into right field. [Immense applause.] Miss Moore ran home. The next striker, Miss Myers, made a one-base hit, which brought herself and Miss Williams home, owing to the futile attempts of the entire opposing nine to pick the ball up from the ground. The next three strikers were put out, and the brunettes went in. Miss Evans, who rejoiced in bright brown hair, was the genuine ball-player of the party. She warmed one to right field and made her second. Then Miss P. Darlington went in and hit a fly to the quondam Eva, Daisy Muir. Daisy looked up at the bright blue sky, and oh, how the old time came o'er her. She murmured softly: "Uncle Tom, uncle Tom, do you see yon band of spirits bright?" Then the wicked ball came down, and hit her on the little finger, and a look of premature old age spread over her countenance. She picked up the ball, and threw it away. Miss Darlington ran home. Miss Stanton and Miss Fenton made base hits, the latter getting around to third.

Then Miss Temple, the belle of the organization, came to the bat. She was tall, graceful, and had handsome dark eyes and a wealth of black hair. "Oh, Daisy!" "Oh, you darling!" "Oh, you sweet thing!" Such were her greetings from the crowd. She regarded them not, but, with her soul full of hope, poked away with the end of her bat at the first ball, and made first base on a masterly fumble by the pitcher. Miss Elliot then came up, and was accidentally put out on first. In the meantime, Miss Fenton had run home on a foul and run back to third, and then finally scored. The determined manner in which the brunettes staid in seemed to sadden the blondes; but, after a series of surprises, they were put out. Score of the first inning—Blondes, 3; brunettes, 15.

It was a discouraging lead, but the blondes did not weaken. They went in and by determined efforts succeeded in scoring 2. They would have made a great many more, but Miss Evans, the brunette catcher, was a mean thing and would not indulge in passed balls like the other catcher, Miss Moore, who was a real nice girl. The best played inning for fielding was the brunettes' third, in which their opponents allowed them to score only 1 run. Toward the end of the game the girls began to show symptoms of sadness and weariness, and doggedly refused to run from one base to another, until it became morally certain that the other side was hopelessly tangled up with the ball. Often when the fielders could not stop the ball in any other way they sat down on it. This was at once effective and picturesque, and never missed gaining a great howl of applause. Once Miss Evans threw to second and put out Miss Brown. Then the crowd informed her that she was a "dumpling" and a "corker." She looked as if she believed it. When five innings had been played and the back hair and brains of the girls appeared to be in a hopelessly demoralized condition, with a tendency on the part of their hose to follow suit, the game was called. The girls heaved long sighs of relief, started for the dressing rooms, and "like an unsubstantial pageant faded, left not a pin behind." The score was 54 to 22 in five innings in favor of the brunettes. They play again tomorrow.

59

Bleachers Collapse on Opening Day
in Cincinnati (1884)

Source: *Cincinnati Enquirer*, May 2, 1884

Nearly every nineteenth-century ballpark was a hastily built wooden structure destined to be short-lived. Usually they were destroyed by fire, decay, or termites. The article below describes the collapse of the bleachers—known as the "bleaching boards"—in Cincinnati's first game in its new park. The collapse was attributed to the weight of fans hurrying to catch streetcars after the Reds' 10–9 loss to Columbus. The club not only repaired the stands in time for the next day's game but continued to play games on that site until Riverfront Stadium was opened during the 1970 season.

The list of injured spectators, along with their addresses, gives students of the game a rare opportunity to sample baseball crowd demographics. Unfortunately, the 1884 and 1885 Cincinnati city directories include only two of the spectators at the addresses provided by the Enquirer. *They were Henry Holthaus, a cigar maker, and Harry D. Armstrong, a printer.*

A MAN-TRAP

Serious Accident at the American Ball Park
The Stands Give Way and Involve Over Fifty People in the Ruins

A very serious accident occurred yesterday at the close of the game between the Cincinnati and Columbus Clubs at the American Ball Park by the giving way of a portion of the buildings. Fifteen or twenty were injured, and three or four very seriously, with a possibility that in one case at least it may prove fatal. The accident caused a great deal of excitement, and the rush that followed brought to the minds of many present the terrible crush and panic that occurred in Robinson's Opera-house several years ago, where so many poor women and children were killed. A portion of the building attached to the cheap seats gave way just as the game closed. The spectators occupying that part of the grounds were hurrying, as is usual, to get outside and catch a street-car. As they passed along the south-east end of the "bleaching board" and came down on the steps there was a loud crack, and the next instant about twenty feet of the platform caved in. Between fifty and sixty people were precipitated to the ground, a distance of about twelve feet. Looking from the grand stand, where a good view could be obtained, the picture was an awful one, and it seems a miracle that some one was not killed outright. There was a promiscuous heap of men and boys struggling hard to get out and save themselves from being crushed to death by the falling timber and the bodies of their companions in misfortune. Two or three of the coolest-headed spectators in the other buildings yelled to the victims to not get excited and to keep still and they would get them out.

This doubtless saved a great many from being trampled to death. As it was, quite a number were crushed badly, and four or five sustained broken limbs and internal injuries which may yet prove fatal. As fast as the wounded could be extricated from the heap by the attaches of the grounds and others who lent a hand they were carried into the bar-room under the grand stand, and Dr. Maley and several other physicians who were on the grounds did all they could to alleviate their suffering. An alarm was turned from a patrol-box, and Patrol Wagons Nos. 4 and 5 responded. Two or three victims were taken away in those conveyances. A list of injured will be found further along in the account.

The cheap seats are not the only part of the ground that seems to be in a weak condition. Yesterday at the opening of the game, when the people were crowding into this building, a portion of it, located in almost the center, creaked and groaned as if it would come down the next moment. There was a rush at that time, and a panic was only prevented by the intervention of the police. A number of people left this part of the park and exchanged their tickets for other seats at this time. On two occasions during the afternoon there was reason for serious alarm. The building is on new-made ground.

The list of wounded, as near as could be ascertained, is as follows:

Henry Henschell, 409 West Seventh Street; right arm broken and internally injured. Removed to the hospital.
Charles Murphy, Chicago; shoulder dislocated and injuries on the head. Removed to the hospital.
James Langdon, Clinton street and Freeman avenue; arm broken and internal injuries. City Hospital.
Henry Holthaus, Baymiller and Hopkins; back injured.
C. Brodbeck, 41 Moore street; a bad cut in the forehead and leg injured.
Jack Benson, 731 Central avenue; back hurt.
Ed B. Carrick, No. 218 Longworth street; head and back hurt; slight.
Harry D. Armstrong, 166 Miller street; leg sprained; slight.
Charles Morris, Columbus, leg sprained.
John Wachter, Pittsburg, leg hurt.
Harry McGrevy, head cut.

There were a number of others who sustained slight injuries.

60

The Championship Series of the United States Concludes (1884)

Source: *New York Times*, October 26, 1884

In 1882 the champions of the NL and the new AA played a pair of postseason games, but no one considered them a true test of the strengths of the respective leagues. In 1884 the

Providence Grays, NL champions, and the Metropolitan Club of New York, the AA flagbearers, played three games "for the championship of the United States." Nonetheless, as the following document reveals, the 1884 series generated little spectator interest. From 1885 through 1890, the pennant winners of the two leagues met in postseason series that ranged in length from six to fifteen games.

CLOSE OF THE BASEBALL SEASON

THE METS BEATEN AGAIN BY THE PROVIDENCE NINE

The baseball season in this vicinity was brought to a close yesterday afternoon when the Providence Club defeated the Metropolitans easily. There were but a few hundred spectators present, and when the League champions gazed on the empty seats they turned up their noses and said they would not play. This displeased the officers of the Metropolitan Club, and Mr. Arthur Bell, the Treasurer, reminded them of the small attendance at the games in Providence, and said he would not disappoint his patrons if they were only 10 persons within the inclosure. This brought Bancroft's pets to their senses, and they unwillingly entered the field. They tried to stop the game by refusing to accept any umpire the Mets would name, and in order not to allow them any loophole by which to postpone the contest the Mets said they would agree to any person Joe Start would name, even if they selected their manager.

The contest was the worst of the series. The Mets played recklessly in the field and failed to give young Becannon any kind of support. Reipschlager distinguished himself behind the bat by making half a dozen errors. He was very kind to the visitors, presenting them with three-quarters of their runs. Foster, of the Saginaw Club, played second base in the absence of Troy. The score is appended.

PROVIDENCE	R	1B	PO	A	E	METROP'TAN	R	1B	PO	A	E
Hines, c. f.	3	1	1	0	0	Nelson, s. s.	0	0	0	1	0
Carroll, l. f.	1	1	0	0	0	Brady, r. f.	1	0	1	0	1
Radbourne, p........	1	1	0	1	0	Esterbr'k, 3d b.	0	2	0	1	2
Start, 1st b.	0	0	6	0	0	Roseman, c. f.	0	2	0	0	0
Farrell, 2d b.	1	1	1	3	0	Orr, 1st b.	0	1	12	0	0
Irwin, s. s.	1	1	2	1	2	Foster, 2d b........	0	0	2	4	1
Gilligan, c.	1	2	4	0	1	Reipschl'g'r, c.	1	0	2	2	6
Denny, 3d b.	2	2	1	2	1	Kennedy, l. f.	0	0	1	1	0
Radford, r. f.	1	0	3	0	0	Becannon, p........	0	1	0	4	0
Total	11	9	18	7	4	Total	2	6	18	13	10

RUNS SCORED IN EACH INNING

Providence	1	2	0	0	4	4—11
Metropolitan	0	0	0	0	1	1—2

Runs earned—Providence, 2; Metropolitan, 0. First base by errors—Providence, 3; Metropolitan, 2. Bases on balls—Providence, 2; Metropolitan, 0. Struck out—Providence, 1; Metropolitan, 2. Left on bases—Providence, 1; Metropolitan, 4. Three base hit—Denny. Two base hit—Esterbrook. Double plays—Kennedy and Foster; Farrell, Irwin, and Start. Wild pitches—Radbourne, 1; Becannon, 1. Passed balls—Reipschlager, 2. Umpire—Mr. Timothy Keefe. Time of game—One hour and twenty minutes.

61

New National Agreement Signed (1885)

Source: *New York Times*, October 18, 1885

In 1885 the NL and AA signed a new National Agreement to replace the 1883 accord. In addition to the reserve clause, the 1885 agreement called for a salary cap of $2,000—known as the Limit Agreement—and a minimum salary of $1,000 per season. In practice, clubs used various subterfuges to evade the salary limit. A small group of New York NL players, led by shortstop John Ward, were so angered that just four days after the publication of the article below they formed a secret organization called the Brotherhood of Professional Base Ball Players. Four years later the Brotherhood formed its own league, the Players' League, which had no salary limits.

THE BASEBALL CONVENTION

A TREATY OF PEACE BETWEEN THE LEAGUE AND THE NATIONAL ASSOCIATION

The Baseball Convention was in active session all yesterday and last night, at the Fifth-Avenue Hotel, and the two great associations succeeded in coming to an amicable settlement. The labors of the day resulted in the ratification by Presidents Young and McKnight of a new national agreement. This document provides that no contract shall be made for the services of any player by any club of the National League or the American Association of professional ball clubs for a longer period than seven months, beginning April 1 and terminating Oct. 3, and that no contract shall be made prior to Oct. 20. It also provides a general rule, "Once a League player, always a League player," and, similarly with the other association, and that when a player is released for 10 days he shall be open to the acceptance of clubs only belonging to the association of which he was a member. After the expiration of 10 days he is eligible to contract with any club. The Secretary of each association is required to transmit immediately to the other a list of all players under contract, and all who were under contract on Aug. 24 last, thus taking in the "big four" [Dan Brouthers, Hardy Richardson, Deacon White, and Jack Rowe, who were transferred to Detroit from Buffalo after the latter club was purchased for $7,000 in the transaction described below.—Ed.] and such players shall be ineligible to contract with any other club member of the other association, provided that the number of such players shall not exceed 12. In other words, one club can only reserve 12 players. No club not a club of either association shall be entitled to membership in either association from any city in which at that date any club member is located. Cincinnati, therefore, will not have a League club next year. But nothing is to prevent any club of either association from resigning its membership in one and gaining admittance into the other.

As to salaries, no club shall pay to any of its players for one season's service a salary in excess of $2,000, nor at a rate in excess of this maximum for any portion of the season, but no player shall receive less than $1,000. No advance money is to be paid to any player prior to April 1 except a sufficient sum in March to provide for his transportation to the city in which his club is located. A board of arbitration, consisting of three duly accredited representatives from each association, shall make, alter, and repeal all necessary rules not inconsistent with the national agreement, and this board shall have sole and final jurisdiction of all disputes and complaints. This is virtually the Saratoga secret agreement of August 24 worked over to prevent such outrages as the purchase of the Buffalo franchise by the Detroit Club, an action which practically destroyed the previous agreement. The American Association elected as its Board of Arbitration C. H. Byrne, of Brooklyn; Zach Phelps, of Louisville; and W. A. Nimmick, of Pittsburg. The eight clubs of the American Association pledged themselves not to resign from or forsake the association they are now in this Winter or next year. For the first time the American Association felt strong enough to assert itself and more than hold its own.

The status of the Eastern and Southern Leagues was referred to the Board of Arbitration. The Metropolitans were given permission to remove to Staten Island next year, and it was understood that Erastus Wiman, of the Staten Island Rapid Transit Company, was at the back of the scheme to have a crack club located there. . . .

62

African American Baseball Clubs (1886)

Sources: *New York Freeman* and *Cleveland Gazette*, August 28, 1886

African American newspapers frequently carried short items on baseball from around the nation. The first three passages are from the Freeman; *the final two are from the* Gazette.

Norfolk, August 24—The Red Stocking baseball club returned from Raleigh, where they engaged the Eclipse and National clubs. The first three of its members who returned gave a very bad account of their treatment on the field and otherwise, but this seems to be denied by those arriving later, who report that they were well treated and looked out for. Three games were played with the Eclipse club, one a tie and one in favor of each club. The game with the Nationals was won by the Norfolk players. The whole matter so far as the financial result was concerned was a failure. The gate-money was not sufficient to defray expense.

Niagara Drippings—The season here seems still to be on the increase. The present week was begun with rain, yet it is very warm. The Buffalo base ball team will be down on the 26th to engage in a game with the Cataract nine. Miss Fayette's garden party was a very pleasant affair. Messrs. Wesley Smith and John Ballard made a short visit to their home last week. There will be a game of base ball played between the International nine and a picked nine next week. Mr. Henry Ball, captain of the Internationals, has his team in pretty good order.

Fort Snelling (Minn.) News—The fort baseball nine played the Billsbury nine of Minneapolis on the 19th inst. The game resulted 9 to 4 in favor of Minneapolis.

Hot Springs, Ark.—The Little Rock and Hot Springs base ball clubs played two games of ball last week. The Hot Springs club won one game, and the Little Rock one. The deciding game was not played.—Jack Allen left for Chicago, Saturday.

Black Diamond City/Wilkes Barre, Pa. A welcome messenger—THE CLEVELAND GAZETTE—The "Cuban Giants" (colored), of Trenton, N.J., vs. the Wilkesbarres (white), at Athletic Park, Friday afternoon, resulted in a victory for the former by a score of 9 to 5. It was shameful, indeed, to see how scrupulous our white journals were after the victory in "rendering unto Caesar the things that were his." The Giants came here well recommended as base ball players and we are gratified to say carried off the laurels.

63

Baseball "Notes and Comments" (1886)

Source: *Sporting Life*, September 8, 1886

Sporting Life *included a regular feature called "Notes and Comments"—a week's worth of gossip, rumor, facts, and opinion listed in the order of the length of the comment. The following is a sample of these comments from one issue. Notice the advertisement for baseball cards, which appeared in every issue.*

Kuehne's smile is perpetual.
Young Nash has at last made a home run.
Rochester's catchers are all more or less disabled.
Send four cents in stamps for a set of our *new* base ball cards.
At this rate it will soon be "Frowning Mickey" and "Howling James."
"Louisville's great red-headed galaxy of ball players" is what they call Jim Hart's aggregation in Pittsburg.
It has been stated by a scientist that the Red Tail, a little bird, will catch 900 flies in an hour. The Red Tail ought to make a record at base ball.
New York has been seriously considering the engagement of Stovey, Jersey City's fine colored pitcher. The question is would the League permit his appearance in League championship games?

More superstitious notions: Gleason, of St. Louis, always comes on the field walking astride the right foul line. Big Brouthers always lays his gloves in a certain spot while he goes into the bench or to the bat, and he allows no one to interfere with them.

New Bedford, Mass., notes:—Manager Bancroft, of the Rochesters, was in town for a few days attending to business connected with the two theatres here of which he is manager. He says he resigned his position as manager of the Rochesters because of the interference of one of the directors, but at a meeting of the association Monday night that director was removed, and he will return to Rochester and stay until September 20. Frank is looking fine, and is in excellent health. . . . . . The New Bedfords and Fall Rivers will play six games for the championship of Bristol County, the initial game taking place in this city Saturday, the 28th inst. . . . . . Fall River is talking strongly of putting a team in the New England League next season, and so is New Bedford. . . . . . The home team will probably take a trip to New Hampshire next month, playing the Concords, Manchesters and other clubs in that State. . . . . . Brown, of your city, who is pitching for the Manchesters, was knocked out of the box Monday by the home team.

64

St. Louis Browns Celebrate World Championship (1886)

Source: *St. Louis Post-Dispatch*, October 25, 1886

The NL had beaten the AA in the postseason championship series in both 1884 and 1885, but in 1886 the Browns helped to establish the credentials of the AA by defeating the Chicago White Stockings four games to two. One of the most celebrated plays of the century, Curt Welch's "$15,000 slide," scored the winning run for St. Louis in the sixth and final game of the series. The Post-Dispatch *article claims, however, that Welch scored on what should have been labeled a wild pitch. Attendance at the series was exceptionally high, averaging about 7,000 spectators per game. Given the winner-take-all format, each St. Louis player received a little more than five hundred dollars.*

THE WORLD'S CHAMPIONS

FRIENDS OF THE BROWNS WILL BANQUET THEM NEXT SATURDAY NIGHT

President and Players to Receive Elegant Scarf Plus—Division of the Game Receipts—Some Good Winnings on 'Change—How the Last Game Was Won—Notes and Gossip

It had been suggested that the most fitting way to finish up the business connected with the world's champion games would be to tender the Brown Stocking Club a banquet, and a few St. Louis friends of the Browns have determined to do so. It is proposed that the banquet take place next Saturday night, and the Elk Club quarters have been mentioned as the probable place. At the banquet each member of the Browns will be presented with a check signed by Mr. Von der Ahe for the amount due him on a division of the game receipts for the six games played in the series. H. Clay Sexton, John J. O'Neill and other well-known citizens whose interest in the national game is proverbial will attend.

A part of the ceremonies will be the presentation to each player of an elegant scarf pin made in mystic style with three shades of gold. A pin will also be presented to President Von der Ahe himself on which will be worked his monogram "C.V.A.," with the letters "St. L.B.," denoting "St. Louis Browns," interlaced in the monogram. The work will be done by the Mermod & Jaccard Jewelry Company, and will be costly and elegant in every respect.

HOW THE GAME WAS WON

The game which won the championship of the world for the Browns was the most exciting one of the six played. The Chicagos scored a run in the second, the fourth and the fifth inning, while the Browns had goose eggs to their credit in all up to the eighth. In that inning Comiskey broke the ice by crossing the plate, having hit safe to right, gone to second on Welch's hit to third, to third on a passed ball and home on Foutz's sacrifice. Welch and Bushong then scored on Latham's three base left field hit. This tied the score. In the tenth inning the ball went by Kelly, the Chicago's catcher, and Welch, who was on third, came home, winning the game, by a score of 4 to 3. There was some discussion as to whether the ball which let in the winning run was a passed ball or a wild pitch. Kelly himself, was asked about it afterwards and said: "I signalled for Clarkson for a low ball on one side and when it came it was high up on the other. It struck my hand as I tried to get it, and I would say it was a passed ball. You can give it to me, if you want to. Clarkson told me that it slipped from his hands."

DIVIDING THE RECEIPTS

The total receipts for the six games played in St. Louis and Chicago by the Browns and White Stockings amount to $13,920.10. From this amount the expenses of the Browns' trip to Chicago and the salaries and expenses of the umpires must be deducted. Then the remainder will be divided by two, and one-half will be distributed equally among the twelve players on the Brown Stocking club, each player receiving a little over $500. The receipts are at present deposited in two banks, the Chicago receipts in a Chicago bank and the St. Louis receipts in a St. Louis bank. Mr. Von der Ahe will write Mr. Spalding for his draft on both for the amount jointly deposited, and after indorsing the drafts will draw the money from the banks in both cities. The umpires receive $100 each and their expenses, and that were paid to-day by Mr. Von der Ahe at the Lindell Hotel.

At the conclusion of Saturday's game President Von der Ahe was overwhelmed with telegrams from nearly all parts of the country congratulating him upon the success of the Browns in winning the championship of the world. The telegrams were characteristic of their senders. One in particular was worthy of note. It was from Mose Fraley at Chicago and read: "Concert of Chicago against solid St. Louis. Give the boys fifty dollars for wine and I will pay same. Let it be yellow label Clivuot."

THRICE CHAMPIONS

The game yesterday at Sportsman's Park between the Browns and Maroons resulted in another victory for the Browns, which gave them another championship, that of the city of St. Louis. The pitchers were Boyle and Foutz. The score was: Browns—Runs, 6; hits 6; total bases, 6; errors, 6. Maroons—Runs, 5; base hits, 9; total (bases), 11; errors, 6.

65

Heavyweight Champion John L. Sullivan Nearly Causes a Riot at a California League Game (1886)

Source: *San Francisco Examiner*, November 15, 1886

In 1886 the nation's best-known athlete was a boxer, not a baseball player. After knocking out Paddy Ryan in San Francisco on November 13, John L. Sullivan, who considered himself a talented ball player, agreed to umpire a California League game between the Greenhood & Morans of Oakland and the Pioneers of San Francisco. His appearance so excited the crowd that the game could not proceed until Sullivan left the field.

Sullivan as an Umpire

John L. Sullivan, the champion pugilist and pseudo ball-tosser, was the drawing card yesterday at the Alameda grounds. It was believed by the management that the announcement that the Trojan would umpire the game between the Greenhood & Morans and Pioneers would attract an unusually large number of spectators, but the immense multitude that swarmed through the gates was not anticipated by the most sanguine. Ladies were charged admission, but escorts and quarters were not lacking. Members of the gentle sex were apparently the most anxious to cast their lovely eyes upon the handsome pug. They came as early as 11 o'clock, and an hour before the game commenced the grand stand was densely thronged with females. At 2 o'clock every seat on the grounds was occupied, and a complete circle was formed about the diamond. When the Pioneers started out to practice the fielders were prevented from taking their positions owing to the proximity of the throng. The sphere was driven far into the field by the batters for the purpose of forcing the people back, but this produced little or no effect. The 2 o'clock train from this city swelled the multitude and it soon became apparent that there would not be sufficient space in the field to play the game. The crush was so great that none of the spectators were comfortable, and nearly all distressed. The lack of foresight in the management in not having more than one entrance came nearly being the cause of many serious accidents which only the good-nature of the crowd prevented. At one time nearly 2,000 people were struggling to get into the grounds through a gateway not three feet wide. Less economy and more thought for the public convenience should be the rule at these grounds. There should be at least five entrances.

SULLIVAN ON DECK

At the regular hour for commencing the contest there were over 18,000 people on the grounds. The scene was a repetition of the one witnessed at the Polo grounds in New York on Decoration Day. Men, women and children were scattered all over the field. The surrounding housetops, trees and fences were hidden beneath the weight of humanity. Finally the spectators became impatient, and began to yell for Sullivan, and all eyes were anxiously turned in the direction of the dressing-rooms, in which it was presumed the great gladiator was ensconced. Shortly before 2:30 o'clock the liliputian form of President Mone was seen bounding over the fence in the rear of the home-plate. He was followed by Pat Sheedy and the only John L. The latter was attired in a neat black suit, with Prince Albert coat, and baseball cap. He walked up to the homeplate, and when the people caught a glimpse of his stately form there was a grand rush in his direction. Men in center field struggled hard to make a home run across the pitcher's bag, and ladies at the initial and third bag made strenuous efforts to reach the same goal. In a few moments Sullivan was in the center of about 2,000 people. He quietly twirled his mustache and maintained a phlegmatic demeanor, while he gazed around like a Roman General surveying the excited and admiring populace upon his return trip across the Tiber at the close of a successful Punic war.

The ball-tossers, who were forgotten for the time, went into executive session at the outskirts of the throng. In the mean time the entire police force of Alameda, consisting of as many as seven men and a short but stout chief, was called out to quell the disturbance. They worked sedulously to scatter the mob, but all in vain.

Fortunately President Mone scored an idea. He argued with himself and arrived at the conclusion that if Sullivan disappeared the crowd would fall back. He accordingly made a suggestion, and Sullivan disappeared. Then the people began to yell their disapproval, but lung power had no effect. Finally a general discussion was inaugurated, and it was decided to clear the field upon condition that the pugilistic novelty be escorted around it so that everybody could view his classic countenance. This proposition was made to President Mone, and he acceded to the demand. Sullivan was informed of the demand and kindly consented. He soon afterward made his appearance in company with Sheedy, and the pair were escorted by a squad of officers around the circle in the field. A crowd of small boys followed and a peanut vender dropped in the rear. During the walk-around females flocked from all quarters and kept apace with the giant and his manager. When they arrived in front of the grand stand everybody arose and saluted the hero at the conclusion of the trip, and the people began to shout and the sounds of rejoicing continued for several minutes.

When Sullivan retired De Witt Court made his appearance and called game. The people however refused to move off the field, and despite the combined efforts of the police officers and ball-tossers the throng remained within twenty feet of the bases. The people in the grand stand shouted to those in the field to move off, and the latter replied with yells of derision. The players were obliged to adopt the rule that a man would be allowed only one base on a ball in the field.

Morris and Carroll, the Pittsburg battery, appeared with the Pioneers. The pitcher was slugged by the Oakland boys, and gauged by nearly every batter. But, no doubt, he did not try to do any effective work in the box. As the spectators interfered with the players many errors were scored, and in consequence the contest excited little interest. Owing to these facts a detailed account of the game is not given.

66 ───

Formation of the National League of Colored Base Ball Clubs (1887)

Source: *New York Freeman*, March 26, 1887

In 1886 the Southern League of Colored Base Ballists collapsed just a few weeks after it was formed. The organizers of the National League of Colored Base Ball Clubs hoped to avoid the same fate by allowing only clubs from large cities to join, and by signing the National Agreement.

COLORED BASE BALL CLUBS

MEETING OF THE NATIONAL LEAGUE IN BALTIMORE

Our Louisville Correspondent Describes the Trip—Delegates Present—Schedule of Games Adopted and Other Business Transacted

LOUISVILLE, Ky., March 19—THE FREEMAN man left for Baltimore to attend the business and schedule meeting of the National League of colored base ball clubs on Friday, March 11, at 2:20 A.M., viz. the O. & M. and C. W. & B. and B. & O. railroads. Arriving at Washington Sunday morning, March 13, your correspondent stopped over several hours to call upon a student at Howard University. Meeting Mr. T. J. Minton and his son, I said I was looking for a young man that I had been told would be among the brightest scholars and orators that Howard had ever produced. Young Mr. Minton paused a moment and then said, "I guess you must be looking for Mr. Chas. S. Morris of Louisville, Ky." He led me to Mr. Morris's room and "Sa'chel," as he signs himself in his newsy letters to the Indianapolis *World* and Detroit *Plain-dealer*, asked me to breakfast with him. He also introduced me to his room mate, Mr. C. A. Douglas from Albany, N.Y., and other students. We took in the city, calling on several and visiting all the prominent places up to 3:30 P.M., at which time I left for Baltimore.

Those forty miles were quickly traveled and I disembarked for the Boston Dining Saloon, and furnished rooms, kept by Mr. and Mrs. A. D. Furby, 228 Camden street. Mr. Furby and wife always make everybody comfortable at their place. The people of Baltimore are gems as far as hospitality is concerned, especially Messrs. J. J. Callis, manager of the Lord Baltimore Base Ball Club, Editor E. J. Waring of the Baltimore *Star* and Wm. H. Barnes, business manager. The *Star* is ably edited and managed. Mr. A. B. Wilson, correspondent of the Baltimore *Daily Sun*, represented that paper at the meeting of the delegates. Those present were: President, Walter S. Brown of Pittsburg; J. J. Callis, vice-president; C. Howard Johnson, secretary; Gilbert Ball and S. K. Governs, Philadelphia; B. M. Butler, New York; A. A. Selden, Boston; Chas. K. O'Donnell, Pittsburg; H. S. Cummings, J. R. Harris, Baltimore; Horace McGee, Cincinnati; Joseph Brown of Washington and C. W. Hines, Sr., of Louisville. . . .

The League closed its two days' session on Tuesday, March 15, by a reception and supper at the Douglass Institute, tendered by the Lord Baltimore Club. Mr. J. J. Callis was master of ceremonies. At the session Tuesday, Messrs. Horace McGee and Joseph Brown, representing Cincinnati and Washington respectively, were admitted as delegates. The umpires appointed were Malachi Adams, Baltimore; Charles Williams, Cincinnati; A. G. Davis, Philadelphia; Elijah Anderson, Louisville and Charles Catling, Pittsburgh. The others will be chosen at an early day. The Reach ball used by the American Association was adopted. Mr. A. J. Reach of Philadelphia will give two gold medals to the players making the highest batting and fielding averages. Additional directors appointed were S. K. Governs, Philadelphia; C. W. Hines, Louisville; Horace McGee, Cincinnati; J. J. Callis, Baltimore; Marshall Thompson, Boston; Ambrose Davis, New York; Charles H. O'Donnell, Pittsburg; Wm. Smith, Washington.

Wednesday morning your correspondent left for Philadelphia. In that beautiful city I spent ten of the happiest hours of my life. My old friends are so numerous there. I shall not name them, for the fear I can't do them all justice alike in such a small space as my letter is to occupy, but in conclusion, it is a puzzle between Baltimoreans and Philadelphians, as to their hospitality.

67

The "Colored League" Opening Day in Louisville (1887)

Source: *Louisville Courier-Journal*, May 8, 1887

The relatively small size of the African American population in northern cities and insufficient income within the black communities hampered the development of black professional baseball.

Nevertheless, the Louisville Falls Citys prepared for opening day of the National League of Colored Base Ball Players in that city by purchasing new uniforms, hiring players from as far away as New York and Detroit, and constructing a new ballpark. The new facility wasn't ready on May 7, when the first game was played, so the contest against the visiting Boston Resolutes was played in Eclipse Park, home of Louisville's AA franchise.

The Resolutes triumphed 10 to 3, but unfortunately only five hundred fans were on hand to see their victory. The small gate fee contributed to the Resolutes' financial problems: there was not even enough money to pay the players' train fares back to Boston. Several of the Resolutes worked as waiters to earn their return-trip tickets. During the nearly two weeks they were stranded in Louisville, both the Falls Citys and Resolutes disbanded; shortly thereafter, the Colored League folded as well.

COLORED LEAGUE

The Boston Resolutes Make Mince-Meat of the Falls City Club

The National Colored League season was formally opened yesterday at the Louisville Base Ball Park. The Falls City team, comprising the best ball-tossers of the city, were defeated with ease by the Boston Resolutes. The game was witnessed by about five hundred people.

The Resolutes are all fine players, especially the dusky little twirler Selden. He struck out thirteen men, and held the Falls Citys down to six hits, two of which were bases on balls. Selden has a most deceptive drop curve, and a most perfect control over the ball. But there are no flies on the other Boston players. Smith is an excellent left-hand throwing catcher, and hits the ball hard enough to burst the cover. Penno, Walker and Williams are all good infielders, and understand thoroughly the fine points of the game.

The weak point of the Falls City team is its execrable base-running. The players hugged the bags as if they were chained to them. They are fairly good fielders, but at the bat are rather weak and unscientific. Gillespie throws a speedy ball, but is a left-hand man and very erratic in delivery. Keiger pitches in good style, and seldom sends a batter to base on called balls. Clark catches well and throws accurately to bases, but Thompson is a trifle weak behind the bat.

The Louisvilles shifted about considerably in the game. Gillespie sent so many men to base on balls that Keiger was put in to pitch after the third inning. The Bostons knocked out four runs in the first inning. They demonstrated a superiority from the very start. The visitors were blanked in the last four innings, however, principally by Keiger's good work in the pitcher's box.

The pitchers made balks and illegal throws quite frequently, but the umpire, Anderson, did not apparently care to exercise his privilege. He made several poor decisions, but they were evenly divided between both sides.

The Falls Citys made their first run in the fifth inning. Thompson led with a hit, stole second, and scored on Garrett's two-bagger. Gillespie was then put out from short-stop to first base, but Garrett dashed home on the play.

The Falls Citys scored their third and last run in the ninth inning. Clark drove a terrific hit past left field, and crossed home-plate before the ball reached the diamond.

Following is the score:

FALLS CITY	AB	R	1B	PO	A	E
Thomas, 1b..............	4	0	1	7	2	0
Armstrong, l. f............	4	0	0	1	0	0
Keiger, r. f. and p..........	4	0	1	0	1	1
Brooks, 2b..............	4	0	0	2	2	2
Clark, c. and 3b...........	4	1	1	6	4	1
Thompson, c. f. and c.......	4	1	1	3	0	0
Jesse, 3b and r. f..........	3	0	0	4	1	1
Garrett, s. s.	3	1	1	2	2	2
Gillespie, p. and c. f.	3	0	1	2	4	0
Totals	33	3	6	27	16	7

BOSTON RESOLUTES	AB	R	1B	PO	A	E
Cross, 1b................	5	2	2	10	0	0
Brown, r. f..............	5	2	4	0	0	0
Penno, s. s..............	5	2	3	0	3	0
Selden, p.	4	1	3	0	6	0
Williams, 2b.............	5	0	1	2	2	0
Walker, 3b..............	5	1	1	1	2	1

BOSTON RESOLUTES	AB	R	1B	PO	A	E
Taylor, l. f.	5	1	3	1	0	1
Terrill, c. f.	5	1	2	0	0	0
Smith, c.	5	0	3	13	0	1
Totals	44	10	22	27	13	3

INNINGS	1	2	3	4	5	6	7	8	9	T
Resolutes	4	2	2	1	1	0	0	0	0—	10
Falls Citys	0	0	0	0	2	0	0	0	1—	3

Earned Runs—Resolutes 5, Falls Citys 2.
Two-Base Hits—Garrett.
Home Runs—Clark.
Double Plays—Clark, Brooks and Thomas, Garrett, Thomas and Thompson.
First Base on Balls—Falls Citys 2, Resolutes (?).
Hit by Pitched Ball—Selden.
Struck Out—Falls Citys 13, Resolutes 3.
Passed Balls—Smith 1, Clark 2, Thompson 4.
Wild Pitches—Gillespie 1, Keiger 1.
Umpire—Anderson.

The Falls City Club will play the Gorhams, of New York city, at the Louisville Base Ball Park this afternoon at 3:30 o'clock. The Gorhams will arrive in the city at noon to-day. The contest will be for championship honors, and will doubtless prove to be a good drawing card.

There were several amusing incidents in the game between the Colored League clubs yesterday. The coaching was superb. One of the Falls City men yelled like a Comanche Indian at a war dance. A collision took place at second base, and the base-runner pretended to be knocked silly. The crowd gathered excitely around him, and in the excitement he jumped up, scampered to third base, and was credited with a clean steal. When Clark made a home run in the ninth inning, the Falls City men were so much enthused and excited over the hit, that it was ten minutes before the game was resumed.

68

World Champion St. Louis Browns Refuse to Play Cuban Giants (1887)

Source: *St. Louis Post-Dispatch*, September 13, 1887

The year 1887 was significant for race relations in baseball. Previously, a few talented African American players had been permitted to play on teams in established leagues. Some, like southpaw pitcher George Stovey and second baseman Frank Grant, even achieved a measure of renown. In 1887, however, baseball executives initiated a behind-

the-scenes campaign to ban black players from their teams. This movement also affected exhibition games between white and black clubs. The article below reports a major league club's refusal to meet the country's preeminent black team.

THAT REVOLT

A Dramatic Account of the Mutiny Among the World's Champions

The Philadelphia Sunday News gives a very dramatic account of the mutiny among the Browns. It might be well to add that the proprietors of the park at which the game with the Cuban Giants was to have been played say they will sue Mr. Von der Ahe for $700. The News says:

The entire St. Louis Club was released last night.

Startling news, isn't it?

Von der Ahe told all the men that they were released and then drove them out of his room at the Continental Hotel.

He was mad enough at the time to suspend them for life and fine them all their back pay.

Here's how it happened.

While Chris was at supper in the Continental Hotel a document was handed to him to which the names of all the St. Louis players were attached with the exception of Comiskey's and Knouff's.

Chris read it, and the breast-bone of a reed-bird stuck cross-wise in his throat. By a superhuman effort Chris swallowed his emotion and the bone went down with it.

But it settled his supper.

The document was a protest signed by the players declaring that they would not go to Harlem Bridge tomorrow to play the Cuban Giants. The protest set forth the fact that they had no objection to playing against a white club, but they drew the color line strongly. Knouff had not signed the paper because he was not there when it was gotten up, and Comiskey knew nothing about it. Gleason was the man who formulated the paper.

After supper Von der Ahe sent for the men to come to his room.

As soon as they had arrived he began to storm and rage at them, and he picked out Jack Boyle as a special mark.

"This is the thanks you give me for my kind treatment of you," Chris declared. "This is the thanks I get for giving you half the gate receipts." Then cooling down a little he asked them one after another if they would change their minds. All declared that they would not, except Gleason, the man who had drawn up the protest. He weakened and said that he would go if the rest would. When the others refused Chris got his Dutch up, and said: "You're all released. Get out of the room." The players left their irate manager in a pretty state of mind. He expects that it will cost him $500 or $600 to settle with the Cuban Giants. He ordered his secretary,

Mr. Munson, to cancel the date by telegraph. Mr. Von der Ahe had engaged two boxes for the club at one of the theaters, but after the trouble he would not take them, but went himself, taking some of his friends with him.

Charley Comiskey feels very much put out by the action of the players, and declares that it would not have happened had he not broken his thumb.

The players held an indignation meeting last night while they ate saur kraut lunch in a saloon on Ridge avenue above Eighteenth street.

69

African American Player Responds to Report of Proposed Ban of Blacks in the Tri-State League (1888)

Source: *Sporting Life*, March 14, 1888

When a report surfaced (later proved false) that the Tri-State League planned to bar black players, Weldy Walker—who with his brother Moses had integrated the AA in 1884—responded with the following letter. Notice that Walker mentions the inequity of the reserve clause, just as John Ward does in his 1887 Lippincott's article (see Document 75). For more information on black players in 1887, see Jerry Malloy, "Out at Home," in The Armchair Book of Baseball II, ed. John Thorn (New York: Charles Scribner's Sons, 1987), pp. 262–85.

WHY DISCRIMINATE?

An Appeal to the Tri-State League by a Colored Player

W. W. Walker, a well-known colored player, requests THE SPORTING LIFE to publish the following open letter to the president of the Tri-State (late Ohio) League:

STEUBENSVILLE, O., March 5—MR. MCDERMITT, President Tri-State League—*Sir:* I take the liberty of addressing you because noticing in THE SPORTING LIFE that the law permitting colored men to sign was repealed, etc., at the special meeting held at Columbus, Feb. 22, of the above-named League of which you are the president. I concluded to drop you a few lines for the purpose of ascertaining the reason of such an action.

I have grievances, and it is a question with me whether individual loss subserves the public good in this case. This is the only question to be considered—both morally and financially—in this, as it is, or ought to be, in all cases that depend upon the public for success—as base ball. I am convinced, beyond doubt that you all, as a body of men, have not been impartial and unprejudiced in your consideration of the great and important question—the success of the "National game."

The reason I say this is because you have shown partiality by making an exception with a member of the Zanesville Club; and from this one would infer that he is the *only* one of the three colored players—Dick Johnson, alias Dick Male, alias Dick Noyle, as THE SPORTING LIFE correspondent from Columbus has it; Sol White, of the Wheelings, whom I must compliment by saying was one, if not *the* surest hitter in the Ohio League last year, and your humble servant, who was unfortunate enough to join the Akrons just ten days before they "busted."

It is not because I was reserved and have been denied making my bread and butter with some club that I speak; but it is in hopes that the action taken at your last meeting will be called up for reconsideration at your next.

The law is a disgrace to the present age, and reflects very much upon the intelligence of your last meeting, and casts derision at the laws of Ohio—the voice of the people—that say all men are equal. I would suggest that your honorable body, in case that black law is not repealed, pass one making it criminal for a colored man or woman to be found in a ball ground.

There is now the same accommodation made for the colored patron of the game as the white, and the same provision and dispensation is made of the money of them both that finds the way into the coffers of the various clubs.

There should be some broader cause—such as want of ability, behavior and intelligence—for barring a player than his color. It is for these reasons and because I think ability and intelligence should be recognized first and last—at all times and by everyone—I ask the question again, why was the "law permitting colored men to sign repealed, etc.?"

Yours truly,   WELDY W. WALKER.

70

"King" Kelly Defends Player "Kicking" (1888)

Source: Mike Kelly, *Play Ball: Stories of the Diamond Field* (Boston: J. F. Spofford, 1888)

Mike "King" Kelly was the most popular baseball player of the 1880s. In 1887, the Chicago White Stockings sold his contract to Boston for $10,000, an enormous sum for that day. After that, Kelly was called "the $10,000 beauty." In the introduction to his book, which was probably ghostwritten, Kelly observed that the fans attended ball games not only for the excitement generated by the game itself but in order to witness the "kicking" of the players.

There are so many exciting incidents in the life of a ball player, that is almost impossible for one to put them on paper. A ball player is a busy individual in the summer months, and in the winter very often he has but little to do. Therefore, when the idea of writing a few reminiscences was suggested to me, I thought it an excellent idea. Here at Hyde Park on the Hudson, where I spend the winter months, one has plenty of time for literary work. There is'nt a great deal to do here in winter. There is plenty of ice boating and "sliding" down the big hill,—"tobogganing" they call it in the big cities, but "sliding" is good enough for Hyde Park,— the entertainments and dances at the engine-house, the billiard tournament at the Hyde Park Club, a most excellent club for young men, founded by Archibald Rogers a few years since, and the meeting of the village gossips at "Pop" Hornung's. So one can see that writing is a most agreeable change from these pastimes.

I will not endeavor to tire my readers with a history of the game in this country. Abler pens than mine have done that. I will simply relate some of my experiences on the diamond field, and give a brief sketch of my career.

There are so many interesting things which occur in the course of a season, that unless one has a particularly retentive memory, he is apt to be at a loss just to know when to begin and where to stop. In these articles I will not bore my readers by discussing rules or the principles of the game. Those of you who have seen a base ball game know just how its played, and what the rules are. Those of you who have never witnessed a game of ball should go at the first opportunity next season. I am willing to wager that after looking at three or four games you will become a regular fiend. I have known men to forsake their business day after day to see their favorite clubs at work. There is excitement enough in two hours to last the ordinary man for as many days.

Many times have I been asked the question, "To what do you ascribe the great popularity of base ball?" This, seems to me, can be answered in just two words, "The excitement." People go to see games because they love excitement and love to be worked up. That is one reason why I believe in "kicking" now and then on the diamond. It may be all right for the newspapers to say that "base ball will become more popular when played without kicking." I disagree entirely with these authorities on this subject. Look at the Chicago Base Ball Club. It has been the most successful in this country. Why? One good reason because they are "chronic kickers," and people flock to see them to witness the sport. You won't find the ordinary man going out to a baseball field when it's 80° in the shade to see two clubs play ball for a couple of hours, without a word being said on either side. The people who go to ball games want good playing, with just enough kicking to make things interesting thrown in.

Of course, because of being the $10,000 beauty, and all that sort of thing, there was more or less excitement regarding my appearance with the Boston club last season. In some towns they had an idea that I was a sort of "Jumbo." Down in Hartford I remember playing a good game, and keeping pretty quiet all the way through it. Yet I played ball just as good as I ever did before. At the conclusion of the game I heard a conversation between two men.

One said, "So that is Kelly, is it? Well, what do you think of him?"

His partner replied, "Well, I firmly believe that he is an overrated player. Why, he didn't kick a it. He can't play ball." You see he wanted more kicking and less ball playing. There wasn't excitement enough in the game, and it made him very sore indeed.

All of which convinces me that a little kicking now and then will greatly please the best of men. . . .

71

A Humorous Look at the Umpire (1888)

Source: Wallace Peck, *A Stitch in Time Saves Nine* (New York, 1888)

Player "kicking" was usually directed at the umpire. As Wallace Peck's satire reflects, the fans helped to make the umpire the game's chief symbolic villain.

The old world of Columbus had its Nine Muses—Clio, Euterpe, Thalia, Melpomene, Terpsichore, Erato, Polymnia, Urania and Calliope; but his new world has discarded these antiques, and substituted a modern list; the Nine Muses of America being the Pitcher, Catcher, Short Stop, First, Second and Third Base, Right, Centre and Left Fielders—these being the deities worshipped by the modern man. The 10th Muse—if such may be allowed—is the Umpire. 60,000,000 Americans know about base ball than The Umpire; and to them he is always exhibiting the symptoms of a simpleton. The Umpire, nevertheless, is a man of parts (particularly after the first few games), and can talk fluently the United States, Base Ball, and Profane Languages. He is as wise as the saloon-keeper who places an ice-water tank outside his shop, with a brass band alongside, to attract the thirsty to its free glasses. He is also as astute as the Jerseyman who first buys his mosquito screens, and then builds his house. Like the members of the nine, The Umpire is the subject of barter, as high as $1.84 having been paid by one club to another for his transfer. The Umpire is born—not made. If he had been made he would have been armored, like a modern cruiser, with a torpedo net alongside. At game time his Opinion is asked to sally forth, and when it appears the audience hoot it; and it soon learns the fighting weight of a Base-Ball Hiss. By and by The Umpire is told that he is a tennis-player gone wrong, at which he leaves the diamond, and takes to driving an ambulance. Some day the base ball crank, in cutting across the graveyard to see a game, feels a twinge as he reads this epitaph:

YE UMPIRE

"First in gore, first in pieces, and
last in the hearts of his countrymen."

72

The Widespread Popularity of Baseball (1888)

Source: Jacob Morse, *Sphere and Ash: History of Base Ball* (1888; reprint, Columbia, S.C.: Camden House, 1984)

In his introduction to the first published history of baseball, Jacob Morse described the tremendous growth in the game's popularity. He noted that baseball was prospering not only in the United States but also in Canada and Cuba.

It can be said, without fear of contradiction, that base ball is the sport of sports in the United States; no other sport furnishing as much or as satisfactory amusement. The game was never so popular and never gained so much ground as last season,— a fact largely due to the excellent influences that surrounded it, and to the ability of the gentlemen who had it in charge. The struggles for the supremacy in the league national championship were closely watched by thousands from the first day of the season to the end, and by admirers not only in this country, but also abroad. Wherever the American chanced to be, he eagerly scanned papers and mails from home which might give him information on the positions of the clubs. So great has been and is the hold of the game in the land, that American students in Berlin have celebrated the Fourth of July by a contest of base ball, while matches in Honolulu in the Sandwich Islands have been of frequent occurrence. The game has found its way into Canada, and has seriously threatened to replace lacrosse, the national sport of that country. A Canadian club, the Torontos, now holds the championship of the International Association, and was one of the strongest in the country at the close of the season. The sport thrives, too, in Cuba, and there are excellent grounds, good clubs, and promising players in Havana. The development, too, of the sport in sections of this country to which it has been comparatively new, has been simply marvellous. Leagues have been formed in the Southern, Western, and North-western States, and beside these organizations, there is scarcely a State that has not a league. Even in far-off San Francisco excitement over base ball is intense, and some of the most desirable players in the country hail from that city. The fever has also struck New Mexico, and the clubs that have introduced the game there attest the great interest manifested in that region. Instead of the game being played out, as many would have it, it has actually increased its hold in the estimation of the public, and in some places has supplanted every rival for popular favor. In Phila-delphia the fever is so great that the city easily supports two clubs at an admission price of but twenty-five cents. New York really has had two clubs, in the New Yorks and the Metropolitans, while the grounds of the Brooklyns are readily accessible to residents of the metropolis. On the days of great matches, it is no exaggeration to say that people come from great distances to witness contests. Nor is the interest in the game confined to those who are present at the matches. There are thousands who are unable to find the time to attend, and there are thousands who cannot

The Excelsior (left) and Knickerbocker (right) clubs before a game, 1858. The umpire, wearing a top hat, is holding the ball. Courtesy of the National Baseball Library and Archive, Cooperstown, New York.

In this eerie lithograph star pitcher Jim Creighton holds the tool of his trade (no date). Courtesy of the National Baseball Library and Archive.

A game of "ice baseball" played in the early 1860s (no date or source). Courtesy of the National Baseball Library and Archive.

A decorative collage of drawings of the 1869 Red Stockings of Cincinnati. Pitcher Asa Brainard displays his underarm pitching style (and his fashionable muttonchop sideburns) in the center. Courtesy of the National Baseball Library and Archive.

Beadle's and DeWitt's were printed by the same company for different audiences. The Beadle's cover features delicate young men (notice the bottle-shaped bat and the split-handed grip) while DeWitt's highlights a hairy-chested, muscular man. Courtesy of the National Baseball Library and Archive.

Number 1.

Price, 10 Cents.

HAND-BOOKS

DE WITT'S

DE WITT'S BASE BALL GUIDE FOR

1877.

For Sale by
The American News Company,
115, 117, 119 and 121 Nassau Street, New York.

A distinguished crowd watches the Red Stockings and Athletics during their 1874 tour of England. Courtesy of the National Baseball Library and Archive.

J C Carbine – W L Hague – W S Hastings – Chas Fulmer – A Devlin – J C Chapman   Snyder – J J Gerhardt – A A Auison –

G W Bechtel – J J Ryan.

In this damaged 1876 photo of the Louisville Grays, we see only one of the four players expelled from baseball the next year—Jim Devlin. Notice the stylish high-top shoes. Courtesy of the National Baseball Library and Archive.

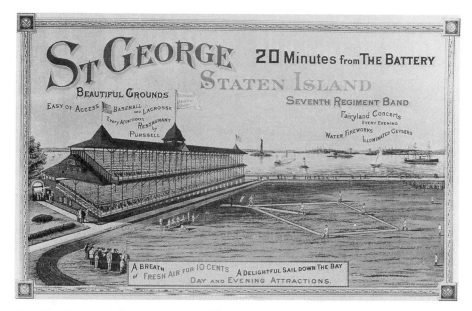

This 1886 lithograph features not only the home park of the Metropolitan (AA) Club but also, in the center background, the Statue of Liberty. Courtesy of the National Baseball Library and Archive.

This action shot, from the 1889 Opening Day game in Philadelphia between the Brooklyn Bridegrooms and the Athletics, shows an attempted steal of second base. Notice the umpire hustling from behind the plate to make the call, and the shortstop waiting for the ball—even with a right-handed batter up. Both the second baseman and the center fielder appear to be backing up the play. Reprinted from *Athletic Sports in America, England, and Australia,* ed. Harry Palmer (Philadelphia: Hubbard Bros., 1889), p. 147. Courtesy of The University Libraries, University of Maryland at College Park.

National League founder William Hulbert (c. 1880). Courtesy of the National Baseball Library and Archive.

The venerable sportswriter Henry Chadwick (1908). Courtesy of the National Baseball Library and Archive.

Sporting Life editor Francis Richter (no date). Courtesy of the National Baseball
Library and Archive.

John M. Ward, Capt. New York B. B. Club.

Newsboy

NEW YORK.

John Ward, from a rare 1888 Newsboy Cabinet tobacco card. Courtesy of the National Baseball Library and Archive.

Controversial owner John Brush (no date). Courtesy of the National Baseball Library and Archive.

afford the expenditure, even though it be slight. Yet these must be counted among the most ardent lovers of the game, and to them, on a holiday, there could be no greater treat than that of witnessing a base ball match. To the business or professional man nothing affords more pleasure than a ball game. Here he can throw off all cares and troubles. He forgets to think about them in the relaxation he enjoys in the excitement of a close contest, and he goes to his home feeling all the better for the few hours spent in the air. It is a medicine to him and a tonic, and it is with a zest that he afterward partakes of his evening meal. The game, too, is purely and thoroughly American, entirely characteristic of our race and times. It had an English origin, 't is true, but the child is as different from the parent as anything that could be imagined. Cricket could never have become an American game. It is too slow, too leisurely, for the American. It could never become national, for how many could spare the time, were they players, to participate in a contest that will take as much as a day, granting that the contest would be finished in this space of time? And even if players could find time, how about the spectators? No, the American would not sacrifice a morning for a cricket game. He is quick and active, nervous and energetic, and he wants his sport to answer the requirements of his temperament. Base ball has answered his purpose admirably. . . .

73

Baseball Promotes "Local Pride" in New York City (1888)

Source: *New York Times*, September 23, 1888

Even though the rosters of professional baseball teams were frequently stocked with players from other cities, the existence of such teams deepened the sense of community among the residents of the cities in which the teams were located. In this editorial, the writer reasons that the way feelings of local pride are awakened is irrelevant as long as the citizens act upon that pride to better their city.

LOCAL PRIDE

A considerable number of intelligent and respectable citizens of New-York are daily disgusted at the evidence of the interest taken by a still more considerable number of persons whom they assume to be less intelligent and respectable in the game of baseball. They regard it as monstrous and absurd that the papers should devote so much space to chronicling the procedures of nine persons of no eminence except for their capabilities of throwing, catching, and hitting balls and of running short distances with rapidity. They deplore the effect of these chronicles upon the young, and they resent the absence from the public prints of matter more interesting to themselves which they assume is displaced to make room for the accounts of baseball matches. Those of them whose disgust has not prevented them from learning anything at all of its subject point out that it is not even a local pride that is properly involved, since the players are mercenaries who may appear this season in the green shirts and scarlet stockings and blue caps of one community, and next year in equally kaleidoscopic raiment betokening a new allegiance.

This is all true, and yet the zealots of baseball, at least in this city, have some reason on their side, though they may not be able to produce it. However illogical it may be that local pride should be aroused by the victories of one team of professional baseball players over another or touched by its defeats, yet, as a matter of fact, that feeling is enlisted on the part of a considerable fraction of the population in the varying fortunes of the so-called "New-Yorks," and we hold that anything whatsoever that can excite the local pride of New-York is so far a good thing. For local pride is much the same thing as public spirit, which at least cannot exist without it, and there is no city in the world that is more deficient in public spirit than New-York, or that ought to welcome more anything that tends to stimulate that quality.

It is in some respects a misfortune for a town to be the biggest in its country, though doubtless it is a misfortune that other towns would gladly assume. Its inhabitants are too apt to assume that its bigness puts it out of competition and that it is superfluous for it to be anything else but big. The New-Yorker who goes to Boston or to Philadelphia or to Chicago is sure to have the excellences and advantages of those towns respectively pointed out to him by the inhabitants thereof, and he is equally sure to regard the indication as "provincial," assuming that the establishment by the census that there are more "head" of New-Yorkers than of Bostonians or Philadelphians renders any other indication of its superiority unnecessary. He is only internationally sensitive. When he goes to London or Paris, or when a Londoner or Parisian is under his charge in his own city, he is apt to wish that he had something else to point out than the bigness in which their cities exceed his own. He would like them to admire New-York, though he is above soliciting the admiration of his countrymen. The Londoner, on the other hand, has not even our international susceptibility, now that the old censuses of Pekin are discredited, and if his American visitor does not like London he will cheerfully agree with him that it is a beastly hole. He has no local pride, and feels himself dispensed from cultivating any.

If New-York were not so big as to be out of competition in that respect it would doubtless be a better place to live in, and anything that brings it into direct competition with other cities, even in so trivial a matter as playing baseball, has wholesome elements. It is not at all municipally important that the New-Yorks should win the championship, but it is important that New-Yorkers should be anxious that their city should excel in anything. When *Iroquois* won the Derby it was plausibly said that the victory raised the United States higher in the estimation of the general mass of Englishmen than any other they had ever achieved. A cynical philosopher, replying to a person uninterested in aquatic sports, who betrayed the same impatience with the inordinate attention paid by the press and the public to the international yacht races that we are now remarking upon with reference to baseball, defended the public interest upon the ground that the *America's* Cup was really the only trophy the country had to show. Possibly a similar remark about the possession of the champion baseball pennant by New-York would be equally exaggerated, but at all events the competition proves that it does not quite suffice for all New-Yorkers that New-York is big. If this sentiment were extended in more rational directions there might actually come an irresistible public demand that New-York should become the best paved, cleaned, and policed city and the most attractive place of residence in the United States. Meanwhile, any stir of local pride is to be welcomed that makes a beginning in the direction of that distant and Utopian end.

74

Poem: "Casey at the Bat" (1888)

Source: *San Francisco Examiner*, June 3, 1888

This chapter closes with the poem "Casey at the Bat: A Ballad of the Republic." Its author, Ernest L. Thayer, penned it for his regular humor column in the San Francisco Examiner. Actor DeWolf Hopper, who recited it countless times on the stage, was largely responsible for popularizing the poem. Few pieces of baseball literature have so effectively captured the emotional power of the game.

CASEY AT THE BAT

A Ballad of the Republic, Sung in the Year 1888

The outlook wasn't brilliant for the Mudville nine that day;
The score stood four to two with but one inning more to play.
And then when Cooney died at first, and Barrows did the same,
A sickly silence fell upon the patrons of the game.

A straggling few got up to go in deep despair. The rest
Clung to that hope which springs eternal in the human breast;
They thought if only Casey could but get a whack at that—
We'd put up even money now with Casey at the bat.

But Flynn preceded Casey, as did also Jimmy Blake,
And the former was a lulu and the latter was a cake;
So upon that stricken multitude grim melancholy sat,
For there seemed but little chance of Casey's getting to the bat.

But Flynn let drive a single, to the wonderment of all,
And Blake, the much despis-ed, tore the cover off the ball;

And when the dust had lifted, and the men saw what had occurred,
There was Johnnie safe at second and Flynn a-hugging third.

Then from 5,000 throats and more there rose a lusty yell;
It rumbled through the valley, it rattled in the dell;
It knocked upon the mountain and recoiled upon the flat,
For Casey, mighty Casey, was advancing to the bat.

There was ease in Casey's manner as he stepped into his place;
There was pride in Casey's bearing and a smile on Casey's face.
And when, responding to the cheers, he lightly doffed his hat,
No stranger in the crowd could doubt 'twas Casey at the bat.

Ten thousand eyes were on him as he rubbed his hands with dirt;
Five thousand tongues applauded when he wiped them on his shirt.
Then while the writhing pitcher ground the ball into his hip,
Defiance gleamed in Casey's eye, a sneer curled Casey's lip.

And now the leather-covered sphere came hurtling through the air,
And Casey stood a-watching it in haughty grandeur there.
Close by the sturdy batsman the ball unheeded sped—
"That ain't my style," said Casey. "Strike one," the umpire said.

From the benches, black with people, there went up a muffled roar.
Like the beating of the storm-waves on a stern and distant shore.
"Kill him; Kill the umpire!" shouted some one on the stand;
And it's likely they'd have killed him had not Casey raised his hand.

With a smile of Christian charity great Casey's visage shone;
He stilled the rising tumult; he bade the game go on;
He signaled to the pitcher, and once more the spheroid flew;
But Casey still ignored it, and the umpire said, "Strike two."

"Fraud!" cried the maddened thousands, and echo answered fraud;
But one scornful look from Casey and the audience was awed.
They saw his face grow stern and cold, they saw his muscles strain,
And they knew that Casey wouldn't let that ball go by again.

The sneer is gone from Casey's lip, his teeth are clenched in hate;
He pounds with cruel violence his bat upon the plate.
And now the pitcher holds the ball, and now he lets it go,
And now the air is shattered by the force of Casey's blow.

Oh, somewhere in this favored land the sun is shining bright;
The band is playing somewhere, and somewhere hearts are light.
And somewhere men are laughing, and somewhere children shout;
But there is no joy in Mudville—mighty Casey has struck out.

—PHIN.

5

The Great Player Revolt, 1887–90

Despite the imposition of a player reservation system in 1879, salaries, and player expectations, rose steadily in the 1880s. The owners attempted to curb rising salaries with the Limit Agreement in 1885, but they failed to enforce its $2,000 salary cap. That same year, John Ward founded the Brotherhood of Professional Base Ball Players as a secret lodge to provide financial aid to sick and indigent "brothers." Initially Ward had no intention of confronting the owners or transforming the Brotherhood into a trade union. However, in 1888 the owners infuriated the players by adopting a salary scale based not only on ability but on personal character. After Ward returned from a round-the-world tour, he and his Brotherhood associates laid the foundations for their own league. Despite careful planning and superior player talent, the Players' League collapsed after its only season due to financial difficulties.

75

John Ward Attacks the Reserve Clause (1887)

Source: John M. Ward, "Is the Base-Ball Player a Chattel?" *Lippincott's Magazine* 40 (August 1887): 310–19

John Montgomery Ward was the Renaissance man of nineteenth-century baseball. He entered the NL in 1878 as a pitcher for the Providence Grays and quickly demonstrated his immense talents. Just two years later he threw the second perfect game in NL history. After being sold to New York in 1882, a sore arm forced him to switch to shortstop, where he starred for the remaining twelve years of his career. In 1887 Ward earned a law degree from Columbia University. He put his legal training to use in the following article, in which he offered an insightful analysis of the history of the player-owner relationship and formulated the grounds for the Brotherhood's opposition to the reserve clause.

IS THE BASE-BALL PLAYER A CHATTEL?

I should like to describe fully the relations which exist between base-ball club and player; but, as this is not possible in a limited article, I will confine myself to a consideration of these relations as they have been induced by the action of the reserve-rule. I will first describe briefly the origin, intent, and effect of the rule; I will then trace in detail its subsequent development; I will show that there has been a complete departure from its original intent, and in consequence a total change in its effect; that abuse after abuse has been fastened upon it, until, instead of being used to the ends for which it was formed, it has become a mere pretence for the practice of wrong. Incidentally, I will touch upon some of the methods employed by clubs in their dealings with players.

The first reserve agreement was entered into by the club members of the National League September 30, 1879. By that compact each club was conceded the privilege of reserving for the season of 1880 five of its players of the season of 1879, and each of the eight clubs pledged itself not to employ any player so reserved by any of the others. The five men so chosen by each club were thus forced either to sign with the club reserving them at its own terms or withdraw to some club not a member of the League; and, as there were no such clubs then in existence, the reservation was practically without alternative. The club thus appropriated to itself an absolute control over the labor of five of its men, and this number has since been enlarged to eleven, so that now the club controls practically its entire team.

The contracts of the players for 1879 contained no reference to any right of reservation by the clubs, nor was any such in contemplation at the time the contracts were signed: so that it was an *ex post facto* rule, and therefore a positive wrong in its inception.

In order to justify this extraordinary measure and distract public attention from the real causes making it necessary, the clubs tried to shift the blame to the players. They declared that players were demanding extortionate salaries, and that the rule was needed as a protection against these. They attempted to conceal entirely that the real trouble lay in the extravagant and unbusiness-like methods of certain managers and in the lack of good faith between the clubs themselves. According to them, the player who accepted a proffered increase of salary was a disorganizer and a dangerous character, from whom protection was necessary, while the club official who offered it was but a poor weak instrument in his hands. Was it really wrong for the player to accept a larger salary when offered? or was not the dangerous factor here the club, which in violation of faith with its associates enticed the player by offering the increase? And was it really against the players or against themselves that the clubs were obliged to combine for protection? The history of base-ball deals between different clubs is full of instances of broken faith, and in most such cases where a player was involved the favorite procedure has been to whitewash the clubs and black-list the player. Yet I do not hesitate to say that I believe base-ball has more to fear from the reckless and improvident methods of some of its managers than from all the faults of all the players.

In the enactment of the reserve-rule the clubs were probably influenced by three considerations: they wished to make the business of base-ball more permanent, they meant to reduce salaries, and they sought to secure a monopoly of the game.

At the close of each season there was always a scramble for players for the following year: the well-balanced and successful team was especially subject to inroads, so that the particularly strong nine of one season was not unlikely to be a particularly weak one the next. The business of base-ball thus lacked stability. There was no assurance to the stockholders of a continuing fixed value to their stock, for the defection of a few important players might render it almost worthless. But with the right of retaining the pick of its players the club was assured of a good team, and the stock held its value.

Again, in this annual competition for players, clubs often paid extravagant salaries to certain very desirable men, and the effect was to enlarge the average scale so that it was assuming undue proportions. But with the privilege of retaining its best men at its own figures, the average salary would be forced down.

The third consideration, which doubtless had some weight, was the desire to create a monopoly. It was just beginning to be seen that base-ball properly managed might be made a lucrative business, though its real fertility was yet scarcely dreamed of. With all the picked players reserved to it and the prestige thus given, it was thought that the League might easily retain the control of the business.

But with the growth of the game in popular favor, and the consequent development of its money-making features, the maintenance of this monopoly became more and more difficult. A rival organization did spring up, and the reserve-rule then lost much of its force, for many of the players were willing to accept the alternative of withdrawing from the League and joining forces with the new Association. The young aspirant developed such strength that it was found impossible to put it down, and the result threatened was a disastrous war in the competition for players and the favor of the public. With great good judgment and the remarkable instinct for self-preservation which has always characterized it, the League agreed with the American Association on the terms of an armistice. This was in the spring of 1883, and in the fall of the same year this armistice was made permanent in the great offensive and defensive alliance known as "The National Agreement." The parties to this were the four base-ball leagues then in existence. Each pledged itself, among other things, that its club members should respect the reservation of players by the club members of every other party, in the same manner as though they were all of the same league.

The effect of this was that a player reserved was forced to sign with the club reserving him, or quit playing ball altogether. These four leagues included all the clubs in the country, and the alternative of withdrawing to another club was thus practically cut off. As new leagues have sprung up, they have been either frozen out or forced into this agreement for their own protection, and the all-embracing nature of the reserve-rule has been maintained. There is now no escape for the player. If he attempts to elude the operation of the rule, he becomes at once a professional outlaw, and the hand of every club is against him. He may be willing to play elsewhere for less salary, he may be unable to play, or, for other reasons, may retire for a season or more, but if ever he reappears as a professional ball-player it must be at the disposition of his former club. Like a fugitive-slave law, the reserve-rule denies him a harbor or a livelihood, and carries him back, bound and shackled, to the club from which he attempted to escape. We have, then, the curious result of a contract which on its face is for seven months being binding for life, and when the player's name is once attached thereto his professional liberty is gone forever.

On the other hand, what reciprocal claim has the player? Absolutely none! For services rendered he draws his salary; but for a continuance of that service he has no claim whatever. The twentieth paragraph of the regular League contract declares that the club reserves the right to release the player at any time, "at its option," by ten days' notice, and that its liabilities under the contract shall thereupon cease and determine. That is to say, the club may hold the player as long as it pleases, and may release him at any time, with or without cause, by a simple ten days' notice; while the player is bound for life, and, no matter what his interests or wishes may be, cannot terminate the contract even by ten years' notice.

The uninitiated in "base-ball law" may say, "If players are foolish enough to sign such contracts they must expect to abide the consequences." But, as a matter of fact, the player has no volition in the case. A provision of the League prescribes a certain form of contract, no other is "legal" according to this "base-ball law," and no club dares offer him any other to sign: that printed form is presented to him with the alternative of signing it or none at all, and under such duress he has nothing to do but submit. At some other time I may write more fully of this contract, the most unique unilateral document extant; but for the present I quote it only to show its connection with the reserve-rule. One of its clauses declares the players bound "by the Constitution of the National League and the Articles and Covenants of the National Agreement:" among these latter is included the reserve-rule, and in this way it is worked into the contract which the player is forced to sign, and which is thereby given a semblance of legality.

This, then, is the inception, intent, and meaning of the reserve-rule in its simplicity: its complicity I will presently describe. It inaugurated a species of serfdom which gave one set of men a life-estate in the labor of another, and withheld from the latter any corresponding claim. No attempt has ever been made to defend it on the grounds of abstract right. Its justification, if any, lay only in its expediency. It was a protective measure which gave stability to the game by preserving the playing strength of the teams, and it acted as a check on the increase of salaries. Its immediate results were clearly beneficial, opposition to it died away, and, notwithstanding the peculiar, not to say servile, position in which it placed the players, they accepted it as for the general good.

But, however satisfactory in its original application, I scarcely believe there will be any one found to justify it in the purposes to which it has been recently applied.

Instead of an institution for good, it has become one for evil; instead of a measure of protection, it has been used as a handle for the manipulation of a traffic in players, a sort of speculation in live stock, by which they are bought, sold, and transferred like so many sheep.

Ideal wrong will always work itself out in practical wrong, and this has been no exception. The rule itself was an inherent wrong, for by it one set of men seized absolute control over the labor of another, and in its development it has gone on from one usurpation to another until it has grown so intolerable as to threaten the present organization of the game. Clubs have seemed to think that players have no rights, and the black list was waiting for the man who dared assert the contrary. Players were cowed into submission, and were afraid even to resort to the courts for a remedy. But all this time there was a strong undercurrent of discontent, and for the past year it has required all the influence of the conservative element of the profession to hold this in check and maintain a sentiment in favor of peaceful and legal reform.

The first mistake was made at the initial attempt to apply the rule. As was to be expected the players chafed at first under the unaccustomed yoke. Hines, of Providence, declared that rather than submit to that club's reservation he would stay idle for a year. The construction was then evolved that even this would not free the player from the reservation,—that, though the term of his *contract* had expired, and though the reservation was so distasteful that he would prefer the loss of a year's salary, yet he would still be held by it. That is to say, the life-estate was indefeasible: the brand of the club once upon the man, it might never be removed by any act of his own. A practical illustration of the working of this construction was given in the case of Charlie Foley. During the season of 1883 he contracted a malady which incapacitated him for play. He was laid off without pay, *though still held subject to the direction of his club*. In the fall he was placed among the players reserved by the club, though he had not been on the club's pay-roll for months. The following spring he was still unable to play, and the Buffalo Club refused either to sign or release him. He recovered somewhat, and offered his services to the club, but it still refused to sign him. Having been put to great expense in securing treatment, his funds were exhausted, and it became absolutely necessary for him to do something. He had offers from several minor clubs, to whom he would still have been a valuable player, but on asking for his release from Buffalo it was again refused. He was compelled to remain idle all that summer, without funds to pay for medical treatment; and then, to crown all, the Buffalo Club again reserved him in the fall of 1884.

The second abuse was a clear violation of the spirit of the rule, and a direct breach of contract on the part of several clubs. A clause in the old form of contract gave the club the right to release any player at any time, with or without cause, by giving him twenty days' notice. Of course this was meant to apply to individual cases and total releases. But several clubs, seeing in this a convenient means of escaping the payment of the last month's salary, gave all their players the twenty days' notice on September 10 and on October 1 dismissed them, instead of on November 1 as the contracts stipulated. One club did not even go to the trouble of giving notice, but, in open disregard of its contract obligations, dismissed its players October 1. Two of the men had courage enough to bring suit, and they recovered judgment, and finally got their full pay; but the others lost the month's wages. But now, the most extraordinary part of all, after formally *releasing* the men, the same clubs claimed and were conceded the right of reserving them for the following year.

The third step was of a more serious nature; for, though no violation of contract, it was the beginning of the present odious system of buying and selling players. As the pecuniary returns of the game increased, the value of the individual player was enhanced: the strength or weakness of one position made a difference of thousands in receipts, and this set the astute managerial mind to work. Some scheme must be devised by which these gaps might be filled. It finally dawned upon him that this continuing claim upon the player's services was much akin to a right of property. Why, then, might this not be bought and sold, as are other rights of a similar nature?

Having found a purchaser, it would only be necessary to obtain the player's consent and the sale might be made. The result was a series of deals by which players were disposed of in this manner. Since the player's consent was obtained, it may be said that he was in no wise injured; but there were really two serious dangers. The first was that the club would be tempted to force the player's consent in one of the many ways at its disposal,—which, in fact, was frequently the case; and the second was in the part which the reserve-rule played in the transaction. If the buying club received a claim for the remaining term of the player's *contract* only, the price would be regulated accordingly and the deal perfectly legitimate. But a fictitious value was always given, because the buying club bought not only the player's services for the unexpired term of his contract, but the right to reserve or sell him again. It is not, then, the ordinary assignment of a legal contract-claim for future service which makes the price, but the anticipated operation of the reserve-rule. The rule is, therefore, being used not as a means of *retaining* the services of a player, but for increasing his value for the purpose of sale. This is a clear perversion of the original intent of the rule. The assertion of any such claim at the time of its adoption would have killed it then and there. The clubs claimed that the right to retain the services of a valuable player was necessary for the conservation of the game, and with that understanding the players tacitly acquiesced in the seizure. They never received any consideration for the concession;

and when the Chicago Club sells Kelly for ten thousand dollars it simply makes that sum out of Kelly, for which it has never given him the slightest consideration. Kelly received his salary from Chicago (or such part as was not taken out in fines), and earned every dollar of it several times over, and yet the Chicago Club takes ten thousand dollars for releasing Kelly from a claim for which it never paid him a dollar, but which it acquired by seizure some years ago.

Abuse number four is another step in the development of this traffic, in that it ignores entirely the player's consent, and the deal is completed without the slightest consultation of his wishes or interests. The selling club first secures the promise of the six clubs not immediately interested to keep hands off the player. The price being then paid by the buying club, the player is notified of his release to that club. By the pledge secured from the other clubs, none of them will employ him, and therefore, no matter how distasteful the change, or how many the reasons for wishing to go elsewhere, he is forced to go to his purchaser or nowhere.

Number five is a further extension of the scope of the reserve-rule, and cuts off entirely the player's only hope for escape. One would naturally suppose that the disbandment of the club with which he was under contract would release the player from all restrictions; and such was indeed the case until within the last year. But with the expected retirement of the St. Louis and Kansas City Clubs a number of first-class players would be thrown upon the market who would command good salaries if left to contract freely for themselves. The avarice of the clubs was equal to the occasion, and the League itself (whatever that may mean) reserved these men and peddled them out at so much per head. Without any regard to the fact that family ties and other considerations bound them to particular localities, the players were disposed of at the will of the League here, there, or anywhere it saw fit, and through the same organized conspiracy were obliged to go as assigned or quit playing ball altogether. The player read in his morning paper that he had been sold to such a club, and in a short time, though the question of terms had not yet been mentioned, he received a notification to report on a certain date. This was all he knew or had to say about the matter. The price demanded by the League for several of these players was more than any club was willing to pay. For instance, in the case of McQuery the amount asked was one thousand dollars, afterwards reduced to seven hundred and fifty dollars. No club being found willing to pay so much, he was held until the 19th of April before being allowed to sign with any club. Though a good player, he was kept out of an engagement, received no salary, lost his opportunities for signing with some League or Association club, and finally was very fortunate to contract with a club of the International League.

The crowning outrage of all came in the shape of a resolution adopted by the American Association at its Cleveland meeting last spring. Though not a League measure, I mention it as showing the spirit of the clubs and the possibilities of the reserve-rule. Not satisfied with the passive conspiracy not to hire a reserved player if he refused to sign with the reserving club, the Association actually declared its intention of black-listing him. For the mere refusal to sign upon the terms offered by the club, the player was to be debarred entirely, and his name placed among those disqualified because of dissipation and dishonesty! Has any body of sane men ever before publicly committed itself to so outrageous a proposition? Fortunately for the dignity of the Association and the interests of the game, no attempt has ever been made to enforce this penalty; if it had, it is just possible that the great reserve-rule might now exist only in the game's history and in the records of the courts.

The last step, which may scarcely be called a development—being rather a natural consequence of the system,—is the practice of "loaning" players. A man is loaned by one club to another on condition that the latter pays his salary and returns him on demand, much the same as a horse is put out to work for his feed.

These are, in part, the relations which exist between base-ball players and the associations by which they are employed. Is there a base-ball official who will claim them to be governed by any semblance of equity? Is it surprising that players begin to protest, and think it necessary to combine for mutual protection?

Encouraged by the apparent inactivity of the players, the clubs have gone on from one usurpation to another until in the eye of the base-ball "magnate" the player has become a mere chattel. He goes where he is sent, takes what is given him, and thanks the Lord for life. The demand exceeding the supply, the growth and cultivation of young players has become an important branch of the business. They are signed in large numbers, and, if they turn out well, are disposed of as a valuable commodity to the highest bidder. If they fail, they are simply released, and the cultivator has been at little expense. Indeed, the whole thing is becoming systematized, and is carried on with the utmost openness; so that it is not unusual to find a news paragraph announcing that such and such players are for sale.

In order to learn the sentiment of some League officials on this point, I approached Mr. John I. Rogers, of the Philadelphia Club. Mr. Rogers is a gentleman of superior intelligence and legal ability, and I was therefore not surprised to find him a rather weak supporter of the system. He freely admitted the injustice of selling a player without the latter's consent, and did not think the League had any right to reserve and sell the players of a disbanding club. He did claim, however, that a club had a right, with the player's consent, to sell its claim upon his future services, for in so doing he declared that the club was simply "compounding the value of those future services."

I have pondered a great deal over out short talk, and I think I know what Mr. Rogers meant by that specious phrase. He meant that a club which has a legal claim *by contract* upon the future service of a player may accept a cash consideration for the release of that claim at any time before the expiration of the term of contract; and in that I agree with him perfectly. I am sure he did *not* mean that a club may sell its claim on the future service of a player when that claim rests not on a legal contract, but simply on the reserve-rule. For such a purpose that rule never gave a claim. It invested the club with a questionable right of reservation for one purpose only,—namely, to retain the services of the player; not at all to sell him. The true consideration in such a sale is not the release of the claim, but the future service of the player. It proceeds, therefore, not from the selling club, but from the player; yet the former takes the cash. Every dollar received by the club in such a transaction is taken from the pocket of the player; for if the buying club could afford to pay that sum as a bonus, it could just as well have paid it to the player in the form of increased salary. The whole thing is a conspiracy, pure and simple, on the part of the clubs, by which they are making money rightfully belonging to the players. Even were we to admit, for the sake of argument, that the reserve-rule does give a right to sell, we naturally ask, What consideration did the club ever advance to the player for this right? What did the Chicago Club ever give Kelly in return for the right to control his future services? Absolutely nothing; and yet that club sells that right, so cheaply acquired, for ten thousand dollars! But, I repeat, it never gave such a right, and any such claim by one set of men of a right of property in another is as unnatural to-day as it was a quarter a century ago. The rule is a special statute of "base-ball law," made for a special purpose; it is of doubtful right when confined to that purpose, and it is of certain and unqualified wrong when applied to any other.

In the case of a sale with the player's consent at a time when he is under contract, the case is complicated. The club may properly sell its contract-claim, but in every such case the same wrongful element will be found to enter. The buying club pays a much larger price than the contract-claim is worth, because it expects to acquire also the right to reserve or sell. The case, analyzed, is this: the amount actually paid for the contract-claim is rightfully given, while every dollar in excess is taken from the player through the wrongful operation of the reserve-rule.

The remedy for these abuses may be difficult to find; the system has become so rooted that heroic treatment may be necessary to remove it; but go it must, like every other, founded upon so great injustice and misuse of power. The only question is, Whence shall the remedy proceed? Shall it come from the clubs, or from the players, or from both conjointly? The interests of the national game are too great to be longer trifled with in such a manner, and if the clubs cannot find a way out of these difficulties the players will try to do it for them. The tangled web of legislation which now hampers the game must be cut away, and the business of base-ball made to rest on the ordinary business basis. There will be little need, then, of extra-judicial rules to regulate salaries, for these will regulate themselves, like those of the dramatic and other professions, by the law of supply and demand; "base-ball law," that wonderful creation which no one individual seems ever yet to have mastered, will be laid away as a curious relic among the archives of the game, and the time-honored and time-proven common law will once more regulate base-ball affairs; "deals" will be confined to legal limits; "phenomenons" and "wonders" will no longer receive advertising salaries, for the careful business manager will keep within justified figures; contracts may be made for periods of more than one season, the leagues will be composed of cities of nearly equal drawing strength, and the percentage system will be re-enacted, thus reducing to a minimum the temptation to compete for players; the players will catch the spirit of the new order; base-ball, to them, will be more of a business and less of a pastime; contract-breaking will be impossible, and dissipation will disappear; the profession of ball-playing will be looked upon as a perfectly honorable calling, and the national game be more than ever the greatest of out-door sports. All of these changes may never come; many of them certainly will. But it will *be* when the game is governed by the law of the land, when its financial conduct is placed in the hands of thorough business-men, when the "greats" and the "onlys," the "rustlers" and the "hustlers," have gone "down the back entry of time."

76

Francis Richter Proposes a Player Reservation System for the Minor Leagues (1887)

Source: *The Millennium Plan of The Sporting Life* (Philadelphia: Sporting Life Publishing, 1888)

In 1887 Francis Richter, the opinionated editor of Sporting Life, *proposed a reorganization of professional baseball that would give minor league clubs the same right to reserve players as that enjoyed by their major league counterparts. The following year Richter's suggestion was officially endorsed by the* NL *and the* AA. *The selection below is taken from Richter's "Millennium Plan," which originally appeared in the December 7, 1887, edition of* Sporting Life.

Complete Reservation by Minor Leagues

PERMITTING EACH MINOR LEAGUE CLUB UNDER NATIONAL AGREEMENT PROTECTION TO RESERVE AT LEAST ELEVEN MEN— A FULL TEAM—FROM SEASON TO SEASON

Argument.—Reservation by minor leagues will operate on them exactly as it does on the big leagues. It will enable the minors to keep salaries within reasonable proportions; stop the annual demoralizing chase after their young players, who, knowing their advantage, now play off competing managers against each other until, under the present insane rush for players, their salaries are forced up far beyond their real worth, with consequent stimulating effect on the salaries of the old players who, of course, are not disposed to accept less remuneration than the untried experimental material. Reservation will relieve the present hardship of starting each year over again with entirely new teams which, from their nature, are unequal, and for that reason must be experimented with all season to the detriment of the players employed who have no sense of security in their positions, and to the hurt of the big leagues which are brought into unprofitable and demoralizing competition with these minor leagues, which, knowing that to achieve success or get out of financial holes they must have winning teams, enter the market, lose their heads, and actually outbid the big leagues. Their very instability makes them reckless. They cannot count on the business from year to year as can most of the big league clubs, and therefore many of them go in to win at any cost, even that of withdrawal at the end of the season. The practical working of events under the present system was strikingly illustrated last season when in at least two of the minor leagues salaries were paid generally equal to, and in many cases exceeding, those paid in the big leagues.

Reservation must be granted the minor leagues by the big leagues as a matter of self-preservation, aside from the toning-down effect it will have on salaries. The fact that players can get as much salary in a minor league, under less severe discipline and without reservation, as they can get in a big league, where the work is continuously exacting and reservation from year to year certain, is certainly not calculated to easily land young players in big leagues or to make old players in big leagues anxious to retain their places therein, or at least indifferent thereto; and to just that extent is discipline loosened. The truth of this was illustrated during the last season when many players were made dissatisfied or indifferent by communications from old confreres who had gone into the minor leagues descriptive of the "very soft snaps" they were enjoying; and is further illustrated at the present time when we see so many players who give every indication of future greatness resolutely refusing the most flattering offers from big clubs, preferring to cast their lot with the minor leagues where the pay is nearly equal, and their work less likely to be over-shadowed. Of course, the minor leagues should not pay these excessive salaries so damaging to themselves and the entire business, but they cannot help themselves so long as they are driven into competition season after season with the big leagues. . . . Reservation will cure this evil.

77 —————————————————————————————————————

The Brush Salary Classification Plan (1888)

Source: *New York Clipper,* December 1, 1888

After the Limit Agreement of 1885 failed to curb escalating salaries, John T. Brush, owner of the Indianapolis club, proposed a plan in which players would be placed into one of five classes based upon their ability and—most troubling to the players—their personal behavior. Brush cleverly arranged for the NL to approve his plan while Brotherhood leader John Ward was engaged on the world baseball tour. When Ward learned of the plan, he returned to the United States and began planning the formation of the Players' League.

. . . The delegates next took up the salary question and decided to make a change that would regulate the players' salaries in the future. The reduction is to be done by grading the players into classes, with stated salaries for each class; and in order to insure the carrying out of the play in good faith by all parties, any violation of the rule will subject both club and player to severe penalties. The full text of the plan is shown in the amendments to the constitution adopted by the League, as follows: Amendment—. . . Section 30. Strike out and insert: "The compensation for all League players for services as players shall be limited, regulated, and determined by the classification or grade to which such players may be assigned by the secretary of the League, after the termination of the championship season, as follows: Class A, compensation $2,500; class B, compensation $2,250; class C, compensation $2,000; class D, compensation $1,750; class E, maximum compensation $1,500. But this section shall not prohibit the payment of extra compensation for the services of one person to each club, as field captain or team manager. In determining such assignment batting, fielding, base running, battery work, earnest team work, and exemplary conduct, both on and off the field, at all times shall be considered as a basis for classification. Each player upon executing a League contract shall make affidavit in form prescribed by the secretary of the League to the effect that the consideration prescribed in said contract includes all salaries, bonuses, rewards, gifts and emoluments and every other form of compensation expressly or impliedly promised him for his services as player during the term of such contract, and satisfactory proof to the secretary of the League of any false statement contained in such affidavit shall, after fair notice to such player, blacklist him, unless the ruling of the secretary be reversed by the board of directors of the League upon proper appeal, hearing and counter proof. The president of each club shall, between the 20th and 21st days of October of each year, file an affidavit with the secretary of the League setting forth the full payment as salary, bonus, reward, gift, emolument and every other form of compensation, express and implied, made to each player in full settlement of his services as player for and during the season then terminating. A violation of the limit to compensation prescribed in section 30 or any false statement in said affidavit, shall, upon satisfactory proof to the secretary of the League, subject to club to which said president belongs to a fine of $2,000 and the release of any player the subject of such illegal compensation or false statement from reservation by such club for the succeeding year, which player, however, will be retained under reservation for such other club as the League may determine. Negotiations for the release from contract or reservation and for services of players other than those of National League clubs shall be carried on exclusively through the secretary of the League or his duly authorized agent. The president, secretary or manager of a club shall file with the secretary of the League, either by letter or telegram, a written offer for the release and salary of said player. If two or more League clubs file an offer for the same player, the offer first received shall have priority of claim to such player until such negotiations fail, when the offer next in order filed shall be entitled to negotiation, and so on in sequential order with any subsequent offers, but no club shall have prior claim to any such negotiation for more than one player not under contract with it as required by another League Club. Negotiations carried on directly or indirectly with any such player except through the secretary of the League shall forfeit all right to contract with and subsequent reservation of such player by the club so offending. *Resolved*, That the amendments to sections 27, 29 and 30 be adopted, to take effect on Dec. 15, 1888, and that the limitations of players' compensation, contained in section 30, shall not apply to players with whom the several League clubs have made contractile obligation for a continuance of salaries or compensation in excess of said limitations, provided that a list of such players, with the amount of compensation so promised, accompanied by pledges against future increase thereof, be filed with the secretary of the League on or before Dec. 15, 1888, and further, that a release of such players by the clubs now entitled to their services shall exclude them from the benefits of this resolution."

78

Albert G. Spalding's Round-the-World Tour Stops in London (1889)

Source: *London Times*, March 13, 1889

Baseball team owner and sporting goods magnate Albert G. Spalding hoped that a round-the-world tour would not only promote the spread of the national pastime internationally, but also promote the sale of his merchandise. This article describes a game played on the last leg of the tour in London.

THE AMERICAN BASEBALL PLAYERS

Fifteen years ago the American national game of baseball was brought under the notice of Englishmen by the visit of teams from Philadelphia and Boston. Exhibitions were given at Prince's Ground, Belgravia, Lord's, Manchester, and other places. The popularity of the game in the United States is marvellous. In the present instance the English matches form only a part of the programme. The players comprise a selection from "All America" and the Chicago team. The party left the United States in October last and they have visited New Zealand, Australia, Ceylon, Egypt, Naples, Rome, Florence, and Paris. Yesterday they made their appearance at Kennington Oval in the presence of about 6,000 spectators. The Prince of Wales witnessed a part of the match and during an interval the players were presented to his Royal Highness. Among the company in the pavilion were also Prince Christian and his son, Prince Albert the Duke of Buccleuch (president of the Marylebone Club), Viscount Oxenbridge (president of the Surrey Club), Lord Lewisham, Lord Rowton, Sir Reginald Hanson, Dr. W. G. Grace, Mr. W. W. Read, Mr. G. J. Bonnor, Mr. Denzil Onslow, &c. Owing to the rain of the morning the turf was heavy, while a mist made the light rather bad; thus, it was not a very favourable day for the teams to give their first exhibition. The spectators appeared to take only a lukewarm interest in the play itself. To those unacquainted with the rules the frequent changes from batting to fielding were distinctly puzzling, while the indifferent light made it difficult at the football end of the ground to follow the ball. In front of the pavilion the piece of turf marked out for the game was diamond shaped.

Within a few minutes of the advertised time the players took the field, and after a little practice the game began. All America, who opened the contest, wore white entirely; while the Chicago men were dressed in gray and black. Baldwin was the Chicago pitcher. Hanlon, Ward, and Brown, the first three on the batting order, were quickly put out, none of them reaching the first base. Healy pitched for America. Ryan scored the first run for Chicago, while a capital hit by Pfeffer enabled Sullivan to obtain a second, and the opening innings ended with an advantage of two runs to Chicago. America did much better at their second attempt. Carroll and Wood both got away, and a vigorous hit by Fogarty enabled them each to complete the round. Fogarty and Manning also scored, and when the innings closed All America had a lead of two runs. After the whole of the players had given several hearty cheers for the Prince of Wales, who just then arrived, the game proceeded. Neither side scored in the next three innings, and at the interval Chicago were still a couple of runs behind. On resuming Manning, Earle, and Fogarty, of America, were put out in succession. In their sixth innings, the Chicago men showed fine form with the bat. Anson made a three-base hit on the right— distinctly the best hit of the afternoon, and which aroused for the first time a little cheering. Another good stroke by Pfeffer enabled him also to cover three bases, and Anson reached home. Misfielding by both pitcher and catcher gave Tener his first base, and enabled Pfeffer to equalize matters. Thus the score was "four all." The figures were unaltered at the end of the seventh innings. America did not improve their position at the eighth attempt, but, on the other hand, there was capital hitting by several of the Chicago men. Anson led off with a three-base hit, while a good stroke by Pfeffer allowed him to get home. The last-named and Tener both scored, after which the disposal of Burns, Baldwin, and Pettitt terminated the innings. America again failed, and Chicago being in a majority of three points did not go in again. Thus Chicago won by seven runs to four. The fielding of both sides was very brilliant and the runners indulged in plenty of sliding on the greasy turf. In the batting department the form was rather disappointing and failed altogether to arouse any general enthusiasm. To-day there is to be a game at Lord's, while Thursday and Saturday are set apart for matches at the Crystal Palace and Leyton.

79

Celebration of the Conclusion
of the Great Tour (1889)

Source: *New York Clipper*, April 13, 1889

Although Spalding's round-the-world tour converted few foreigners to baseball, it cap-
tured the imagination of fans in the United States. At the conclusion of the trip a huge
celebration was held in New York City. Among those present were actor DeWolf Hopper,
who recited "Casey at the Bat," and Mark Twain. Perhaps inspired by Twain's oratory,
master of ceremonies Abraham G. Mills told the audience that "patriotism and research
had established the fact that the game . . . was American in its origin." According to the
Clipper, "this stimulated staccato cries from some of the feasters of 'no rounders,' and the
English claim that America's national game was prehistorically the English game of
'rounders' was forever squelched."

The party left San Francisco, California, Nov. 18 last, and arrived in New York April
6. After dinner the tourists, or most of them, went over to Brooklyn in carriages to
witness the game between the New York and Brooklyn teams. In the evening the
players and many friends occupied six of the eight boxes at Palmer's Theatre. The
house was so full that a new sign had to be put on the front of the theatre:
"Positively no more money taken tonight." Not even admission tickets were sold at
the box office. The boxes were decorated with flags, and from the proscenium arch
hung an emblem of flags of all nations, with a gilt eagle and a shield with crossed
bats, a pair of baseball gloves and a catcher's mask. Fun began when DeWolf
Hopper, coming on with his household goods under his arm, remarked, "I always
did hate this moving, and it's worse than ever this year, now that I've got to take all
the things away from the Polo Grounds." Digby Bell coming on a moment later,
informed the audience that he had "been with the boys around the world," and
alleged that his "ambition is to get something to eat and see a game of ball." This
sort of thing kept up all through "the May Queen," until in the last act DeWolf
Hopper added this to his topical song:

> Our twenty American athletes who roamed
> In climes that are foreign have now returned home.
> They've played the world over before crowds and courts,
> They've shown effete Europe the noblest of sports,
> They've shown the old foreigners how to have fun
> With the mystical curve and the lively home run,
> And now let's greet them with our main and might.

Then he went to the wing and marched back with a campaign transparency
inscribed "Welcome Home, Boys" and, striding across the stage, sang the last line:
"Do you catch on? If you do it's all right."

A glass of beer was handed him as he reached the other side of the stage, and he blew the foam off, and waving it toward the boys in the boxes, remarked, as he drank, "Here you are, fellows." That completely upset the house, and it was some moments before he could get a hearing again, to remark dryly as he rubbed imaginary foam from his lips: "I always did like that verse." Then he said a few sentences appropriate to the occasion, and started to recite "Casey's at the Bat." This pleased the audience still more, and when he was done they insisted on having more. "Sa-ay, I'm a Henglishman, y'know; rounders beats base ball. Don't ask me to sing any more about it." The applause still continuing, he advanced to the footlights as in a burst of confidence, and when everyone was quiet, remarked, in his driest tones: "Don't fail to see the game in Brooklyn Monday. I'm going to umpire." There were repeated calls during the evening for Anson and Ward, but neither responded, although both were in the house. . . .

WORDS OF WELCOME

At 10 o'clock A. G. Mills called the diners to order, and announced that the speechmaking of the evening was in order. Before announcing the toasts, he read letters of regret from Gov. Hill, Gov. Bulkeley, of Connecticut, and H. P. Carter, the Hawaiian Minister. He also read a letter from Mayor Grant. When Mr. Mills had finished reading the letters, he said that every type of manly sport was represented in the gathering before him. But they were there to pay particular tribute to the great game and some of its most celebrated exponents. It was truly the national game, and Mr. Spalding and his men had given it world wide reputation. Mr. Mills wanted it distinctly understood by his audience that patriotism and research had established the fact that the game which develops the lungs of the spectators, more than any other in the annals of the world's sports, was American in its origin. This stimulated staccato cries from some of the feasters of "no rounders," and the English claim that America's national game was prehistorically the English game of "rounders" was forever squelched. Then Mr. Mills paid a blooming and resonant tribute to Mr. Spalding, and said it had been left to him to evolve the scheme of taking the baseballists around the world, a feat in pluck unparalleled in the history of athletics. The boys were not only star baseball players, but they were, in every sense, representatives of American manhood and citizenship.

Mayor Chapin of Brooklyn was introduced as the representative of a city that was possibly the birthplace of baseball and he was gloriously cheered. He had not played the game in twenty-five years. Just about that time he discovered that baseball was not his mission in life. He had sought his livelihood in an easier and less dangerous game.

Mayor Cleveland of Jersey City gave his welcome for the 200,000 Jersey City-ites, and then the health of A. G. Spalding was drunk standing, the band coming in with "Hail to the Chief."

Mr. A. G. Spalding was enthusiastically greeted. He said he felt lost among so many gifted orators, but he did very well, as he proceeded to give an epitome of the famous tour. It had all been told at length, he added, by the newspapers whose enterprise had sent correspondents with them around the world. The trip was a success, he said, and much of the success was due to the business manager, Mr. Leigh Lynch.

They had twenty-eight banquets in twenty-four days in Australia, and still lived.

Mr. Spalding closed by touching on the joy of the boys on getting home and the cheerful reception give them down the bay at four o'clock last Saturday morning. They had gone away Americans and had come back better ones, and Mr. Spalding wished he were a Depew or a Dougherty so that he might tell his gratitude for this reception and banquet.

Capt. Anson, of the Chicagos, was then introduced as "the greatest general of the ball field." He remarked: "They say I have pretty good qualities for kicking, and, if I could kick out of making any remarks here I would do so. I believe this is the proudest moment of my life. I am proud of having been captain of one of the teams, and I am proud of the manner in which we have been received abroad, and the kind patronage we have received. We are sorry that we have not with us our associate, Ed. Williamson, whom everybody loves, and whom we were obliged to leave abroad."

Capt. John Montgomery Ward, of the All Americas, was called upon as a skillful ballplayer, an accomplished writer, and a man who has added dignity to the profession. He said: "We are about to complete a delightful trip and a delightful experience and I assure you we have seen it in first class style. In Honolulu, in New Zealand, in Australia, in France and England, and, in fact, in every country we have visited, we have received cordial hospitality."

Mr. Mills called upon Mr. Leigh A. Lynch, the business manager of the tour, to say a few words, and Mr. Lynch amused the boys very much with reference to the untold part of the trip.

A letter from H. A. P. Carter, the Hawaiian Minister, was read by Mr. Spalding. It expressed the utmost good feeling for the American ball players.

"Mark Twain" was introduced as a native of the Sandwich Islands. In the course of a witty speech he said: "Yes, and I would envy them somewhat of the glories they have achieved in their illustrious march about the mighty circumferance of the earth, if it were fair; but, no, it was an earned run, and envy would be out of place. I will rather applaud—add my hail and welcome to the vast shout now going up from Maine to the Gulf, from the Florida Keys to frozen Alaska, out of the throats of the other 65,000,000 of their countrymen. They have carried the American name to the uttermost parts of the earth, and covered it with glory every time. That is a service to sentiment; but they did the general world a large practical service, also, a service to the great science of geography. Ah, think of that! We don't talk enough about that—don't give it its full value. Why, when these boys started out you couldn't see the equator at all; you could walk right over it and never know it was there. That is the kind of equator it was. Such an equator as that isn't any use to anybody; as for me, I would rather not have any equator at all, than a dim thing like that, you can't see. But that is all fixed now; you can see it now; you can't run over it now and not know it's there; and so I drink long life to the boys who ploughed a new equator round the globe stealing bases on their bellies!"

Mr. Spalding read a letter from Senator Cantor announcing the passage of the Polo Grounds bill, and the boys cheered again and again.

80

Player Strike by Louisville Players (1889)

Source: *Louisville Courier-Journal*, June 15, 1889

In the midst of the 1889 season, Louisville owner Mordecai Davidson appointed himself field manager. His Draconian measures in disciplining his players resulted in a one-day strike in Baltimore. Immediately afterward the strikers formed the first chapter of the Brotherhood in the American Association, but when tensions eased the chapter was dissolved. By this time Davidson had been forced to sell the franchise to the AA, which forgave most of the fines he had levied.

IN A NEW ROLE

Members of the Louisville Base Ball Club Strike On Their President-Manager
Davidson Fined Cook and Shannon and the Others Took Up Their Fight
An Unsuccessful Round Robin From the Players
Brought Threats of More Fines
Amateurs Supplant Three Strikers, and Rain
Prevents the Baltimore–Louisville Game

EVEN A WORM WILL TURN, ETC.

Baltimore, June 14.—(Special.)—Quite a little sensation was created in this city to-day among the patrons of baseball by the announcement that the players of the Louisville club intended to refuse to play the game which they were scheduled to play with Baltimore this afternoon, or to go to the grounds. In other words they had "struck" on account of heavy fines imposed on two members of the team by Manager Davidson for bad playing in Thursday's game and brought to a climax by his emphatic refusal to remit the fines. The public generally in this city, and the local players, sympathize with the Louisville men in the affair, but consider that they have acted thoughtlessly and hastily. Manager Davidson was in New York to-day, and, of course, has taken no action in the matter as yet.

The story of the trouble is as follows: On Thursday night Manager Davidson fined Second-baseman Shannon $25 for a fumble and a disastrous wild throw, and Cook also got $25 for stupid base-running. Shannon's general playing in that game was very good, and one of his plays was the most brilliant of the game, which abounded in good points. It was a one-handed jumping catch of a hard hit liner by which he made a double play and retired the side when the Baltimores appeared certain to score. Cook's fault was not a great one, and was as much due to bad coaching as to his own faulty judgment.

When the Louisville club returned to Pepper's Hotel, where they were staying, there was trouble in the camp. The fines were imposed and Raymond narrowly escaped a similar assessment. The players held a consultation and drew up a "round robin" signed by all of the players except one, asking for the remission of the fines. A prompt refusal followed, and in the storm of indignation, while Manager Davidson was waiting for a train for New York, the players rehearsed their grievances and soon informed Mr. Davidson, with all the emphasis they could add to it, that if the fines were not remitted there would be no Louisville–Baltimore game on Friday, for their club would not even go to the grounds. Both sides were wrought up to a high degree of excitement, the manager smarting under the storm of satire and ridicule from the press which has everywhere assailed him, and the players feeling acutely the injustice which they considered the manager had displayed. Davidson, unfortunately, met angry and resolute men with stern measures, and instead of pacifying them, tried to frighten them. Instead of remitting the fine he told them sharply that if they lost to-day's, Friday's game he would fine every man on the playing team $25 each, and that if they refused to play he would fine each of them $100.

With this exchange of threats Manager Davidson left the men and took the train for New York. This morning all the players seemed determined not to go to the grounds. They had notified President Wykoff of the situation, and in answer to their friends in this city who inquired of them what they were going to do, answered that they were all going swimming this afternoon, either at the Ferry bar or at the Natatorium. Capt. Wolf and a few of the cooler heads thought better of the case as the day wore on, and Ramsey, Vaughn, Wolf, Weaver, Stratton and Gleason consented to play. There are always a few semiprofessionals lounging around base ball centers here, and three of them were engaged for the day to don Louisville uniforms and play with that team. Their names are Mike Gaul, John Traffley and Charles Fisher. The other Louisville players held to their original resolution. The game commenced at the regular time, Ramsey pitching and the three volunteers in the outfield. Ramsey was batted all over the field for two innings, the Baltimores making five runs to the Louisvilles none, when a heavy, long shower put an end to the game.

Nothing was heard from President Wykoff by the players, in answer to their dispatches. Umpire Gaffney tried Thursday to pacify the men, but without avail. Hecker described the situation to-night to the correspondent as follows: "When we got to Columbus Ehret and Vaughn had hard luck. Ehret had a wild pitch or two. Vaughn had one or two passed balls for which Davidson fined them each $25. But the fact is that if each had played perfectly they could not have won. While we were at the depot there, Browning, Raymond and Wolf became involved in a quarrel. One word brought on another and Wolf finally, called Browning a vile name, although my wife was in hearing. Raymond interfered, and Davidson coming up, fined all three $25 each. On the way to Philadelphia on the cars Davidson remarked, 'Some fellow will be unfortunate enough in Philadelphia to make errors, and they will cost him $25 or $50 more.' To-morrow," continued Hecker, "will be one month and two pay days since we received our salaries. In Brooklyn Davidson fined Browning $100, but he deserved that, and not long ago Mr. Davidson said to us, 'I expect to get about $1,000 of your salaries on this trip.' Several men have already been fined. Davidson has been offered $7,500 for the club, but wants $9,000. What we need is somebody to lead us. We don't know what a sacrifice hit is by this time."

The striking players are Hecker, Browning, Shannon, Raymond, Ehret and Cook. They are acting very quietly, but appear very determined and look to the American Association for a remedy for their troubles.

81

A Controversial Game in Brooklyn (1889)

Source: *Brooklyn Eagle*, September 8, 1889

Late in the AA pennant race of 1889, the second-place St. Louis Browns met the league-leading Brooklyn Bridegrooms. Holding a 4–2 lead in the eighth inning, the Browns started to stall, hoping that the umpire would call the game on account of darkness. When this tactic failed, the Browns left the field and the umpire awarded the game to Brooklyn. Brooklyn subsequently won the Association pennant by two games. This account from the Brooklyn Eagle *vividly describes the crowd and its behavior. Notice the presence of women, an overflow crowd permitted to stand in a roped-off section of the outfield, and an activity surprisingly similar to "the wave" of the 1980s and 1990s.*

FORFEITED BY ST. LOUIS

A Game Which Proved a Disgraceful Exhibition
Brooklyn's Rivals Left the Field Before the End of Yesterday's Contest,
and Have to Endure a Score of 9 to 0—New York and Boston Win—
The Record to Date

Not in the history of professional ball playing in this city has the game received such a blow to its continued favor with the best patrons of the national game as was given it yesterday at Washington Park at the hands of the St. Louis Club players and the club's president, the latter of whom sat on the bench and aided and abetted Captain Comiskey and his gang in their ball playing tricks on the field and in their bold and impudent exhibition of the bulldozing work through which they have gained so many of their victories this season. Hundreds were present yesterday who, on witnessing the disgraceful conduct of the visiting team in the closing part of the contest, declared that if that was professional ball playing they would have nothing to do with it.

Everything went on with comparative quiet, despite some disreputable tricks the visiting team resorted to, until the sixth inning, and, when that had ended, with the St. Louis team one run ahead, then did the bully captain of the gang and his lieutenants begin to resort to the ways which had won them victories at home time and again. They entered upon a line of tactics to delay the game which the umpire was made powerless to prevent, simply because every fine inflicted was paid by the club, and the penalty was therefore completely nullified, and the umpire rendered helpless to enforce the rules. But at last his patience gave out, and when he refused to acquiesce in their impudent demand that he call the game on account of darkness, and that, too, before sundown, and they took up their bats and left the field, they insultingly ignoring his decision, he very properly, and under a legal interpretation of the constitutional laws of the association, decided the game forfeited to the Brooklyn Club by a score of 9 to 0, and with the added penalty of a $1,500 fine for leaving the ground before the legal close of the contest, and this amount the "boss manager" will have to pay out of his own pocket.

Never before have the Brooklyn team met with so hearty and enthusiastic a reception as they did when they marched on the field to engage in their preliminary practice. The St. Louis players had preceded them, and as they went on the field only a slight reception was given the champions compared to that they met with last Spring on the same field.

Everything was propitious for a grand contest. The weather was all that could have been desired, and as for the attendance it exceeded in numbers and surpassed in character every previous gathering seen on the grounds, except on a holiday occasion. Not a seat was at command at 3 P.M., and at the hour for calling play standing room was at a premium, over fifteen thousand people being within the inclosure. An extra force of police were on hand in case of an emergency, but their services were not needed, except when the crowd inadvertently rushed on the field in the seventh inning. The attendance of ladies was so large that the overflow of the fair sex had to find seats on the bleaching boards. The outfield was inclosed by a roped boundary and a cordon of police kept the crowd from encroaching. In fact everything was done by President Byrne to afford the contestants a fair field under the circumstance of so vast an assemblage of spectators. By 4 P.M. seats on the edge of the fence were sought for until a fringe of people encircled the grounds.

THE GAME

. . . In the sixth inning fungo hits to the outfield disposed of the first two batsmen and Clark's foul fly ended the inning. On the other side O'Neill opened with a safe bounder to center. On Comiskey's sacrifice the runner was forwarded, and Robinson's safe bounder to center sent O'Neill home, thereby tying the score. Fuller's two bagger to left field then sent Robinson home with the leading run, and then Milligan ended the inning, leaving St. Louis in the van by 3 to 2. Now came the tug of war as Brooklyn went in to their seventh inning at 5:40 P.M. with a cloudy atmosphere, but the sun still well up in the west. Caruthers opened at the bat and after two balls had been called a strike was declared, on which Caruthers threw up his arms as if the decision was an outrage. The next ball nearly hit him, and as he went to the base on balls Milligan did the kicking act. The St. Louis captain now began his bulldozing tactics to delay the game into darkness and kept up arguments on the subject with the umpire, despite fines, for delay. Smith then went to the bat and he purposely got in the way of a pitched ball and ran to first. Another delay occurred on this discussion, the Brooklyns playing into Comiskey's hands in this inning. Then Smith made an effort to balk the catcher and a third argument delayed the game still further. This was just as objectionable as the St. Louis tricks. It was now 5:50 P.M. and the umpire noted the time and got ready to call the game in case Comiskey did not resume play promptly. With Caruthers on third and one man out O'Brien came to the bat, but after two strikes he fouled out to Latham. Collins now came to the bat, and he hit apparently safe to center field, but Duffee made a wonderful catch and a blank was drawn. Comiskey had thus far successfully worked his tactics of delay, and he intended to win the game by it. The eighth inning was then played with the result of blanks to both sides, and once more Comiskey and his gang tried to bulldoze the umpire. But he adhered to his determination to have the game played out as long as he himself could see the ball. Despite over half an hour's intentional delay by the visitors, it was only 6:18 P.M. when the Brooklyns went to the bat in their ninth inning, and when Smith reached base on an error by Milligan, Comiskey called his men in, who took up the bats and marched off the field, to the disgust of every impartial spectator on the field, he contemptuously disregarding the umpire's call to the St. Louis field to play ball. Goldsmith took his watch, waited the legal time, and, the St. Louis players not returning, he then and there gave the game to Brooklyn as forfeited by 9 to 0, and with this decision goes all bets, as also the penalty of the $1,500 fine which the St. Louis Club must pay to Brooklyn. Here is the score of the game:

BROOKLYN	R	1B	PO	A	E		ST. LOUIS	R	1B	PO	A	E
O'Brien, l. f.	1	1	1	0	1		Latham, 3b.	1	2	3	2	0
Collins, 2b.	1	1	4	2	2		McCarthy, r. f.	0	0	3	1	1
Foutz, 1b.	0	2	12	1	0		O'Neill, l. f.	1	2	1	0	0
Burns, r. f.	0	0	1	0	0		Comiskey, 1b.	0	0	4	0	0
Pinkney, 3b.	0	1	1	2	0		Robinson, 2b.	1	1	0	2	1
Corkhill, c. f.	0	0	0	0	0		Duffee, c. f.	1	1	3	0	1
Clark, c.	0	1	4	3	0		Fuller, s. s.	0	1	3	1	1
Caruthers, p.	0	0	0	4	0		Milligan, c.	0	2	7	1	0
Smith, s. s.	0	0	0	2	0		Chamb'l'in, p.	0	1	0	1	0
Total	2	6	24	15*	3		Total	4	10	24	8	4

	1	2	3	4	5	6	7	8	
Brooklyn	2	0	0	0	0	0	0	0	—2
St. Louis	0	0	0	0	1	2	1	0	—4

*Error in original; should be 14.—Ed.

Earned runs—Brooklyn, 1; St. Louis, 2. First base by errors—Brooklyn, 4; St. Louis, 1. Battery errors—Brooklyn, 1; St. Louis, 5. Left on bases—Brooklyn, 8; St. Louis, 6. Stolen bases—Brooklyn, 4; St. Louis, 2. Total bases—Brooklyn, 7; St. Louis, 13. Struck out—Brooklyn, 3; St. Louis, 3. Chances for catches—Brooklyn, 12; St. Louis, 6. Sacrifice hits—Brooklyn, 1; St. Louis, 3. Double play—St. Louis, 1. Runs batted in by safe hits—Collins, 1; Foutz, 1; Milligan, 1; Robinson, 1; Fuller, 1. Bases on balls—By Chamberlain, 3. Passed balls—Clark, 1; Milligan, 2. The game ended at 6:18 P.M. Attendance—15,143. Umpire—Goldsmith. Time of game—2 hours and 25 minutes.

SCENES AND INCIDENTS

It would take the pen of a Dickens or a Collins to describe the scenes and incidents of yesterday's contest. Nothing like it has ever been seen in this vicinity, and there was more excitement to the square inch than ever seen before. People hereabouts, aware of the importance of the three games of the series, began passing through the gates at an early hour, and by 3:30 o'clock even standing room could not be obtained on the grand stand. In fact not another person could get anywhere near the little box office leading to the reserved seats. The bleacheries were black with people and on the pathways surrounding these seats the people were jammed together in one immovable mass, and the only time they could gather themselves together was when the excitement got the best of them and everybody was forced to throw up their hands and were compelled to sway about like a wave on the ocean from the irresistible and frenzied throng. The banks back of the fielders were littered with a multitude, and even on the high fences venturesome enthusiasts perched themselves on a precarious and dangerous footing. The rays of the sun, when not obscured by the threatening clouds, poured down on the sweltering mass with terrible intensity, and the crowd shed their coats and vests, but the perspiration still poured from them like small rivers. The excitement as the game progressed, made it worse for them, for they shouted, yelled, stamped and acted in a general way like mad men till they were utterly exhausted.

No words can describe the scenes and excitement which prevailed throughout. Imagine nearly sixteen thousand people worked up by the appeal of one of the Brooklyn players, who wrote to the EAGLE some time ago beseeching the home patrons to "root" for their success. They came there to do it, and it is safe to say that if some of the spectators, the majority of whom were staid, dignified and phlegmatic citizens, could have a slight idea of the manner in which they acted, frenzied by the outrageous actions of the St. Louis team, they would utterly refuse to believe how they behaved.

When the Western players marched off the field they were the recipients of such hooting, cat calls, hisses and adjectives not nice to print that it made them look around in alarm, and it is safe to say that they will never forget the scene, nor will their ears stop tingling for some time with the volume of sound which met them.

An amusing incident happened at this point of the game. One of the waiters, back of the third base line, with a tray loaded with glasses of beer, became so enthused that he forgot himself, with disastrous results. He leaned out over the railing and evidently wished to clap his hands in approval of the runs scored. The tray fell to the ground below the stand, the glasses were smashed to pieces and he was out of pocket for a pretty penny. This made the crowd yell with ghoulish glee and amused them while Comiskey brought in his original mule play. Latham was spiked at this juncture and another delay ensued.

When Latham went in for St. Louis he showed the effects of his injury. After unsuccessfully trying to bunt the sphere he mumbled to himself, walked around the home plate like a chicken with its head cut off and then tried again. Pinkney's fumble enabled him to reach the initial bag, but Clark's deadly throw to second rendered him hors de combat. How the crowd did guy him! McCarthy, one of the worst ruffians on the field, then tried his kicking propensities on Goldsmith, but without avail. When he came in hissing and indescribable shouts which greeted him, and which must have convinced anyone but one of his caliber how detestable he was held in the spectators' opinion, went up from the multitude. He did not mind it, apparently, for with an air of sang froid he lifted his cap and smiled his approval.

In the second inning Chamberlain showed his qualities as a pitcher by striking out Clark, Smith and O'Brien on his curves. But Caruthers followed him in just as good work, retiring three heavy hitting Missourians on his drop curve balls. For fully three minutes the air resounded with deafening applause for Bob, and he looked proud. The Brooklyn team had several opportunities to score after this point, but by some stupid base running or bad coaching and a lack of a little hit they could not make another run.

Latham, the clown, who always caused unlimited merriment by his antics and hippodromes, did not begin his funny tricks until the sixth inning, when the St. Louis team had scored. He woke up then and made the spectators laugh at his witty sayings and repartee. At one time, while at the bat, he yelled to McGunnigle, the Brooklyn manager, who was showing signs of nervousness, to stop pulling his moustache and not to hoodoo him. Again, just as O'Neill was about to meet a ball, he said: "Oh! look at that hit," and the remark was well timed, too, for the left fielder cracked out a ball which enabled one of his fellow players to cross the plate. When the Missourians tied the score he turned flipflaps, stood on his hands and rolled over the ground in a perfect paroxysm of delight. Of course, the spectators looked distressed, but they had to laugh at the clown's antics nevertheless.

At the end of the eighth inning the St. Louis players on the bench, reinforced by two or three of their followers, took out a few tallow candles and lit them. They evidently thought that they had the game well in hand and were holding a wake over the Brooklyn corpse. They grew hilarious over the scene and it required Manager McGunnigle and a policeman to remove the St. Louis men who were on the bench.

The scene when Umpire Goldsmith declared the game forfeited beggared description. Cheers rent the air, mingled with hoots and derisive shouts for St. Louis.

A youth who had allowed his enthusiasm to get the better of him became involved in a quarrel with a bystander, but was arrested.

Manager McGunnigle and Tom Burns had an animated discussion on the players' bench when the latter hit a slow bounder to Comiskey and did not run on it. The St. Louis captain fumbled it, and had Burns run on the hit he would probably have reached the first bag and perhaps saved a shut out in the inning when two men were on bases.

On the elevated trains the mass of people coming home was simply terrific. It was a jostling, turbulent crowd, and a number of hats were crushed and some clothing torn. Altogether, the game will not be forgotten in some time by those who witnessed it.

Bob Ferguson, one of the association umpires, came on from Baltimore, where he was scheduled to judge yesterday's Cincinnati–Baltimore game. He sat in the press box and was an interested spectator of the contest. Ferguson evidently did not envy Goldsmith's position for the day, but was content to watch the plays.

82 ───

A Players' League Proposed (1889)

Source: *Chicago Tribune*, September 10, 1889

Throughout the 1889 season the Brotherhood secretly discussed plans for forming a new league. John Ward and Albert L. Johnson, a Cleveland streetcar magnate, provided leadership for the movement. In the following article, Tribune *reporter Frank H. Brunell, who would later become secretary and treasurer of the new Players' League, analyzes the Brotherhood's grievances and proposed remedies.*

THAT BASEBALL COMBINE

How the Johnson Scheme Looks in the Light of Recent Stories

Some of the alleged details of the plan by which Albert L. Johnson of Cleveland is to become the head of a combination of league players, members of the brotherhood, and arrayed against the league on account of the classification law and sales system, drop out from day to day. An Indianapolis ball player tells the half concealed story. It runs this way in effect:

Johnson has been working the scheme for some time. John M. Ward, president of the brotherhood, is "in" with him. Johnson is to be the head and business man of the combination. Each of the dissatisfied players is to sign a contract with him. Thus a trust is to be formed and the cream of the baseball talent to be cornered.

When the various league clubs offer their players contracts for 1890 they will be rejected. The players signed by Johnson are to be apportioned among the present league towns except Pittsburg and Indianapolis. A new national league is to be formed. Brooklyn has already been selected in place of Pittsburg, and Cincinnati is to replace Indianapolis, according to the present idea of the schemers.

THE TRIBUNE's Indianapolis correspondent writes:

"Ward seems to be acting in good faith and hopes to see the plan work out, but it is equally well known, so my informant says, that Johnson realizes that such a great scheme can never be carried through successfully, but he hopes to make something out of it by selling the release of the players back to the clubs from which they jumped, the players being given a percentage of the purchase money. The Boston, New York, Chicago, Philadelphia, and the players of all other big clubs are to be drawn into the trust, and it is said that an effort will be made to get Comiskey and several more of the prominent players of the American association into the scheme. The gentleman who gave me these facts, if they are facts, was in a position to know, and although I laughed at him and tried to show him how absurd such a move would be, he said he got his information from a source that could not be questioned. He maintained that, whether the scheme was ever carried through or not, it was now under consideration and would be attempted. Johnson left Cleveland some time in the early part of last week, and the gentleman who was in that city says that he is now in New York or Boston conferring with some of the leading brotherhood men and at the same time getting contracts with as many players as possible."

HOW THE SCHEME LOOKS

The more the story is probed the more it assumes spectral hue. Johnson is well known in baseball circles. He is a businessman of a good many interests. There is little of the visionary about him. While he might be induced to handle the Cleveland corner of the trust if there was a promise of financial success, he certainly would not handle it nationally. He also knows enough of baseball to know how slim are the chances for such a scheme being successful. The history of baseball has proven the weakness of the player on the side of self. The most acute management has usually failed to keep the members of a team under proper control. There is certainly no hope of making such a trust on the cooperative plan. The teams that lose money outnumber those making steady profits in a proportion of at least two to one. If men could be secured in each of the cities included in the plan who would back each club financially there might be a chance for success. But this would be a mere transfer of managers, as in the old Union association—a dire failure—because men who would find the money for such an enterprise would also be apt to look for a chance of some profit.

Then again, would the owners of the present league franchise be apt to stand calmly by and allow the new combination to usurp their various fields? Not at all. Certainly all the men now in league teams would not join the combination. Perhaps the places of the plotters could be filled. The American association managers, for the sake of their own preservation, would be apt to aid the league men, and out of the opposition teams in the various cities occupied by the combination a ruinous fight would ensue, with the chances against the Johnson–Ward teams. In New York, Chicago, Boston, and Philadelphia the fight would certainly be made on these lines and with these chances. A glance at the scheme as it is said to stand today gives one the "bluff" idea.

AN OLD PROJECT

The outlines of the plan are not new. Two years ago a similar project was talked of in brotherhood quarters. John Ward was behind it and Erastus Wiman of New York, who then owned the Metropolitan franchise in the American association, was put into the exalted position now occupied, by A. L. Johnson. Mr. Wiman has since said that such a plan was laid before him, but that he did not embrace it or take nearly as much interest as did "the mysterious capitalist," so much talked about by Mr. Ward and his confrères. It was a "bluff" at the league magnates and brought to the players some concessions in the way of modifications of a cast-iron and unfair contract.

Since then a new necessity for a new "bluff" has arisen. The classification law, which aims at ultimate reduction of all salaries to $2,500 per season and less, has been at work for a season. The members of baseball stardom do not like it. From the first the stars who control the brotherhood, have used all their influence to beat it down. The Johnson play is the last device in the way of a sledgehammer on this classification law. It will be used during the winter and may serve its purpose. The classification law is likely to be modified or wiped out in any event, and no fair-minded man has any love for the sales system. If, however, the chimerical structure credited to Johnson, Ward & Co., should be reared and opened for business it will have to go on its own hook and furnish a better article of baseball than the opposition affair. There is little sympathy in the public support of baseball. The game is popular because it is flattering to local pride and is honest, clean, and sharp. Only winning teams make money for this reason. But the chances are that the Johnson–Ward scheme is a threat to the magnates who are hesitatingly considering the breaking down of the classification law and abolition of the sales system.

83

The "Brotherhood Manifesto" (1889)

Source: Elwood Roff, *Base Ball and Base Ball Players* (Chicago, 1912), pp. 86–87

The following statement released November 4, 1889, and probably written by John Ward,
summarizes the Brotherhood's position regarding the owners and their abuse of the
reserve clause. The author emphasizes that the players had made every effort to reach a
peaceful solution with the owners and were forming their own league only as a last
resort. He portrays the NL *as a monopoly "stronger than the strongest trust," which had*
to be broken.

TO THE PUBLIC:

At last the Brotherhood of Ball Players feels at liberty to make known its
intentions and to defend itself against the aspersions and misrepresentations which
for weeks it has been forced to suffer in silence. It is no longer a secret that the
players of the League have determined to play next season under different management, but for reasons which will, we think, be understood, it was deemed advisable
to make no announcement of this intention until the close of the present season;
but now that the struggles for the different pennants are over, and the terms of our
contracts expired, there is no longer reason for withholding it.

In taking this step we feel that we owe it to the public and to ourselves to explain
briefly some of the reasons by which we have been moved. There was a time when
the League stood for integrity and fair dealing; to-day it stands for dollars and
cents. Once it looked to the elevation of the game and an honest exhibition of the
sport; to-day its eyes are upon the turnstile. Men have come into the business for
no other motive than to exploit it for every dollar in sight. Measures originally
intended for the good of the game have been perverted into instruments of wrong.
The reserve rule and the provisions of the national agreement gave the managers
unlimited power, and they have not hesitated to use this in the most arbitrary and
mercenary way.

Players have been bought, sold and exchanged as though they were sheep
instead of American citizens. "Reservation" became with them another name for
proprietary right in the player. By a combination among themselves, stronger than
the strongest trust, they were able to enforce the most arbitrary measures, and the
player had either to submit or get out of the profession in which he had spent years
in attaining proficiency. Even the disbandment and retirement of a club did not
free the players from the octopus clutch, for they were then peddled around to the
highest bidder.

That the players sometimes profited by the sale has nothing to do with the case,
but only proves the injustice of his previous restraint. Two years ago we met the
League and attempted to remedy some of these evils, but, through what has been
called League "diplomacy," we completely failed. Unwilling longer to submit to

such treatment, we made a strong effort last spring to reach an understanding with the League. To our application for a hearing they replied "that the matter was not of sufficient importance to warrant a meeting," and suggested that it be put off until fall. Our committee replied that the players felt that the League had broken faith with them; that while the results might be of little importance to the managers, they were of great importance to the players; that if the League would not concede what was fair we would adopt other measures to protect ourselves; that if postponed until fall we would be separated and at the mercy of the League, and that, as the only course left us required time and labor to develop, we must therefore insist upon an immediate conference.

Then, upon their final refusal to meet us, we began organizing for ourselves and are in shape to go ahead next year under new management and new auspices. We believe it is possible to conduct our national game upon lines which will not infringe upon individual or natural rights. We ask to be judged solely upon our work, and believing that the game can be played more fairly and its business conducted more intelligently under a plan which excludes everything arbitrary and un-American, we look forward with confidence to the support of the public and the future of the national game.

NAT. BROTHERHOOD OF BALL PLAYERS

84 _____

The NL Responds to the Manifesto (1889)

Source: Albert G. Spalding, *America's National Game* (1911; reprint, Lincoln: University of Nebraska Press, 1992), pp. 273–77

When presented with the "Brotherhood Manifesto," the NL, led by Albert G. Spalding, immediately formulated a response and a strategy to combat the threat. Spalding, along with Boston magnate John Day and New York magnate John Rogers, rebutted the charges leveled in the manifesto by recounting the history of the NL from management's perspective. In Spalding's view, the owners were the saviors of the game, protecting it from the numerous offenses of willful, selfish players. In order to fulfill their mission, Spalding and his fellow owners had to stop the Brotherhood in its tracks. In their campaign to suppress the player uprising, the owners tried to influence public reaction by appealing to fears of anarchism and labor unions.

TO THE PUBLIC

The National League of Base Ball Clubs has no apology to make for its existence, or for its untarnished record of fourteen years.

It stands to-day, as it has stood during that period, sponsor for the honesty and integrity of Base Ball.

It is to this organization that the player of to-day owes the dignity of his profession and the munificent salary he is guaranteed while playing in its ranks.

The good name of this League has been assailed, its motives impugned and its integrity questioned by some of the very men whom it has most benefited.

The League therefore asks the public to inspect its record and compare the following statement of facts with the selfish and malicious accusations of its assailants:

The National League was organized in 1876 as a necessity, to rescue the game from its slough of corruption and disgrace, and take it from the hands of the ball players who had controlled and dominated the "National Association of Professional Base Ball Players."

No effort was made by the old Association to control its members, and the result was that contract-breaking, dissipation and dishonesty had undermined the game to such an extent that it seemed an almost hopeless task to attempt its rescue.

The League, upon its organization, abolished pool-selling and open betting on its grounds, prohibited Sunday games and prohibited the sale of liquors. A better class of people were invited to attend the exhibitions, and a more systematic way of conducting the game was introduced. But the old customs and abuses were not to be crowded out without a struggle. At the end of the season of 1876, two of the strongest clubs, the Mutuals, of New York, and the Athletics, of Philadelphia, were arraigned before the League for violating their scheduled engagements. This was the first crisis the League was called upon to meet, and the world knows how promptly and vigorously it faced the issue by expelling those two prominent clubs, representing, as they did, its most populous and best-paying cities. The following season, 1877, was a disastrous one financially, and ended with but five clubs in the League, in one of which, Louisville, were players publicly accused of dishonesty. The League promptly investigated these charges, and when the four players of that club—Devlin, Hall, Craver and Nichols—were proven guilty of selling games, they were promptly expelled and have never been reinstated. These two steps, boldly taken, when the League was struggling for existence, settled the question as to a club's obligations to the League, and forever banished dishonesty from the ranks, stigmatizing the latter as an unpardonable crime.

The struggle for existence for the next three or four years was desperate, and at each annual meeting there occurred vacancies difficult to fill, because of the almost certain financial disasters threatening clubs in the smaller cities.

Finally, as a check upon competition, the weaker clubs in the League demanded the privilege of reserving five players who would form the nucleus of a team for the ensuing season. This was the origin of the "reserve rule" and from its adoption may be dated the development of better financial results. The system of reserve having proven beneficial, both to clubs and players, the reserve list was increased to eleven, and then to fourteen, or an entire team. Under this rule the game has steadily grown in favor, the salaries of players have been more than trebled, and a higher degree of skill has been obtained.

Out of, and as an incident to, "reservation," arose releases for pecuniary considerations. The right of reservation being conceded, the club's claim on the player's continuous services must be of some value. But, except in cases of disbanding or retiring clubs, that right has never been transferred without the player's cooperation and consent, usually at his request, and for his own pecuniary emolument.

In the exceptional case of the disbandment or retiring of a League club, the involuntary transfer of a player to a new club was the subject of complaint by a committee of the Brotherhood, in November, 1887. But, after several hours' conference with the League Committee, the former were obliged to admit that such involuntary transfer was essential to the welfare, if not the existence, of the League, and, while it might work apparent hardships to one or two individuals, its abolition would imperil the continuance of full eight club memberships and the employment of perhaps thirty fellow players. The Brotherhood Committee, therefore, wrote into the contract they had formulated that 15th paragraph, by which each signing player expressly concedes such involuntary transfer of the right of reservation to his services from his club—if it should disband or lose its League membership—to "any other Club or Association," provided his current salary be not reduced.

And the necessity for such power of preserving the circuit of a League, by approximately equalizing its playing strength, is recognized by the new League, which the seceding players have temporarily organized; for they give this "extraordinary power" of transferring players, with or without consent, and with or without club disbandment, to a central tribunal of sixteen, whose fiat is final.

In view of those facts and concessions, the use of such terms as "bondage," "slavery," "sold like sheep," etc., becomes meaningless and absurd.

At the annual meeting of the League in November, 1887, the Brotherhood asked and received recognition upon the statement of its representatives that it was organized for benevolent purposes and desired to go hand in hand with the League, in perpetuating the game, increasing its popularity and elevating the moral standard of its players. They disavowed any intention or desire to interfere with the business affairs of the League, the salaries of players or the "reserve rule," simply asking that the contract be so revised that it, in itself, would indicate every relation between a club and its individual players.

This "Brotherhood Contract," then accepted and adopted, has never been violated by the League, either in letter or spirit, and we challenge proof in contradiction of this declaration.

To correct a misapprehension in the public mind as to the alleged "enormous profits" divided among stockholders of League clubs, it may be interesting to know that during the past five—and only prosperous—years, there have been paid in cash dividends to stockholders in the eight League clubs less than $150,000, and during the same time League players have received in salaries over $1,500,000. The balance of the profits of the few successful clubs, together with the original capital and subsequent assessments of stockholders, is represented entirely in grounds and improvements for the permanent good of the game, costing about $600,000.

The refusal of the Brotherhood Committee to meet the League in conference at the close of the season proves incontestably that the imperative demand for a conference in mid-summer, to redress grievances that have never yet materialized, was a mere pretext for secession.

They knew there was no urgency for the consideration of their claims, and knowing that the League could not, without sacrifice of time, money and other conflicting interests, convene its clubs in mid-summer, and anticipating and desiring a refusal, to cover the conspiracy, which it now appears was then hatching, they started the organization of a rival association while receiving most liberal salaries from their employers. Under false promises to their fellow players that they would only secede in the event of the League refusing them justice, they secured the signatures of the latter to a secret pledge or oath to desert their clubs at the bidding of their disaffected leaders. Upon the publication of their plot, September 7, 1889, they and their abettors denied, day after day, that there was any foundation for the story, and repeatedly plighted their words that the League should have a chance to redress their alleged grievances before they would order a "strike."

How false their promises and pledges, how evasive, contradictory and mendacious have been their every act and deed, from first to last, we leave to the readers of the daily and weekly press for verification.

An edifice built on falsehood has no moral foundation, and must perish of its own weight. Its official claims to public suport are glittering generalities, that lack detail, color and truth, and the National League, while notifying its recalcitrant players that it will aid its clubs in the enforcement of their contractual rights to the services of those players for the season of 1890, hereby proclaims to the public that the National Game, which in 1876 it rescued from destruction threatened by the dishonesty and dissipation of players, and which, by stringent rules and ironclad contracts, it developed, elevated and perpetuated into the most glorious and honorable sport on the green earth, will still, under its auspices, progress onward and upward, despite the efforts of certain overpaid players to again control it for their own aggrandizement, but to its ultimate dishonor and disintegration.

By order of the National League of Base Ball Clubs,

	A. G. SPALDING	
	JOHN B. DAY	} *Committee.*
PHILADELPHIA, November 21, 1889.	JOHN I. ROGERS,	

85

Formation of the Players' League (PL) (1889)

Source: *New York Times*, December 17, 1889

This article describes the meeting that resulted in the formation of the Players' League. Notice that the meeting attracted dozens of ball players looking for new positions. In the end, the Players' League signed nearly all of the more prominent NL players, including thirteen future Hall of Famers, to contracts for the 1890 season.

THE BALL PLAYERS MEET

A LARGE GATHERING IN THE FIFTH-AVENUE HOTEL

THE MEN ASSURED OF THEIR SALARIES BY THE ADOPTION OF A GUARANTEED PLAN YESTERDAY

Ball players with national reputations, ball players with local reputations, and ball players of all calibres, from the League star to the minor Association substitute, assembled in the corridors of the Fifth-Avenue Hotel yesterday when the Brotherhood meeting was called.

Prominent among those present were John Chapman of Syracuse, P. T. Powers of Rochester, W. W. Burnham of Worcester, Chris Von der Ahe and Congressman J. J. O'Neill of St. Louis, Thomas Daly, Brooklyn's new catcher; Agent Fullenweider of Detroit, ex-President Stearns of Detroit, Frank White, Edward Donnelly of London, Ontario; W. Collins of the Athletics, Robert Ferguson, W. W. Bunnell, and a host of others connected with the national game in all sorts of capacities.

Chris Von der Ahe, the "boss" President of the famous Browns, who has a reputation for talking German with an English accent, was the centre of attraction. He strode up and down the corridors of the hotel, and puffed away vigorously at a fragrant cigar. The situation did not appear to trouble him in the least. He chatted pleasantly, and seemed to think that the Brotherhood could not get along without his team. Von der Ahe has many followers who are of the same opinion. While St. Louis has not made a formal application for membership, it is said on excellent authority that the Players will ask the Browns to join them and drop the Pittsburg Club. In the latter city things are not as they might be, and the Brotherhood officials are seriously thinking of allowing the old League men to have full sway in the Smoky City. The genial Chris says that he wants to join the Brotherhood if for nothing else than to play in cities as an attraction against the Brooklyns and Cincinnatis. "The League people thought that they were great drawing cards," he said. "Why, my men can draw thousands to their hundreds."

Another prominent figure was that of Michael Dorgan, the old right-fielder of the Giants. He came down from his home at Syracuse to attend the meeting, and looks ruddy and years younger than he did when he was playing here. Dorgan has given up the billiard business and will be seen on the diamond once more next season. "I don't know exactly where to play," he said, "but I am entertaining several offers. I am a Brotherhood man and would like to be with the boys. Of course if that is impossible I will have to do the next best thing. I do not want to play in a minor league. I will be with the big fellows or I won't be there at all." During the day it leaked out that Left-fielder Hornung and Sam Crane had signed League contracts with the New York Club. Arthur Irwin said that he was after Hornung for a Brotherhood club, but he was out-generaled by the officials of the Giants.

Before the Brotherhood men were called together there was a meeting of the Brooklyn Club for the purpose of electing officers and forming a permanent organization. The officers elected were: President—Mendell Goodwin; Vice President—E. F. Linton; Secretary—J. J. Wallace; Treasurer—S. M. Chauncey; Directors—Mendell Goodwin, Linton Wallace, S. M. Chauncey, and John Montgomery Ward. As soon as the result of the meeting was known the delegates all adjourned to Parlor F, and after the door was securely locked and a glance cast over those present to see that there were no outsiders inside, Chairman Johnson called the meeting to order and business began, with John Ward acting as secretary.

The following delegates were present: New-York, Edward Talcott and William Ewing; Boston, J. B. Hart and Dan Brouthers; Philadelphia, John Vanderslice and George Wood; Cleveland, Albert Johnson and John Stricker; Chicago, John Addison and Fred Pfeffer; Buffalo, M. Shire and John Rowe; Brooklyn, E. F. Linton and Ed Andrews; Pittsburg, C. F. Buiner and Edward Hanlon.

As soon as the meeting was called to order Col. McAlpin, the Chairman of the Committee on Constitution and By-Laws, read his report. Each section was discussed, but only a few changes were made. The object of the new organization is to foster and elevate the national game of baseball and establish the championship of the world. According to the by-laws no player can be transferred unless the Board of Directors receives his consent in writing. Another section says: "The business of the League which shall consist of one stockholder who is not a player and one player who may or may not be a stockholder elected and designated by the Directors of each of the corporation members of this League." Ward, while reading off this section, said in a casual way that all the members of the New-York Club are stockholders in the enterprise. To make the enemies of the Brotherhood who are circulating the report that the men cannot hold anybody responsible for their salaries forever hold their peace, John Addison of Chicago presented the following resolution, which was adopted unanimously:

> *Resolved,* That each member of this League shall guarantee and positively agree to pay to each player employed by it the salary fixed by his contract upon his request, and that there be raised a fund of $40,000 to be contributed by the members deposited with the Treasurer of the League as a guarantee for the performance of each member of this League of its contracts to pay salaries.

Ward said that under the rule the players have a double guarantee that they will receive their salaries, something never attempted by the great moral National

League. "I for one," he said vehemently, "am not the least fearful of my salary, and in saying that I think that I voice the sentiment of all the boys. Our guarantee will be deposited in a few weeks, and will not come out of the gate receipts, as many may suppose." "Eddie" Talcott of the New-York Club and Col. McAlpin said that they favored the scheme, as they wanted to assure the boys that their money will be forthcoming even if the Brotherhood is not a grand success.

It was decided to tax each club $1,500 a year for the expenses of the Secretary and Treasurer. The umpires will be paid out of a separate fund. About 6 o'clock Judge Bacon took the constitution and by-laws to examine them carefully and see if they contained any flaws.

The following is the official list of players now under contract with the clubs of the Players' League as announced by the Secretary last night:

New York.—Ewing, Brown, Keefe, Crane, O'Day, Connor, Richardson, Whitney, O'Rourke, Gore, Slattery.

Brooklyn.—Ward, O'Connor, Cook, Weyhing, C. Murphy, Tucker, Bierbauer, Bassett, Seery, Andrews, McGeachy.

Boston.—Radbourn, Kilroy, Daley, Swett, Brouthers, Quinn, Nash, Richardson, Stovey, Kelly.

Philadelphia.—Milligan, Cross, Hallman, Buffinton, Sanders, Foreman, Cunningham, Husted, Farrar, Myers, Shindle, Mulvey, Wood, Thompson, Clements, Delehanty.

Pittsburg.—Fields, Miller, Staley, Galvin, Maul, Morris, Beckley, Dunlap, Kuehne, Hanlon.

Cleveland.—Faatz, Stricker, Zimmer, Sutcliffe, Snyder, O'Brien, Beckley, Gruber, Twitchell, McAleer, Radford, Larkin, McKean.

Buffalo.—Mack, Clark, Ferson, Krock, G. Keefe, Carney, Wise, J. Irwin, Rowe, White, Hoy, Beecher.

Chicago.—Darling, Farrell, Boyle, Tener, Baldwin, Dwyer, Bartson, Pfeffer, Williamson, Latham, Bastian, Van Haltren, Ryan, Duffy.

Six of the players have also signed contracts with the National League, namely, Clements, Delehanty, Beckley, Miller, McKean, and Mulvey.

At the evening session the following officers were elected: Col. F. A. McAlpin of New-York, President; John Addison of Chicago, Vice President; Frank H. Brunell of Chicago, Secretary and Treasurer. The Central Board will be made up of the delegates to the present convention. The Playing Rules Committee is as follows: B. F. Hilt, Julian Hart, W. Ewing, John Ward, and F. Pfeffer. The Schedule Committee, drawn by lot, is Brooklyn, Cleveland, Philadelphia, Buffalo, and Chicago. A legal committee will be appointed to-day.

The meeting adjourned until 10 o'clock this morning.

86

A History of the Player Revolt from the Players' Perspective (1890)

Source: *Players' National League Base Ball Guide*
(1890; reprint, St. Louis: Horton, 1989), pp. 7–10

Brotherhood secretary Tim Keefe recited the history of the organization from its inception in 1885 to the eve of the 1890 season.

THE BROTHERHOOD AND ITS WORK

Secretary Tim Keefe's Narration of the Birth and Progress of the Brotherhood of Base Ball Players

On the 22nd day of October, 1885, the following preamble was drawn up and signed by the players of the New York Base Ball Club:

We, the undersigned, professional base ball players, recognizing the importance of united effort and impressed with its necessity in our behalf, do form ourselves this day into an organization to be known as the "Brotherhood of Professional Base Ball Players." The objects we seek to accomplish are:

To protect and benefit ourselves collectively and individually.

To promote a high standard of professional conduct.

To foster and encourage the interests of the game of Base Ball.

John M. Ward, G. G. Gerhardt, William Ewing, Roger Connor, Daniel Richardson, Michael Welch, Michael C. Dorgan, Jas. H. O'Rourke, T. J. Keefe.

John M. Ward was chosen president of the new organization, committees were formed, the work of the different committees, after a short period, was finished, and the foundation of the substantial and famous organization known as the "Brotherhood of Professional Base Ball Players" was laid.

In the year 1886 President Ward and the New York Chapter, began to organize chapters in the different cities where National League clubs were located. The first chapter to join the national organization after the New Yorks was that of Detroit. The latter chapter joined on the 11th day of May, 1886. It was made up of the following players: H. Richardson, Ed. Hanlon, J. C. Rowe, S. Thompson, S. Crane, Jas. Manning and C. Baldwin. Chas. Bennett, Chas. Ganzell, D. Brouthers and Chas. Getzein joined at the next meeting. Our next stopping place was Chicago, and on May 15th, 1886, the names of Fred Pfeffer, Ed. Williamson, and Frank Flint were proposed for membership in the new organization. The staunch trio was unanimously elected. Later on in the season the names of M. J. Kelly and Jas. McCormick were added to the roll of the Chicago Chapter of the Brotherhood.

On May 19, 1886, we arrived at Kansas City. The latter city contained a League team that season, and at a meeting held in that city the names of Paul Radford,

J. Donnelly, M. McQueery, Jas. Whitney, M. Hackett, and Chas. Bassett were proposed for membership and unanimously elected. The names of Chas. Briody, Pete Conway, Dave Rowe and Jim Lilly were added to the list. Kansas City formed a very substantial chapter.

On May 29th, 1886, the chapter that contained the star deserters of the world was formed at a meeting at the Polo Grounds. The names of H. Boyle, E. Seery, P. Cahill, John Glasscock, George Myers, Fred Dunlap, Jerry Denny, Alex McKinnon and John Healy of the St. Louis Club were proposed for membership in the new organization. All the men were unanimously elected and all swore on the word of God to protect and work for the interest of the Brotherhood. The names of John Kirby, Jos. Quinn, Frank Graves and Chas. McGeachy were afterwards added to the rolls of the St. Louis Chapter.

The New York Chapter visited Boston June 12, 1886, and, at a meeting held in that city, the names of John Morrill, Chas. Radbourn, Jos. Hornung, Ezra. B. Sutton, Rich Johnston, Con Daily, Tom Gunning, Chas. Buffinton, William Nash, Sam Wise, Tom Poorman, Ed Tate, John Burdock, W. Stemmyer, P. Dealy and C. Parsons were proposed. Each was unanimously elected to membership of the local organization named the Boston Chapter.

The next important meeting was held at Philadelphia, July 12, 1886. There the names of C. Bastian, Arthur Irwin, Chas. Ferguson, W. Clements, W. Titcomb, George Wood, Ed Andrews, and Jas. McGuire were proposed and unanimously elected to membership. The names of Jos. Mulvey, W. Gleason, A. B. Sanders, E. J. Delehanty, Pete Wood, W. Hallman, Sydney Farrar, and Jas. Fogarty were added to the list later on and the organization christened the Philadelphia Chapter.

July 15, 1886, at a meeting held at Washington, D.C., the names of Paul Hines, Cliff Carroll and Ed N. Crane were proposed for Brotherhood membership. All were elected. Dupee Shaw and Bernard Gilligan were afterwards added to the membership of the organization known as the Washington Chapter. In the fall of 1886 John Farrell, W. Kreig, S. Houck, D. Oldfield, W. Goldsby, F. Gilmore, H. O'Day, John McGlone, J. Henry, Con Mack and George Shock were proposed and duly elected.

In the following year (1887) the Kansas City Club retired from the league, some of the players going to Indianapolis and some to Washington and the St. Louis Chapter also disbanded, its principal men going to form the Indianapolis Chapter.

Clubs disbanding and changing from one city to another, also young players joining the ranks, produced a change in the membership of the different chapters every year. At a meeting, held by the New York Chapter Aug. 4, 1887, at Chicago, the formation of a new League contract, the buying and selling of players, a time limit on the service of a player in one city, and a player's injuries were all discussed at length, and a meeting of the Executive Council suggested.

Aug. 24, 1887, at a meeting held at the Polo Grounds, the names of S. Barkley, F. Carroll, Ed. Morris, Geo. Miller, J. C. Coleman, Jas. Galvin, E. Dalyrmple and W. Kuehne were proposed and unanimously elected to membership to a new local organization known as the Pittsburg Chapter. The names of J. Fields, W. Sunday, Al Maul, H. Staley, and Lauer J. Beckley were afterwards added to this chapter.

A close review of the national game and matters in general since the formation of the Brotherhood in 1885, shows conclusively that the organization has been a benefit to the great American game. The Brotherhood has gained the objects for which it was organized, viz; to place the game on a high standard; to foster and encourage the interest in it, and to promote a high standard of professional conduct. It has also purged the game of most of its disagreeable features in the past even though such work called out severe measures. But severe cases require heroic treatment. Heroic treatment was necessary in order to rid the game of the disagreeable features and the fetters that bound it and its exponents, such as the selling and buying of players, the reserve rule, the classification system and the clumsy transferring of players. The Brotherhood was forced by the arbitrary actions of the National League to secede from the latter organization last year. The National League refused to meet the executive committee of the Brotherhood and the movement, out of which grew the Players' National League was the only course left for the Brotherhood to consistently pursue. The number of cases whereby the members of the Brotherhood have been benefitted by the organization are too numerous to recite. The only conclusion that a thoroughly informed and fair minded person can reach after a glance at the Brotherhood's work is that it has benefitted and will continue to benefit and elevate the game in the future far more than the braggart National League ever claimed to have done in the past. The Brotherhood's work of refining will be done in the face of opposition. That done by the Brotherhood came naturally and out of no particular effort on the part of that organization. In the day when the National League had a chance to show what it cared for the game when not associated with its own profit, the National League's exhibition was a mean and miserable one. No means, however dirty and enervating, were not called into play to wreck the Brotherhood and its kindred organization, "The Player's National League." Both stand and will live on to a glorious old age.

T. J. KEEFE.

87

A History of the Player Revolt from the Owners' Perspective (1890)

Source: *Spalding's Official Base Ball Guide, 1890* (reprint, St. Louis: Horton, 1989), pp. 14–17

The author of this rebuttal focuses on the crucial role of a "master mind" in the Brotherhood (John Ward), claiming that he and his fellow conspirators obtained compliance with their aims by instituting a "system of terrorism" on the "weaker" members of the organization.

THE LEAGUE PLAYERS' REVOLT OF 1889

The chapter of League history covering the revolt of the League players, which was inaugurated in New York in 1889, is one which not only began a new era in professional club management, but it also exhibits some of the peculiar characteristics of the majority of the fraternity in a very striking light. The fact, too, that the secession movement had its origin in the New York Club's team of players, which club had petted its players for years, only emphasized the fact of the ingratitude for personal favors done, which marks the average professional ball player. The revolt of the League players unquestionably grew out of the ambitious efforts of a small minority to obtain the upper hand of the National League in the control and management of its players. Added to this was the desire for self-aggrandizement which influenced a trio of the most prominent of the players, headed by one man who was the master mind of the whole revolutionary scheme from its inception in connection with the Brotherhood to its consummation in the organization of the Players' League, and it was the former organization which the leaders of the revolt used as a lever to lift them into the position of professional club magnates.

The methods adopted by the originator of the revolutionary scheme were of a character well calculated to mislead the majority of the players. It would not have done to have openly seduced the players of the League from their club allegiance, so it was deemed necessary to first combine all of their players under the banner of the Brotherhood organization, the ostensible objects of which were the mutual benefit of its members, and to assist those who needed aid from sickness or misfortune. This was a very plausible plan, and apparently devoid of guile. But in building up the Brotherhood, care was taken to bind its members by an iron clad oath, something unnecessary in the case of an organization designed exclusively to serve benevolent purposes. This oath in fact was the carefully disguised seed of the revolt, from which was developed the full grown plant of the Players' League. Once having gathered the League players within the fold of the Brotherhood, the chief conspirator soon began to throw aside the mask of his disguise, and securing the co-operation of the more intelligent of his confreres in aiding the revolt, the quartette of leaders assumed the direction of its affairs. These "big four" of the great strike, correctly estimating the weakness of character and lack of moral courage of the average Brotherhood member, knew that he would be loth to break the oath of allegiance to the Brotherhood, however he might be willing to violate his National League obligations, and they went quietly to work on this basis to complete their plans looking to the ultimate declaration of war upon the League, and the establishment of the rival Players' League.

It is a fact which cannot be gainsaid, that fully two-thirds of the members of the Brotherhood, up to the close of the League campaign in 1889, had never contemplated the disruption of the National Agreement and the organization of the Players' League as the outcome of the Brotherhood scheme, or they would not have joined it. Naturally enough, the players' sympathies were with the success of the Brotherhood as an association of players for benevolent objects. But not until they had been influenced by special pleadings, false statements and a system of terrorism peculiar to revolutionary movements, did they realize the true position they had been placed in, and then a minority, who possessed sufficient independence and the courage of their convictions, returned to their club allegiance in the National League.

A step in the progress of the revolt which the leaders found it necessary to take, was that of securing the services of such journalists in each League Club city as would lend their pens as editors of Brotherhood organs. This movement was deemed essential in order to bring a special influence to bear on such capitalists among the wealthy class of patrons of the game as were eager to join in a movement calculated to give them a share in the "big bonanza profits" of the money making League Clubs. Another use these writers and organs were put to in forwarding the interests of the leaders, was that of denouncing every player who was independent enough to think for himself in the matter of the revolt as a "deserter" or a "scab." Of course this system of terrorism had its effect on the weaker class of the Brotherhood, and the result was that only a minority refused to become slaves of the Brotherhood; and thus was started the Players' League of Professional Ball Players.

The original plan of organization of the Players' League, embraced co-operation by the players in the matter of gate receipts and profits, and one of the inducements held out to the players to secede from the League Clubs, was the alluring one of sharing in the proceeds of the season's games. The bait proved to be a tempting one and it was readily taken; but after the League had been started and the bulk of the players had committed themselves by overt acts to the revolt, the leaders, in order to secure the required financial aid of sympathetic capitalists, receded from their plan of co-operation, and a change was made in the new League's constitution, the new feature introduced being that of obliging each player to depend upon the gate receipts for the payment of his salary after all necessary expenses outside of the salary list had been paid. This new clause proved distasteful to several players who had taken the oath of allegiance to the Brotherhood, but who had not legally signed Players' League contracts, and these men were not slow in returning to the League, after discovering the trickery they had been subjected to by the leaders. But others lacking in moral courage and who still have faith in the movement made to make them magnates instead of $5,000 a year "slaves," still remained obedient to their Brotherhood task masters.

In the working up of the scheme of organizing a Players' League, all sorts of efforts were made by the leaders of the revolt to enlist the sympathies of the base ball public in their behalf. Circulars were issued, and newspaper articles appeared, emanating from the "head center" of the rebellion, alleging extraordinary grievances as the cause of the secession from the League ranks. But the effect of these pen missiles was largely offset by the statements made on behalf of the National League, which clearly set forth the true position of affairs, and plainly showed the treachery, mendacity and false pretenses persistently set forth by the leaders and their organs to bolster up the revolt.

The leaders had originally declared that there war was against the National League, and that only; but when their plan of campaign met with its first failure, resort for recruits for their revolutionary army was had to the ranks of the American Association, and the temporary disruption of this organization was due to the influence exerted by the revolt. This was the return made to the Association for the neutral position they had occupied in the differences which had occurred between the League and the Brotherhood. Had the Brotherhood followed the honorable course of holding a conference with the League at the end of the championship campaign—the only appropriate time for such a conference—there is no questioning the fact that every grievance, real or imaginary, alleged by the Brotherhood, would have received due consideration by the League, and all enactments calculated to antagonize the best interests of the players would have been removed from the League's statute books, for it was too plainly to the interest of the National League to place their club players in the position of making their interests and welfare identical with those of the National League, not to have done all they could to make their rules equitable.

88

The Reserve Clause Overturned in Court (1890)

Source: *New York Times*, January 29, 1890

A key tactic designed to combat the PL was to sue its players for violating the reserve clause in their contracts. The owners started the process by suing John Ward for breach of contract. As reported below, the judge ruled that the standard NL contract lacked "mutuality" and therefore was not enforceable, because owners could release a player after giving him ten days' notice, but the player was bound to his team as long as the team chose to reserve him. A brief editorial follows the article.

WARD WINS HIS FIGHT

AN INJUNCTION AGAINST HIM DENIED

A DECISION BY JUDGE O'BRIEN WHICH GIVES GREAT PLEASURE TO THE BROTHERHOOD—THE OTHER SIDE

Judge O'Brien of the Supreme Court handed down yesterday his decision on the application of the Metropolitan Exhibition Company (New-York Baseball Club) for a preliminary injunction to restrain John M. Ward from playing baseball with any other club during the season of 1890. The application was based on an agreement made by the defendant with the plaintiff on April 23, 1889, by which he gave it his services for 1889, and containing a clause by which he gave it his right to reserve his services for 1890.

While refusing to grant the injunction because the case can be determined on its merits before the opening of the baseball season of 1890, Judge O'Brien sustains the view of the meaning of the reserve clause held by the plaintiff. He also decides against the defendant's contention that as a general rule an injunction will not be granted in aid of a contract for personal services. Following is a part of the decision:

"One of the principal questions discussed on the argument was as to the meaning of this word 'reserve' as used in the contract. On the part of the plaintiff it is claimed that the meaning of this word is clear and unambiguous, requiring no explanation, being used in its ordinary sense of 'to hold, to keep for future use.' The defendant, on the other hand, claims that this word, which was not a new one to the parties, has a history. . . . That it had always been used in a particular sense, and, in order to ascertain that meaning, reference must be had to the history of the word. That if resort is had to such history it will result in a construction to be given to the contract which shall determine that when the defendant accorded the right to reserve his services that it was not thereby meant that he was absolutely pledged or bound to plaintiff, but that his services were reserved to the exclusion of any other member of the league of baseball clubs. . . . It is sufficient to say that whether we have regard to the history of the word as used in the various contracts or give it its ordinary and well-accepted meaning, we shall arrive at the same conclusion as to the meaning of the word adverse to the defendant's contention and in favor of the meaning given to it by the plaintiff."

Justice O'Brien having said that a preliminary injunction should not be granted in these cases except on "facts and circumstances showing that a contract exists which is reasonably defined and certain," proceeds to consider the forms with this requirement. After considering the reserve clause and supplemental contract he says:

"Not only are there no terms and conditions fixed, but I do not think it is entirely clear that Ward agrees to do anything further than to accord the right to reserve him upon terms thereafter to be fixed. He does not covenant to make a contract for 1890 at the same salary, nor upon the same terms and conditions as during the season of 1889. . . . The failure of the existing contract to expressly provide the terms and conditions of the contract to be made for 1890 either renders the latter indefinite and uncertain, or we must infer that the same terms and conditions are to be incorporated in the one to be enforced, which necessarily includes the reserve clause, for no good reason can be suggested, if all the others are to be included, why this should be omitted. Upon the latter assumption the want of fairness and of mutuality, which are fatal to its enforcement in equity, are apparent under such circumstances each of the parties is bound."

Every player, he says, who signs such a contract is bound for the season, and to make another such contract for the ensuing season, while the club, by the provisions of paragraph 17, may terminate the contract at any time and in any place, "leaving the player to make his way home as best he can."

After quoting Fry to the effect that a contract to be specifically enforced by the court must be mutual, and that a party not bound by the agreement itself has no right to call on a court of equity to enforce specific performance against the other contracting party by expressing his willingness in his bill to perform his part of the engagement, the Justice says:

> "It will thus be seen that I do not fully concur in the claims made by the plaintiff that the probability of finally succeeding is of the strongest and most certain kind. Upon either one or both of the grounds considered, but principally upon the ground that the contract is indefinite and uncertain, does there arise a serious doubt as to the plaintiff's being accorded on the trial the relief asked for."

After saying that the case can be tried in Special Term and decided at least a month before the opening of the baseball season, which will secure every possible right of the plaintiff, the Justice concludes:

> "While, therefore, I think that this is not a case in which a preliminary injunction should be granted, it is proper that the rights of the parties should be determined by a trial before the ball season begins, and to that end, on application made, I shall assist in securing a speedy trial, upon which a final and deliberate judgment upon the rights of the parties can be pronounced."

Judge O'Brien's opinion caused a feeling of joy among the Brotherhood men and their followers. Ward, of course, felt jubilant.

"Now that the case has been practically settled," he said, "we will go to work and complete our task of organizing the strongest baseball association in the country. I don't know just what course our enemies will pursue, but it is safe to predict that the Brotherhood will come out on top. The temporary injunction asked for was simply a bluff. The League men know that the players know little or nothing about law and that they could coerce our players. In some instances they have been successful, but the men who have been brave enough to hold out in spite of the inducements offered in the shape of League gold will reap their reward, and they deserve it. As to the deserters from our ranks, I don't know what we will do. That matter will be decided upon in a few days, but the probabilities are that we will not molest them. We do not want traitors in our ranks. We want honest, conscientious ball players, and I am proud to be able to state that we have about one hundred of them on our roster now."

The League men regard the opinion, strange to say, as a victory. "We will push this case and get a definite decision as soon as possible," said President Day of the Giants after a consultation with his counsel. "The Judge's reason for refusing to grant a temporary injunction is apparent. He is evidently of the opinion that there is ample time between now and the opening of the baseball season to have a trial and for that reason a temporary injunction is not necessary. In that respect I agree with him."

Mr. Day says that preparation will be made at once to get the case on the calendar of the February term, so that a decision can be secured in good season.

There was a large crowd of League and American Association magnates in town last night. They are here to attend the meeting of the Arbitration Committee in the Fifth-Avenue Hotel to-day. All of the League men share the opinions of Mr. Day, and they are positive that the Brotherhood will receive a set back.

The decision of Judge o'BRIEN in the case of DAY against WARD, which is really the case of the Baseball League against the Players' Brotherhood, is decidedly discouraging to the League. It holds that the "reserve clause" in the contract of the League with the players does not really reserve. In substance this clause seems merely to be an agreement to make another agreement if the terms of the second agreement are satisfactory to both parties. It is therefore either superfluous or void. As Judge o'BRIEN intimates, there does not seem to be anything in the contract to prevent the baseball player from putting upon his services a price which nobody would think of paying, and of discontinuing his services if his terms are not met. The scheme of the players for managing themselves does not look very promising from a commercial point of view, but if Judge o'BRIEN's decision is sustained there does not seem to be any obstacle from a legal point of view to their trying the experiment.

89

Baseball's Contribution to the Economy (1890)

Source: *Harper's Weekly*, May 3, 1890

Here O. P. Caylor, a prominent sportswriter who had been hired by Albert Spalding to edit a new pro-NL weekly, the New York Sporting News, *explains the importance of baseball as a business enterprise. In comparison to the great steel, oil, and manufacturing industries, however, baseball's impact on the economy was minuscule.*

. . . In concluding, it might not be amiss to note the tremendous strides professional base-ball has taken during the last fifteen years, until it has become an established business all over the United States. There are at this time about one hundred professional clubs banded together under the National Agreement. These one hundred clubs give employment to about fifteen hundred players, whose average salary is perhaps $1000 a season, making a total amount paid in salaries of

$1,500,000. Besides the National Agreement clubs there are the eight Brotherhood clubs, embracing about one hundred and twenty players, whose salaries will aggregate $250,000, swelling the grand total to 1620 players and $1,750,000 in salaries.

These clubs during the season will travel about 450,000 miles by rail. Each club will carry from twelve to sixteen men in their journeying around, which means railroad tickets representing 6,300,000 miles. At an average of 2½ cents a mile, the cost of travel alone, not including sleeping-car accommodation, will be found to amount to something like $157,500—quite a neat drop in the earnings of the American railroads.

There is another class of business which profits from this base-ball playing—the hotels. During one-half of the playing season, about eighty days of each year, every club has its team on the circuit, and the players are for the most part quartered at the very best hotels. Not less than $200,000 is spent in this way among the various hotels in cities which support base-ball clubs. Probably $100,000 would be a small estimate of the rents paid by the clubs for their grounds, and certainly $200,000 would not more than pay the miscellaneous expenses, such as sleeping-car fares, carriage hire, advertising, salaries of ground employés, treasurers, and gatekeepers, and the purchase of supplies.

Add it all together, and you will have nearly two and a half-million of dollars paid out by professional base-ball clubs each year. It is not unlikely that these figures are too small to be correct, nor is it a hazardous guess to say that the profits of the whole season among all the clubs, over and above expenses, will reach a quarter of a million dollars. Then we find the American people paying each season $2,750,000 for their amusement in base-ball. Three spectators, on an average, will represent a dollar. So that we have a total attendance during the season of about eight millions of people. Divide this up into one hundred and thirty playing days, and you will arrive at the conclusion that the average daily attendance in America on base-ball games where admission fees are charged is over fifty thousand. This season, I believe, it will exceed sixty thousand.

It is not an unreasonable estimate to say that every day during this summer five million Americans will examine the columns of their favorite newspapers to see the result of the professional base-ball games of the previous day.

90

The Demise of the PL (1890)

Source: *New York Times*, November 13, 1890

After a tumultuous season in which NL games were sometimes pitted against PL games on the same day in the same city, the PL collapsed. With one or two exceptions, every franchise in both leagues lost money. Although the details of the PL's demise remain unclear, note that the players were excluded from the meetings in which an apparent agreement was reached between the NL and the PL investors. As Albert G. Spalding put it later, the "monied men met with the monied men."

Also included is a brief note on a separate meeting of the PL in Pittsburgh.

END OF THE BASEBALL WAR

A COMPLETE VICTORY FOR THE NATIONAL LEAGUE MEN

CONSOLIDATIONS IN NEW-YORK, BROOKLYN, AND PITTSBURG, AND CHICAGO WANTS TO SELL OUT TO SPALDING

It required but one season to end the existence of the Players' Baseball League. As was foreshadowed in THE TIMES a few weeks ago, the new organization has died a natural death. The New-York, Brooklyn, and Pittsburg Clubs have consolidated or agreed upon terms, the famous ten-thousand-dollar beauty has signed a contract with the Boston League Club, the Chicago Brotherhood team is anxious to sell out, and players of the calibre of Williamson and Ryan are knocking for admission into the League fold.

All this news leaked out at the meeting held in the Fifth Avenue Hotel yesterday. As a rule, baseball men are as silent as oysters, but yesterday they made a new departure. They were very communicative and as happy as clams. They told of the downfall of the Players' League without shedding tears, and assured everybody that the national game next year would be on its old footing. That malady, known in the baseball world as mismanagement, caused the death of the Players' League. Blunder after blunder has been made, and to-day the Players', who a year ago were very enthusiastic, are a sorry lot. They have lost faith in the moneyed men, and are willing to go back to their old clubs. It is only just, however, to say that the sudden collapse of the new organization must not be attributed to John Ward, the founder of the Brotherhood. If his ideas had been carried out the chances are that the Players' League would be in a prosperous condition to-day. But the financial men stepped in, and their ignorance of baseball, coupled with their desire for notoriety, has caused the ruin.

The Board of Directors, which consists of Messrs. Robison of Cleveland, Day of New-York, Byrne of Brooklyn, Nimick of Pittsburg, and Secretary Young, met early in the morning. The report of Secretary Young was the first business which came before the Board of Directors, and after it was approved Mr. Young was elected to succeed himself as Secretary for another year. The board then formally awarded the championship of the League for 1890 to the Brooklyn club, which had won the largest percentage of games during the season. A petition from Paul Hines claiming salary due him from the Pittsburg Club was referred to President Byrne of Brooklyn for adjustment. The Pittsburg club, in its own behalf, says that instead of owing him money he drew $100 in excess of his salary.

Subsequent to the adjournment of the Board of Directors the joint Committee on Playing Rules, with Messrs. Day, Spalding, and Rogers of the League and

Managers Powers and Barnie of the American Association, were together for an hour, during which time they altered Sections 1, 2, and 3 of Article xxviii, and Section 6 of Article xlviii. The first-mentioned sections give a club the privilege of having one or all of its surplus men on the players' bench in uniform, and allow the substitution of any or all of them at any time during a game. This rule takes the place of the one formerly providing that only two men shall be in uniform. If a player is retired from the game once he cannot be returned. The change in Rule 48 does not call for the retirement of a player in running from the home plate to first base on a hit if he goes outside the three-foot limit line while the ball is fielded to first base, as heretofore.

It was after noon when the regular meeting of the National League was called. There were present John B. Day of this city, C. H. Byrne and Gus Abell of Brooklyn, M. J. Nimick and J. P. O'Neill of Pittsburg, F. De Robison, George Howe and David Hawley of Cleveland, John I. Rogers and A. J. Reach of Philadelphia, A. H. Soden and W. H. Conant of Boston, A. G. and Walter Spalding of Chicago, and John T. Brush of Indianapolis. Beyond adopting reports of several committees, nothing of importance was transacted. The committees for next year were selected as follows:

Schedule—C. H. Byrne of Brooklyn, F. De Robison of Cleveland, A. J. Reach of Philadelphia, and a representative of the Cincinnati Club to be named hereafter.

Playing Rules—J. B. Day of New-York, John I. Rogers of Philadelphia, and President Young.

Board of Arbitration—President Young, John B. Day of New-York, and John I. Rogers of Philadelphia.

During the meeting the Pittsburg delegates announced officially that they had come to an agreement with the Players' League officials of that city on a basis of 50 per cent. each. The players selected are as follows: First base, Beckley; second base, Laroque; third base, Miller; short stop, Corcoran; right field, Burke; centre field, Hanlon; left field, Fields; pitchers, Staley, Galvin, J. Smith, and Maul; catchers, Mack, Decker, and Berger. The only change likely to occur in the above list, he said, is at second base. A manager has not been engaged as yet, but either Harry Spence or W. W. Burnham will be selected. It leaked out that the proprietors of the club have offered Ward a handsome salary for next season. If he is engaged Corcoran will cover second and Laroque will probably be released.

During the meeting A. G. Spalding startled the delegates by producing a telegram from Col. McAlpin saying that the Chicago Players' Club would sell for $25,000. This is $10,000 more than Spalding is inclined to pay, but he will consider the matter. This confession of weakness caused rejoicing in the League camp. It was intensified later on when Spalding showed dispatches from two of his deserters, Ryan and Williamson, asking to be taken into the fold once more.

Both the Boston and Chicago Clubs have been gunning for the services of

"Mike" Kelly. He is one of the best drawing cards in the profession, and naturally the competition for his services is great. Spalding offered Kelly $5,000 for his season's work but it was learned that Kelly had signed a contract offered by the Boston League Club, but he still has the document in his possession. To a TIMES reporter last night Kelly said that he would stand by the Players' League to the end, but in the event of its dissolution he would look after Kelly. He will not do anything definite until he hears from the leaders of the Brotherhood. Some very tempting offers have been made this player, but he has been steadfast and refused to desert his colleagues.

Two applications were received from Cincinnati for the franchise of that city. One headed by John T. Brush and John Kilgore will be given the preference. The deal is to have Brush to consolidate with the recent purchasers of the Red Stockings on a half-and-half basis. If this cannot be done, Brush will indulge in a game of freeze-out, and the present Cincinnati Club will probably be out in the cold.

A committee, composed of Messrs. Ward, Johnson, and Prince, left Pittsburg last night to confer with the League delegates. The meeting will take place to-day.

THE PLAYERS' LEAGUE MEETING

PITTSBURG, Penn., Nov. 12.—At the session of the National Players' League in this city to-day President McAlpin formally presented the resignation of the New-York Club. An opinion from Judge Bacon of New-York was read to the effect that at the time the agreement was entered into between the New-York Players' League Club and the National League club of the same city it was understood that the two leagues were to consolidate. As this had not yet taken place, the agreement between the New-York clubs would not stand.

No action was taken on the resignation, and a committee consisting of Ward, Prince, and Johnson was appointed to attend the National League meeting now in session in New-York for the purpose of placing the matter of consolidation before it. The committee will leave to-night for New-York. The Players' League club of this city was not represented at to-day's meeting, and the matter of Pittsburg's resignation was laid on the table. The meeting then adjourned, to assemble at the call of the Chairman. As the matter now stands, the feeling is strongly in favor of consolidation, as all admit that the baseball war has been a failure.

6

The Tumultuous 1890s

The decade began inauspiciously with the collapse of the PL following the 1890 season and the demise of the AA one year later. The NL responded to these changes by reorganizing itself into a twelve-team circuit, adding four former AA franchises. The expansion resulted in an unbalanced league in which three teams—Brooklyn, Baltimore and Boston—won every pennant for the rest of the decade, with the other nine teams finishing far behind. With only one surviving major league, postseason championships failed to interest fans or players, especially since the same teams were involved nearly every year. In addition, the 1883–97 depression adversely affected all professional baseball.

Yet an offensive explosion fueled by the increase of the pitching distance to the modern 60′6″ standard and innovative, aggressive tactics introduced by a fresh set of stars made for exciting baseball. By the turn of the century, with economic recovery underway, there were positive signs that the sport might regain lost ground and enter a new era of prosperity.

Prospects for Local Baseball in Louisville (1891)

Source: *Louisville Courier-Journal*, April 5, 1891

Histories of baseball usually focus on the professional game, particularly the major leagues. The following article discusses the prospects of amateur and semiprofessional baseball in Louisville. Notice that the local city league planned to charge a gate fee and to play in the city's big league park.

The organization of the City League is about completed. It will be composed of four clubs. The Eclipse Club, the East End Browns and the representatives of two big local business concerns make up the league. It is the desire of the organization to play at Eclipse Park, while the Louisvilles are absent. John Kelly has promised to give them an answer in regard to this matter by to-morrow at noon. It is almost certain that the park will be obtained. A meeting of the City League for the purpose of completing the organization will be held at Reccius' Sporting Head-quarters to-morrow night. A schedule will be arranged and other details agreed upon. The league will play twenty-five cent ball. There is little doubt that the movement will be a success. There is plenty of disengaged local talent in the city, to make four clubs, which will give good exhibitions of ball-playing. Such organizations exist in all the other big cities, and the fact that there has not been one before this in Louisville is due to the absence of any attempt at organization rather than to the failure of public patronage.

In one respect last year's base ball season in this city was very remarkable. While the Louisvilles stood first and the large attendance at the games showed undoubted great local interest in the sport, there were few amateur clubs in the city than had been for many years. This statement is almost paradoxical, as it would seem that interest in professional ball implied a like interest in amateur ball. Yet such was not the case.

This year there will be a largely increased number of city clubs. The old Acme's are going to reorganize. They until last year had played good ball from season to season. There can not be too many amateur clubs in the city. Already several teams have been organized and have issued challenges to any club whose members are under "twenty, eighteen, fifteen or twelve years," as the case may be.

The "Pirates" Earn Their Name (1891)

Source: *Philadelphia Press*, February 15, 1891

After the demise of the PL, *the clubs in the remaining major leagues went through the formality of reserving, and then re-signing, their 1889 players. Somehow, the Philadelphia Athletics neglected to reserve two of their best players, slugger Harry Stovey and star infielder Louis Bierbauer. Stovey and Bierbauer acted quickly, signing contracts with* NL *clubs in Boston and Pittsburgh, respectively. Although the* AA *protested, an interleague committee headed by their own representative, Allan "White Wings" Thurman, awarded Stovey and Bierbauer to their new* NL *teams. The* AA *again prepared for war, but it was so weak after the financial losses it had suffered in the* PL *conflict that it collapsed after the 1891 season. Meanwhile, Athletics supporters angrily labeled Pittsburgh magnates "Pirates" for stealing Bierbauer, a name Pittsburgh supporters grew to appreciate.*

SPORTING NEWS

Bierbauer Will Go to Pittsburg and Stovey Will Remain in the League

WAGNER SAYS IT'S AN OUTRAGE

CHICAGO, Feb. 14 (SPECIAL)—It was 3 o'clock this morning when the National Board adjourned. It had taken it from 8 o'clock until that time to reach a decision in the cases of Stovey and Bierbauer. The other cases caused but little discussion. At 11 o'clock this morning the board announced that it was ready to give its decisions, and invited all the base ball people in the rotunda of the auditorium to be present. Among those who accepted the invitations were: Von der Ahe, Anson, Cushman, of Milwaukee; President Beck, of Sioux City; Gillette, of Milwaukee; Gus. Schmelz, Billy Harrington, Director Cohn, of Columbus; Jim Hart, Baron Hach, Billy Barnie, Arthur Irwin, J. Walter Spalding, Davis Hawley, A. G. Spalding, Van Horn, of Denver; John T. Brush, and others. J. Palmer O'Neil and Ned Hanlon were also interested spectators.

President Thurman announced the decisions, prefacing them with a long speech, in which he said that the board had conducted its investigation with the care and accuracy which marks a court of justice. He touched on the Stovey and Bierbauer cases first, and the decision was briefly as follows:—

BIERBAUER TO PLAY IN PITTSBURG

The neglect of the Athletic Club to reserve Bierbauer on October 10, 1890, for the season of 1891, in accordance with the fourth section of the National Agreement, then governing the case, released him from reservation and from the jurisdiction of the National Agreement, but a majority of the board think that if the approval of the report of the Conference Committee by both the League and Association implied an intent and, understanding that all club members of both leagues and associations except the new Association Club of Philadelphia should waive the right to negotiate for the services of Bierbauer and other former Athletic players then that understanding would amount to an estoppel of the Pittsburg Club from making the contract now under consideration, but as it is not susceptible of proof that such agreement of waiver was so universally implied, we are all reluctantly compelled to sustain the contract of Bierbauer with the Pittsburg Club. Stovey's case was decided in the same way.

This decision was signed only by John I. Rogers and Thurman. Mr. Krauthoff entered a minority report. He claimed that the proceedings which culminated in the adjustment of the recent difficulties in base ball circles were of such a character that all the National League and Association Clubs waived their strictly legal rights to contract with these players and left the Philadelphia Association Club free to do so.

Connie Mack, the Buffalo catcher, was also given to Pittsburg. It was announced that on investigation it was found that Arthur Irwin's agreement with Mack had been made some weeks before the Boston Club was admitted to the American Association, hence the club practically did not exist at the time. The Pittsburg contract, on the other hand, was in good form, and the player was awarded to the Smoky City.

LYONS WILL BE A BROWN STOCKING

The case of Denny Lyons, who was claimed by Chicago and St. Louis was cut off in short order. The Chicago Club holds a contract signed by Lyons with the Chicago Brotherhood Club. It was declared that such an organization did not exist now, and the player was given to St. Louis, with whom he has since signed. Powell, of Spokane Falls, was released from reservation, his club having failed to pay him back salary on the time promised.

J. Palmer O'Neil was in the seventh heaven of delight to-night, and the Association men are a disgruntled set. J. Earl Wagner said that it was an outrage. The League had pretended that it was willing to do anything to help the Association, and at the first chance had taken advantage of a technicality to sign two of the Association players. By the decision, however, he is left in undisturbed possession of Hoy, for whom no claim was made. Wagner made a last effort to secure Pickett to-day, but failed, and the player signed with Kansas City.

THE BOARD COMPLETES ITS WORK

The National Board finished its work at 8:30 to-night. A new form of contract was adopted, to be used in all leagues under the National agreement control. The copy of it calls for a seventh months' term, with a clause giving clubs the option to retain the player for the ensuing year. The record calls for a twelve months' contract by which the player can be paid each month of the twelve. By this means clubs will have control of the player during the entire year.

The minor leagues were divided into four classes, with different grades of protection. Class A has protection for contract and reservation. Class B has protection but any club in the three major leagues* can at any time during the season draw on this league for a player, with the latter's consent, and by paying a stipulated price. Class C gives protection for contract only. Class D protects a contract, but any of the grades above it can draw on it for a player during the season by paying a stipulated sum.

The control of the umpires in the three major leagues was turned over to Nick Young, and he will sign and assign them to duty. A form of questions was drawn up which each manager must draw up and send to the chairman of the board the fifth of each month, showing the character of every player in each club, and listing their imperfections of every kind. The list is a very comprehensive one. The matter of appointing official scorers was left to the various clubs, but Nick Young will compile all official records of all leagues under the control of the National agreement.

The Association men were terribly warm over the decision to-day, and swore vengeance, but they are cooler to-night and no break is possible. Billy Barnie was the most rabid of the set.

The League held a conference to-day, all the clubs but Boston being represented. It was decided at the League meeting in March, to adopt the equal division of gate receipts. The sales system was taken up and all the clubs agreed to sign a clause to do away with it. The meeting backed Brush up in his work in Cincinnati, and instructed him to go ahead and organize his club irrespective of Al Johnson. The National Board's next meeting will be in New York in March.

*The three "major leagues" are the NL, the AA, and the Western Association, which cosigned a new National Agreement drafted after the 1890 season. The WA was never considered equal to either the NL or the AA.—Ed.

93

The NL Reorganizes and Expands
to Twelve Teams (1891)

Source: *Indianapolis Journal*, December 19, 1891

The AA lost the baseball war, and with its collapse at the end of the 1891 season the NL added four of the stronger AA clubs to its roster. As a concession to these clubs, the NL allowed them to maintain their customary twenty-five-cent admission fee—half the NL rate—as well as their policy of selling alcohol at games. At the same time, the NL adopted another AA practice—playing games on Sundays in those cities whose laws permitted such practices.

THOSE "MAGNATES" ADJOURN

Most Memorable Meeting in the History of Base-Ball Is Over
New Organization with a Twelve-Story Name Promulgates Its Constitution—
Dividing Up the Players

The base-ball "magnates" finished their work last night and most of them left the city.

Gray-eyed skeptics will be inclined to doubt if in six months from now, any one will allude to the new twelve-club affair, which cunning John Brush and the other cunning members of the League have launched from the Bates House this week, "The National League and American Association of Professional Base-ball Players." For convenience it will no doubt become simply the "N. L. and A. A. of P. B. B. P." Any one threatened with paresis can receive a special dispensation, perhaps, whereby they will be permitted to call it the "National League," or, if in a hurry to catch a train, the "League" will be sufficiently explicit. The magnaminity displayed by the old League members of the new league, who outnumber their Association brethren two to one, in incorporating the word "association" in the name of the consolidated offspring, goes to show how very generous this set of alleged cold-blooded magnates can be where they have it in their hearts. The ten years during which the American Association fought the League were cycles of tribulation to the latter body. Now, since the League has made a meal of its belligerent rival, old scores are wiped out and all is forgiven.

The new League promulgated its constitution yesterday, in which it appears that the four Association teams are assessed something like $10,000 each toward the fund raised to buy out the other clubs. In addition to this, 10 per cent. of their gate receipts will be appropriated to assist in raising a sinking fund of $25,000, which will eat a goodly hole in their profits the first year. The new League is formed, ostensibly, to endure ten years, and a cunning clause says that it cannot disband without a unanimous vote of the twelve clubs. This at first glance would seem to indicate the old League is satisfied with a twelve-club League. However, whatever virtue there may be in that idea is spoiled further on by the provisions of Section 8 of the constitution. The Association clubs which were frozen out prophesied that the twelve-club League would resolve itself into an eight-club league inside of a year, and that Von der Ahe and his Association friends who played double in the treacherous deal would then find themselves once more in the cold. Section 8 verifies this apprehension. It says that the membership of any club may be terminated for any one of the following reasons:

First—By resignation duly accepted by a three-fourths vote of all the clubs in meeting duly convened.

Second—Failure to present its nine at the time and place agreed upon to play any championship game, unless caused by unavoidable accident in traveling.

Third—Allowing open betting, or pool-selling upon its grounds, or in any building owned or occupied by it.

Fourth—Playing any game of ball with a club that is disqualified or ineligible under this constitution.

Fifth—Offering, agreeing, conspiring, or attempting to lose any game of ball, or failing to immediately expel any player who shall be proven guilty of offering, agreeing, conspiring or attempting to lose any game of ball, or of being interested in any pool or wager thereof.

Sixth—Disbandment of its organization or team during the championship season.

Seventh—Failing or refusing to fulfill its contracted obligations.

Eighth—Failing or refusing to comply with any lawful requirement of the board of directors.

Ninth—Willfully violating any provision of this constitution, or the legislative or playing rules made in pursuance thereof.

Without attempting to be facetious, the feline is released from the reticule in the first subdivision of that section. "By resignation duly accepted by a three-fourths vote of all the clubs" gives the power of dropping the four Association clubs into the hands of the eight League clubs, and one other whose vote could be easily purchased and paid for out of the $25,000 sinking fund. John Brush must have written that clause.

Section 48, regulating the price of admission, is interesting and reads as follows:

The general admission fee to all championship games shall be 50 cents, but each club shall designate a part of its grounds, and provide seats thereon, the admission fee to which shall be 25 cents, and all division of percentages shall be made on the basis of 50 cents, except as to that part of the grounds the admission fee to which is fixed at 25 cents, and as to such part of said grounds, all division of percentage shall be on the basis of 25 cents.

This permits the 25-cent towns—Philadelphia, Baltimore, Washington, Louisville, St. Louis, and possibly Pittsburg—to have 25-cent base-ball if they so desire, and they do, while the larger cities can keep within the constitution by marking off a plat no larger than a box-stall, containing a few splint-bottom chairs, and selling a few tickets to the poor relations of the directors for half price.

The two strikingly new features of the National League and American Association of Professional Base-ball Players—namely, the double championship-series scheme and Sunday base-ball—will not be touched on until the spring meeting of the League. An oral understanding, however, was had regarding the same. The matter of players' contracts, number and salaries of umpires, and other minor matters will be arranged at the same time. Although pool-selling and gambling will be prohibited on the grounds under the new constitution, there was no penalty attached to selling beer, which will give Von der Ahe and others lacking scruples on this point free license to engage in the trade, the League meanwhile conniving at the traffic.

Little besides placing the new League on its feet remained to be done yesterday. The representatives of the frozen-out clubs remained in the city until evening to get their clutches on the checks for the amounts which represented the compromise price paid for their clubs, after which they departed for their homes. The first business of the new League was the election of officers. President N. E. Young, of Washington, was re-elected president and treasurer of the new League. Zach Phelps, of Louisville, president of the assimilated American Association, was given an honorary snap as counselor of the new League, in conjunction with John I. Rogers, of Philadelphia, attorney for the old League. The new board of directors is composed of John Brush, of Cincinnati; Hart, of Chicago; Von Der Ahe, of St. Louis; Von der Horst, Baltimore, George Wagner, of Washington, and Conant, of Boston. The schedule committee is composed of Hart of Chicago; Von der Ahe, of St. Louis; and Byrne, of Brooklyn. Ex-President Phelps and President Nick Young were selected as the arbitration committee to apportion the players not signed to the clubs yet desiring players to fill out their quota of fifteen. Chicago, Baltimore and Cleveland will hold their claims for players already having under contract all the men they want at present. President Young declined to make public the list of players asked for and assigned to the different clubs, giving as his reason that the League wanted to give the different managers an opportunity to obtain contracts with the men. Al Reach and John I. Rogers, of Philadelphia, were appointed as a "jollying" committee to issue a statement to minor leagues explaining the purposes and policy of the new league, and also to lend assistance to the establishing of minor leagues.

It was given out that the new League is heartily in favor of a central league, as outlined in the Journal Wednesday, taking in Detroit, Buffalo, Columbus, Indianapolis, etc. There is a strong inclination of the Chicago people, however, to organize a new American association which, if done, might include clubs in Chicago, St. Louis, and, possibly, one or two other cities now gobbled by the League. Before leaving for home last night, the Chicago people said a new association circuit was very seriously considered, but that no actual steps had yet been taken. Sam Morton, secretary of the old Chicago Association club, is perhaps the prime mover in the new scheme, and his experience in the past in connection with the Western league as one of the owners of the Minneapolis club leaves room for belief that a new association will be a fact in the no distant future.

Regarding the disposition of players, there are some whose fate is already settled. New York put in a bid for Amos Rusie, who had signed with Chicago for $6,250, the exact terms of which deal are now made known for the first time. Chicago said she would not lay claim to the brilliant twirler—Chicago is always against paying fancy salaries—and with this announcement John B. Day, of New York, claimed that Rusie should, therefore, be returned to the Giants. The claim was allowed. His contract with Pfeffer, which will have to be honored, however, it is said, will insure Rusie the same salary.

Roger Connor, who had signed with the Athletics, will remain in Philadelphia, while Danny Richardson, the Gotham second-baseman, goes to Washington. Johnny Ward will captain and manage the Brooklyn team, as last year. There is already considerable kicking over the proposed manner of disposing of the players and some trouble is likely to be experienced.

Fred Pfeffer will not return to Chicago. This, he says, is final, and none doubt him. No less than five clubs entered a claim for Pfeffer, but it is doubtful if he will play ball next season. He says he would prefer Chicago to all other places, but he will never play under Anson again, and St. Louis would like mighty well to get him, but he would prefer going to some Eastern club—New York or Boston. It is barely possible that he may stand in Danny Richardson's shoes in New York.

President Brush held a suspicious conference with President Art, of Chicago, as did Captain Comiskey with Pfeffer, and it is believed he is after the great second baseman, but Fred said last night he would not play in Cincinnati.

94

The NL Adopts a Split-Season Format (1892)

Source: *New York World*, March 4, 1892

After the demise of the AA, the "World Championship Series" was no longer possible. At the NL meeting described below, the "double championship-series scheme," known today as the split-season format, was formulated as a substitute. The winner of each half was to meet in a postseason series to determine the NL championship. However, the NL abandoned the split-season format, and the new 154-game schedule, after the 1892 season. This article also suggests how important scheduling was to the profitability of NL teams.

AN ALBUM FOR AL SPALDING

The League Favors the Great Chicago Financier

SECRETARY EBBETS'S SCHEDULE ADOPTED UNANIMOUSLY

The Season to Be Divided into Two Parts, Consisting of Seventy-seven Games Each—Many Conflicting Dates for New York and Brooklyn—Messrs. Byrne, Young and Phelps Chosen as the New National Board

The first spring meeting of the new baseball league came to an end yesterday afternoon. Charley Ebbets's schedule was adopted, a new National Board was elected and a bouquet was thrown at A. G. Spalding in the shape of an album containing engrossed resolutions. A vote of thanks was tendered to Mr. Ebbets for the great amount of work he did in preparing the highly acceptable and perfectly fair schedule, and also to George Munson, of St. Louis, for his assistance in the matter. It was resolved to hold the League's annual meeting in New York next fall, and then the delegates dispersed to their twelve different homes.

Two short sessions were held in parlor F of the Fifth Avenue Hotel yesterday. At the morning session Col. John I. Rogers presented the souvenir album to J. W. Spalding, who received it for his brother. The resolutions confer upon A. G. Spalding honorary membership in the League, and jolly him into believing that he is immaculate.

The new National Board was also elected at the morning session. The first nominee was Col. John I. Rogers, of the Philadelphia Club. The Colonel has been identified with the governing bodies in baseball as long as such have existed. But he has decided to shake off the cares of office, and absolutely declined to accept. Then Messrs. Young, Phelps and Byrne were selected. Subsequently, when the board organized, Mr. Byrne was chosen Chairman and Mr. Young Secretary and Treasurer. The offices carry no salary.

The schedule was taken up at the afternoon session, which lasted about two hours. The schedule was explained in detail and was accepted unanimously and without a single change. Each club got pretty nearly what it asked for in the way of holiday and Saturday assignments, and the weaker clubs got just as much as the more powerful.

At the beginning of the season each club will open the grounds of one other club, and no two Association clubs will be brought together on such occasions. The same rule is observed on the holiday dates, when it will be observed no two Association clubs come together.

The season is divided into two parts, according to the instructions given at the Indianapolis meeting. President Hart, of Chicago, wanted two unequal seasons, one of eighty-eight games and one of sixty-six. He was soon convinced that two seasons of seventy-seven games each was the better plan, and the latter prevailed. Each club will play seven games with each other club in each season. In the first season a club will play four games at home and three abroad with a certain club and the reverse in the second season, thus evening up.

The first season will open April 12 with New York in Philadelphia, Brooklyn in Baltimore, Boston in Washington, Pittsburg in Cincinnati, Cleveland in Louisville and Chicago in St. Louis. On April 21, Baltimore opens in Boston, Philadelphia in Brooklyn, Washington in New York, St. Louis in Pittsburg, Cincinnati in Cleveland, and on April 23, Louisville in Chicago.

The first division of 77 games closes July 13, 93 days from the opening date. Deducting 13 Sundays, this leaves but 80 playing days. The second division begins July 15 and ends Oct. 15, just 93 days, less 13 Sundays, leaving, as in the first division, but 80 days to play the 77 games. The holiday assignments are as follows:

Clubs	Memorial Day	Independence Day	Labor Day
Boston	Cleveland	Cincinnati	Louisville
Brooklyn	Cincinnati	Louisville	St. Louis
New York	St. Louis	Chicago	Chicago
Phila'phia	Louisville	St. Louis	Cleveland
Baltimore	Pittsburg	Pittsburg	Cincinnati
Washington	Chicago	Cleveland	Pittsburg
Pittsburg	Baltimore	Baltimore	Washington
Cleveland	Boston	Washington	Phila'phia
Cincinnati	Brooklyn	Boston	Baltimore
Louisville	Phila'phia	Brooklyn	Boston
Chicago	Washington	New York	New York
St. Louis	New York	Phila'phia	Brooklyn

The Baltimore and Pittsburg clubs have agreed to reverse the usual order of things, so far as their holiday games are concerned. Instead of playing in Baltimore Memorial Day they will play in Pittsburg and vice versa on Independence Day. The Washingtons and Pittsburgs will play in Pittsburg Labor Day.

The assignments for other holidays and special dates are: New York in Philadelphia, Brooklyn in Baltimore and Boston in Washington on Good Friday; Brooklyn in Philadelphia, Boston in Baltimore and New York in Washington on Easter Monday; St. Louis in Philadelphia and Chicago in Baltimore on Whit-Monday; Philadelphia in Boston on Bunker Hill Day; Cincinnati, St. Louis and Louisville in Chicago during the Democratic Convention in that city; Cleveland and Louisville in Washington during the annual meeting of the League of American Wheelmen; Chicago in Baltimore on the anniversary of the battle of North Point; New York and Brooklyn in Washington during the Grand Army convention; Chicago, Louisville, St. Louis and Cleveland in Pittsburg while the exposition is open. Each club has at least one Saturday at home and abroad with each other club.

The mileage is very evenly divided. According to Mr. Ebbets's calculations the total mileage of all the clubs for the season will amount to 162,335 miles, an average of 13,528 per club. The distance each club will have to travel is as follows: Boston, 13,384; Brooklyn, 13,320; New York, 12,053; Philadelphia, 12,873; Washington, 12,388; Baltimore, 12,321; Chicago, 14,369; Cincinnati, 14,052; Pittsburg, 13,691; St. Louis, 14,976; Louisville, 14,501; Cleveland, 13,502.

The New York Club has nothing to complain of in the schedule this year. Its opening, holiday and Saturday dates are all first class. And Brooklyn is not far behind in this respect.

The New York and Brooklyn clubs will conflict oftener than usual this season because of the peculiarities of the twelve-club schedule. In the past two years New York and Brooklyn have played at home on the same dates only when the Western clubs were here. Now it is different. Of the seventy-seven home games the two clubs will conflict in sixty-three.

95

A Scoreless Tie in the First Game
of the Championship Series (1892)

Source: *Cleveland Plain Dealer*, October 18, 1892

During the 1892 season, critics attacked the split-season format and the postseason play-off between the champions of each half as a sham. What incentive would the champion of the first half have to play its best in the second half of the season, they argued, since it was guaranteed a spot in the play-off? Their predictions proved accurate: first-half leader Boston coasted through the second half of the season, then mauled Cleveland 5–0 in the play-off after Cy Young and Jack Stivetts, two of the finest pitchers of the decade, battled each other in an eleven-inning scoreless opener.

NOT A SINGLE RUN

DID EITHER TEAM MAKE IN ELEVEN INNINGS

A Wonderful Game at League Park—The First Contest in the Series of Nine for the League Pennant of 1892 Results in a Draw—Sensational Fielding and Magnificent Pitching Make the Game Interesting—A Big Crowd

CLEVELAND 0–BOSTON 0

The first round in the fight for the little piece of bunting that represents so much to base ball teams and to base ball patrons is over and the two gladiators last night rested on their arms, neither having gained an inch of advantage. It was the greatest struggle in the history of the game in Cleveland, and it was also one of the greatest in the history of base ball itself. It was real base ball that was played—scientific playing for runs. That none of these runs came was not the fault of any player. All surely worked hard enough for them.

For eleven innings of the most wonderful kind of playing the men worked to get one runner across the plate. For two full hours of desperate labor they did their utmost to win. At the end of that time neither side had scored that much needed run and then the umpires decided that it was time to let the people go home to supper. Hostilities were suspended with the first game of the series a draw. If yesterday's game is a sample of the kind of ball that these two teams are to put up in this series, they are sure to be the greatest games ever played. Surely yesterday's was one of the greatest. Not only was it close at all times, but it was crowded to the brim with the most brilliant of plays. In fact there were so many pieces of sensational fielding that the spectators finally became accustomed to them and took them as a matter of course. All the afternoon they were kept busy applauding the good plays and let it be said to their credit that the good ones made by the Boston players as well as those made by the men in Cleveland uniforms were applauded. In the sixth inning when Long by a wonderful running catch robbed Childs of what should have been a two-base hit, the hand clapping and the cheering was just as hearty as when McAleer robbed Duffy of a double later on in the game. The people wanted to see the Cleveland team win, but they were not so biased as not to appreciate good ball playing. That is one good feature about Cleveland crowds. And that crowd was a big one as well as an enthusiastic one. There were in round numbers 6,000 people in the stands and scattered back of the ropes that were stretched around the field. In action, as well as in size, it was a holiday crowd. That the people were satisfied with the game, even if Cleveland did not win it, was shown by the nature of the comment heard as the crowd was dispersing. "The best game I ever saw," was the general verdict.

The game was a pitcher's battle from start to finish. Still the ball was hit hard enough by both teams to keep the fielders busy and that kept up the interest. Big Jack Stivetts was in the box for the Boston's and it was a model game that he pitched. In the eleven innings only four hits were made off him. At times he was hit hard, but Boston fielders were always in the way of the ball. He was finely caught by Kelly, whose throwing to bases was splendid. Young was the big Boston man's opponent and if Stivetts pitched a good game, the Clevelander did fully as well. Boston managed to make five hits off Young but the one extra hit was more than offset by the fact that Cy made every Boston man hit the ball—he did not give a base on balls—while Stivetts sent four Clevelanders to first without their hitting at the ball. The fielding on both sides was wonderful. The visitors failed to make a single error while the Clevelands made two. Childs' was a most excusable one and that of Zimmer cost nothing. Just before the game started, President Young of the national league appointed Emslie and Snyder as the day's umpires. They alternated behind the bat and on the bases and both umpired satisfactory ball.

Childs was the first man up in the inning and as usual he had his eye with him. He was very patient and pretty soon Mr. Emslie told him that he might walk down to first base. Then happened an unfortunate thing. Burkett was told to bunt, and he tried hard enough. But, sad to tell, the bunt was a fly right into Stivetts' willing hands, and Childs was caught off first. In the Boston half Long lifted a safe hit over the second base bag. McCarthy fouled out to Zimmer, and then came a piece of that daring base running that Boston newspapers are so fond of telling about. Long took a lead of about a mile off first. He was surprised that the Cleveland players were not at all rattled by this exhibition of daring, and that before he could get back to the bag Zimmer had thrown him out. Then Duffy lifted a neat single into right field and was caught in a bold attempt to steal second.

McKean started the second with a safe hit to left. Virtue bunted and put him on second base. On Stivetts' throw to Long, McKean was declared out and then McAleer was given a base on balls. He stole second, but was left there when O'Connor struck out. Not a Boston runner reached first in their half.

With two out in the third Childs was given a base on balls, but his attempt to

steal second was fatal. The Boston men were again unsuccessful in getting a runner
to first. In the fourth McKean was sent to first on balls, but Virtue was thrown out
by Kelly on Jake's little hit in front of the plate. There were two out in the Boston
half of the fourth when Duffy sent a slow, teasing grounder to Childs. The Kid
fumbled it and Duffy was safe. He stole second and when Zimmer threw the ball
into center field he went to third. That was the first time that a runner on either
team had reached that base. Instead of rattling Young it made him pitch all the
harder. Kelly hit three times at the ball. He did not hit the ball, however, and was
out.

Three Clevelanders went out in order in the fifth. For Boston Nash, who was the
first man up, hit safely to left field. Lowe in an effort to put Nash on second hit the
ball too hard and Nash was thrown out at second by Young. Lowe took that base on
a passed ball and with only one out things began to have a dangerous look for
Cleveland. Tucker hit to Young and was thrown out at first, Lowe taking third.
Then Quinn retired the side on his grounder to McKean.

In the sixth with two men out, Burkett hit to center for a single base. Davis
struck out. McCarthy waited until there were two out for Boston and then he made
a single. Zimmer's good throw stopped him in his wild race for second. In the
seventh neither team got a man to first and the same thing happened in the eighth.

Cleveland came very close to crowding a runner over the plate in the ninth.
Childs sent a fly to Lowe but Burkett beat out a bunt hit. Davis sent a hot grounder
to Tucker. It was too swift to handle and Davis reached first, Burkett taking second.
McKean sent a smoking hot one to Long who threw Davis out at second, Burkett
taking third. While Quinn was talking to the umpire about his decision Burkett
made a dash for the plate. Quinn's throw was good and Kelly put the ball on the
runner. Boston went out in order. The tenth and eleventh were unproductive for
Cleveland, not a runner in the two innings reaching first. It was the same way for
Boston in the tenth. In the eleventh after Lowe and Tucker had gone out, Quinn
sent a short fly to center field that fell safe. But Stivetts sent a fly to O'Connor and
the game was over. Though neither side had won the crowd was satisfied that it had
seen the best game on record and went home contented. The score:

CLEVELAND	AB	R	BH	SH	SB	PO	A	E
Childs, 2b.	3	0	0	0	0	2	4	1
Burkett, l. f.	4	0	2	0	0	0	0	0
Davis, 3b.	4	0	1	0	0	1	3	0
McKean, s. s.	3	0	1	0	0	2	1	0
Virtue, 1b.	4	0	0	1	0	15	0	0
McAleer, c. f.	3	0	0	0	1	3	0	0
O'Connor, r. f.	4	0	0	0	0	3	0	0
Zimmer, c.	4	0	0	0	0	7	3	1
Young, p.	4	0	0	0	0	0	4	0
Totals	33	0	4	1	1	33	15	2

BOSTON	AB	R	BH	SH	SB	PO	A	E
Long, s. s.	4	0	1	0	0	2	6	0
McCarthy, r. f.	4	0	1	0	0	0	0	0
Duffy, c. f.	4	0	1	0	1	1	0	0
Kelly, c.	4	0	0	0	0	8	2	0
Nash, 3b.	4	0	1	0	0	1	2	0
Lowe, l. f.	4	0	0	0	0	2	0	0
Tucker, 1b.	4	0	0	1	0	15	0	0
Quinn, 2b.	4	0	1	0	0	3	5	0
Stivetts, p.	4	0	0	0	0	1	4	0
Totals	36	0	5	1	1	33	19	0

Cleveland	0	0	0	0	0	0	0	0	0—0
Boston	0	0	0	0	0	0	0	0	0—0

Total bases on clean hits—Cleveland 4, Boston 5.

Double plays—Stivetts–Tucker; Long–Quinn–Kelly.

First base on balls—By Stivetts 4 (Childs 2, McKean, McAleer); by Young none.

First base on errors—Duffy.

Left on bases— Cleveland 4, Boston 3.

Struck out—By Stivetts 7 (Davis, Virtue, O'Connor 2, Young 3); by Young 6 (McCarthy, Kelly, Nash, Tucker, Quinn, Stivetts).

Passed ball—Zimmer.

Time—2:00.

Umpires—Emslie and Snyder.

NOTES OF THE GAME

It was a game for one's life.

President Young and wife, and President Soden of the Boston club saw the great game.

There never will again be such a struggle for a game that means so much for its winner.

In the fourth an easy fly fell between Nash and Kelly that either could have taken.

Nash got in two good stops and throws and Davis was right in line with the Boston third baseman.

The Boston players are the wildest and wooliest lot of kickers that ever played on a Cleveland diamond. They kick with neither rhyme nor reason and seem to do it on general principles.

The crowd numbered only a few short of 6,000. It was the best natured and fairest crowd that ever saw a base ball game. The grand stand was bright with ladies. They hooted as heartily for the Clevelands to win as did the men folks.

"Let the dance go on" was Kelly's comment as Umpire Emslie said play. Mike played a good game behind the bat but in a hitting way he was very weak. But then that was no disgrace for many a better batter than Mike is now, found trouble in hitting the curves of Stivetts and Young.

McKean made his great play in the first inning. Duffy was on first with two out and started to steal second. Zimmer's throw was high and to the left of the bag. McKean reached over with one hand, pulled down the ball and put it on the Angel Child in time to get him out. Mac got plenty of deserved applause for the fine play.

96

A Revolutionary Rule Change: 60′ 6″ (1893)

Source: *New York Times*, March 8, 1893

The most significant rule change in the history of baseball was enacted at the NL meeting described below: the magnates agreed to increase the pitching distance by five feet, making the pitcher start his motion from a mark 60′ 6″ from home plate. The pitcher previously had been positioned in a "pitcher's box" that started fifty feet from the plate and ended with a line five and a half feet farther back, from which the pitcher had to initiate his motion. After the back line was moved back, it was replaced with a pitcher's rubber.

Other important changes instituted at this meeting include the introduction of players' benches and the decision not to charge an at bat to batters on a sacrifice. However, prominent players and officials successfully argued against giving the same reward to those who hit fly balls that advanced runners. Sacrifice flies were not recognized until 1908, and then only when they scored a runner. The modern definition of a sacrifice fly was instituted in 1926.

DISCUSSING NEW RULES

MEETING OF THE NATIONAL BASEBALL LEAGUE

MODIFICATIONS ASKED OF THE MEASURES PROPOSED BY THE COMMITTEE ON PLAYING RULES—NO NEW DEALS REPORTED— VIEWS OF THE PLAYERS

Baseball men of all calibres, from the prosperous looking magnate to the meek and humble minor league player, filled the corridor of the Fifth Avenue yesterday. They sat on the lounges usually occupied by office seekers and political strikers and wandered about the hotel renewing acquaintances made on the ball field. It was the annual meeting of the National League and American Association of Baseball Clubs, and everybody was anxious to learn what deals would be consummated and the nature of the changes in the rules.

Nearly everybody left the hotel disappointed. The delegates sat in Parlor F for over eight hours and discussed the proposed changes suggested by the Playing Rules Committee, but beyond inducing the committee to modify some of the changes, little or nothing was done. Toward the latter part of the session the newspaper men, players, managers, and umpires present were called in and asked to give their views on the changes suggested. These will be acted upon to-day.

Prominent among those present were: Manager Powers, Gen. Dixwell, Frank Hough, F. C. Richter, Arlie Latham, Charles Buffinton, Charles Bassett, Harry Stovey, Joseph Hornung, C. C. Hart, Samuel Altmeyer, William Gleason, John Sharrott, Thomas E. Burns, W. W. Burnham, Frank Selee, Harry Wright, John Troy, Patrick Tebeau, J. M. Ward, Wilfred Carsey, Nick Engel, Michael Tiernan, William Collins, Charles Jones, William Sharsig, William Barnie, H. H. Diddle-bock, John Chapman, E. F. Stevens, F. L. Fulenwider, C. D. White, Charles Ebbets, J. J. Franklin, W. W. Newell, L. D. Fassett, J. D. Maloney, and Jeremiah Sullivan.

When the meeting was called the clubs were represented as follows: New-York, Cornelius Van Cott and E. B. Talcott; Brooklyn, C. H. Byrne; Boston, A. H. Soden, W. H. Conant, and J. B. Billings; Washington, F. S. Elliott; Baltimore, H. R. Vanderhorst; Pittsburg, A. K. Scandrett and W. W. Kerr; Louisville, J. H. Ruckstuhl; Cleveland, Frank De H. Robison; St. Louis, Chris Von Der Ahe; Chicago, James A. Hart; Cincinnati, J. T. Brush. Mr. Von Der Ahe was compelled to leave for home early on account of the reported low condition of his son, who was run over a couple of weeks ago by a cable car in St. Louis.

The playing rules were acted upon after the routine business was finished. The proposition to put the pitcher back eight feet led to a heated discussion. Mr. Robison was opposed to making any changes, and he asked the committee to inform those present what good could be wrought from the innovations, as he termed them. Then a vote was taken, and Boston, Cleveland, Pittsburg, Chicago, St. Louis and Louisville voted against the changes. Then it was suggested to move the pitcher back five feet, and with that end in view the following rule was drafted:

"RULE 5. Strike out the old rule and substitute 'the pitcher's boundary will be a rubber plate 12 inches long and 4 inches wide, with the surface even at the distance of 60 feet 6 inches from the outer corner of home plate, so that a line drawn from the centre of second base will give six inches upon either side.' "

Mr. Robison appeared to be the only person present who opposed this rule. He intimated that the Brooklyn delegate on the Playing Rules Committee, if he had his way, would place the pitcher at second base.

"The members of the Playing Rules Committee," he said, "do not know the difference between a flat bat and a round one or a round ball and an oval one," a remark that caused Napoleon Byrne to get red with anger.

To do away with the rows and disputes on the field caused by a claim of balk or illegal delivery, the following rule will be passed:

"RULE 27. The pitcher shall take his position facing the batsman, with both feet square on the ground, one foot in front of and in contact with the pitcher's plate, defined in Rule 5. He shall not raise either foot unless in the act of delivering the ball, nor make more than one step in such delivery. He shall hold the ball before the delivery fairly in front of his body and in sight of the umpire. When the pitcher feigns to throw the ball to a base, he must resume the above position and pause momentarily before delivering the ball to the bat."

"RULE 30. A balk shall be any motion made by the pitcher to deliver the ball to the bat without delivering it."

By Rule 27 it will be seen that no restrictions are to be placed on the pitcher. So long as he keeps one foot on the rubber plate in the twelve-inch space, he can go through all the contortions that he pleases. The unrestricted steps, too, will materially assist some pitchers who were cramped somewhat and their effectiveness was diminished in the old five-and-a-half-foot box. The balk, too, was made very plain.

In the future the players of one team will not be allowed to mingle while on the field with those of the opposing nine. Two benches will be provided on each ground, one for the home team and the other for the visitors, and only the Captain and his assistant will be allowed to go out of a twenty-five-foot boundary. The flat bat was abolished by the substitution of the following for Rule 13: "The bat must be made round and of hard wood, and may have twine on the handle or granulated substance applied not to exceed 18 inches from the end. No bat shall exceed 42 inches in length."

Perhaps one of the best changes made in the rules was the agreement arrived at to score a sacrifice hit as "no time at bat," as is done when a player gets his base on balls, is hit with a pitched ball, or sent to first on an illegal delivery. This is done with a view of promoting more team work among players. Some of the record seekers always claimed that they could not sacrifice to advantage. In reality they did not care to, as it impaired their batting record, and in many instances the record of a player in this respect is an important factor in getting a big salary. The "sluggers," as they are termed, are seldom out of work. This change was suggested by President Young, who claims that it will make a .300-per-cent-batter out of some men who have never been higher than .250 in the list.

A sacrifice will be allowed a man when he purposely strikes a ball so as advance a runner which does not result in a base hit. Some present thought that a long fly caught by an outfielder should be credited as a base hit, but Capt. Ward opposed it. He claimed that any time a player hit to the outfield he was looking for a base hit. Harry Stovey and Capt. Tebeau were of the same opinion. The probabilities are that a sacrifice will be allowed only when an infielder in his own territory handles the ball.

J. J. Franklin, President of the Board of Aldermen of Buffalo; W. W. Newell of Binghamton, L. D. Fassett of Albany, W. W. Burnham of Providence, and J. D. Maloney of Troy are here to ask protection for the Eastern League. Last year $1,500 was paid into the treasury of the big organization for protection, but the League clubs are engaging the Eastern players indiscriminately on the plea that the smaller association did not carry out its contract in letting the men go before Oct. 1. In order to reduce expenses the clubs were disbanded on Sept. 15. Barnett, the clever

Binghamton pitcher, has been engaged by the St. Louis team in spite of the fact that his old club has a contract with him for the season of 1893.

The Eastern League claims that an injustice has been done them, and they will make a vigorous howl if their requests are not complied with.

This afternoon the Globe Trotters Club will be organized at a meeting to be held in the Arena. Only those who journeyed around the world with the Chicago-All America Combination are eligible for membership. After a collation the members and their friends will witness the performance of "Ninety Days" at the Broadway Theatre. Pfeffer, Ryan, Anson, and Williamson sent regrets. Those who promised to be present are J. M. Ward, Captain of the All-America Club; W. I. Snyder, George Wright, A. G. Spalding, Edward Crane, Thomas Burns, Robert Pettit, Thomas Daly, S. Goodfriend, H. Palmer, Edward Hanlan, and George Wood. A. G. Spalding's wife and mother, Mrs. Anson, and Mrs. Williamson, who accompanied the players on the trip, will be made honorary members.

The new Arbitration Committee will be composed of Messrs. Young, Soden and Vonderhorst.

Capt. Ward has signed contracts with Harry Lyons and McQuaid, a California outfielder. He is a brother of the umpire, and is said to be a first-class man.

97

A Fourth of July Game in Sitka, Alaska (1893)

Source: *Sitka Alaskan*, July 8, 1893

This article reveals the symbolic importance of baseball in small towns across America, especially in a distant port like Sitka. The impromptu game may have pitted sailors and seafarers (the Neptunes) against the town's settlers (the Daisies).

THE GLORIOUS FOURTH

Early in the morning the national colors were waving from the many flagstaffs, the gunboat Pinta and the Coast Survey steamer Patterson dressed ship, and a general holiday was observed. No arrangements for a public celebration having been made, a stillness, as can be observed on every Sunday morning, reigned over the town until precisely at Noon, the guns of the water battery boomed forth the national salute, the chimes of St. Michael's Church commenced to ring merrily in honor of the day, and the cling-clang of the Fire Alarm Bell joined in and marred the harmony of the Russian Church's bells.

At 2 o'clock, in the afternoon, a base ball game was played which lasted for over two hours and a half, attracting young and old to the Parade Ground to witness the friendly contest. Mrs. C. S. Johnson kept the score of the game, and we are able, through her kindness, to give the following result:

Score of Base Ball game, July 4th. Neptunes—Runs 7. Indian Joe 1 run, in 1st inning; J. Burns 2 runs, in 1st and 2d innings; Ed Haley 1 run, in 1st inning; Alex. 1 run, in 6th inning; Carpenter 1 run, in 6th inning; Porter 1 run, in 2d inning.

Daisies—Runs 12. N. Bolshanin 1 run, 1st inning; Hope 2 runs, in 1st and 4th inning; T. Haley 1 run, in 1st inning; Jack 3 runs in 1st, 3d, and 6th innings; Larianoff 1 run, in 3d inning; J. Kaznakoff 2 runs, in 3d and 5th; Tealer, 1 run, in 3d; Dixon, 1 run in 5th innings.

The day closed with a display of fireworks on board the Pinta, and another in front of the residence of Mr. Adolph A. Meyer, the pyrotechnic effects of both of which were much admired.

98

Ban Johnson's Career as a Baseball Executive Launched (1893)

Source: *Indianapolis Journal*, November 22, 1893

Byron Bancroft (Ban) Johnson covered sports for the Cincinnati Commercial-Appeal between 1887 and 1894. His days as a journalist ended when he was chosen president of the revived Western League. By singlehandedly arranging the league's schedule, strongly supporting his umpires, and working tirelessly to keep ailing franchises afloat, Johnson was soon hailed as the most successful league president in the nation.

EIGHT CLUBS NAMED

Western Baseball League Completes Its Organization
Sioux City the Last Club Taken In—Ten Per Cent Sinking Fund—
Schedule Committee

Yesterday the promulgators of the Western Baseball League met in secret session in Room 2 of the Grand Hotel, and were in session nearly all the afternoon and night. Ben [sic] Johnson, of Cincinnati, presided, and was elected president, secretary and treasurer of the league. Messrs. Cushman, Long and Manning were appointed as a committee on constitution and by-laws, and were in consultation over the work all afternoon.

The discussion over the eighth city to be taken into the League was hot, and "long." John S. Barnes, who is representing Vanderbeck, of Detroit, made a hard fight for Omaha, but the financial condition of the Sioux City club loomed up so much better that that city was taken in. This makes the league comprise Minneapolis, Kansas City, Milwaukee and Sioux City in the West, and Indianapolis, Toledo, Grand Rapids and Detroit in the East. Omaha and Lincoln both went by the board.

The committee on constitution is still out, and is considering the proposition of assessing each club $500, to be held as a guaranty of good faith. During the season 10 per cent. of the net receipts will be reserved as a sinking fund. When this reserve amounts to $8,000 the guaranty will be taken down. The board of directors will be elected to-day and the schedule committee appointed. The annual fall meeting will be held in October each year in the city holding the championship for the year. The question as to players has not been settled, but that will not be a difficult one, as there are plenty in the market. Sioux City is lined up with a good team. Milwaukee, Minneapolis and Toledo have good clubs to draw from.

Mr. Brush is in a position to make Indianapolis the champion if he so desires, as he owns the Cincinnati team, and can sign any National League players for the home team who are a little too shaky for the League.

99

Henry Chadwick Argues for Sacrifices over Slugging (1894)

Source: *Spalding's Official Base Ball Guide*, 1895 (reprint, St. Louis: Horton, 1989), pp. 102–4

Although the 1893 increase in the pitching distance resulted in an unprecedented offensive explosion, Henry Chadwick, editor of Spalding's Guide, *was not an advocate of "slugging." He continued to urge players to become more proficient in bunting and place hitting. Chadwick felt that adding five and a half feet to the pitching distance would make it easier for hitters to execute successful bunts.*

The Batting of 1894

THE TEAM-WORK AT THE BAT

It goes to the credit of the leading teams in the pennant race of 1894 that the first three clubs did better team-work at the bat, and more of it, than any previous trio of the kind known in the annals of the League. In fact, competent managers and captains of teams have learned in recent years, by costly experiment, that one of the most potent factors in winning pennants is the method of handling the ash known as good *team-work at the bat*, the very essence of which is devoting all the batsman's efforts to *forwarding runners by base hits*, and not by each player's going to the bat simply to build up a high record of base hits without regard to forwarding runners on base. Suppose the first batsman in a game to take his position at the bat makes a two or three-bagger at the outset. Of course the object of the batsman who succeeds him would be to send the runner home the best way he can, either by a base hit or a sacrifice hit. In striving to do this, the very worst plan is to try solely for a home run hit, as it only succeeds once in thirty or forty times, and not that against skilful, strategic pitching. Time and again were batsmen, last season, left on third base after opening the innings with a three-bagger, owing to the stupid work of the succeeding batsmen in trying to "line 'em out for a homer," instead of doing real team-work at the bat.

Of course, good "sacrifice hitting" is part and parcel of team-work at the bat, but this kind of hitting was not done to any special extent last season by a majority of the League batsmen.

SACRIFICE HITTING

There is one thing about the point of play in batting known as "sacrifice hitting" which is not as thoroughly understood as it should be. A majority of batsmen seem to be of the impression that when they are called upon to forward a base runner by a "sacrifice hit," all they have to do is to go to the bat and have themselves put out, so that the base runner at first may be able to reach second base on the play which puts the batsman out. This is a very erroneous idea of the true intent of a sacrifice hit. No skilful batsman ever goes to the bat purposely to hit the ball so as to have himself put out; that would be a very silly move. On the contrary, he takes his bat in hand every time, with the primary object of *making a base hit* if he possibly can; but in trying for this strongest point in batting, he proposes to make the desired hit in such a way that if he fails to make the base hit he will at least hit the ball in that direction in the field which will oblige the fielders to throw him out at first base. With this object in view he will always strive for a safe hit to *right field,* especially by means of a hard "bounder" in that direction, so as to force the second baseman to run to right short to field the ball, in which case the runner at first base will be able to steal to second on the hit in nine cases out of ten. Another good effort for a sacrifice hit is to *bunt* the ball so that it may roll towards third base, out of reach of the baseman or pitcher. A third sacrifice hit is that of a long high ball to the outfield, which admits of a chance for a catch, but so far out in the field that the runner will have an opportunity to steal a base on the catch. This latter point won't work, of course, when two men are out; moreover, it should be the last point aimed at.

A great deal of bosh has been written—mostly by the admirers of "fungo" hitting—about sacrifice hitting being something that should not be in the game, just as these fungo-hitting-advocates try to write down *bunt* hitting—the most difficult place hit known to the game. This class of writers think that the very acme of batting skill is the home run hit, a hit which any muscular novice in batting on amateur fields can accomplish without difficulty, and where more home runs are made in a single season than in two seasons by the best managed professional teams. The effort to make home runs leads to more chances for catches by out-fielders in one game than there are home runs made in fifty. The exhaustion which follows a home run hit, with its sprinting run of 120 yards at full speed, is entirely lost sight of by the class of patrons of the game who favor home runs. One season, a few years ago, the tail-end team of the League excelled all its rivals in scoring home runs, while the pennant-winning team took the honors and the prize solely on account of its excellence in team-work at the bat. The mere record of the best averages in scoring base hits in batting seems to be regarded by the majority of "cranks" in base ball as the only sound criterion of good batting. This is one of the fallacies of the game, as such a record is unreliable. The only true criterion of good batting is the record which shows the players who excel in the batting which forwards runners; and this record the existing scoring rules, up to 1895, did not admit of, the champion batsman being regarded as the one who excels in his base-hit average, without regard to the runners his base hits forwarded. For instance, one batsman in a game will make three three-baggers, and forward but a single runner by his three hits, while another batsman by a single base hit, a good "bunt" hit and a telling "sacrifice" hit, will forward *four runners*; and yet by the existing scoring rules the record batsman carries off all the honors in the score, and the team-worker at the bat does not get the slightest credit for the effective batting he has done.

100

The Page Fence Giants Play the Cincinnati Reds (1895)

Source: *Cincinnati Enquirer*, April 12, 1895

Although African Americans had been driven out of organized baseball almost completely by the mid-1890s, black and white clubs continued to play exhibition games against each other. The Page Fence Giants, who represented the Page Woven Wire Fence Company of Adrian, Michigan, were one of the most powerful of the black barnstorming teams of the era. The Giants featured John (Bud) Fowler, a legendary figure in black baseball who had been playing since at least 1872. Sporting Life *reported in 1885 that "those who know say there is no better second baseman [than Fowler] in the country." Notice the* Enquirer*'s typically casual use of racial stereotypes and the sense of pride the Giants evoked in black spectators.*

"COME SEVEN"

"And Then Come 'Leven"
It Was a Lively Game All Around
The Reds Vanquished the Colored Giants
Second Game With the Same Team This Afternoon
History of an Old Timer—Bud Fowler's Long Siege on the Diamond

"Come seben! Come eleben!"

The colored troops fought nobly, but they couldn't reach the desired goal. Consequently the stock of red-fire, Roman candles and skyrockets that was to have lighted up the sky above Little Buck, Big Buck and Ral-Row last night can now be purchased at bargain-counter rates.

Every colored barber, every wine boy, every palace car porter and every member of the local colored population of the male gender who could get off yesterday afternoon was on the seats at the Cincinnati Park when time was called for the game between the Reds and the Page Fence Colored Giants.

Such a shouting and a jubilating hasn't disturbed the ambient air of the Millcreek Valley in many a day. It was a little cold around the outer edges yesterday, but it was warm, mighty warm, among "dem hot gentlemen up in the pavillion."

The Reds won the game, but it is in the nature of a coincidence that the victory should be achieved by figures that are dear to the hearts of colored folk. Could a more appropriate score for the game have been made than 11 to 7? While the local team won the game they didn't have a picnic doing it. The colored players gave them an argument right from the start.

Along about the third inning, when the score stood 2 to nothing in favor of the Giants, you could have tossed a ripe Georgia watermelon or a fat possum, done to the last turn, down among that gang of colored rooters in the pavillion and they would have kicked it aside and gone on looking at the game. About this time you couldn't get close enough to the players to hand them a ripe peach.

All jokes aside, it was a great game. Bud Fowler, the veteran, has got together a great team of players. They will win more games than they will lose. Brooks, the center fielder, made three wonderful catches. Malone, the third baseman, played in good style, and Bud Fowler wears his 47 years like a young blood. He showed yesterday that he hasn't forgotten how. They are good coachers, and put up a scrappy game of ball. Hoy and Hogriever carried off the honors for the Reds. Big Hank Spies played first in Captain Ewing's place, and played it well.

The first two innings were uneventful. In the third the colored boys made two runs. Hopkins, Burns, Miller and Taylor hit out for singles in rapid succession and two runs were the result.

The Reds finally got down to business in the fourth. Holliday got a base on balls. Hoy then cranked out a beauty to deep center for three bases. Smith hit down to third and a throw was made for home. In attempting to run Hoy down Malone hit him in the back and he scored. Merritt went out on a fly, but Hogriever sent Smith home with a clean single.

In the fifth the home team increased the lead. A safe hit by McPhee and an error by Taylor, bases on balls by Smith and Merritt and safe hits by Hogriever and Parrott netted five runs.

The colored team scored three runs in the sixth. Two of them were gifts from Umpire Sheridan. After one hand was out Brooks, Malone and Nelson hit for singles, scoring one run. With men on second and first, Hopkins hit down to Parrott. The latter turned around with the ball in his hand and didn't know what to do with it. He finally threw to first and Spies went it back to third in time to cut off Malone, but the umpire wouldn't allow it. Then Burns hit for a single and two runs were scored. The Reds made two runs in the sixth on hits by Spies and Holliday and a two-bagger by Hoy.

THE SCORE:

CINCINNATI	AB	R	1B	PO	A	E
Latham, 3b	5	1	1	2	2	0
McPhee, 2b	3	1	1	3	1	0
Spies, 1b	5	1	1	9	2	0
Holliday, cf	4	2	1	2	0	0
Hoy, lf	5	3	4	2	0	1
Smith, ss	3	2	0	1	4	2
Merritt, c	2	1	0	4	2	0
Hogriever, rf......	5	0	3	1	0	0
Parrott, p	3	0	1	1	2	0
Phillips, p	1	0	0	1	0	0
Totals	36	11	12	26*	13	3

GIANTS	AB	R	1B	PO	A	E
Taylor, 1b	4	0	1	9	0	2
Fowler, 2b........	4	0	0	6	2	1
Johnson, ss	5	1	1	0	5	1
Brooks, cf	4	2	1	3	0	0
Malone, 3b	5	1	3	1	3	0
Nelson, lf	4	1	1	1	1	1
Hopkins, rf.......	4	1	1	0	1	0
Burns, c	4	1	2	4	1	0
Miller, p	3	0	2	0	3	1
Howland, p	1	0	0	0	2	1
Totals	38	7	12	24	18	7

*Declared out for not touching base.

Innings	1	2	3	4	5	6	7	8	9	
Cincinnatis	0	0	0	3	5	2	1	0	x—11	
Page Fence Giants	0	0	2	0	0	3	2	0	0—7	

Two-Base Hits—Hoy, Johnson, Malone. Three-Base Hit—Hoy. First Base on Balls—McPhee 2, Holliday, Smith 2, Merritt 3, Taylor, Brooks. Passed Balls—Brooks 2. Time—2:05. Umpire—Sheridan.

What Old Hickory Jim was to the turf Bud Fowler, the second baseman and Captain of the Page Fence Giants, is to the baseball world. There are old-timers, and again there are all old-timers, but such veterans as Candy Nelson and Adrian C. Anson are young bloods as compared to this relic of the game. Fowler has been playing baseball for the past 20 years, and he is yet as spry and as fast in his actions as any man on his team. He has not charley horses or stiff joints, but can bend over and get up a grounder like a young blood. Bud has played match games for trappers' furs. He has been rung in to help out a team for the championship of a mining camp and bags of gold dust. He has played with cowboys and the Indians. He has crossroaded it from one town to another all over the Far West, playing for what he could get and taking a hand to help out a team. He used to be a pitcher, then he became a catcher. Finally, in case of an emergency, he would get in and play either position just as the occasion required. When the baseball business was dull he would get out and turn a trick as a sprinter. Bud can do 100 yards close to even time, and has brought home the coonskins many a time by the use of his legs.

But first started in this business with the Mutuals, of Washington, D.C., in 1869. He has played every season since that time. Not only has he played every season, but more. For the last 11 years he has put in the winters at Los Angeles, Florida, Cuba or New Orleans, and played ball every winter. Bud talked entertainingly in THE ENQUIRER office about his experience on the diamond. It is taking a peep back in the swaddling clothes days of the national game to hear this relic of the year of the famous undefeated 1869 Reds talk. He has played in all the state, interstate, international, Western, Pacific, Northern Pacific and Lake Leagues that were ever organized. Bud Fowler was 49 years old the 10th of last month, but to look at him you would set him down to be not more than 25. After 25 summers and 11 winters in the harness he hasn't even broken a finger joint to show what business he has engaged in. Altogether he is a wonder. Fowler attributes his remarkable condition to the fact that he has always taken care of himself. Wine, women, and song have played a very little part in the life of this veteran of the diamond. Go out and see him play second base this afternoon.

Whenever the Giants score a good point the gang of colored rooters in the pavillion would loosen up and let out a few links of voice. A gang of Sioux Indians in the throes of the Ghost or Green Corn Dance couldn't give this crowd any pointers in the yelling line. Along about the third inning, when the score was 2 to 0 in favor of the colored team, they were "tuned up" in fine style.

The big glove rule has no terrors for the Page Fence Giants. Every man on the team except the catcher and first baseman plays bare-handed.

The colored Giants play their last game to-day and leave for Grand Rapids to-night. Holland, formerly of the Chicago Colored Unions, will pitch for the Giants, and is said to have speed equal to Rusie's. Rhines or Foreman will do the pitching for the home team.

John Ward Explains the Hit-and-Run Play (1896)

Source: *Spalding's Official Base Ball Guide, 1896* (reprint, St. Louis: Horton, 1989), pp. 89–90

One of the most ingenious offensive tactics is the hit-and-run play. Here Henry Chadwick reports that John Ward credited Tommy McCarthy and several other Boston players with perfecting the play around 1893. However, Ward, in his 1888 book Baseball: How to Become a Player *(Philadelphia: Athletic Publishing; reprint, Cleveland: Society for American Baseball Research, 1993, pp. 133–34), had already described how the play should be executed.*

Excellence in base-running has become one of the most necessary adjuncts to the winning of pennants. It is questionable if, in the annals of the League, there has ever been such good work done in base-stealing as by the Boston team of 1893. That it was the strongest element of their success in winning the championship that year goes without saying. That most scientific of professional ball players, John M. Ward, in commenting on the Bostons' team-work in this respect in 1893, said:

"I have never, in my twelve years' experience on the diamond, seen such skilful playing. The Boston players use more head-work and private signals than any other team in the country, and that alone is the reason why they can win the championship with such apparent ease. McCarthy is the chief schemer. He is the man who has introduced his new style of play into the team and he has been ably assisted by Nash, Duffy, Long, Lowe and Carroll. These men have the utmost confidence in one another's ability to carry out instructions, and they work together as one man. 'Team-work in the field' used to be a prime factor in a pennant-winning team, but now 'team-work at the bat' is the latest wrinkle and the Bostons have it down fine.

"One thing that has facilitated their innovation is an ability to *bat scientifically* and run bases more swiftly than players of other teams. But to this ability must be added head-work, a complete system of signals and confidence in themselves and one another. I have made a careful study of the play of this team, and I find that they have won a great many games by scoring nearly twice as many runs as they made hits."

The Bostons led all the League clubs in 1893 in both base-stealing and run-getting, and their total runs scored exceeding 1,000, while the tail-end club barely scored 700. Ward, in his description of their combination that year of team-work at the bat with skilful base-running, said:

"Say, for instance, that they have a man on first and nobody out. Under the old style of play a sacrifice would be the proper thing. Then the man on first would reach second while the batsman was put out. The Bostons, however, work this scheme: The man on first makes a bluff attempt to steal second, but runs back to first. By this it becomes known whether the second baseman or the short stop is going to cover second for the throw from the catcher. Then the batsman gets the signal from the man on first that he is going to steal on a certain pitched ball. The moment he starts for second the batsman just pushes the ball for the place occupied only a moment before by the infielder who has gone to cover second base. That is, if the second baseman covers the bag the batter pushes the ball slowly to right field; if it is the short stop, the ball is pushed to left field. Of course, it takes a skilful batter to do this, but they have such hitters on the Boston nine. Now, when that ball is pushed to the outfield, the man who has already started to steal second just keeps right on to third, while the batsman is safe at first. Then the trick is tried over again, and in most cases successfully. The man on first makes another bluff to steal, and when the batsman learns who is to cover second base, he pushes the ball out again, the man on third scoring, the man on first reaching third, and the batsman gaining first."

The Bostons did not equal their play of 1893, in this important respect, in 1894, and hence their defeat that year after winning the pennant three times in succession. And they played with still less effect in team-work in 1895, and therefore had to be content with sixth place in the race.

Boston and Baltimore Conclude an Epic Pennant Race (1897)

Source: *Baltimore Sun*, September 28, 1897

The 1897 season featured one of the tightest pennant races in major league history. Despite accumulating two separate seventeen-game winning streaks, the Boston Beaneaters could not distance themselves from the Baltimore Orioles. During the final month of the season, the teams jockeyed for the front position, but neither team could gain an advantage of more than one game. In the penultimate game of the season, Boston outslugged Baltimore 19–10. With this decisive win, the Beaneaters regained the lead.

The teams then contended for the Temple Cup, first offered by Pittsburgh sportsman William C. Temple in 1894 to the winner of the postseason series between the first- and second-place NL teams. The Cup series failed to excite much fan interest, and after the Orioles won the 1897 series 4–1 over Boston, the series was discontinued. No postseason championship series would be attempted until the 1903 World Series.

BOSTON ON TOP

An Extraordinary Concourse Of People Turns Out To See The Orioles Defeated By 19 To 10

30,000 SEE THE ROUT

Heavy Hearts Of The Multitude And Joy For A Few

VICTORS ARE CHEERED

Visitors' Band Plays Maryland And The Glad Hand Is Shown

HEAVY BATTING ALL AROUND

But Baltimore Makes A Mistake In The Pitcher's Box
Corbett, Nops, Hoffer And Amole All Put In To Pitch, While Nichols Works Out The Whole Game—Details Of The Contest—How The Crowds Passed Into Union Park And How They Looked And Acted While There—The Attendance For The Series Breaks All Records—Men From The Hub Go Away With Hearts That Are Warm Toward This City

It was a colossal affair in all its horrible, heartrending features. The excitement was stupendous, the interest so big as to roll like a tidal wave all over the land, the expectations were huge on both sides, the throng was enormous and even the score of 19 to 10 was big, while the difference by which the Boston Baseball Club walloped the champion Orioles, of Baltimore, was too large for comprehension— in this latitude.

After the novelty of sitting in so vast a concourse as thirty thousand persons in one great circle, the realities of the hour came home with reflection, and while some few hearts from Boston town were running over with the happiness of victory, the tear-blurred eyes of still thirty thousands beheld a misty vision of an ocean of faces, and a meteoric shower of two-base hits from Boston bats, while some tiny white-clad champions were chasing the leathern balls to the ends of the earth, even as little children run to find where the lustrous rainbow's arch rests upon the land that they may gather the golden treasures there.

Let us drop a tear and go on, and let it be a hot and scalding tear, for verily Boston is hot stuff, and her beans are smoking. Let her light her bonfires and regild her State House dome and send forth some modern Paul Revere to ride and spread the news.

All honor to the victors, and to the vanquished, too. For Baltimore and Boston have met twelve times, and each has won half of the battles. Three times in succession has Baltimore gained the pennant, and three times successively was that sign of championship flung to the breeze by Boston. Had Oriole pitchers been in condition or more successfully selected yesterday the air would have rung with shouts of gladness, but disappointed as the home partisans were, there is more cause for gladness, for they were fair and generous and sportsmanlike enough to cheer old Boston for the victory so gallantly won—so gamely earned. Were ever two teams so evenly matched before? Cheer up, Baltimore. Those who gave honor to your conquerors are with you in defeat. You will not be defeated until the season is over, and one game lost by Boston may give you the championship.

IN THE PUSH

What a struggle for life it was to get into Union Park yesterday; what a battle to get out again. From every quarter the thousands came and packed Huntingdon avenue for blocks. Long lines, waiting for tickets, extended to the east as far as the York road, and another line stretched its length westward to Charles street, while new entrances were formed and still other files of surging, struggling humanity were formed to find their way into the inclosure through the clubhouse door and the wagon gates.

Once there was a crash. The eastern-most wagon gate, on Huntingdon avenue, was pushed from its foundation, and two thousand persons, some with tickets and some without, some with the cheapest pasteboards and some with grandstand cards, burst through the new opening and dashed madly into the grounds, not caring what positions they had or had not bought, but intent only upon getting into the grounds to see the baseball game of a century—the last on earth, it seemed to be.

Inside, the seats filled as if by magic. Only in the ladies' stand was there a slow filling up, but most of the seats here were reserved, and it took a manful and muscular effort of escorts to get their ladies through the thick fringe along the top and entering tier without playing havoc with hats, dresses and ribbons.

Meanwhile, the crowds poured in upon the field. When the gates upon the bleachers' side opened there was a wild scramble across the turf for good places on the front line of the right field. Some fell and were trodden upon by those behind, but these picked themselves up, brushed out their kinks and joined the chase.

But now there is a wild roar of the gathered multitude. Horns sang out a long, loud refrain, cowbells and bazoos were sounded and cheers arose, for the Boston rooters 150 strong had arrived. Another such outburst and the Boston players came through the gates, and there was music by the rooters' band.

HOT TIMES IN OLD TOWN

As the catchy strain, with its pleasant swing, struck the ear, everybody knew it was "Hot Times in Old Town." Every horn in the thousands in the park, and every other engine of noise, including stove-pipes and tincans filled with stones, kept time with the music, and those who had only brought their voices along sang in a sort of inharmonious melody. Cheers rent the air after this, and then the band played "Maryland, My Maryland."

By this time the view from one of the upper boxes in the middle of the grand stand took in a wonderful picture. There were the mass of faces on the bleachers, and broad circle of people extending around the deep ball park, down one side, across centre field and up again to the grand stand; the thousands on the house-tops outside of the grounds, the thick cluster of men in shirt sleeves along the top of the bleacher railings, the men and boys perched high upon the grand stand rafters and the hundreds of others who seemingly hung upon nails and studded all the fences and obscured every advertising sign.

This picture remained unchanged until the close. When the last Oriole had been put out and the game was among the lost, the rope barriers were dashed aside, and the crowds in the twinkling overspread the whole field. So thick was the mass that from the topmost seats the entire green-sward was blotted from view.

Pellmell toward the visiting players dashed the greater portion of the crowd, and about them and their encouraging friends from Boston occurred the most striking scenes of the afternoon.

THE BLOW THAT HURT FATHER

It was a terrific charge, but the Bostonians had been too long in Baltimore to misinterpret the intention of the sway which was massing about them. The band was playing "The Blow Nearly Killed Father," when the crowd gave three hearty cheers for Boston and its club and rooters. The tune switched to "Maryland, My Maryland," and the crowds from far and near cheered again and again in recognition of the fact that the Massachusetts boys had captured Maryland for the day. Then the band played "Dixie," and the Northerners and Southerners tried to outdo each other with cheering.

The Boston players had been hauled up into the stand by their admirers from home, who embraced them in a delirium of happiness. From this place, where they overlooked the shouting Baltimoreans on the ground below, they threw out dozens of little bags filled with beans, as if to get rid of ballast and sail higher still into the clouds of victory. . . .

103

The Brush Purification Plan (1898)

Source: *Sporting Life*, January 15, 1898

During the 1890s NL owners became increasingly concerned about complaints arising from unruly player behavior. "It is impossible for a respectable woman to go to the games of the National League without running the risk of hearing language which is disgraceful," complained veteran George Wright in a Sporting Life *interview. According to sportswriter Hugh Fullerton, "the Baltimore park reeked with obscenity and profanity." In response to such protests, in 1898 John T. Brush obtained a resolution calling for the dismissal and blacklisting of any player who used "filthy" or "obscene" language. The net result of the Brush resolution on player behavior was apparently negligible. Notice Brush's distinction between "profane" and "obscene" language.*

BRUSH EXPLAINS

THE PURPORT OF HIS BLACKLISTING RESOLUTION

He Says Its Scope Has Been Misunderstood and That Obscene Players Only Are to be Made the Victims of Capital Punishment

Cincinnati, O., Jan. 11.—The apostle of reform, Mr. John T. Brush, has departed for Indianapolis. However, he left behind him information that will enlighten many critics who are benighted on the subject of the proposed rule for the punishment of players using obscene language on the ball field. The resolution introduced by Mr. Brush at the recent League meeting and which was passed by unanimous vote is generally misunderstood, and the author of it, as well as the League in general, is being roundly abused in consequence. Editor Charles Zuber had a talk with Mr. Brush on the subject Monday and he corroborated what the "Times-Star" said some time ago, namely: that there would be various grades of punishment according to the offense; that the extreme penalty would be life-long expulsion.

PUBLIC MISAPPREHENSION

"The resolution appears to have been generally misunderstood," said Mr. Brush. "In the first place, it calls only for punishment for obscene language. You know there is a difference between profane and obscene language. Profane language is printable—at least characters can be used to make it understood in print. On the other hand, obscene language is unprintable and cannot be used by gentlemen. Profane language, used in the heat of an argument, will not drive people away from ball games. Obscene language will, and it is to put a stop to that which will drive people away from the games that the resolution was introduced and will be passed. It does not touch on any other rowdy actions of players on the field, as there are existing rules covering

THE MINOR OFFENSES.

"And it should be understood, too, that every breach of this rule does not mean life-long expulsion from the League, for it does not. It is only in extreme cases that full penalty will be inflicted. Minor offenses will be treated with milder punishment. In connection with this general belief that the extreme penalty would be inflicted in every case it has been argued that it would be wrong to deprive a player of his livelihood because he offended. Obscene language will drive people, especially ladies, away from games as quickly as would dishonest play. Twenty years ago the League put a stop to crooked ball playing by blacklisting Craver, Hall, Devlin and Nichols for life, because they accepted bribes to lose games. And there has been no selling of games since that time. One example would have done as well as the four. They were blacklisted to purge the game of all crookedness that might be contemplated by players at any time.

ONE EXAMPLE WILL SUFFICE

"In the present the use of obscene language threatens the game as did crookedness twenty years ago. And only one example is needed to put a stop to the threatening evil of to-day. We must have clean base ball, and if the players can not be made to understand this by arguments and threats, they must be made to feel it by severe punishment." Comment is unnecessary. Mr. Brush's remarks should receive the indorsement of every fair-minded critic who has the interest of the game at heart. There is no excuse whatever for the use of obscene language on the field.

7

The Birth of the American League
and the Origins of the World Series,
1899–1905

Aided by the return of prosperity and continued squabbling among NL owners, Ban Johnson made bold plans for transforming his Western League into a major league. Following the 1899 season he renamed his loop the American League (AL); the following year he planted franchises in Chicago and three other cities just vacated by the NL—Cleveland, Baltimore, and Washington, D.C. After declaring the AL a major league in 1901, Johnson launched a frontal assault on the senior circuit by urging its players to defect to the AL.

Johnson's success in attracting NL players, and in planting a franchise in New York in 1903, persuaded the war-weary NL to sign a new National Agreement with the AL. This opened the door for the resumption of a postseason championship series between the two league pennant winners. Although Pittsburgh and Boston played such a series following the 1903 season, the "World Series" was not officially established until 1905.

104

Western League Disbanded and Renamed the American League (AL) (1899)

Source: *Chicago Inter-Ocean,* October 12, 1899

When Ban Johnson transformed his Western League into the American League he did not seek independence from the National Agreement, but he did ask the NL to exempt his league from the draft for two years and to double the draft price to $1,000. This article analyzes not only the initial AL meeting but also the conflicts within the NL ownership.

CHANGE THE NAME

Old Western Is Now the New American League

NEW DEAL IN BASE BALL

Chicago Will Be Represented in the Western Circuit
The Good Mr. Brush Figures in the New Scheme—
Details of Yesterday's Meeting of Western League

A brand new baseball league was organized at a meeting held in the Great Northern hotel yesterday afternoon. By a unanimous vote the members of the Western league decided to change the title of their organization, and at the same time extend the scope of their operations.

The old Western league is dead, and in its place is a new organization which has been officially named the American league. This new league will consist of the following cities: Chicago, Kansas City, Milwaukee, Indianapolis, Minneapolis, Detroit, Buffalo, and either Cleveland or Toronto.

In addition, in securing a foothold in this city these magnates of the West have secured several other favors from the men who control the premier baseball organization of the country. To begin with, the new American league has asked for a revision of the much-talked-about drafting rule. President Johnson, the official head of the organization, has been instructed to present a formal request to the National board of arbitration for a revisal of the drafting rule which now prevails in the National league. Johnson will ask that the new league be allowed to hold its players for two years, and that the drafting price be increased from $500 to $1,000. This request will, in all probability, be granted, and the new league recognized as the legitimate successor of the old American association. The changing of the name and the concessions which will be granted by the major organizations constitute the first move in a very clever game of baseball politics. The old league people know that Ban Johnson and his associates hold the balance of power in baseball, and they make no secret of their desire to keep their Western brethren in line.

Every concession that has been made or will be made to the old Western league people is with the idea of retaining this organization under the national agreement. There is precious little sentiment involved. The old league men are frightened by this talk of a rival league, and they realize their danger.

THIS IS THE SITUATION

Here is the situation in a nutshell. The good Mr. Brush of Indianapolis still shapes the policy of the national league. During the last ten days this ever-amiable autocrat has been busy making baseball history. He began by grasping the hand of Andrew Freedman and convincing that good looking, but erratic individual, that "things are seldom what they seem in baseball." After taking up with Freedman, the good man from Indiana sprung another surprise by shattering the more or less famous Brush–Hart–Robison syndicate.

Brush has broken with Robison for all time, and his relations with Hart are strained, to say the least. Robison practically ruined baseball in St. Louis, and even his best friends admit that Mr. Hart has put in a rather disappointing season in Chicago. Brush never had any use for losers, and all things considered, his latest move will not startle the men who follow the politics of the national game. There are men in the Western league who are of more than passing value to Brush. He knows that with Freedman in New York and the proper men at the head of a second club in Chicago, the National league will be in a position to laugh at the efforts of the men who are endeavoring to form a rival organization.* He knows, furthermore, the only way to keep the Western league people in line is to give them a fair showing, both as regards territory and the protection of their players.

As a result, Brush and his new associates, who, by the way, are Eastern men, have agreed to give the Western league a club in Chicago, and it may possibly be, if the rival league people manage to make good, that this territory will be extended, and that a club in St. Louis, owned and managed by Comiskey, will form the eighth club in the new Western circuit. If Brush had his way he would make Comiskey the official head of the St. Louis major league team, for both he and Becker, the St. Louis grocer, who owns a large block of stock in the St. Louis club, have tired of Frank Robison. The only obstacle in the way of consummating the deal is that Comiskey will not consider any salary offers. . . . The story of yesterday's proceedings follows:

CHANGE THE NAME OF THE LEAGUE

The meeting did not begin until late in the afternoon, but the delegates managed to transact considerable business before they adjourned.

*The "rival organization" was the AA, which several were attempting to revive. This effort—unrelated to a similar attempt in 1894—seemed to be succeeding until Cap Anson, after being chosen as the AA's first president, abandoned the upstarts. For details see David Pietrusza, *Major Leagues: The Formation, Sometimes Absorption, and Mostly Inevitable Demise of 18 Professional Baseball Organizations, 1871 to Present* (Jefferson, N.C.: McFarland, 1991), pp. 135–44.—Ed.

When President Ban Johnson called the meeting to order these men answered to the roll: W. F. C. Golt and Robert Allen of Indianapolis, James Franklin of Buffalo, Charles Comiskey of St. Paul, M. R. Killilea, Connie Mack and F. C. Gross of Milwaukee, G. A. Van Derbeck of Detroit, James H. Manning of Kansas City, and C. H. Saulpaugh of Minneapolis. Comiskey of St. Paul held the proxy of Loftus of Grand Rapids.

Five minutes after the meeting had been called to order Golt of Indianapolis offered the formal motion that the name of the organization be changed and that it be called the American league. This motion was promptly seconded by Franklin of Buffalo, and it was passed unanimously.

Then President Johnson was authorized to make the necessary changes in the constitution to meet the requirements of the new condition. Johnson was also instructed to draft resolutions of respect to the late Arthur O'Malley, who was Tom Loftus' partner in Grand Rapids. Johnson was also instructed to write a letter to the National board of arbitration asking for a revisal of the drafting rule.

The pennant was formally awarded by the board of directors to Indianapolis, who announced that the clubs had finished in this order: Indianapolis, Minneapolis, Detroit, Grand Rapids, St. Paul, Milwaukee, and Buffalo and Kansas City a tie for last place. The annual report of President Johnson was read and approved. This report showed that as regards receipts Minneapolis finished first, with Kansas City a close second. Then came Indianapolis, Milwaukee, Detroit, Buffalo, Grand Rapids, and St. Paul in the order named.

The fines imposed by umpires and collected by Mr. Johnson during the season amounted to $205. It was decided to hold the schedule meeting in Chicago on March 1.

Before the regular league meeting, the board of directors, consisting of the representatives of the St. Paul, Grand Rapids, and Buffalo clubs held a meeting, at which only routine business was transacted. The board of directors for 1900 will consist of Van Derbeck of Detroit, Golt of Indianapolis, Manning of Kansas City, and Saulpaugh of Minneapolis.

The question of a new circuit was not formally considered yesterday, but the matter will be taken up at the session to be held this morning, and it is safe to predict that before the meeting adjourns the men most interested will decide on the make-up of the circuit for next year. This much is certain, there will be a club in Chicago, with Tom Loftus at the head of it. A strong team will be placed on the field, and the games will be played on the South Side. A non-conflicting schedule and the support of the national league will, in all probability, make the new club a winner from the start. The eighth club will be located in either Cleveland or Toronto, and Comiskey will be in charge.

Ten per cent of the total receipts of the year were divided among the clubs of the league in the following order: Minneapolis, Kansas City, Indianapolis, Milwaukee, Detroit, Buffalo, Columbus, Grand Rapids (tied), and St. Paul.

105

Honus Wagner and Other Lousville Stars Transferred to Pittsburgh (1899)

Source: *Louisville Courier-Journal*, December 9, 1899

Apparently anticipating that the NL *would be reduced from a twelve-team to an eight-team loop, Louisville's principal owner, Barney Dreyfuss, purchased a controlling interest in the Pittsburgh franchise. On December 8, 1899, he "traded" Louisville stars Honus Wagner, Rube Waddell, Fred Clarke, and Deacon Phillippe, along with nine other players, to the Pirates for $25,000 and several nondescript players (one of whom, Jack Chesbro, later would achieve stardom). Apparently the* Courier-Journal *was unaware that Dreyfuss controlled both clubs. At any rate, the newspaper tried valiantly to put the best "gloss" on the transaction.*

THE NEW COLONELS

General Impression That Louisville Got Much the Best of the Deal

The big deal was all the talk in sporting circles last night, and the consensus of opinion was that Louisville had not been left with such a bad team after all. The team is as strong as it was three years ago, as a glance at its make-up will show. Dexter, Hoy and Ketcham constitute a strong outfield, both in hitting, fielding and rungetting. Wills was good enough for first base last year. O'Brien, while an old-timer, played second for Pittsburg, and while he is not as strong a man as Ritchey, he will do very well. Madison is said to be a good young shortstop, and Billy Clingman is the equal of any third baseman in the country.

As regards batteries, the new team will not be strong. In fact, this is its weak point. Nothing is known of Gould here, and he may or may not do. Chesbro, Dowling and Magee, if the team plays here, will probably do most of the pitching.

Of course, it is too early to talk about selecting a manager, as the team was only made up yesterday afternoon, but President Pulliam, in all probability, will act as manager as well as President, while either Clingman or Dexter will likely be made Captain.

At first glance it seems that Pittsburg has all the good players, but one has only to think over them for a short time to understand that the local nine is stronger than Baltimore was at the beginning of last year, and infinitely stronger than Cleveland was at any time during the season.

By some of the disappointed fans it will probably be said that Mr. Pulliam's team will not draw well. This may be true, but it is certain that this team will draw better than a minor league team would, for the simple but emphatic reason that Mr. Pulliam's team will play against the stars of the country, whereas a minor league team would play only against the teams and players of the respective league to which it belonged. For the sake of the local enthusiasts of the game it is to be hoped that Mr. Pulliam's team will be allowed to play here, for then the enthusiasts would at least have a chance to see Freddie, Hans, Leach, to say nothing of the other stars, play; while, if Louisville was represented by only a minor league team, the fans who wanted to see the big League stars perform would have to go to Cincinnati or some other big League city to witness the sport.

In Pittsburg, according to the Courier-Journal's special correspondent, those in a position to know think that the circuit will be reduced at the coming meeting of the League. Of course, this is problematical. If it is reduced the Louisville players will be disposed of. If it is not reduced Mr. Pulliam will run his team here until the end of the ten-year agreement, and do the best he can with it.

It is the general impression among the fans that the Louisville magnates got none the worst of the Pittsburg deal. Mr. Pulliam is on his way home with a check for $25,000. It is true that the local club has lost thirteen of its best players, but it has six youngsters, a team as good as Baltimore was at the beginning of last season, and a franchise to dispose of. Mr. Kerr, of Pittsburg, while he probably did not let Mr. Dreyfuss have a controlling interest in the Pirates, let him have enough stock to make Barney a decided factor in the management of the club's affairs, as the fact that he will be President proves. With such a team in the Smoky City and playing Sunday ball it seems a certainty that those interested will make big money next year.

106

NL **Reduced to an Eight-Team Circuit (1900)**

Source: *New York Times*, March 9, 1900

Led by Andrew Freedman, the controversial owner of the New York Giants, the NL reduced the number of its franchises from twelve to eight in 1900. The move eliminated weaker franchises as well as the worst cases of "syndicate baseball" (instances of persons owning a controlling interest in more than one big league club). On the other hand, the reduction to eight teams left Cleveland, Louisville, Washington, D.C., and Baltimore without big league baseball, a situation soon exploited by Ban Johnson.

EVENTS OF A DAY IN THE FIELD OF SPORT

Baseball Circuit Reduced to Eight Clubs

FREEDMAN WINS HIS FIGHT

McGraw and Robinson of Baltimore Will Probably Play in New York

At the session of the National League and American Association of Baseball Clubs at the Fifth Avenue Hotel last night the League circuit was cut down to eight clubs.

Syndicate baseball, which Andrew Freedman, President of the New York Club, condemned and started a crusade against, was abolished by the elimination of Cleveland, Louisville, Washington, and Baltimore from the circuit.

The reduction of the circuit is the salvation of baseball, as one manager announced after the session, and there is now predicted a general revival of the great American game throughout the country.

Just what it cost the eight clubs that now make up the League to bring about the reduction could not be learned last night. The League bought the franchises only, with the exception of the Washington Club, and the clubs can dispose of their players at their own figures. The Washington Club has been purchased outright, and its players will be distributed among the eight clubs.

The reduction of the circuit will mean a revival of the old time enthusiasm in New York. Mr. Freedman announced a few days ago that New York would get the best team possible when the League abolished syndicate baseball and cheap politics. The Baltimore players are now free to be disposed of, and if the remarks made after the meeting by C. H. Ebbets of the Brooklyn Club are any indication, McGraw and Robinson, with other Baltimore players, will come to New York. When Mr. Ebbets was asked if negotiations would begin with the New York Club for the purchase of the players, he said:

"We have not considered the disposal of these players as yet. I know that Mr. Abell wants to have McGraw in Brooklyn, but McGraw aspires to be a manager-captain, and now that Baltimore is out of the League he has a chance of having his fondest hopes realized."

McGraw certainly cannot be a manager in Brooklyn, as the Brooklyn Club would no more think of disposing of "Ned" Hanlon than it would of getting out of the League. Every other club but New York has its manager under contract, and as it was reported in Baltimore last week that when McGraw and Robinson signed contracts conditions were named whereby these players would consent to play in New York if the circuit was reduced there is every reason to believe that these two players will wear New York uniforms eventually.

As the National League retains territorial right in the four cities eliminated, it is very probable that Baltimore and Washington will become Eastern League cities, while Cleveland and Louisville will enter the Western League.

The session of the League began at 3 o'clock yesterday afternoon, when the Circuit Committee went into session. The representatives of the Cleveland, Washington, Louisville, and Baltimore Clubs were conferred with. At 6 o'clock the committee announced that its report was ready, and at 9 o'clock the League convened to hear the committee's recommendations. Chairman John T. Brush's report showed that all but the Washington Club consented to a money consideration for their franchises.

It was decided that the money to be paid for the franchises should be raised by setting aside a percentage of all gate receipts until the obligation is liquidated. A new National agreement calling for eight clubs will be drawn up to-day.

John T. Brush said after the meeting that the committee's report was adopted unanimously, and every one will now start in and place the game of baseball on a sound basis.

Harry Van Der Horst, who until a few days ago strenuously objected to giving up his Baltimore franchise, said that he consented to the deal very reluctantly, but as it was the only means of bringing about harmony and a revival of the sport, he gave in to the pleadings of his associates. It transpired after the session that "Nick" Young had only a ten-club schedule prepared, so it will be at least two weeks before the final plans of the season can be made.

The League will meet again this morning.

107 ———

Inaugural AL Game Played in Detroit (1900)

Source: *Detroit Free Press*, April 20, 1900

The following account captures much of the pageantry with which Detroit opened its season against Buffalo in the newly named American League. Notice that Detroit invited Charlie Bennett, one-time star catcher for the team who had lost both legs in a railroad accident in 1894, to attend the game as an honored guest. Detroit's mayor opened the game with a ceremonial pitch to Bennett.

BASKET OF FRESH GOOSE EGGS

BUFFALO PRESENTED IT TO THE UNWILLING TIGERS
DETROITERS HAD ALL SORTS OF THINGS DONE TO THEM
DIDN'T EVEN HAVE THE FUN OF REGISTERING A HIT
DOC AMOLE PITCHED A WONDERFUL GAME OF BALL
GIVEN GILT-EDGED SUPPORT BY HIS TEAM MATES
CROWD OF 5,000 HAD NO CHANCE TO CHEER THE TEAM

Mayor Maybury and Charley Bennett Opened the Season of 1900

If there is anything in that old gag about a bad beginning insuring a good ending, then Ban Johnson might just as well pack up the pennant and express it to James D. Burns on the first train. For the Tigers made a start yesterday such as was never equalled in the history of baseball. It is impossible to imagine anything more harrowing than the calamity that befell the Detroit players in the opening game with Buffalo, and if the familiar saying holds good, when they get fairly on their stride it should be like finding money to walk away with the championship of the American League.

Think of it! The biggest crowd that ever attended an opening game in Detroit since the days of the famous Big Four gathered in the grand stand, on the bleachers, in carriages, and swarmed around the outskirts of the gardens. It was distinctively a Detroit crowd. They came there to cheer and root for the Tigers, filled to the brim with enthusiasm, but not once after greeting the players as they came upon the field and paying a graceful and hearty tribute to that great catcher of seasons gone by, Charlie Bennett, did they have even a slight opportunity to turn loose that pent-up loyalty of the noisy and unmistakable variety. For the Buffalo club, Ald. Jim Franklin's pennant winners, not only won the game, but shut the Tigers out, the final score being 8 to 0.

That was an awful blow—"it nearly killed" Burns and Stallings, while the players did not feel exactly jubilant—but the loss could have been borne much more easily had insult not been added to injury. Doc Amole, a young man who throws with the wrong hand, was the direct cause of the insult. He was in grand form, had all sorts of curves and speed and kept the Tigers guessing so effectually that only once in the game was there anything that approached a base hit. It is sad to lose the opening game of the season; sadder still to be shut out, and positively mournful to be sent back to the club house with the batting average of each and every man badly punctured; but that is exactly what Doc Amole did, and the act will never be forgotten so long as baseball lives. Perhaps the wound will heal sufficiently to allow forgiveness to be granted and due credit allowed the twirler for his wonderful feat; but forgotten, never!

AMOLE'S WORK WAS GILT-EDGED

No-hit games are events that are seldom seen, and when such a feat is accomplished it is generally along in the middle of the season, when the pitchers have rounded into the finest kind of form. For that reason, the performance of Southpaw Amole will go on record as one of the seven wonders of the national game and Manager Hanlon, of the Brooklyn team, will wonder what caused him to release a man with an arm that is capable of such deeds the day the flag falls for the long-drawn-out race. While it is quite true that the Detroit men were handicapped by lack of practice and have not found their "batting eyes" as yet, it is equally true that such gilt-edged work is not expected of a pitcher, and too much credit cannot be given Amole for his masterly effort of Thursday, April 19, 1900.

A more desirable day could not have been made to order than was Thursday, with its bright sunshine and balmy spring breezes, and the streets were thronged when the parade moved away from the Russell House. The players of the Detroit club, wearing their new and neat white uniforms with black trimmings, were seated on one coach, while the plain gray of the Buffalo men adorned the top of another coach. City officials and newspaper men were in carriages, while Frank McDonald's "Hot Air" club was a feature of the street display, with the little German band to assist the tin horns of the rooters in noise making. On Woodward avenue the Elks joined in, about 400 strong, and when the park was reached, fully an hour before the game commenced, the gates had already been thrown open and the seats were being rapidly filled.

At 1 o'clock the Bisons took the field for preliminary practice and fifteen minutes later the Tigers scampered out to their positions and did some pretty work. When the gong announced the hour for play to commence, the players of both teams marched to the plate, in company front, with Magnate Burns at the head of his team and Magnate Franklin accompanying the Bisons. At the sight of Charlie Bennett, accompanying Mayor Maybury to the home plate, the crowd could not restrain a cheer, but quickly quieted down and listened attentively to the brief address of the chief executive of the city. In a few well-chosen words Mayor Maybury referred to the popularity of the game, the loyalty of Detroit people to their team, and the necessity of clean baseball, expressing the hope that no fault would be found with the Detroits along that line this season. The patrons were complimented on their fairness to visiting teams, and then the formality of introducing the famous catcher was gone through with.

PITCHER MAYBURY—CATCHER BENNETT

When Charlie Bennett doffed his hat, cheer after cheer was lustily given, the mayor paying a deserved and handsome tribute to the man Detroit learned to love so well in the National League days. Bennett then took his place behind the plate, and the mayor, with a new ball in his hand, started for the pitcher's slab. He wanted to pitch the short distance, but was urged to take the regular position, and that proved his undoing as a twirler. His speed was good, but he was shy on control, and after failing to pitch it within Bennett's reach in four attempts, he moved up several feet closer to the plate. The first trial from that distance was also a failure, but the sixth ball pitched went straight into Bennett's hands, and the season was officially opened.

108

Formation of the Players' Protective Association (1900)

Source: *Sporting Life*, June 16, 1900

Francis Richter, editor of Sporting Life *and formerly a strong supporter of the Brotherhood, here sympathetically reports the founding of the Players' Protective Association. Members of the Association, like their Brotherhood counterparts a decade earlier, were unwilling to join any labor organization. Aware of the fate of the Brotherhood, association officers made clear that they did not intend "to antagonize the League in any way." Still, the association faded out of existence in 1902.*

PLAYERS ORGANIZE

THE LONG-EXPECTED PROTECTIVE UNION MATERIALIZES

The Ball Players, in Self-Protection Against the Constantly Growing Tyranny of the Base Ball Trust, Propose to Fight It With Powerful Counter-Organization

Slowly but surely the League magnates who have been for some years industriously sowing the wind are beginning to reap the whirlwind. One manifestation of that is the organization of a players' union, in order to counteract the despotic policies and grasping methods of the little coterie of ancient fossils who are gradually running the League and even the national game to death. The players have at last learned that the only way to meet the League Trust is with counter organization, as in these piping times of trusts the individual cuts no more figure in base ball than in any other line of business. The wonder is that union for self-protection against intolerable oppression has been so long delayed, considering the constantly growing exactions and usurpations of power by the magnates. These gentry probably realize the potentialities of the players' union even more fully than do the players at present. At any rate this new movement, added to the steadily progressing, though secret, work of organizing the new American Association for next year will doubtless give the League Trust something to think of and worry over besides watching the turnstiles.

ORGANIZATION EFFECTED

According to the programme laid out in April last three delegates from each National League team met at the Sturtevant House, in New York city, on Sunday, June 11, and organized the "Protective Association of Professional Base Ball Players." The delegates to the meeting were as follows:

New York—Davis, Doyle and Mercer.
Brooklyn—Keeler, Kelley and Jennings.
Boston—Duffy, Collins and Clarke.
Philadelphia—Delehanty, Donahue and Murphy.
Pittsburg—Zimmer, Ely and O'Brien.
Cincinnati—Corcoran, Irwin and Phillips.
Chicago—Griffith and Callahan.
St. Louis—Young, Burkett and Heldrick.

Ryan, of Chicago, was also expected to be present, but he was called away to his home, at Clinton, Mass. McGraw, of St. Louis, was unable to attend because of injuries received at the Polo Grounds in the game on Saturday, which will lay him up for at least some weeks.

Daniel Harris, representing Samuel Gompers, President of the American Federation of Labor, was present, and he explained matters to the players. He said that the proposed union would not necessarily be compelled to affiliate itself with the American Federation of Labor, but whether it did or not, it would receive the moral support of his organization. Harris showed the players that they had many grievances, which, if handled in the proper way, could be rectified without any great amount of trouble. He went over the ground so thoroughly that the delegates informed him that after they had formally organized they might join the federation represented by him. Harris then withdrew, and the Protective Association of Professional Base Ball Players was organized.

PROCEEDING CAUTIOUSLY

Following a long discussion it was voted not to affiliate the association with the American Federation of Labor as yet. The delegates thought that it would be better to feel their way before taking any such summary action. They further decided that it would be well to keep the good will of the American Federation of Labor, and at the same time it would not be advisable to antagonize the National League in any way. The affiliation may come later, but the players thought it advisable to feel their way before taking any positive step in that direction. This point was decided by vote.

ACTING WISELY

Officers were elected, including a president, vice president, secretary and treasurer, but by a unanimous vote it was agreed that their names should not be made public. A committee on by-laws was also elected, and it was voted to secure as legal adviser one of the following: Harry Taylor, formerly of the Louisville Club, now a lawyer in Buffalo; Michael J. Sullivan, formerly of the New York Club, now an attorney of Boston, and William Goeckel, of last year's Philadelphia team, but now practicing law at Wilkesbarre.

SOME FEATURES

Each club has a chairman for the players, as follows: Kelley, of Brooklyn; Davis, of New York; Duffy, of Boston; Delehanty, of Philadelphia; Griffith, of Chicago; Corcoran, of Cincinnati; Ely, of Pittsburg, and Burkett, of St. Louis. While the majority of players of each team have joined the new association, it is understood that it is not compulsory for any man to become a member. The association will hold another meeting in New York during the next trip East of the Western clubs, when it is believed an attempt will be made to enlist the support of all players in the minor leagues, for it is argued that if the latter are not included the association will not be effective when the proper time arrives.

Hugh Jennings, of the Brooklyn Club, was appointed a committee of one to talk to the newspaper men after the meeting, which adjourned shortly after 6 o'clock. Jennings said:

"It was the sense of the meeting not to antagonize the League in any way. Justice and fair dealing are what we want. The organization takes in about all the League players. A League player does not have to join now, however. Nor would a player be tabooed if he did not join. If he has a grievance, however it would be his alone and not ours. Later minor league players will be taken in.

"In case of any unfair treatment afforded to one of our men, I do not say that the Protective Association would order strikes, but I do say that we would resort to harsh measures. Players have been oppressed year in and year out by the magnates of the National League, and they have been helpless. But with our Protective Association in full sway we are confident that the magnates in future will see fit to so negotiate with players that there will be no greivances.

"When we have perfected our organization and have included all of the minor leagues we will be in a position to dictate terms, which, let it be understood, will not be unreasonable in any way. Mr. Harris, representing President Gompers, told us that we would not have to support any other unions in the way of being called out and that our dues would be merely nominal. We think very favorably of affiliating ourselves with his organization, but action has been deferred for the present."

Mr. Jennings further said, that judging from the spirit displayed by the delegates the new players brotherhood would be a sure go, as the delegates were a unit in the belief that the time had arrived for the players to protect themselves against further outrages.

It is said that the president of the Protective Association is either Duffy of Boston or Griffith of Chicago. The work of organization is not to stop with the National League, but to include all the ball players of the country, and organizers are now, and have been for some considerable time, at work in the minor leagues. There is little doubt that in a very short time the American and Eastern leagues will be formally organized as chapters of the new Players' Protective Association.

109

Formation of the National Association of Professional Base Ball Leagues by the Minor Leagues (1901)

Source: *Sporting Life*, September 14, 1901

With the NL-AL baseball war in full swing, the minor leagues decided to take the "unselfish advice" Sporting Life editor Francis Richter had first offered in his 1887 "Millennium Plan." They established a representative organization designed to protect their own interests. The National Association of Professional Base Ball Leagues still exists today. The organization operated independently of the major leagues until it subordinated itself by signing the National Agreement in 1903.

FULLY INDEPENDENT

THE MINOR LEAGUES DECIDE TO STAND ALONE

A Great Combination Formed Under a National Agreement With Able Officials—A Union That Will to an Extent Revolutionize and Benefit the Sport

By Editor Francis C. Richter

At last the minor leagues, after decades of needless degrading servitude, profiting by the unselfish advice of "Sporting Life," have thrown off the fetters long imposed upon them by selfish and arrogant power, and now stand before the world as independent members of the great base ball body of which they form the rock bottom, just as the common people form the solid base of all nations, all societies and of civilization itself.

In convention assembled, last week in Chicago, all the minor leagues of this great country effected an organization for mutual offense and defense, upon their own terms, with their own officers and their own Board of Arbitration, under their own National Agreement; and, happily, without any entangling alliance with either of the grasping, selfish major leagues.

So far as can be judged, at this distance and time, the new National Agreement is broad, equitable and sufficiently elastic to embrace without friction all the minor leagues henceforth under its aegis. The operation thereof is also entrusted to capable, experienced and fair-minded men such as the able Mr. Powers and the energetic Mr. Hickey, who, the one as Chief Executive of the new Association and the other as Chairman of the Board of Arbitration, will find a fruitful and pleasing field for their undoubted organizing and administrative talents.

On the lines laid down the new "National Association of Professional Base Ball Leagues" cannot fail to be a brilliant and permanent success if the minor leagues will now but adhere firmly and unselfishly, under all conditions, to their own Agreement; and particularly uphold their own Board of Arbitration in all of its rulings as regards territory and players—particularly the latter, as it will require time, unswerving resolution and rigid adherence to all decrees of the Board to inculcate into the player mind the new fact that the time for ignoring minor league rights and wishes has gone by, that their decrees are to be strictly enforced, and that betrayal or defiance of minor league laws and rules means *swift, sure and permanent punishment.*

The minor leagues are particularly to be congratulated upon steering clear of both of the warring major leagues with their perpetually conflicting interests, between which they would ultimately have been ground as between the upper and nether mill stone. This was the case when the old League and Association exploited the base ball world for their own aggrandizement and profit, until the rapacious old League finally devoured its own ally peacemeal under cover of the very elastic old agreement; and history would have soon or late repeated itself in our day.

The present independent organization of the minor leagues is the best thing for all the leagues, and, therefore, for base ball, all things considered. Ultimately the two warring major leagues must get together. Then, if the minor leagues hold together and perfect their present organization, we shall have a novel and ideal condition; for, with the major leagues operating under a new agreement and all the minor leagues working under their own agreement, there will be between the two great divisions of the base ball world—the major and minor—such an exact balance of power as will *compel* mutual respect, tolerance and fair dealing, and thus open up the happiest era base ball has ever enjoyed.

Major leagues, from their very nature, never have yielded, and probably never will yield, to anything but force, or fear inspired by force, and this can only be effected by a body of approximate strength. This the minor leagues are only *collectively,* and, therefore, in union they have secured the most potent weapon of self-protection. They have done well so far, and "Sporting Life" takes pleasure in congratulating them upon a step it has long urged upon them. Now let them persevere unflinchingly in the good work. Furthermore, if "Sporting Life's" further assistance is needed—and without doubt it will be—let them not hesitate to request the help of this long-established and independent organ, not of any particular league or clique, but of the great game of base ball.

110

John J. McGraw Defects to the NL (1902)

Source: *Baltimore Sun*, July 8, 1902

Ban Johnson declared war on the NL in 1901 by declaring his American League a major league. Over seventy NL players, lured by higher salaries and greater freedom, jumped to the new league. One of these players, John McGraw, the new player-manager and part owner of the AL's Baltimore franchise, soon proved difficult for Johnson to control. In the spring of 1902 Johnson, known for his unflinching support of his umpires, suspended McGraw indefinitely for abusing an umpire. In this article the Sun *reporter explains why McGraw then decided to defect to the NL.*

GOOD-BY, M'GRAW

Orioles' Manager To Take Charge of New York Club

JOHNSON'S NAGGING TOO MUCH

Will Get As Big A Salary As Was Ever Paid A Baseball Player— Wants Baltimore To Give Release

Manager John J. McGraw, of the Baltimore baseball team, exploded a baseball bomb yesterday when he admitted that he has been negotiating with Andrew Freedman for several days with an eye to taking the management of the New York National League team and expects to start for New York tonight to assume his new duties.

McGraw was thoroughly incensed when he was suspended by President Ban Johnson, of the American League, because he refused to go to the clubhouse when put out of the game by Umpire Connolly in the eighth inning of the contest with Boston in Baltimore on June 28. The game was forfeited to Boston because the manager refused to obey the umpire.

The offense occurred on Saturday, but the suspension was not received until Monday. In the interim McGraw declared that if he were suspended he would never again play in the American League, and intimated that he would go to the National League. Little or no attention was paid to the remarks at the time, as McGraw was extremely angry, and not even his closest friends thought he was doing more than blowing off steam.

Immediately after the announcement of his suspension certain ingenious baseball writers began to puff hard at their pipes and dream about McGraw going to New York and building up the team in that city, which is at the tail end of the National League race and badly in need of a capable head. The pipe was finally smoked out, and the dreamers took another turn, but their first vision was correct, and McGraw will become a National League manager today. He said yesterday afternoon:

"When I said that I would never play again in the American League if Johnson suspended me, I qualified my statement by saying that it applied as long as Johnson is head of the organization. It would be merely foolishness for me to stay here any longer as things stand now. I am not allowed to play, for as soon as I get in the game I am harassed and nagged by the umpires until I am put out. The consequence is that I am drawing a salary from the club for services which I cannot perform, while all the time I could be making good money elsewhere.

"Mr. Freedman made overtures to me through a mutual friend while we were in Boston. It was not Horace Fogel, who is getting players for the New York team. The identity of the party I do not care to disclose. Since then I have been in touch with Mr. Freedman and know pretty well what is expected.

"I am to get a contract calling for as much money as any ball player ever drew and am to have practically unlimited funds at my command for securing players which will put New York well up in the National race instead of down at the bottom.

"I understand that Mr. Freedman intends to spend the summer in Europe and think that he intends to let me have entire charge of the team in his absence, with the right to sign and release players as the occasion demands.

OFF TO GOTHAM

"I shall most probably go to New York tomorrow night to meet Mr. Freedman, and expect to sign the contract with him right away. If I do, I shall then go immediately to Chicago to take charge of the team and to play my position at third base. Yes, I know the troubles that some other managers have had in New York, but I think that I will have no difficulty in getting along. I will have a contract that will secure me, and do not see that I have reason to fear.

"Although my playing will be with the New York team, I will keep my home and business in Baltimore. I like this city. I have hundreds of friends here, and nothing but the attitude assumed by President Johnson could make me leave. I expect to furnish a home here in a short while and make this my permanent headquarters.

"The Baltimore team has not drawn so well at home this year as we anticipated, but that is largely due to the actions of Johnson. To show how his high-handed proceedings have cut down the gate receipts you have only to look at the comparatively small crowd Baltimore drew in Boston on July 4. Johnson had suspended Collins, one of the most gentlemanly players that ever appeared on the diamond, for a trivial offense. Collins is immensely popular, and the people were so disgusted with Johnson's actions that they simply stayed away from the American League game, and hundreds of them are now going to see the Boston Nationals instead.

"I cite Boston simply to show how Johnson can keep down the attendance. In Baltimore it has been just the same way. Our men have been suspended or put out of the game for things that passed unnoticed in other teams. As a consequence the team was always disarranged, it was necessary to constantly shift the batting order, the machine work in the field was broken up, the batting tricks became confused and the men did not work together properly on the bases.

"The umpires have made it a point to speak to me in the most dictatorial, humiliating manner, a manner no man could stand without resenting it, and I would be a fool to stay here and have a dog made of myself by a man who makes no pretense of investigating or giving a hearing to both sides. They have not waited for some overt or covert act on my part, but have assumed the initiative and have haughtily delivered orders to me about how I should play the game, as if I did not know my business.

SAMPLE OF OPPRESSION

"As an instance, I will take the case of Johnstone on the day when I was last put out. I went up to the bat in the first inning and drew a line as a mark for my feet. Johnstone immediately took another bat, drew another line and said:

" 'Now you get over that line and I will call you out.'

"The whole thing was done in such an insolent manner that I could not have been blamed for calling him down, but I contented myself with remarking that it was my place to play and his to umpire.

"The suspension itself was unwarranted and putting me out of the game even more so. Seymour had run from second base and past third. When it became necessary for him to return to second he did not touch third. He was touched with the ball on second and called out by Connolly. As soon as I had the play explained to me I called Seymour off the bag, although 99 out of every 100 of the spectators did not think he was out. While returning to the bench I noticed that Connolly was standing on the line between first and second. I remarked:

" 'Connolly, you had better get out of the line; somebody will jump into you and spike you.'

"I used no expletives, nor did I do anything else that would warrant my being sent to the clubhouse, yet Connolly in a most insulting way ordered me off the field. I made up my mind right there that I would no longer stand for being made a dog and refused to go. My suspension followed.

"Against a combination like that it is impossible for me to work here and so I am going to New York.

"The Baltimore team, as a result of bad luck and of Johnson's actions, is not making money, and it is probable that one or two of the high-priced players now on the team will have to be dropped in order to save expenses. This does not necessarily mean that the Orioles will make a poorer showing than they are making now, but only that one or two of the men who were signed as much for drawing cards as for their playing will have to give place to fellows who can put up a good game, but are not in a position to demand so much money.

"I have several men already in mind for the New York club if I go there, but can announce nothing now. I certainly will not draw on the Baltimore team. I would not do that, because of my friendship for the people here, and because it would not be right. Another thing, I still retain my interest in the Baltimore club, and from purely selfish motives if from no other, I would refrain from taking or advising any steps to make it weaker."

A NOTABLE REMOVAL

McGraw's retirement from Baltimore marks the first shifting of a man of his importance from the American to the National League, as against the number of prominent National Leaguers who have joined forces with the American.

McGraw took an extremely active part in the formation of the American League team in Baltimore. He and Robinson put up a goodly sum to start subscriptions for the stock, and it was largely due to the confidence of the public and moneyed men of the community in the integrity and ability of this pair that funds were raised to support the team. Baltimore was recognised as a keynote of the American League, and without a team here the Eastern end of the circuit would have been in such bad shape that it is doubtful whether the league would have been launched as a major organization.

Ever since the formation of the league McGraw has refused to take part in its politics and has made no effort to build up a faction for controlling the organization. Despite the modest position he assumed, it has been felt all along that Johnson was inimical to him and to Baltimore generally.

BASED ON HIS REPUTATION

McGraw's one-time reputation for hot-headed action on the field was apparently used as a club with which to smash his career in the league which he did so much to form. Umpires have persistently applied the rules more strictly to him than to other men in the league. Fouls have been called strikes on him, and all a player has had to do to get home from third was to yell that McGraw held him, and the run was allowed as a matter of course; he has been nagged while batting, and when making the legitimate protests to an umpire which were justified by his position as manager, the occasion has been seized to put him out of the game.

But the loss of McGraw by no means carries with it the downfall of the team. The organization will continue right along under the joint management of Kelley and Robinson, and they should make it a success. From a playing standpoint McGraw's absence will not be felt so badly, as he has been in the game so little that the team has become accustomed to getting along without him. At the opening of the season his leg was weak and he did not play. Next he was suspended, then Harley, of Detroit, spiked him out and put him out of the game for five weeks, and finally came the suspension of June 28.

111

The NL and the AL Sign a Peace Agreement (1903)

Source: *Sporting Life*, January 17, 1903

The warring NL and AL reached a peace settlement on January 10, 1903, in which each league agreed to honor the contracts and territorial monopolies of the clubs in the other league. Although the leagues would operate independently of each other, the new National Agreement they signed in September 1903 created a three-man commission, composed of the two league presidents and a jointly selected third member, to oversee all of "organized baseball." In effect, the commission served as a judicial body that would resolve disputes between teams and leagues, both major and minor, that had signed the National Agreement.

SETTLEMENT SECURED; PEACE PROCLAIMED!

THE POPULAR DOUBLE LEAGUE SYSTEM SCORES A SPLENDID TRIUMPH

The Warring Major Leagues Reach an Agreement in Which Each League Fully Preserves Its Autonomy

By Francis C. Richter

Below will be found details of the ever-memorable joint conference of the National League and American League Committees, at Cincinnati, January 9 and 10, which resulted in settling the great major league war by a mutually satisfactory compromise, thus once more restoring complete peace to the base ball world and assuring a brighter and better era for the national sport than it has ever before enjoyed:

THE JOINT CONFERENCE

The Amalgamation and Territorial Restriction Questions Settled

President Ban Johnson's final proposition to Chairman Herrmann that the two committees meet with the understanding that all consolidation propositions be sidetracked and the conference be confined to the question of players' contracts, conflicting dates and inter-league competitions [exhibition games—Ed.] proved acceptable and Mr. Herrmann on the 7th inst., wrote Mr. Johnson to call a joint meeting at a time and place to suit his own convenience. Mr. Herrmann stated that his committee had received power to act, but he reserved the right to communicate with all of the National League magnates by wire on any subject before final action be taken. This was agreeable to Mr. Johnson, and he accordingly issued a call for a meeting on January 9 in Cincinnati. In the meantime Mr. Herrmann named President Pulliam as the fourth member of the League Committee.

In Joint Convention

The American League delegates met at the Grand Hotel, and the National League delegates at the St. Nicholas Hotel, where each party went over the situation with such other magnates as were present. On the afternoon of January 9 the two committees went into joint session at the St. Nicholas Hotel and remained in conference with the exception of a brief recess for lunch until late at night. When they adjourned for the day the territorial question had been settled definitely, and only the player question remained to be disposed of. Notwithstanding Ban Johnson's condition that the amalgamation question be side-tracked, it was brought up by the National League people and was then given its quietus by the American Leaguers, after a very full discussion.

The Amalgamation Scheme

It is understood that the National League men had a consolidation proposition under which the Eastern circuit was to have been Boston, New York, Brooklyn, Philadelphia, Baltimore and Washington, the Athletic club to buy out the Philadelphia club and Henry Killilea to vacate Boston for cash and the Baltimore franchise in the twelve-club league. This would have left the American people in control of Philadelphia, Washington and Baltimore. In the West Pittsburg, Cincinnati and Chicago were to be held by the National League interests and Cleveland, St. Louis and Detroit by the American League interests.

As To Territorial Restriction

When the National League scheme had been discussed in all its phases President Johnson flatly put a stop to all further discussion on that subject by declaring that the American League would not consider for a moment any proposition looking to an amalgamation of the two organizations and reiterating what he has maintained all along, that the American League was committed to the maintenance of two separate and distinct organizations, working in harmony only in the matter of respecting each other's contracts. When it was made evident to the National's representatives that the American delegates were a unit in opposing amalgamation, the former then got down to the territorial question, with a view to restricting the American League to its present territory. The upshot of this discussion was that the American League refused to consider New York, which it had already entered, but agreed to keep out of Pittsburg, in the interest of peace, if the player question could be settled to mutual satisfaction.

The American League and the World Series 263

On the Basis of Two Leagues Dwelling Together in Harmony

With the amalgamation scheme squelched and the territorial question settled provisionally the joint committee on Saturday 10th tackled the player question. This was a hard job and throughout the discussion the National League men were kept very busy with long distance phone calls with the out-of-town magnates. The rub came over the division of the fifteen players signed and claimed by both leagues. After very full discussion of each case a division was finally made by which the American League got Delehanty, Crawford, Davis, Elberfeld, Keeler, Conroy, Donovan, Lajoie and Fultz, and the National League received Willis, Leach, H. Smith, Hulswitt, Mertes, Bowerman and Mathewson. That much agreed on everything else was easy. Each League then submitted a full list of its players, which are to be considered reserved. It was also agreed that all money received by awarded players should be returned to the clubs losing them.

An Agreement Formulated

The rest of the afternoon was spent in discussing the minor matters of non-conflicting schedule, uniform playing rules and interchange of exhibition games. The terms of a new National Agreement were also discussed and Messrs. Johnson and Pulliam were appointed a committee to formulate such an agreement with the assistance of President P. T. Powers of the National Association of Professional Leagues. The work of the Joint Committee was then formulated into a joint and full agreement which was signed by all of the conferees. This was then typewritten and given out to the press, the delegates in the meantime holding a jollification meeting, after which they caught the night trains for their respective homes. . . .

Credit Where It Is Due

Each of the eight conferees did his full duty toward bringing about a mutual agreement, but the greatest factor in the settlement was the confidence inspired by the "new man in base ball," President Herrmann of the Cincinnati Club; also his close personal relations with Ban Johnson, the two having been friends from boyhood. Without Herrmann's personality and reputation for fair dealing it is doubtful if anything would have come of the conference which began in mutual distrust. After the first session everybody relied on Herrmann's judgment and ability to carry out

HIS PEACE PROGRAMME,

and he never let up an instant. After the ways had been well greased on the first day Herrmann on Saturday would not let the conference adjourn or take a recess or do anything else until the articles of agreement were signed for each of the sixteen clubs in the two major leagues. The visiting conferees were unanimous in saying that Garry Herrmann led them into the promised land, and while Herrmann is the president of a National League club the American conferees were most enthusiastic in according him credit for the result.

Somers Also Strong

Another man who inspired universal confidence and became a strong factor in bringing about mutual concessions and good will was the "young Napoleon" from Cleveland, Charles W. Somers. He arrived in Cincinnati ahead of his colleagues from Chicago, and not only talked peace with Herrmann from the start, but gave the Cincinnatian valuable assistance and support in smoothing over rough places and rounding sharp corners. It may be said, however, that Herrmann held the whip-hand of his own committee owing to the fact that he held territory that the American League could, and would, gladly have used in its business, in case the National League should put Herrmann into the mood of shifting his club into the opposition camp. At the same time Mr. Herrmann also held a check on the American League which held him in greater respect as a fighter than any other League magnate.

112

The Tragic Death of Ed Delehanty (1903)

Source: *Buffalo Express*, July 8, 1903

The circumstances of Ed Delehanty's death on July 3 have never been clearly established. Mike Sowell, author of July 3, 1903 *(1992), suggests that Delehanty was despondent over the magnates' decision to award him to the Washington* AL *club instead of the New York* NL *team, which had already paid him a salary advance greater than his annual salary with Washington. Faced with the prospect of repaying the advance and remaining with Washington, he appparently fell into a state of depression. After abandoning his club and getting drunk, he was thrown off a train at the Canadian border. It is believed that while attempting to walk across the International (railway) Bridge spanning Niagara Falls, Delehanty fell through an open draw and drowned in the river below.*

MAY HAVE BEEN ED DELEHANTY

Friends of the great Ballplayer fear he was Man drowned in Niagara

WENT OFF THE BRIDGE

**Delehanty disappeared from Detroit last Thursday,
the Day of the Accident here**

It is now feared by the friends of Ed Delehanty, the ballplayer, that he was the man who fell to his death in the Niagara River, off the International bridge about midnight on Thursday, July 2d.

Last Thursday Delehanty, who is connected with the Washington club of the American League, disappeared mysteriously from his club, which was playing a three-day engagement in Detroit. He has not been seen since, and might have been swallowed up by the earth so effectual has been his disappearance.

Previous to his departure Delehanty had been drinking, it is reported, and had acted strangely, so much so that his comrades of the ball club were much disturbed as to his safety.

Last Thursday night a man weighing about 160 pounds, smooth shaven, described as about 40 years old by the night bridge watchman, Sam Kingston, was reported to have been put off a Michigan Central train for drunkenness at Bridgeburg, the Canadian terminus of the International bridge. The man is reported to have started to run across the bridge, on which foot passengers are not allowed. When stopped by the night watchman, Kingston says the man threatened him, and then ran on across the bridge, in the darkness, plunging through the draw, near the American end, which had just been opened to permit the Ossian Bedell, the Grand Island steamer, to pass. Nothing remained to identify the man except his hat, which may throw some light on the Delehanty theory today when his friends see it.

The hour of the disappearance of Delehanty at Detroit and the appearance of the man on the bridge, directly on the route which Delehanty would probably have taken on his road east, are circumstances which create a very powerful coincidence.

Delehanty is reported to have started drinking at a hard clip when his club struck Cleveland on June 25th, and had been going hard since until he disappeared in Detroit on July 2d. His mental condition at this time is reported to have worried his fellow players, who made him take hot baths and tried to get him straightened out. He is reported to have talked of self-destruction and one report says he drove Pitcher Lee of his team out of his room with a big knife. His condition excited such alarm that his mother and two little brothers left Cleveland to care for him. Delehanty slipped out of their sight and left Detroit with no belongings other than the clothes he wore.

Delehanty telegraphed to his wife in Philadelphia on Tuesday to meet him in Washington last Friday, as the team would return home that night. She went there, only to ascertain that he had not joined the team when it left Detroit. Before he telegraphed, however, he wrote a letter to his wife, in which he inclosed an accident insurance policy, with the comment that he hoped that something dreadful would happen to the train on which he rode.

Several points of his conduct indicate that he has taken his life, for he was said to be verging on insanity the day he disappeared. He left his mother and brothers in Detroit without money to pay their bills or buy transportation back to Cleveland. Manager Loftus settled these matters, and the family left for their home. Mrs. Delehanty is now stopping at The Oxford in Washington, where several of the ballplayers live, and is greatly distressed at the absence of her husband, for he has never acted so strange or surprisingly as at this time.

Delehanty's name will live in baseball history as one of the greatest. He is known as a batsman of marvelous strength, leading the league at times and always ranking high. Last winter he was the center of a big row between the National and American leagues. Signed with Washington of the American League, Delehanty broke his contract and also signed with the New Yorks of the National League, and accepted a sum of advance money said to have been $4,000. The American League won out for possession and Delehanty had to make good the big sum of advance money to New York and play with Washington for a smaller salary. It is said he has been anxious to leave the Washington club.

113

Richter Condemns Minor Leagues for Subordinating Themselves to the Major Leagues (1903)

Source: *Sporting Life*, September 19, 1903

Francis Richter, editor of Sporting Life, *believed that the National Agreement of 1903 represented a sharp setback for the minor leagues. The new agreement essentially brought all of minor league baseball under the umbrella of the major leagues, for it permitted the major league clubs to draft players from the minors at a set price. On the other hand, it recognized the territorial monopolies of minor league clubs and their right to hold a player's contract until he was drafted. Richter does not address the minor leagues' fear that, without an agreement with the major leagues, they could have their rosters freely raided by major league franchises without receiving any compensation.*

THE MINOR LEAGUES YIELD TO THE MAJORS

AND ACCEPT THE AGREEMENT, SUGAR-COATED WITH TRIFLING CONCESSIONS

Failing to Secure Their Just Demands, and Fearing to Go It Alone Any Further, They Give Up the Battle After a Feeble Fight

By Francis C. Richter

The National Association delegates to the Cincinnati Conference on National Agreement furnished the minor league world with an amazing and stunning surprise. Contrary to instructions and universal expectations, they permitted themselves to be completely overridden, yielded on every important point and, for a few minor concessions, signed the very agreement which they had so bitterly denounced, and which they had declared they would never accept without radical modifications. As we were not present at the meeting, we are unable to say whether the major league delegates employed bluffs, blandishments or hypnotism to whip the National Association delegates into line so easily and quickly. Certain it is, however, that the minor leaguers yielded every important proposition they had formulated and accepted what little the majors chose to give them. The few concessions made by the major leaguers are of no immediate importance or future value, and the document as accepted by the minor leaguers is substantially the charter formulated at Buffalo, with all of the imperfections and inequities pointed out by "Sporting Life" maintained unimpaired. At this writing it is not clear why the National Association delegates sacrificed so much for so little, and their surrender can only be explained on the supposition that the major leaguers had the whip-handle somehow. How the minors surrendered is detailed below. In this connection the statement given out to the local press by Chairman Herrmann is most illuminating: he certainly made little effort to sooth feelings or gloss over a humiliating and melancholy surrender. However, if the National Association is satisfied with the work of its delegates, nobody else has any right to kick; we certainly have no further protest to make, as it is not our funeral.

The National Association having, in return for a few unimportant concessions, been irrevocably committed by its representatives to the new National Agreement, promulgated at the Buffalo Conference and slightly amended at Cincinnati, that document now embodies the supreme law of base ball to which all must bow, willy nilly, and despite the manifold defects in the law pointed out in a previous issue. The fact that it is a powerful aid to the aggrandizement of the major leaguers and a correspondingly severe debaser of the minor leagues cuts no ice, now that the minor leagues have accepted anew a serf's burden. The new agreement will, at least, serve the useful purpose of restoring some degree of order to the entire base ball world, re-establishing needed discipline in the ranks, and enabling all leagues and clubs for some years to recover from the demoralization and recoup the losses of the past three years of war and anarchy.

How long the new agreement will stand supreme depends entirely on circumstances. It may last a decade, or only two years. The growth of abuses, the exigencies and ambitions of leagues, and the possible consolidation of the major leagues are all important factors in the consideration of longevity. This is the fourth National Agreement made in two decades [see Documents 56, 93, and 106—Ed.]. Following precedent, the present agreement will also be broken just as soon as a powerful party thereto finds it profitable or desirable to do so, or when conditions become so harsh as to compel a break away. History always repeats itself, and base ball moves in cycles just as do all other things on this mundane sphere. But, for a time, at least, we shall have rest from war and rumors of war. For this relief much thanks!

114

Boston and Pittsburgh Agree to Play a "Post-Season Series" (1903)

Source: National Baseball Library and Archive, Cooperstown, New York

On September 13, 1903, the New York Times *printed the following release: "Barney Dreyfuss, owner of the Pittsburg club, and Henry Killilea, owner of the Boston club, of the American League, are so confident that their clubs will win the championship of the National and American Leagues, respectively, that they have agreed upon a meeting to arrange a series of games this Fall for what they term the 'championship of the United States.' The meeting is expected to be held this week, and the cities mentioned where games are to be played are New York, Boston, Chicago, and Pittsburg." Although the two owners had contacted each other about such a series as early as July, the document below was not drafted and signed until September 16. Notice that the agreement pertains only to the two clubs, not to their leagues.*

It is hereby agreed by and between Pittsburg Club of the National League and the Boston American League Club of the American League as follows:

1,—That a post season series shall be played between said base ball clubs consisting of a series of 9 games, if it be necessary to play that number before either club should win 5 games, said series however to terminate when either club shall win 5 games.

2,—Said games to be played at the following times and places:
At Boston, Mass., Oct. 1, 2, & 3   (Thursday, Friday and Saturday)
At Pittsburg, Pa.,   " 5, 6, 7 & 8 (Monday, Thuesday [sic], Wednesday and Thursday)
At Boston, Mass.,   " 10 and 12 (Saturday and Monday);
providing however, in the event of the weather being such as to prevent a game being played on either of said days, such game shall be postponed until the next succeeding day when the weather will permit such game to be played where scheduled. And in that event there shall be a moving back of the aforesaid schedule for the day or days lost on account of said inclement weather.

3,—Each club shall bear the expense of the games played on their respective grounds, excepting the expense of umpire.

4,—Each club shall furnish and pay the expenses of one umpire to officiate during said series and it is agreed that the umpire so agreed upon to be furnished shall be O'Day from the National League and Connelly [sic] from the American League.

4½ No player to participate who was not a regular member of team Sep 1, 1903 [hand-written addition—Ed.].

5,—The minimum price of admission in each city shall be 50 cts. and the visiting club shall be settled with by being paid 25 cts. for every admission ticket sold.

6,—A statement to be furnished the visiting club after each game, final settlement to be at the close of the series.

The respective captains of each team shall meet with the umpires above designated before the beginning of the series to agree upon a uniform interpretation of the playing rules.

IN WITNESS THEREOF the parties hereto have caused these presents to be signed by their respective Presidents this 16 day of September, A.D. 1903.

In Presence of   PITTSBURGH ATHLETIC CO.
                               Barney Dreyfuss
                                       President.

                               BOSTON AMERICAN LEAGUE BALL CLUB
                               Henry Killilea
                                       President.

115

The First Game of the World Series (1903)

Source: Boston *Globe*, October 2, 1903

After both clubs threatened to pull out because of injuries to key players, the "world's championship" series commenced in Boston. The opening game featured a pitching match between Boston's Cy Young and Pittsburgh's Deacon Phillippe. Although Phillippe won this game and two others in the series, Boston claimed the first World Series of the twentieth century by a 5–3 margin. This article also contains one of the earliest known references to a "Texas leaguer" hit, which in this instance was a home run.

PITTSBURG A WINNER IN THE FIRST CLASH

Boston Beaten By a Score of 7–3
"Cy" Young Is Off Edge And Is Bumped Hard
More Than 16,000 Persons See Opening Contest
Boston the Favorite in the Game Scheduled for Today

With Cy Young in the box and more than 16,000 persons looking on, the Pittsburg club won from Boston by a score of 7 to 3 in the first game in the series for the world's championship, at the Huntington-av grounds yesterday.

The crowd, which encircled the field, was held well back by ropes and a small army of policemen, and the best of order prevailed. Both teams received liberal applause for good work.

The Boston players evidently were a little nervous, as is usually the case with teams on the home grounds in an important series. As the game progressed, however, Collins' boys got into their stride, and played grand ball when it was too late to overtake the Pirates.

Cy Young was hit hard. He fell considerably short of his best work, lacking speed, his winning ingredient. With Young off edge, the home players were carrying a big handicap.

Phillippi [sic] was in rare good form, but weakened perceptibly as the game drew out, withering under a brace of triples by Freeman and Parent, and finishing at a much slower clip than the one at which he started, although he had no trouble with O'Brien and Farrell, who were sent in to bat for the Boston battery in the ninth when there were two men on bases.

Pittsburg had all the luck and a shade the better of the umpiring, as Connolly favored Phillippi on strikes, while O'Day had no close plays on the bases.

The Boston infield outplayed Pittsburg's. Ferris, after making two bad fumbles and giving the visitors four runs at the start, pulled himself together, and with Collins and Parent, put up a superb article of baseball.

Criger, who is probably the greatest catcher living, had a bad day, making two poor throws to second and having a passed ball on a third strike.

But for the misplays of Ferris and Criger and a bad piece of fielding by Freeman in allowing a line hit to pass under him for three bases, the Pittsburg men would have another story to send home.

Because the Boston boys failed to play up to their natural gait from start to finish, and slipped a shoe in the first game, it need not be assumed that it will occur again.

Fred Clarke carried off the honors of the day in left field. He covered ground like a cyclone, and three times pulled in line drives that were marked for three bases. His marvelous work cut off at least three runs, and the chances are that not another man playing ball today would have connected with any one of the three great running catches made by him. It was ground covering with a vengeance. He was off with the swing of the bat besides pretty nearly calling the turn on the batsman.

Beaumont and Stahl made clever catches, but outside this work of Clarke and Beaumont, and two pretty plays by Ritchie the visitors were not offering anything sensational in the way of fielding.

Ferris, Parent and Collins played fast ball, one play by Criger to Ferris and back to the plate, where they got their man was a classic.

Phillippi apparently took things easy, as he well might, with the start of four runs in the first inning. These runs were started after two men were out and Cy had two strikes on Tommy Leach. The latter and Sebring did the hitting for the Burgers, the little third base man clipping off four safe ones, which is pretty good work for a light batsman.

Sebring got in one clean hit and two lucky ones, Lachance failing to go out and stop his first grounder, and his home run coming from a Texas leaguer; Stahl thinking the ball would roll into the crowd and failing to go after it, thus making a gift of a run.

The crowd had little chance to cheer until "Buck" Freeman lined one up against the right fence in the seventh, and Parent followed with one into the crowd in left for three bases. The cheering was like the roll of thunder, and was tuned up for business when shut off by one of Clarke's great running catches clear over in center field.

After the game one club looked just as good as the other, the difference yesterday was in the pitcher's box, and it's not often that Uncle Cyrus fails to land the money, even if he is a bit fat.

INTO THE CROWD—THREE BASES

After making ground rules, giving three bases for balls hit into the crowd on fair ground, Tommy Connolly took his place behind the bat and Hank O'Day on the bases. Here was a pair of umpires who know their business, and the players never undertook to question their decisions.

Cy Young started off by disposing of the clever Beaumont on a fly to Stahl. He then forced Fred Clarke to pop up a weak fly to Criger. Leach was in for two strikes and then tapped one of Young's straight ones past Freeman for three bases. Wagner threw his bat at a wide out curve and sent it safe to left, Leach scoring. On the first ball pitched the Pittsburg man was off for second like a shot and landed safely, as Criger was a bit slow and Ferris was very much surprised.

It was evident that the visitors were going to force Criger to show his speed, and by doing so they made the Boston man look like a fur overcoat in July.

Bransfield hit a merry grounder at Ferris, and after evading several stabs the ball rolled up Hobe's sleeve, while Bransfield was safe at first. Bransfield went down to second, and Criger threw the ball out to center, Wagner scoring and Bransfield going to third. Ritchey drew a pass, and off he went for second. This time Criger made a bluff to throw down and turned the ball to Collins, but Branfield was hugging the base. Sebring came in with a timely line single to left, and two runs were scored. Phelps struck out, but got first on Criger's passed ball. Phillippi, the ninth man up, fanned, and the home team started in on a big contract.

Dougherty and Collins struck out. Stahl scratched a single to left, and Freeman flied out to right.

BEAUMONT STRIKES OUT

Beaumont opened the second inning with a strikeout. Clarke hit one down the left line and was thrown out by Dougherty while trying for two bases. Leach flied out to left.

Phillippi got a round of applause by striking out Parent, Lachance and Ferris, the only men who went to bat in Boston's half.

In the third Collins made a fine catch of Wagner's fly. Bransfield lined one to right that Freeman came in for and then allowed to go through him to the crowd for three bases. Bransfield scored on Sebring's single past Lachance.

Boston went out in order.

Beaumont opened the fourth with a grounder that was fumbled by Ferris. Clarke and Leach singled, scoring Beaumont. Wagner flied out to Parent, and Bransfield forced a man at second, Ferris making a clever running assist.

Collins hit a ball into the crowd along the left line, but was called back and then hit a fierce liner that Clarke made a grand catch of. Stahl flied out to center. Freeman hit one too warm for Bransfield. Parent hit to Leach and the ball was thrown wild, but luckily for Pittsburg it hit the fence back of first base. Lachance flied out to Ritchey.

In the fifth Collins made two fine assists at first. Phelps singled; then Phillippi flied out to Ferris.

Boston went out in order.

With two out in the sixth Leach singled and Wagner drew a base on balls, only to be forced by Bransfield, Ferris making another fine assist. For the fourth time Boston went out in order.

In the seventh Parent made a pretty assist off Ritchey. Sebring hit a weak fly over Ferris that rolled nearly to the ropes, the Boston outfielders taking their time in fielding it and permitting a home run.

Freeman hit the fence in right for three bases and scored on Parent's drive into the crowd in left for three sacks. Lachance made a fine bid for a hit, but Clarke was there for a great catch. Ferris was hit by a pitched ball. Then the Boston battery turned in a double strikeout.

Parent made a grand assist off Beaumont in the eighth. Clarke flied out to Freeman. Leach hit for three bases, and Wagner drew a pass. Then the best play of the game took place. Wagner started for second, and Criger drove the ball to Parent, but Ferris saw Leach start for home and intercepted the ball and lined it back to Criger for an out.

Boston went out in order.

BRIEF RALLY IN THE NINTH

The visitors went out in order in their half of the ninth.

For Boston, Freeman was safe on Wagner's fumble. Parent singled. Lachance made one more fine try for business, but Clarke again came across the field like a flash and took the ball over his head. Ferris dropped one safe in center and Freeman scored. O'Brien was sent up for Criger, and struck out. Farrell hit the ball to the pitcher and was thrown out at first, and the game was over.

The crowd gathered on the field and many good-sized bets were paid over.

The Pittsburg players were surrounded by their friends and escorted to their carriages, a well pleased lot of ball players, while the Boston men looked anything but discouraged over the loss of game number one. The score:

PITTSBURG	AB	R	BH	TB	PO	A	E
Beaumont cf	5	1	0	0	4	0	0
Clarke lf	5	0	2	2	3	0	0
Leach 3b	5	1	4	8	0	1	1
Wagner ss	3	1	1	1	1	2	1
Bransfield 1b	5	2	1	3	7	0	0
Ritchey 2b	4	1	0	0	1	2	0
Sebring rf	5	1	3	7	1	0	0
Phelps c	4	0	1	1	10	0	0
Phillippi p	4	0	0	0	0	2	0
Totals	40	7	12	22	27	7	2

BOSTON	AB	R	BH	TB	PO	A	E
Dougherty lf	4	0	0	0	1	1	0
Collins 3b	4	0	0	0	2	4	0
C Stahl cf	4	0	1	1	2	0	0
Freeman rf	4	2	2	4	2	0	0
Parent sw	4	1	2	4	4	2	0
Lachance 1b	4	0	0	0	8	0	0
Ferris 2b	3	0	1	1	2	4	2
Criger c	3	0	0	0	6	1	2
Young p	3	0	0	0	0	1	0
*O'Brien	1	0	0	0	0	0	0
†Farrell	1	0	0	0	0	0	0
Totals	35	3	6	10	27	13	4

*Batted for Criger in ninth. †Batted for Young in ninth.

Innings ...	1	2	3	4	5	6	7	8	9
Pittsburg	4	0	1	1	0	0	1	0	0—7
Boston	0	0	0	0	0	0	2	0	1—3

Home run, Sebring. Three base hits, Leach 2, Bransfield, Sebring, Freeman, Parent. Stolen bases, Wagner, Bransfield, Ritchey. Bases on balls, off Young, Wagner 2, Ritchey. Struck out, by Young—Beaumont, Clarke, Ritchey, Phelps, Phillippi. By Phillippi—Dougherty, Collins, Stahl, Parent, Lachance, Ferris 2, Criger, Young, O'Brien. Hit by pitched ball, by Phillippi, Ferris. Umpires, O'Day and Connolly. Time 2h 5m. Attendance 16,242.

T. H. Murnane.

116

NL and AL Formally Agree to Play
Annual World Series (1905)

Source: *Spalding's Official Base Ball Guide, 1905* (reprint, St. Louis: Horton, 1992), pp. 333–35

After the New York Giants refused to meet AL champion Boston in a World Series after the 1904 season, they were attacked for both arrogance and cowardice. Stung by these charges, Giants owner John Brush led efforts to make the World Series the official culmination of the baseball season. Brush's action paid off, as his Giants won the first "official" World Series against the Philadelphia Athletics in 1905. Furthermore, the World Series was embraced by a nation of baseball fans as a "fall classic."

WORLD'S CHAMPIONSHIP SERIES

Rules and Regulations Governing the Contest for the Professional Base Ball Championship of the World and games played between National and American League Clubs. Approved by the National Commission February 16, 1905, and adopted by the National and American Leagues, February 16, 1905.

Agreement to Play

Section 1. The pennant-winning club of the National League and the pennant-winning club of the American League shall meet annually in a series of games for the Professional Base Ball Championship of the world.

The Emblem and Memento

Sec. 2. The emblem of the Professional Base Ball Championship of the World shall be a pennant, to be presented to the victorious club each year, and an appropriate memento, in the form of a button, to be presented to each player of the victorious club. Both shall be selected by the National Commission. The cost of the pennant and the buttons shall be paid by the Commission.

To be Played Under Supervision of National Commission

Sec. 3. The games shall be played under the supervision, control and direction of the National Commission.

When to be Played

Sec. 4. The event shall take place at the end of the championship season of each year. Seven games shall constitute a complete series.

Playing Rules Authorized by the National Agreement

Sec. 5. The games shall be conducted according to the playing rules as provided for by the National Agreement.

Where to be Played

Sec. 6. The National Commission shall promulgate a schedule for the event. Three games shall be scheduled in each of the cities of the contesting clubs. The Commission shall determine by lot where the first three games shall be played. In case it becomes necessary to play the seventh game to decide the event, the Commission shall determine the city in which the game is to be played.

Representatives of Contesting Clubs and Notice to Players

Sec. 7. The clubs entitled to contest for the World's Honors shall be represented by the Presidents of their respective leagues and clubs. The Secretary of the National Commission will be required to notify all of the players of the contesting teams that they will be held amenable by the Commission to all rules governing base ball and will be subject to discipline regardless of contracts.

When to Terminate—Winning Club

Sec. 8. The clubs shall continue to play each day according to the authorized schedule until one of them has won four games, when the contest shall end, and the club winning shall be entitled to fly the emblem or pennant of the World's Championship during the ensuing base ball season, and the players thereof shall be permitted to wear the memento or button as long as they please.

Right to Terminate the Series

Sec. 9. The National Commission shall reserve to itself the right to terminate the series at any time that it deems the interest of base ball demands it, and to declare one of the contesting clubs the winner of the Championship regardless of previous performances.

Guarantee of Contesting Clubs

Sec. 10. Each of the clubs participating in the event shall guarantee to the National Commission in such manner as the latter may prescribe that they will faithfully carry out all of the provisions of these rules and regulations, and such others as the Commission may hereafter make to govern the games, and that they will not exercise an arbitrary right or privilege of abandoning the series until it has been completed or the Championship determined.

The Umpires

Sec. 11. There shall be two umpires, who shall be invested with the authority and discretion that the playing rules confer, and they shall observe the same general instructions with reference to maintaining order and discipline upon the ball field during these contests that govern them in the performance of their duties in all other games in their respective leagues.

Umpires—How Selected

Sec. 12. The President of the National League and the President of the American League shall each select one umpire from their respective leagues, and the umpire so chosen shall be assigned to duty and be subject to the orders of the Chairman of the National Commission.

Compensation of Umpires

Sec. 13. The compensation of the umpires shall be fixed by the National Commission.

Expenses—How Adjusted

Sec. 14. The expenses of the National Commission pertaining to these games, the salaries of the umpires, and other miscellaneous and contingent expenses in connection therewith shall be paid out of the funds to be received by the Commission from these games. Should these funds prove insufficient for this purpose, the balance shall be paid out of the regular funds of the Commission; and should there be a surplus in these funds, it shall be credited each year to the regular funds of the Commission. All other expenses of both clubs, such as hotel bills and traveling expenses, balls, advertising, policing of grounds, ticket sellers and takers, incidentals, etc., shall be paid by the club incurring the same. Should any difference arise at any time as to the latter expense, the same shall be submitted to the Commission for adjudication, and its final shall be conclusive.

Constitutional Rights of the Clubs

Sec. 15. Each contesting club shall preserve its constitutional rights during games played upon its own grounds with reference to the conduct of its business affairs in connection therewith, but the visiting club shall also be allowed its inherent rights and whatever representation and facilities it may require to properly protect the interests of the club and its players: Provided, however, that the captain of the home team should not be accorded the privilege to determine whether the grounds are fit. This authority will be delegated to the umpires. If they fail to agree, the umpire whose turn it is to officiate behind the plate will decide as to the condition of the ground.

Rates of Admission

Sec. 16. The rates of admission and the conditions governing the same shall be fixed by and be under the control of the National Commission.

Division of Receipts

Sec. 17. The receipts from the games shall be divided as follows:

First. Ten (10) per cent. of the gross receipts from all games shall be paid to the National Commission.

Second. Forty (40) per cent. of the balance from the first four games shall form a pool for the players of the two teams, to be divided seventy-five (75) per cent. to the winner and twenty-five (25) per cent. to the loser of the contest.

Third. After the ten (10) per cent. deductions for the Commission, and the forty (40) per cent. which forms the players' pool from the first four games, the balance of the gross receipts shall be divided equally between the two teams.

Fourth. The amount to be paid into the players' pool as provided by this section shall be paid to the Commission, and the same shall be distributed to the players through the Secretary of the Commission.

Adjustment of Salaries After the Contract Season

Sec. 18. In the event that the schedule for a World's Championship series extends beyond the players' contract season, then the salaries of the players who properly belong to the contesting clubs shall continue, at the contract rate, to the end of the series of games scheduled, although only four or more games be played.

Free List Suspended

Sec. 19. The free list shall be suspended during the contest except to representatives of the press and club officials of the two leagues.

Time of Presentation of Pennant and Buttons

Sec. 20. The pennant and buttons shall be presented to the victorious club and its players, each year, by the National Commission, which is authorized to arrange for all of the details of such presentation.

Disputes to be Settled by the Commission

Sec. 21. All questions arising out of the playing for the World's Championship not provided for herein nor covered by the playing rules shall be dealt with and decided by the National Commission.

All Clubs to Agree to these Conditions

Sec. 22. All clubs of both leagues hereby agree absolutely to conform strictly to all the articles of these rules, and in any cases not herein provided for to conform to the decisions of the National Commission.

Rules to Apply to Other Games

Sec. 23. These same rules may apply to all other games played between National and American League clubs, upon application being made to the National Commission, except as to the division of receipts exclusive of the amount to be paid to the National Commission, which shall be mutually agreed upon between the clubs participating in such games: Provided, all players shall be paid at their contract prices for all games of this character that they are obliged to play after the expiration of their contracts.

Players to be Notified

Sec. 24. After the adoption of this Agreement by the National and American Leagues, copies of the same shall be prepared by the respective leagues and sent to the President of each club, who shall, on or before the 10th of March of each year, mail a copy to each player of his club.

8

Postscript: The Origins of the Creation Myth

During most of the nineteenth century the origins of baseball were undisputed: baseball had evolved from a variety of ball games played by children, the English game of rounders in particular. English-born Henry Chadwick and virtually all other baseball writers accepted the rounders-to-baseball evolution. Chadwick even used this development to claim that baseball was the American national game, as the transformation had been initiated and completed entirely by Americans.

By the end of the century, however, the notion that the national pastime was even slightly tainted by foreign influence offended many, Albert Spalding in particular. Following the round-the-world baseball tour of 1888–89, which Spalding hoped would demonstrate the virtues of baseball—and, by extension, of the United States —Abraham G. Mills, the former president of the National League, seized the occasion of a banquet in honor of the Spalding troupe to reject the rounders theory. According to the *New York Clipper*, Mills said that "patriotism and research had established the fact that the game . . . was American in origin," to which some of the feasters responded by crying, "no rounders." Thus, continued the *Clipper*, "the English claim that America's national game was prehistorically the English game of 'rounders' was forever squelched."

Finally, in 1905, apparently in response to a letter from Chadwick, Spalding decided that something had to be done to resolve the matter. He named a commission to investigate, and called for help and information from anyone with knowledge of the origin of the game.

One of the many respondents was a retired mining engineer in his eighties, Abner Graves, who recalled that the game had been created in his hometown of Cooperstown, New York, in 1839 by an older playmate, Abner Doubleday.

Even though the game Graves described was clearly not the same game the Knickerbockers and other pioneering baseball teams played, Spalding and his commission quickly heralded Graves's letter as providing the answer to their quest. In its final report in 1908, the commission officially declared Doubleday the inventor of baseball. Although every element of the Doubleday creation myth has been thoroughly disproved, the myth remains so attractive to fans and writers alike that it survives to this day.

117

A. G. Spalding Requests Formation of a Special Committee to Investigate the Origins of Baseball (1905)

Source: *Spalding's Official Base Ball Guide, 1905* (reprint, St. Louis: Horton, 1992), pp. 3–13

In 1905 Albert G. Spalding used the opening pages of his Guide *to formally "request" (the word hardly seems fitting for a man of Spalding's considerable influence in baseball circles) that a commission be convened to settle the question of baseball's national origins. Not surprisingly, the request was immediately granted.*

The commission members were all men Spalding knew well. Nick Young and Arthur Gorman were both associated with the National club of Washington, which lost to Spalding's Forest City club in a famous 1867 game (see Document 30). Morgan Bulkeley was designated the NL's first president at the behest of Spalding's cohort William Hulbert. Al Reach and George Wright knew Spalding as a rival player and sporting goods manufacturer, before Spalding secretly bought control of their respective companies. A. G. Mills served as NL president after Hulbert's death in 1882, but Spalding held the reins of power, as he did when Young succeeded Mills. Spalding's chosen commission head, James Sullivan, was the publisher of Spalding's Official Base Ball Guides.

In his request, Spalding urged anyone who had "any proof, data or information he may possess or can secure bearing on this matter" to send it to a special commission so that the issue could "be settled for all time." Spalding himself favored an evolutionary theory of baseball's origins, but he traced the game to the colonial game of "One Old Cat" rather than to the English rounders. By hypothesizing that "some ingenious American lad naturally suggested that one thrower be placed in the center of the square," thereby altering One Old Cat in a novel way, Spalding provided an opening for the invention of a creation myth.

WHAT IS THE ORIGIN OF BASE BALL?

Did it Originate From the English Game of ROUNDERS, The Colonial Game of ONE OLD CAT, The New England and Philadelphia Game of TOWN BALL Or WHAT?

Nineteen hundred and five completes the sixtieth year of the life of base ball, for it dates its birth from the organization of the original Knickerbocker Base Ball Club of New York City, September 23, 1845, at which time the first playing rules of the game were formulated and published by that club.

There seems to be a conflict of opinion as to the origin of Base Ball. I think the game has arrived at an age and at a point in its development when this mooted question should be settled in some comprehensive and authoritative way and for all time.

Some authorities, notably Mr. Henry Chadwick, claim that Base Ball is of English origin and was a direct descendant of the old English juvenile pastime called "Rounders," while others claim that it was entirely of American origin and had nothing whatever to do with Rounders or any other foreign game.

While I concede that Mr. Chadwick's Rounder theory is entitled to much weight because of his long connection with Base Ball and the magnificent work he has done in the upbuilding of the game for upward of fifty years, yet I am unwilling longer to accept his Rounder theory without something more convincing than his oft-repeated assertion that "Base Ball did originate from Rounders."

"FATHER" CHADWICK CHALLENGED

For the purpose of settling this question I hereby challenge the Grand Old Man of Base Ball to produce his proofs and demonstrate in some tangible way, if he can, that our national game derived its origin from Rounders.

Mr. Chadwick, who, by the way, is of English birth, and was probably rocked in a "Rounders" cradle, says, in support of his theory, that "there is but one field game in vogue on this continent which is strictly American in its origin, and that one is the old Indian game of Lacrosse, now known as the Canadian national game. Base Ball originated from the old English schoolboy game of Rounders, as plainly shown by the fact that the basic principle of both games is the field use of a bat, a ball and bases."

I have been fed on this kind of "Rounder pap" for upward of forty years, and I refuse to swallow any more of it without some substantial proof sauce with it. . . .

MR. CHADWICK'S ROUNDER THEORY ATTACKED

Having read from boyhood, principally, the writings of Mr. Henry Chadwick that our American game of Base Ball originated from Rounders, and having been taunted with this statement around the world, generally spoken in derision of our game, and having actually played in a game of Rounders, I am now convinced that Base Ball did not originate from Rounders any more than Cricket originated from that asinine position.

About the only tangible argument that I ever heard advanced by Mr. Chadwick or any other authority tending to prove that Base Ball *did* originate from Rounders is the following:

In a recent letter to me Mr. Chadwick says: "You cannot go back on the fact that Base Ball derived its origin from the old English game of Rounders because the basic principle of both games is the field use of a bat, a ball and bases."

Admitting that this is so as far as it applies to Base Ball, as a matter of fact this does not altogether apply to Rounders, for its basic principle is the field use of "a bat, a ball, posts or stakes and a hole."

This kind of reasoning might as well apply and would prove quite as conclusively that Cricket also originated from Rounders, because the basic principle of both games is the field use of "a bat, a ball and stumps or stakes"; *or*, that Golf originated from Rounders, because the basic principle of both games is the field use of "a bat, a ball and a hole"; *or*, that Lacrosse originated from Rounders, because the basic principle of both games is the field use of "a bat, a ball and posts."

Just imagine the argument you would get into and the touchiness an Englishman would show if you told him that his favorite game of cricket derived its origin from Rounders; *or*, the Scotchman's indescribable flow of words if you stated that his ancient game of Golf originated from Rounders; *or*, the American Indian's grunt if it was explained to him that his game of lacrosse originated from Rounders.

Now, boil down together the Englishman's indignation, the Scotchman's huff and the Indian's grunt into one composite mass and you have my feelings and that of every lover of Base Ball when a claim is made that our great American national game of Base Ball originated from Rounders.

BASE BALL IS OF AMERICAN ORIGIN

My investigation and research so far inclines me to the opinion that Base Ball did have its origin in the old colonial game of "One Old Cat." "One Old Cat" was played by three boys—a thrower, catcher and batsman. The latter, after striking the ball, ran to a goal about thirty feet distant, and by returning to the batsman's position without being put out, counted one run or "tally." "Two Old Cat" was played by four or more boys with two batsmen placed about forty feet apart. "Three Old Cat" was played by six or more boys with three batsmen, the ground being laid out in the shape of a triangle. "Four Old Cat" was played by eight or more boys with grounds laid out in the shape of a square. "Four Old Cat" required four throwers, alternating as catchers, and four batsmen, the ball being passed from one corner to the next around the square field. Individual scores or tallies were credited to the batsman making the hit and running from one corner to the next. Some ingenious American lad naturally suggested that one thrower be placed in the center of the square, which brought nine players into the game, and which also made it possible to change the game into teams or sides, one side fielding and the other side batting. This was for many years known as the old game of "Town Ball," from which the present game of Base Ball may have had its origin.

One prominent Base Ball writer claims that he can prove that one of the founders of the old Knickerbocker club came onto the field one day in the early forties with the original game of Base Ball worked out and described on a sheet of paper, and that this game was tried and liked so well that the game was adopted then and there, and the Knickerbocker club was organized to put it into effect.

If such an ancestry can be established for Base Ball every American friend of the game will be delighted.

While "One Old Cat," or "Town Ball" may not rank much higher in the ancestral scale than "Rounders," yet they strongly appeal to the lover of our national sport as distinctively American games.

THE OLD KNICKERBOCKER CLUB OF NEW YORK: THE FIRST BASE BALL TEAM

In looking over the early history of Base Ball I find the names of eleven New York gentlemen who were the founders of the original Knickerbocker Club, names that should be honored and remembered as the founders of our national game by the million base ball players of the present day. They are as follows: Col. James Lee, Dr. Ransom, Abraham Tucker, James Fisher, W. Vail, Alexander J. Cartwright, Wm. R. Wheaton, Duncan F. Curry, E. R. Dupignac, Jr., Wm. H. Tucker and Daniel L. Adams.

Are not some of these gentlemen still living? Or possibly some of their heirs might throw some light on the early history and especially the origin of Base Ball.

A SPECIAL COMMISSION TO INVESTIGATE THE ORIGIN OF BASE BALL PROPOSED

In order to gather this information I would suggest, and hereby respectfully request, that Mr. James E. Sullivan, President of the American Sports Publishing Company, 15 Warren Street, New York City, take the initiative in the work of collecting all possible facts, proofs, interviews, etc., calculated to throw light on this subject, and when collected submit same to a special Board of Base Ball Commissioners or Judges, with the understanding that this board will impartially examine all the evidence of whatever nature and promulgate their decision as to the origin of Base Ball.

I would nominate for that Board: Ex-Governor Morgan G. Bulkley [sic], now United States Senator from Connecticut, and the first President of the National League; Hon. Arthur P. Gorman, United States Senator from Maryland, an old ball player, and ex-President of the famous old National Base Ball Club of Washington, D.C.; Mr. A. G. Mills of New York, an enthusiastic ball player before and during the Civil War and the third President of the National League; Mr. N. E. Young of Washington, D.C., a veteran ball player and the first Secretary and afterward the fourth President of the National League; Mr. Alfred J. Reach of Philadelphia, and Mr. George Wright of Boston, both well-known as two of the most famous ball players in their day, and such additional names as Mr. Sullivan or the above-named Board may deem it advisable to add. Mr. Sullivan to act as Secretary of this Commission.

As all of these gentlemen are interested in Base Ball I feel quite sure they will be willing to act in this capacity, and I am certain that their decision as to the origin of our national sport will be accepted by everyone as final and conclusive.

I would strongly urge that everyone interested in this subject transmit as soon as possible to Mr. Sullivan, 15 Warren Street, New York any proof, data or information he may possess or can secure bearing on this matter, with the hope that before another year rolls around this vexed question as to the actual origin and early history of the great American national game of Base Ball may be settled for all time.

118 ──

Special Base Ball Commission Appointed (1906)

Source: *Spalding's Official Base Ball Guide, 1906* (New York: American Sports Publishing), p. 6.

Albert Spalding appointed the members of the "Special Base Ball Commission." Rather than hiring researchers or having the commission members themselves examine newspaper files, published memoirs, children's books on games, or other possible sources, the commission relied upon the evidence provided by old-timers scattered across the nation.

THE ORIGIN OF BASE BALL

In the 1905 issue of SPALDING'S OFFICIAL BASE BALL GUIDE, a controversy arose as to the origin of the American National Game of Base Ball, between the veteran Base Ball writer, Mr. Henry Chadwick, and Mr. A. G. Spalding, the latter claiming that Base Ball was distinctively of American origin, while Mr. Chadwick contends that it was of English origin. In order to settle the matter definitely—and it is to be hoped for all time—a Special Base Ball Commission was appointed, consisting of the following gentlemen, viz.: Ex-Governor Morgan G. Bulkeley, of Connecticut, now United States Senator from that State, and the first President of the National League; Hon. Arthur P. Gorman, United States Senator from Maryland, and an old ball player and Ex-President of the famous old National Base Ball Club of Washington, D.C.; Mr. A. G. Mills, an enthusiastic ball player before and during the Civil War, and the third President of the National League; Mr. N. E. Young, of Washington, D.C., a veteran ball player, and the first Secretary and afterward President of the National League for many years; Mr. Alfred J. Reach, of Philadelphia, and Mr. George Wright, of Boston, both well known as two of the most famous players of their day. Mr. James E. Sullivan, of New York, the present Secretary of the Amateur Athletic Union of the United States, has acted as Secretary of the Commission, and has collected a mass of evidence on the subject.

This evidence is now being formulated into proper shape which, together with briefs in support of both sides of this interesting controversy, will soon be laid before the Commission for their consideration and decision. As the decision will not be rendered in time to be published in this year's GUIDE, it will be given in full, together with the evidence, in SPALDING'S GUIDE of 1907.

The question as to the real origin of Base Ball has created widespread interest, especially from old timers, as evidenced by the mass of correspondence that has been received by Secretary Sullivan, and the verdict of the Commission is awaited with much interest by the Base Ball public.

119

Abner Graves Identifies Abner Doubleday as the "Father of Baseball" (1908)

Source: Robert Henderson, *Ball, Bat and Bishop: The Origin of Ball Games* (New York: Rockport Press, 1947), pp. 184–85; reprinted by permission of Albert G. Spalding Collection, Rare Books and Manuscripts Division, The New York Public Library, Astor, Lenox, and Tilden Foundations

Abner Graves's letter provided the special commission, and Albert Spalding, with the answer to their prayers. It described how future Civil War general Abner Doubleday invented the game of baseball from scratch while growing up in the idyllic village of Cooperstown, New York. Thus the origin of baseball was located in small-town America, courtesy of an American hero. The game Graves described, however, required eleven men per team and featured "soaking," the practice of retiring a runner by striking him with the ball between the bases. While this game resembled several of the games played prior to the emergence of the "New York game," it was not the fully developed game of baseball as Spalding later claimed.

The American game of base ball was invented by Abner Doubleday of Cooperstown, N.Y., either the spring prior or following the "Log Cabin and Hard Cider" campaign of General William H. Harrison for the presidency. Doubleday was then a boy pupil of Green's Select School in Cooperstown, and the same, as General Doubleday, won honor at the battle of Gettysburg in the Civil War. The pupils of Otsego Academy and of Green's Select School were then playing the old game of Town Ball in the following manner:

A "tosser" stood close to the "home goal" and tossed the ball straight upward about six feet for the batsman to strike at on its fall, the latter using a four-inch flat-board bat. All others wanting to play were scattered about the field, far and near, to catch the ball when hit. The lucky catcher took his innings at the bat. When a batsman struck the ball he ran for a goal fifty feet distant and returned. If the ball was not caught or if he was not "plunked" by a thrown ball, while running, he retained his innings, as in Old Cat.

Doubleday then improved Town Ball, to limit the number of players, as many were hurt in collisions. From twenty to fifty boys took part in the game I have described. He also designed the game to be played by definite teams or side. Doubleday called the game "Base Ball," for there were four bases to it. Three were places where the runner could rest free from being put out, provided he kept his foot on the flat stone base. The pitcher stood in a six foot ring. There were eleven players on a side. The ball had a rubber center overwound with yarn to a size somewhat larger than the present day sphere, and was covered with leather or buckskin. Anyone getting the ball was entitled to throw it at a runner between the bases and put him out by hitting him with it.

I well remember some of the best players of sixty years ago. They were Abner Doubleday, Elihu Phinney, Nels C. Brewer, John C. Graves, Joseph Chaffee, John Starkweather, John Doubleday, Tom Bingham and others who played at the Otsego Academy campus; although a favorite place was on the "Phinney Farm," on the west shore of Otsego Lake.

120

The Final Report of the Commission (1908)

Source: *Spalding's Official Base Ball Guide, 1908*
(New York: American Sports Publishing), pp. 35–49

The following excerpts include the briefs prepared by Henry Chadwick, Albert G. Spald-
ing, and John Ward as well as the final report of the special commission. Although
Chadwick accurately described the commission's work as a "piece of special pleading
which lets my dear old friend Albert escape a bad defeat," its conclusions were quickly
accepted as established truth. Even if Chadwick had taken the commission more se-
riously and had included in his testimony the arguments and information he had
advanced in earlier articles like "The Ancient History of Base Ball" (see Document 29), it
probably would have been ignored.

The Origin of Base Ball

BY JAMES E. SULLIVAN

Secretary Special Base Ball Commission

In the GUIDE of 1905 there appeared an article from Mr. A. G. Spalding, taking
issue with Mr. Henry Chadwick, as to the origin of Base Ball.

Mr. Chadwick has contended for many years that the present American game
of Base Ball derived its origin from, and was a direct descendant of the old English
schoolboy game of "Rounders," while Mr. Spalding contends that Base Ball is
distinctively American, in origin as well as development, and has no connection
whatever with "Rounders" or any other foreign game.

As these well-known Base Ball authorities could not reach an agreement between themselves on this question, it was good-naturedly decided by the contending forces to refer the whole matter to a Special Base Ball Commission for full
consideration and decision. . . .

This controversy as to the origin of Base Ball, and the appointment of a commission of such high standing, aroused considerable public interest, especially
among the old-timers of the game. The Secretary was deluged with communications from different parts of the country, all having a more or less bearing on this
question. For the past three years the Secretary has conducted an extensive correspondence in collecting data and following up various clues, suggested by this
correspondence, that would aid the Commission in arriving at a decision as to the
origin of the game. Having collected all the data and evidence it was possible to
obtain, the Secretary compiled the whole matter together, and at the close of 1907
laid it all before the Special Base Ball Commission for its consideration and decision. The members of the Commission have spent several months in going over

the mass of evidence collected, which has finally resulted in a unanimous decision by the Commission *that Base Ball is of American origin, and has no traceable connection whatever with "Rounders," or any other foreign game.*

The Secretary has recently received notice of this final decision, just in time to promulgate it for the first time in this issue of the GUIDE. . . .

The thanks of the Base Ball public are due the members of the Special Commission for the time and thought they have given to this subject, and their decision should forever set at rest the question as to the Origin of Base Ball.

MR. HENRY CHADWICK'S ARGUMENTS IN SUPPORT OF HIS "ROUNDER" THEORY

BROOKLYN, N.Y., August 1, 1907

GENTLEMEN:

In relation to the existing controversy between Mr. A. G. Spalding and myself as to the origin of the established American game of Base Ball, I shall be "brief and to the point" in my discussion of the question at issue between us; and, in presenting my argument, I shall not occupy even an hour of your valuable time, inasmuch as the facts I present for your impartial consideration are simply incontrovertible.

In the first, the basic principle involved in the point at issue is the use of a ball, a bat, and of bases, in the playing of a game of ball; and, secondly, the date of the period when this self-same basic principle was first carried into practical effect on the field of play.

Now I claim, on behalf of my English clients, that the established American national game of BASE BALL had for its origin the old English school-boy game of "Rounders," and that this latter game existed in England as far back as two centuries ago; and, in fact, it is a question at issue in England as to whether "Rounders" did not antedate the time-honored game of Cricket itself. Suffice it to say, however, that the fact that "Rounders" was played by two opposing sides of contestants, on a special field of play, in which a ball was pitched or tossed to an opposing batsman, who endeavored to strike the ball out into the field, far enough to admit of his safely running the round of the bases, so as to enable him to score a run, to count in the game—the side scoring the most runs winning the game—fully identifies the similarity of the two games. This, in fact, was the basic principle of the old English game of "Rounders," and it is, to this day, the basic principle of the American national game of Base Ball.

As to the various methods of playing the two games, and the difference in their respective details of play, that matter in no way affects the question of the origin of the American game of Base Ball.

In regard to the point, made by the opposing counsel, in which he refers to the game of ball played in "Colonial" days, I claim that the Canadian national game of "Lacrosse," a game played by the aborigines of North America, and the old English game of Cricket, played in New York as far back as 1751, were the only games of ball known to our Colonial ancestry in the old revolutionary period he refers to. So his argument in that regard falls to the ground "as dead as a door nail," as the saying is.

On this statement of incontrovertible facts I present my clients' case to your final judgment, feeling confident that your decision will be in my favor.

Very respectfully yours,

HENRY CHADWICK,

Counsel for the Defence.

MR. A. G. SPALDING CONTENDS THAT BASE BALL
IS OF AMERICAN ORIGIN

POINT LOMA, CAL., July 28, 1907.

GENTLEMEN:

I claim that the game of Base Ball is entirely of American origin, and has no relation to or connection with any game of any other country, except in so far as all games of ball have a certain similarity and family relationship.

While it is to be regretted that the beginning of Base Ball is more or less shrouded in mystery, I believe ample evidence has been collected that will convince the most skeptical that Base Ball is entirely of American origin, and had its birth and evolution in the United States. The game is so thoroughly in accord with our national characteristics and temperament that this fact in itself tends to confirm my opinion that it is of purely American origin, and no other game or country has any right to claim its parentage. . . .

I am aware that quite a general impression exists in the public mind that Base Ball had its origin in the English schoolboy game of Rounders, which has been occasioned largely, if not entirely, by the very able Base Ball writings of my esteemed and venerable friend, Mr. Henry Chadwick, who for the past forty years has continued to make the assertion that Base Ball had its origin in "Rounders," without as yet producing any satisfactory evidence to sustain his theory. Mr. Chadwick has done so much for Base Ball, especially in its early struggling days, that I regret the necessity of disagreeing with him on any Base Ball subject, but my American birth and love of the game would not permit me to let his absurd "Rounders" theory pass unchallenged. If Mr. Chadwick had been born in this country, and not in England, he might be as totally ignorant of Rounders as the rest of us, but it so happened that before he came to this country, when he was about ten years of age, he had seen or possibly played in a game of Rounders, but I do not recall that he claims to have ever seen or played a game of Rounders since his arrival in America, nor have I ever seen or heard of his producing any convincing proof in support of his contention. . . .

A careful search has failed to find a copy of any printed "Rounders" rules published previous to 1845, when the Knickerbocker Base Ball Rules first made their appearance. Any modern rules of Rounders should not be accepted as evidence, for it is well known that friends of that game have in recent years appropri-

The Origins of the Creation Myth 289

ated bodily many of the Base Ball rules, and, in fact, a noticeable effort has been made to make Rounders as much like Base Ball as possible in everything except in name. There is no doubt but that the present-day game of "Rounders" has derived much of its modern origin from Base Ball, and I am as equally positive that our Base Ball of 1845 derived none of its origin from the ancient game of Rounders. Whatever similarity may be found between ancient Rounders and early Base Ball does not in itself constitute evidence that the latter game derived its origin from the former, and therefore should be treated simply as a coincidence and not as an established fact. The fact that not even one scrap of evidence has been produced showing that the game of Rounders was ever played in the United States, or that it was even known by name, clearly substantiates my position in declaring that Base Ball was not derived from Rounders, but is of American origin.

While the evidence that has been collected and that will be submitted to the Commission is not as complete and definite as I should like to have it, yet under the circumstances and at this late date it is the best and only evidence obtainable, but I believe it is amply sufficient to warrant the Commission in deciding that Base Ball is of American origin and in no way connected with Rounders or any game of any other country. The tea episode in Boston Harbor, and our later fracas with England in 1812, had not been sufficiently forgotten in 1840 for anyone to be deluded into the idea that our national prejudices would permit us to look with favor, much less adopt any sport or game of an English flavor.

Having, in my opinion, by the evidence submitted to your Honorable Commission, established the fact that Base Ball was of purely American origin, it now becomes necessary, if possible, to determine just how it did come about. . . .

At some time in the remote past, to accommodate a greater number of players, and to change the individual players of the "Old Cat" games into competing teams, probably some ingenious American boy figured it out that by placing one thrower in the center of the "Four Old Cat" square field and having one catcher, with the players divided into sides, this desired result would be accomplished. This style of game produced what has become generally known as "Town Ball," which was played in this country for many years before Base Ball appeared, and in fact was played up to and for several years after Base Ball was established by the Knicker-bocker Club in 1845. "Town Ball" derived its name from the fact that it was generally played at "Town Meetings." Mr. H. H. Waldo, of Rockford, Ill., one of the pioneers of the West and one of the early promoters of Base Ball, said: "I came West in 1846, and found 'Town Ball' a popular game at all town meetings, and I have no doubt it acquired its name from this fact. The number of players on a side was unlimited, and it was the custom of the losing side to buy the gingerbread and cider. I have always regarded the game of Base Ball as now played as a modification of 'Town Ball.' I never heard of Rounders. We had too much national pride in those days to adopt anything that was English in our sporting life." . . .

I would call the special attention of the Commission to the letters received from

Mr. Abner Graves, at present a mining engineer of Denver, Colo., who claims that the present game of Base Ball was designed and named by Abner Doubleday, of Cooperstown, N.Y., during the Harrison Presidential campaign of 1839, which antedates the organization of the old Knickerbocker Base Ball Club of New York City by six years, when the first printed rules were promulgated. It also antedates by three years the first authentic account of games of Base Ball being played in a desultory sort of way by the young business men of New York City in 1842. While it has generally been conceded that New York City was the birthplace of Base Ball in 1842, this account of Mr. Graves tends to locate its birth at Cooperstown, N.Y., in 1839, and General Abner Doubleday its designer and christener.

In this connection it is of interest to know that this Abner Doubleday was a graduate of West Point in 1842, and afterward became famous in the Civil War as the man who sighted the first gun fired from Fort Sumter, April 12, 1861, which opened the War of the Rebellion between the North and South. He afterward became a Major General in the United States Army and retired from service in 1873, and died January 26, 1893.

Mr. Abner Graves was a boy playmate and fellow pupil of Abner Doubleday at Green's Select School in Cooperstown, N.Y., in 1839. Mr. Graves, who is still living, says that he was present when Doubleday first outlined with a stick in the dirt the present diamond-shaped Base Ball field, indicating the location of the players in the field on paper, with a crude pencil memorandum of the rules for his new game, which he named "*Base Ball.*" As Mr. Graves was one of the youths that took part in the new game under Doubleday's direction his interesting and positive account of this incident is certainly entitled to serious consideration.

Personally, I confess that I am very much impressed with the straightforward, positive and apparently accurate manner in which Mr. Graves writes his narrative, and the circumstantial evidence with which he surrounds it, and I am very strongly inclined to the belief that Cooperstown, N.Y., is the birthplace of the present American game of Base Ball, and that Major General Abner Doubleday was the originator of the game. It certainly appeals to an American's pride to have had the great national game of Base Ball created and named by a Major General in the United States Army, and to have that same game played as a camp diversion by the soldiers of the Civil War, who, at the conclusion of the war, disseminated Base Ball throughout the length and breadth of the United States, and thus gave to the game its national character. The United States Army has certainly played a very important part in the early development of Base Ball, and in recent years the United States Navy has become the emissary that is planting the seeds of the game in every foreign land, which must result in making the American national game of Base Ball the universal sport of the world. The intrinsic merits of the game itself can be depended upon to overcome all prejudice and opposition that may show itself. . . .

Respectfully submitted,

A. G. SPALDING

NEW YORK, June 19, 1907.

MY DEAR ALBERT:

I have carefully read over the letters and manuscripts you sent me bearing on the question of the origin of Base Ball, and I am very much in sympathy with your effort to obtain some exact information upon that question. I fear, however, that your efforts must, in the nature of the case, meet with failure, though your investigations may result in throwing some side lights upon the inquiry.

The game of Base Ball had its origin in this country so many years ago that the living witnesses have long since passed off the green sward and the circumstances surrounding its inception were undoubtedly such that no written records or memoranda of any kind were ever made. Base Ball was originally a boy's game. We know this much, at least, from the rules for the purpose of making it a manly pastime. When, in about the year 1842, or earlier, Dr. D. L. Adams, Alexander J. Cartwright, Colonel James Lee, Duncan F. Curry, E. R. Dupignac, William F. Ladd and other prominent business and professional men of New York City, seeking some medium for outdoor exercise, turned to the boy's game of Base Ball, there was not a code of rules nor any written records of the game, and their only guide to the method of playing was their own recollection of the game as they themselves, when boys, had played it and the rules of the game then in existence, which had come down, like folklore, from generation to generation of boys. Indeed it was not until several years later, upon the organization of the Knickerbocker Ball Club in 1845, that the rules of the game were first put in writing. Some years later, twenty to be exact, I had occasion to look this matter up and was fortunately able to talk personally with several of the original members of the Knickerbocker Club, then still living. Mr. William F. Ladd was at that time a jeweler in Wall Street, a fine, handsome old gentleman, eighty-four years of age, with an intellect as clear as a jewel. He told me many interesting incidents about those early days of the game. One of these was that Col. James Lee, who was, at the time of the organization of the Knickerbocker Ball Club, about sixty years of age, was one of the moving spirits in the organization of that club. That Col. Lee had told him that he, Col. Lee, had played Base Ball as a boy; that it was upon the recollection of Col. Lee and other men of mature years among that little coterie of health-seeking enthusiasts, that the rules were formulated. Another interesting tale told me by Mr. Ladd was that the reason they chose the game of Base Ball instead of—and in fact in opposition to—cricket was because they regarded Base Ball as a purely American game; and it appears that there was at that time some considerable prejudice against adopting any game of foreign invention.

In the infancy of sport in this country New York, Philadelphia, and Boston were the three principal centers and an examination of the earliest records in each one of these sections will disclose the same old popular game of Cat Ball as played among the boys. The rules of Cat Ball, as some of your correspondents point out, were exceedingly simple, such as any crowd of boys of ordinary intelligence, possessing a ball and bat, might easily evolve. From Cat Ball to the Knickerbocker game of Base Ball is only a step, though the game may have been passed through several intermediate stages. The old game of "Scrub" lies between Cat Ball and Base Ball, though whether it preceded or followed the game of Base Ball in point of time no man can now say. . . .

Those who have sought to attribute its origin to the English game of "Rounders" were persons who became acquainted with Base Ball years after its inception as a sport for adults, and they have ignored entirely so much of the early history of the game as we have been able to find. But most important of all it seems to me they overlook the great dissimilarity between the original central and controlling ideas of the two games. The great feature of Rounders, that from which it derives its name, is "the rounder" itself, meaning that whenever one of the "in" side makes a complete continuous circuit of the bases, or, as we would call it in Base Ball, a "home run," he thereby reinstates the entire side; and it then becomes necessary to begin all over again to retry each one of the side at bat, until all of them have been put out, such being one of the rules of that game. Not one of these detractors of the American game has ever shown or claimed that any such rule ever had a place in the game of Base Ball; yet it is not only fair but reasonable to suppose that, if Base Ball were a descendant of the English game of Rounders, there would be some place somewhere in Base Ball of this distinctive feature of the other game. As I have said before, however, all exact information upon the origin of Base Ball must, in the very nature of things, be unobtainable. Boys do not make records of the rules of their boyish games and we have never had in this country the "Year Books" or a "Badminton Library" to do the work for us. America has no "Stonehenge" and therefore we are handicapped in any discussion of this nature by the entire absence of contemporary data. But from what investigations I have made and from such information as I have been able to get from one source and another, and from the innate probabilities, I have never had any doubt myself but that Base Ball was a purely American game.

Yours very truly,

JOHN M. WARD

FINAL DECISION OF THE SPECIAL BASE BALL COMMISSION

NEW YORK, December 30, 1907.

MR. JAMES E. SULLIVAN, Secretary, Special Base Ball Commission, 21 Warren St., New York City.

DEAR SULLIVAN:

On my earliest opportunity, after my recent return from Europe, I read—and read with much interest—the considerable mass of testimony bearing on the origin of Base Ball which you had sent to my office address during my absence. I cannot say that I find myself in accord with those who urge the American origin of the game as against its English origin as contended for by Mr. Chadwick, on "patriotic ground." In my opinion we owe much to our Anglo-Saxon kinsmen for their example which we have too tardily followed in fostering healthful field sports generally, and if the fact could be established by evidence that our national game, "Base Ball," was devised in England, I do not think that it would be any the less admirable nor welcome on that account. As a matter of fact, the game of ball which I have always regarded as the distinctive English game, i.e., cricket, was brought to this country and had a respectable following here, which it has since maintained, long before any game of ball resembling our national game was played anywhere! Indeed, the earliest field sport that I remember was a game of cricket, played on an open field near Jamaica, L.I., where I was then attending school. Then, and ever since, I have heard cricket spoken of as the essentially English game, and, until my perusal of this testimony, my own belief had been that our game of Base Ball, substantially as played to-day, originated with the Knicker-bocker club of New York, and it was frequently referred to as the "New York Ball Game." . . .

As I have stated, my belief had been that our "National Game of Base Ball" originated with the Knickerbocker club, organized in New York in 1845, and which club published certain elementary rules in that year; but, in the interesting and pertinent testimony for which we are indebted to Mr. A. G. Spalding, appears a circumstantial statement by a reputable gentleman, according to which the first known diagram of the diamond, indicating positions for the players, was drawn by Abner Doubleday in Cooperstown, N.Y., in 1839. Abner Doubleday subsequently graduated from West Point and entered the regular army, where, as Captain of Artillery, he sighted the first gun fired on the Union side (at Fort Sumter) in the Civil War. Later still, as Major General, he was in command of the Union army at the close of the first day's fight in the battle of Gettysburg, and he died full of honors at Mendham, N.J., in 1893. It happened that he and I were members of the same veteran military organization—the crack Grand Army Post (Lafayette), and the duty devolved upon me, as Commander of that organization, to have charge of his obsequies, and to command the veteran military escort which served as guard of honor when his body lay in state, January 30, 1893, in the New York City Hall, prior to his interment in Arlington.

In the days when Abner Doubleday attended school in Cooperstown, it was a common thing for two dozen or more of school boys to join in a game of ball. Doubtless, as in my later experience, collisions between players in attempting to catch the batted ball were frequent, and injury due to this cause, or to the practice of putting out the runner by hitting him with the ball, often occurred.

I can well understand how the orderly mind of the embryo West Pointer would devise a scheme for limiting the contestants on each side and allotting them to field positions, each with a certain amount of territory; also substituting the existing method of putting out the base runner for the old one of "plugging" him with the ball.

True, it appears from the statement that Doubleday provided for eleven men on a side instead of nine, stationing the two extra men between first and second, and second and third bases, but this is a minor detail, and, indeed, I have played, and doubtless other old players have, repeatedly with eleven on a side, placed almost identically in the manner indicated by Doubleday's diagram, although it is true that we so played after the number on each side had been fixed at nine, simply to admit to the game an additional number of those who wished to take part in it.

I am also much interested in the statement made by Mr. Curry, of the pioneer Knickerbocker club, and confirmed by Mr. Tassie, of the famous old Atlantic club of Brooklyn, that a diagram, showing the ball field laid out substantially as it is to-day, was brought to the field one afternoon by a Mr. Wadsworth. Mr. Curry says "the plan caused a great deal of talk, but, finally, we agreed to try it." While he is not quoted as adding that they did both try and adopt it, it is apparent that such was the fact; as, from that day to this, the scheme of the game as described by Mr. Curry has been continued with only slight variations in detail. It should be borne in mind that Mr. Curry was the first president of the old Knickerbocker club, and participated in drafting the first published rules of the game.

It is possible that a connection more or less direct can be traced between the diagram drawn by Doubleday in 1839 and that presented to the Knickerbocker club by Wadsworth in 1845, or thereabouts, and I wrote several days ago for certain data bearing on this point, but as it has not yet come to hand I have decided to delay no longer sending in the kind of paper your letter calls for, promising to furnish you the indicated data when I obtain it, whatever it may be.

My deductions from the testimony submitted are:

First: That "Base Ball" had its origin in the United States.

Second: That the first scheme for playing it, according to the best evidence obtainable to date, was devised by Abner Doubleday at Cooperstown, N.Y., in 1839.

Yours very truly,

A. G. MILLS

We, the undersigned members of the Special Base Ball Commission, unanimously agree with the decision as expressed and outlined in Mr. A. G. Mills' letter of December 30.

MORGAN G. BULKELEY

NICHOLAS E. YOUNG

AL REACH

GEO. WRIGHT

Bibliography

Among the best contemporary accounts of nineteenth-century baseball are: Adrian C. Anson, *A Ball Player's Career* (Chicago: Era, 1900; reprint, Mattituck, N.Y.: Amereon, 1993); Henry Chadwick, *The Game of Base Ball* (New York: George Munro, 1868; reprint, Columbia, S.C.: Camden House, 1983); Mike Kelly, *Play Ball: Stories of the Ball Field* (Boston: J. F. Spofford, 1888); Jacob Morse, *Sphere and Ash: History of Base Ball* (Boston: J. F. Spofford, 1888; reprint, Columbia, S.C.: Camden House, 1984); and Charles Peverelly, *The Book of American Pastimes* (New York, 1866).

Histories of nineteenth-century baseball begin with Albert G. Spalding, *America's National Game* (New York, 1911; reprint, Lincoln: University of Nebraska Press, 1992). Other good early histories include Francis Richter, *Richter's History and Records of Base Ball* (Philadelphia: Dando, 1914); Elwood Roff, *Base Ball and Base Ball Players* (Chicago, 1912); and Alfred Spink, *The National Game* (St. Louis: National Game Publishing, 1910). The first two scholarly histories of the game—Harold Seymour, *Baseball: The Early Years* (New York: Oxford University Press, 1960; reprint, 1989), and David Q. Voigt, *American Baseball: From Gentleman's Sport to the Commissioner's System* (Norman, Okla., 1966; reprint, University Park: Pennsylvania State University Press, 1983)—are still the most comprehensive books available on the subject. Two recent general histories of baseball are Benjamin G. Rader, *Baseball: A History of America's Game* (Urbana: University of Illinois Press, 1992), and Charles Alexander, *Our Game: An American Baseball History* (New York: Henry Holt, 1991).

In the last twenty years a variety of scholars and researchers have produced books on specific aspects of nineteenth-century baseball, and sports in general, including: Melvin Adelman, *A Sporting Time: New York City and the Rise of Modern Athletics, 1820–70* (Urbana: University of Illinois Press, 1986); Warren Goldstein, *Playing for Keeps: A History of Early Baseball* (Ithaca, N.Y.: Cornell University Press, 1989); George Kirsch, *The Creation of American Team Sports: Baseball and Cricket, 1838–72* (Urbana: University of Illinois Press, 1989); Jerry Lansche, *Glory Fades Away: The Nineteenth-Century World Series Rediscovered* (Dallas: Taylor, 1991); Peter Levine, *A. G. Spalding and the Rise of Baseball: The Promise of American Sport* (New York: Oxford University Press, 1985); David Pietrusza, *Major Leagues: The Formation, Sometimes Absorption, and Mostly Inevitable Demise of 18 Professional Baseball Organizations, 1871 to Present* (Jefferson, N.C.: McFarland, 1991);

Steven A. Riess, *Touching Base: Professional Baseball and American Culture in the Progressive Era* (Westport, Conn.: Greenwood, 1980); and William J. Ryczek, *Blackguards and Red Stockings: A History of Baseball's National Association, 1871–1875* (Jefferson, N.C.: McFarland, 1992).

The two best sources for statistical information are *The Baseball Encyclopedia: The Complete and Official Record of Major League Baseball,* ed. Joseph Reichler (New York: Macmillan, 1992), and *Total Baseball,* ed. John Thorn and Pete Palmer (New York: Outlet Book Co., 1993). Other valuable reference books include Arthur Ashe, *A Hard Road to Glory: A History of the African-American Athlete, 1619–1918* (New York: Amistad, 1988); *The Baseball Chronology,* ed. James Charlton (New York: Macmillan, 1991); Paul Dickson, *The Dickson Baseball Dictionary* (New York: Avon, 1989); Bill James, *The Bill James Historical Abstract* (New York: Villard, 1986); David L. Porter, *The Biographical Dictionary of American Sports: Baseball* (New York: Greenwood, 1987); *Baseball: A Comprehensive Bibliography,* comp. Myron J. Smith (Jefferson, N.C.: McFarland, 1986; rev. ed., 1993); *The Official Encyclopedia of Baseball,* ed. Hy Turkin and Sherley C. Thompson, with revisions by Pete Palmer (New York: A. S. Barnes, 1951); and Joel Zoss and John Bowman, *Diamonds in the Rough: The Untold Story of Baseball* (New York: Macmillan, 1989).

The following organizations kindly provided permission to reprint documents appearing in this collection: The New York Public Library, Astor, Lenox and Tilden Foundations; The *Baltimore Sun*; The *Boston Globe*; Camden House; The *Chicago Tribune*; *Detroit Free Press*; Globe Information Services; Kentucky Department for Libraries & Archives; The *New York Times*; The *Plain Dealer*; The *Providence Journal-Bulletin*; Spalding & Evenflo Companies; *St. Louis Post-Dispatch*; Times Newspapers Limited; University Microfilms.

Index

golf, 284
Golt, W. F. C., 246
Gompers, Samuel, 254, 255
Goodfellow, E. T., 120
Goodfriend, S., 227
Goodwin, Mendell, 194
"goose eggs," 250
Gorman, Arthur P., 280, 284, 285
Gorman, H., 100, 101
Governs, S. K., 147
Grand Rapids (Mich.) clubs, 246
"grandstand cards" (tickets), 238
Grant, Frank, 150
Graves, Abner, 285–86, 291
Grenelle, William H., 17
Griffith, Clark, 253, 254, 255
Gross, F. C., 246
Guelph (Ont., Canada) clubs, 100

Haldeman, John, 101
Haldeman, Walter N., 101
Hall, George, 102–9, 190, 241
Hamden (N.Y.) clubs, 2
"hands lost/out," 12, 13, 18, 19, 29, 70, 76
Hanlon, Ned, 122, 124, 174, 194, 196, 207, 211, 227, 249, 251
Harrington, Billy, 211
Harris, Daniel, 254, 255
Harris, J. R., 147
Hart, C. C., 225
Hart, James, 141, 211, 216, 218, 225, 245
Hart, Julian B., 194, 195
Hartford clubs, 93, 94, 95, 98, 132, 154
Hawley, David, 207, 211
Healy, Egyptian, 174
Hecker, Guy, 179, 180
Henderson, A. H., 131
Herancourt, G. L., 120
Herrmann, Garry, 262, 263, 264, 265, 268
Hickey, Thomas J., 256
Higham, John, 91, 110, 111
Hilt, B. F., 195
Hines, C. W., 147, 148
Hines, Paul, 110–11, 122, 123, 138, 165, 197, 206
"hippodrome," 49, 77, 96, 101, 184

Hoboken (N.J.) clubs, 10, 14, 15, 19, 20, 21, 44, 45, 47, 49
Hoffer, Bill, 237
Hogriever, George, 232
holidays, 57–59, 121, 145, 157, 181, 218, 219
Holliday, Bug, 232
"home bye," 9
"home goal," 286
Hopper, DeWolf, 159, 175–76
Hornung, Joe, 194, 225
Hot Springs (Ark.) clubs, 141
Hough, Frank, 225
Hough, O. R., 84, 88
Howe, George, 207
Howell, William P., 23, 24
Hoy, Dummy, 232
Hulbert, William, xvii, 83, 90, 93–95, 96, 101, 114, 115, 280
Hulswitt, Rudy, 264
Huntington Avenue grounds (Boston), 270

Indianapolis clubs, 62, 132, 171, 246
"innings" (singular), 3, 11, 12, 26, 33, 49, 286
"in-party" (batting team), 3
International Association, 92, 99–101, 119, 167
Iowa Indians, 11
Ireland, George, Jr., 17
Irwin, Arthur, 194, 211, 212
Irwin, Charlie, 253

Jackson, Jas., 131
Jackson, Thomas F., 23, 24
Jamaica (Long Island) clubs, 35
Jennings, Hugh, 253, 255
Jersey City clubs, 21, 22
Johnson, Albert, 185, 186, 187, 194, 213
Johnson, Ban, xviii, 228, 243, 244, 246, 248, 255, 259, 260, 261, 262, 263, 264
Johnson, C. Howard, 147
Johnstone, Jim, 260
Jones, Charley, 225
junior clubs, 45, 46
Justin, R., Jr., 23

Milligan, Jocko, 182

Mills, Abraham G., 130, 175, 176, 279, 280, 284, 285, 295

Milwaukee clubs, 246

Minneapolis clubs, 141, 246

minor leagues, 127, 170–71, 213, 216, 224, 247, 248, 256–57, 267–68

Moncrief, James, 17

Mone, John, 145, 146

Morrisania (N.Y.) clubs, 21, 22, 32, 80

Morton, Sam, 216

Mott, John W., 23, 24

"muffin games/players," 46, 69, 71

"mule play," 184

Mumford's meadow (Rochester ball ground), 2

Murnane, Tim, 110, 111, 274

Murphy, Morgan, 253

Murray, John, Jr., 17

Mutrie, James, 120, 121

Nash, Billy, 197, 222, 223, 235

National Agreement: of 1883, 127, 128–30, 163; of 1885, 139–40; of 1900, 249; of 1903, xviii, 243, 256, 262, 264, 267–68; and the AL, 243–44; and championship series, xviii; and contracts, 212–13; and minor leagues, 170, 256, 267–68; and the National Association of Professional Base Ball Leagues, 256; and the National League of Colored Base Ball Clubs, 146; and the PL, 199; and players' salaries, 139, 140; and reserve clause, 127, 128, 139, 164, 188, 211; size of membership, 204–5; and Western Association, 213

National Association of Base Ball Players (NABBP), 16, 18, 22–25, 52, 53–54, 55, 72, 77–78, 80, 82, 88

National Association of Junior Ball Players, 46

National Association of Professional Base Ball Leagues, 256–57, 267–68

National Association of Professional Base Ball Players (NA), xvii, 83–88, 97, 98, 99, 190

National Commission, 275, 276, 277, 278

National League (NL): and the AA, 119; and African American players, 141; and the AL, 246, 261, 262–65; and the Brotherhood, 198; John Brush and, 245; and championship series, 142; characteristics of, xvii, xviii, 83, 96–99; contracts, 114, 164, 172–73; formation and reorganization of, xv, 83, 96–99, 186, 187, 213–17, 248–50; model player contract, 111–13; and the National Agreement, 139, 163; and the PL, 206, 207; and the players' revolt, 188–89, 189–92, 199–201; and players' salaries, 114, 171; and reserve clause, 113, 114–15, 162–64, 168, 170; and rule changes, 224–27; Tripartite Agreement, 128, 129, 130

National League of Colored Base Ball Clubs, 146–47

National League of Colored Base Ball Players, 148

Nava, Sandy, 122, 123

Negro Leagues, 115

Nelson, Candy, 233

Newark clubs, 45, 120, 121

New Bedford (Mass.) clubs, 142

Newell, W. W., 225, 226

New England League, 142

New Haven clubs, 22, 92, 93, 94, 98

New York clubs, 11–13, 16, 19, 20, 21, 27–29, 30–32, 45, 73–77, 93, 95, 141, 150, 161, 175; and associations, 80, 100, 120, 132, 258–61; and championships, 137–39

"New York game," 26, 294

New York State Base Ball Association, 80–81

Nichols, Al, 99, 102–9, 190, 241

Nichols, Kid, 110, 237

Niebuhr, Fraley C., 17

night baseball, 115–16

Nimmick, M. J., 206, 207

Nimmick, W. A., 140

Nops, Jerry, 237

Norfolk clubs, 140

Young, Cy, 220, 221, 222, 224, 253, 270, 271, 272

Young, Nick: and the NA, 84, 85, 86, 88; and the National Agreement, 139; and the NL, 206, 207, 216, 227, 250; and origins of baseball, 280, 284, 285, 295; as pitcher, 221, 222–23; and rule changes, 226; and umpires, 213

Zanesville (Ohio) clubs, 153

Zettlein, George, 99, 107

Zimmer, Chief, 221, 222, 224, 253

Zorras (Canadian club), 9